NEW ENGLAND'S
BEST TRIPS
32 AMAZING ROAD TRIPS

This edition written and researched by

Mara Vorhees
Amy C Balfour, Paula Hardy, Caroline Sieg

✓ Top Tips	📖 History & Culture	📷 Essential Photo
🔗 Link Your Trips	👨‍👩‍👧 Family	🏃 Walking Tour
💬 Tips from Locals	🍷 Food & Drink	🍴 Eating
↪ Trip Detour	🌳 Outdoors	🛏 Sleeping

☎ Telephone Number	@ Internet Access	🍽 English-Language Menu
⊘ Opening Hours	📶 Wi-Fi Access	👪 Family-Friendly
P Parking	🥗 Vegetarian Selection	🐾 Pet-Friendly
⊖ Nonsmoking	🏊 Swimming Pool	
✴ Air-Conditioning		

Routes
- ▬▬▬ Trip Route
- ▬▬▬ Trip Detour
- ▬▬▬ Linked Trip
- ▬▬▬ Walk Route
- ▬▬▬ Tollway
- ▬▬▬ Freeway
- Primary
- Secondary
- Tertiary
- Lane
- Unsealed Road
- ✖ Plaza/Mall
- Steps
-)= = Tunnel
- Pedestrian Overpass
- Walk Track/Path

Boundaries
- — ·— International
- ------ State/Province
- ╥╥╥ Cliff

Population
- ✪ Capital (National)
- ◉ Capital (State/Province)
- ● City/Large Town
- • Town/Village

Transport
- ✈ Airport
- +⊕+ Cable Car/ Funicular
- P Parking
- +⊕+ Train/Railway
- ⊕ Tram
- Ⓜ Underground Train Station

Trips
- 1 Trip Numbers
- 9 Trip Stop
- 🚶 Walking tour
- ↪ Trip Detour

Highway Route Markers
- 〔97〕 US National Hwy
- 〔5〕 US Interstate Hwy
- 〔44〕 State Hwy

Hydrography
- River/Creek
- Intermittent River
- Swamp/Mangrove
- Canal
- Water
- Dry/Salt/ Intermittent Lake
- Glacier

Areas
- Beach
- Cemetery (Christian)
- Cemetery (Other)
- Park
- Forest
- Reservation
- Urban Area
- Sportsground

PLAN YOUR TRIP

ON THE ROAD

MASSACHUSETTS 29

CONTENTS

Maine
p273

Vermont
p157

New Hampshire
p215

Massachusetts
p29

Connecticut &
Rhode Island
p91

Contents cont.

Classic Trips

Look out for the Classic Trips stamp
on our favorite routes in this book.

Vermont Green Mountain landscapes are enchanting in autumn

WELCOME TO
NEW ENGLAND

You've read the history books, seen a few photos, maybe enjoyed a bowl of clam chowder. But to see and do the best of New England – to really experience the history, artistry and diversity of this formative region – you have to get in your car and drive.

These 32 road trips wend their way along the storied New England coastline. They cruise the dynamic city streets of Boston, Portland and Providence. They roam over country roads and circle sparkling lakes, traversing the rolling Berkshire Hills, the forested Green Mountains and the alpine Whites.

So rev up your engine. Mount spectacular summits and ogle eye-popping fall foliage. Feel ocean breezes and taste salty air. Chow down on crispy clams and fresh farm produce. Drive through history, following the writers and revolutionaries who changed the world. And if you've only got time for one trip, make it one of our eight Classic Trips, which take you to the very best of New England. Turn the page for more.

→

NEW ENGLAND

Classic Trips

26

WHAT IS A CLASSIC TRIP?

All the trips in this book show you the best of New England, but we've chosen eight as our all-time favorites. These are our Classic Trips – the ones that lead you to the best of the iconic sights, the top activities and the unique New England experiences. Turn the page to see the map, and look out for the Classic Trip stamp throughout the book.

3 Cape Cod & the Islands
Don't miss charming Brant Point Lighthouse as the ferry pulls into Nantucket harbor.

26 Maritime Maine
Meander down to Rockland's thriving waterfront.

27 Acadia Byway Slip on your shades and take a sunset drive to the summit of Cadillac Mountain.

27

9

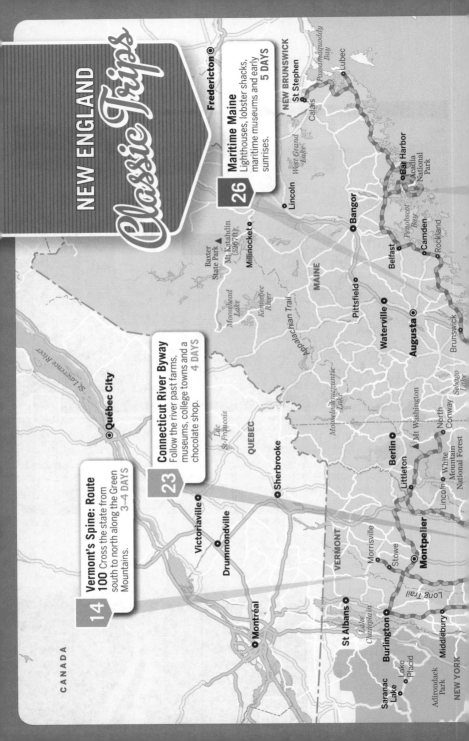

NEW ENGLAND
Classic Trips

14 | **Vermont's Spine: Route 100** Cross the state from south to north along the Green Mountains. **3–4 DAYS**

23 | **Connecticut River Byway** Follow the river past farms, museums, college towns and a chocolate shop. **4 DAYS**

26 | **Maritime Maine** Lighthouses, lobster shacks, maritime museums and early sunrises. **5 DAYS**

CANADA

Québec City

St Lawrence River

Rivière Richelieu

Victoriaville

Drummondville

Sherbrooke

QUEBEC

Lac St-François

Fredericton

NEW BRUNSWICK

St Stephen
Calais
Passamaquoddy Bay
Lubec

West Grand Lake

Lincoln

Baxter State Park
Mt Katahdin (5267ft)

Millinocket

Moosehead Lake

Kennebec River

Appalachian Trail

MAINE

Bangor

Bar Harbor
Acadia National Park

Belfast
Penobscot Bay
Camden
Rockland

Pittsfield

Waterville

Augusta

Brunswick

Mooselookmeguntic Lake

Sebago Lake

Mt Washington
White Mountain National Forest
North Conway

Berlin
Littleton
Lincoln

Montpelier

Montréal

St Albans
Lake Champlain

Morrisville
Stowe

Burlington

VERMONT

Long Trail

Middlebury

Saranac Lake
Lake Placid
Adirondack Park

NEW YORK

27 **Acadia Byway**
Swoop up Cadillac Mountain, then roll past cliffs on Mt Desert Island. **3 DAYS**

20 **Ivy League Tour** History, architecture and traditions are highlights during tours of New England's Ivies. **5 DAYS**

1 **Coastal New England** The ultimate coastal drive connects fishing villages, trading ports and naval centers. **6–8 DAYS**

3 **Cape Cod & the Islands**
Slow, meandering route with beaches, oysters and art. **5–7 DAYS**

13 **Fall Foliage Tour**
The ultimate fall foliage trip, featuring dappled trails and awesome views. **5–7 DAYS**

100 km
50 miles

ATLANTIC OCEAN

Casco Bay

Portland
Kittery
Hampton
Gloucester
Marblehead
Boston
Provincetown
Plymouth
Cape Cod National Seashore
Cape Cod Bay
Sandwich
Hyannis
Nantucket Sound
Nantucket
New Bedford
Newport
Rhode Island Sound

Lake Winnipesaukee
NEW HAMPSHIRE
Plymouth
Concord
Newport
Manchester
Concord
Brattleboro
Hanover
Connecticut River

MASSACHUSETTS
Northampton
Springfield
Providence
RHODE ISLAND
Manchester
Hartford
CONNECTICUT
Waterbury
Norwich
New London
New Haven
Connecticut River
Long Island Sound

Pittsford
Rutland
Lake George
Manchester
Bennington
Williamstown
Wilmington
Great Mountain National Forest
October Mountain (1962ft)
Pittsfield
Great Barrington
Albany
Woodstock
Appalachian Trail
Sherman
Lake Candlewood
Bridgeport
Stamford
NEW YORK
New York
Hudson River

New England's best sights and experiences, and the road trips that will take you there.

NEW ENGLAND
HIGHLIGHTS

Cape Cod National Seashore

The outer edge of Cape Cod is a collage of sand dunes, salt marshes and seaside forest, home to prolific bird and marine life. Since the 1960s, this wild world is all preserved under the auspices of the Cape Cod National Seashore. Drive along the shoreline on **Trip 3: Cape Cod & the Islands**, stopping to climb historic lighthouses, swim at wind-whipped beaches and stroll along scenic boardwalks.

TRIPS 2 3

Cape Cod National Seashore Gateway to the beach

Fall Foliage A Vermont road, ablaze with autumn color

Fall Foliage

New England is radiant in autumn, when farm stands overflow with freshly harvested produce and leaves sparkle with brilliant bursts of yellow and red. On **Trip 13: Fall Foliage Tour** or **Trip 15: Cider Season Sampler**, drive through vivid streamers of seasonal foliage – stopping to chug fresh-pressed cider or pluck a patch of berries – before the earth goes to sleep under a thick blanket of snow.

TRIPS 5 6 13 15

Acadia National Park

The Precipice. The Beehive. Thunder Hole. Is this a James Bond movie or Acadia National Park? The dilemma on **Trip 27: Acadia Byway**: stop to explore or keep on driving? Park Loop Rd, with its gentle curves and crafted viewpoints, was designed with drivers in mind. It tugs you forward. But the adventures pull you sideways. So drive it twice – first without stopping, then to explore.

TRIP 27

Appalachian Trail

The AT traverses 14 states and more than 2100 miles. Five of those states and 730 of those miles are in New England. **Trip 13: Fall Foliage Tour** offers access to the Berkshires; **Trip 22: White Mountains Loop** hits the peaks of the White Mountains; and **Trip 29: Maine Highlands** traverses – yes – the Maine highlands.

TRIPS

5 6 12 13 20 22 29 32

Lighthouses West Quoddy Light, Maine

BEST BEACHES

Herring Cove, Cape Cod National Seashore
Miles of secret sand dunes are perfect for strolling and sunbathing. **Trips** 2 3

Hammonasset Beach A 2-mile-long pine-backed beach set amid salt marshes and meadows. **Trip** 10

North Beach Burlington's lakeside stretch of sand is a rewarding surprise in landlocked Vermont. **Trips** 15 18

Sand Beach Ponder the Milky Way at an evening ranger talk at Acadia National Park. **Trip** 27

Lighthouses

More than 60 lighthouses pepper Maine's coast. Their historic importance is evident on **Trip 26: Maritime Maine**, which curves past fishing villages, ports and maritime museums. But their vital connection to local lives doesn't grab you until you visit on a fog-thick morning, with waves smashing against the rocks. When the foghorn wails and you drop your camera, only then can you begin to understand.

TRIPS 3 26 27 31

15

White Mountains The majestic Presidential Range

White Mountains

Gamblers have Vegas. Gourmands have San Francisco. And hikers have the White Mountains, a region of soaring peaks and lush valleys that covers one quarter of New Hampshire. More than 700,000 acres are protected in the White Mountain National Forest. As you'll see on **Trip 22: White Mountains Loop**, this wilderness is made accessible by the Appalachian Mountain Club, which manages the hut-to-hut hiking network.

TRIPS 21 22

BEST HIKING TRAILS

Mt Greylock Climb the mountain, then climb the War Veterans Memorial Tower for glorious views of five states. **Trips** 6 13

Appalachian Trail Kent's 5-mile river walk beside the Housatonic is part of this historic trail. **Trips** 12 13

Burrows to Forest City Loop The 6-mile trail rewards wanderers with views of Camel's Hump. **Trip** 16

Jordan Cliffs Climb ladders to scale a cliff near Jordan Pond. **Trip** 27

17

Ivy League Universities Harvard University

Vermont Farms Farmer sorting harvested pumpkins

Ivy League Universities

New England is home to four of the eight Ivy League universities. Steeped in tradition, these institutions are known for academic excellence and rich histories. Study up on **Trip 20: Ivy League Tour**, starting on the bucolic green of Dartmouth College, with subsequent stops at the more urban campuses of Harvard, Brown and Yale.

TRIPS 1 10 20

Colonial History

New England's rural hinterland presents a rich tableau of the country's Colonial history. On **Trip 9: Quiet Corner** or **Trip 12: Litchfield Hills Loop**, trace the footsteps of Revolutionary heroes, human rights activists, religious thinkers and reformists, and discover that these bucolic hills are anything but quiet.

TRIPS 9 11 12

Vermont Farms

From apple picking and artisanal-cheese sampling to pumpkin-carving contests, Vermont farms welcome visitors and encourage you to learn how they produce the fare that lands on your plate. Experience it to the max on **Trip 15: Cider Season Sampler**, when the fall harvest spins it into full action and all the leaves erupt in red, yellow and copper.

TRIPS 15 16 18

19

Mansions of Newport

Newport's natural beauty has long attracted wealthy holidaymakers. As early as the 18th century Manhattan's 'society' families flocked here for relaxing escapes, purchasing generous parcels of land and erecting sumptuous summer mansions. On **Trip 7: Rhode Island: East Bay**, take our walking tour down ritzy Bellevue Ave and admire Italianate palazzos, French chateaux and English manors, cloned from steeple to cellar.

TRIPS 1 7 8

Maritime New England

The southeastern corner of Connecticut is unlike any other in New England. The heritage of its seafaring days lives on in the country's largest maritime museum, Mystic Seaport, and the US naval base in Groton, visited on **Trip 1: Coastal New England**. Come for seafaring tales, as well as cruises in tall ships, wooden-boat regattas and restaurants serving seafood.

TRIPS 1 7

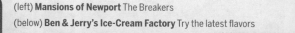
(left) **Mansions of Newport** The Breakers
(below) **Ben & Jerry's Ice-Cream Factory** Try the latest flavors

Ben & Jerry's Ice-Cream Factory

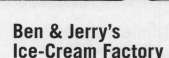

After winding your way up the scenic curves and rural villages on **Trip 14: Vermont's Spine: Route 100**, there's only one thing left to do – eat ice cream at Chunky Monkey HQ, aka the Ben & Jerry's Factory. Take a tour and learn how two schoolmates turned a $5 ice-cream-making correspondence course into the state's most delicious export.

TRIP 14

BEST DRIVING ROADS

Mohawk Trail The region's oldest scenic byway follows a former Native American footpath. **Trip** 6

CT 169 The National Scenic Byway takes in farms and 200-year-old villages. **Trip** 9

Hwy 2, Champlain Islands Bridges, water views and desolate islands take you off the beaten path. **Trip** 18

Kancamagus Highway The river hugs the road on this cruise through leafy mountain panoramas. **Trips** 13 22

21

Maine Get stuck into fresh lobster (Trip 26)

Seafood

As a rule, when in New England, one should eat as much lobster as possible. But there's more to life than the celebrity crustacean. There are also crabs, clams, oysters, scallops and fresh flaky fish.

3 Cape Cod & the Islands Feast on clams, oysters and seafood galore at some of the region's best restaurants.

4 Around Cape Ann Pull up a picnic table for fried clams and steamed lobsters at a waterfront clam shack.

7 Rhode Island: East Bay Eat fried clams at the beach or slurp them raw at Newport's bars.

26 Maritime Maine Lobster rolls, fried haddock and clam chowder – look for the shacks and no-frills eateries along the coast.

Outdoor Activities

Rolling hills and rocky peaks; rushing rivers and glass-like lakes; windswept beaches and sandy dunes: this is what draws millions of outdoor adventurers to New England.

6 Mohawk Trail Surf the Deerfield rapids, hike the Berkshire hills and climb to the top of Massachusetts' highest peak.

13 Fall Foliage Tour Go zip-lining in Bretton Woods or cruise on a 43ft schooner.

14 Vermont's Spine: Route 100 Venture to higher altitudes on abundant trails and zippy gondolas.

22 White Mountains Loop Embrace the views on a hut-to-hut hike amid New England's highest peaks.

27 Acadia Byway Hike, bike, kayak and stargaze on Mt Desert Island, a multi-sport mecca.

Beer & Wine

Despite the region's Puritan roots, modern-day New Englanders like to get their drink on. The region is now home to a host of microbreweries and wineries where you can wet your whistle, but don't drink and drive!

10 Connecticut Wine Trail Tour Connecticut's Atlantic-facing vineyards for award-winning Cabernet Franc.

17 Robert Frost Country Sample organic brews and titillating meads, with a dose of poetry in between.

18 Lake Champlain Byway Pull yourself away from the lake to visit Vermont's most famous microbrewery and its first winery.

28 Old Canada Road The Liberal Cup and the Kennebec River Pub & Brewery are mug-lifting members of the Maine Beer Trail.

Provincetown Catch frolicking whales off the coast (Trip 3)

Art & Architecture

New England's art and architecture span the centuries, from historic homes to modern marvels, and from university collections to contemporary-art museums.

3 Cape Cod & the Islands Artists inspired by the sea display their craft at galleries along Old Kings Hwy.

6 Mohawk Trail Take in Deerfield's collection of period homes and Mass MoCA's ever-changing exhibits.

10 Connecticut Wine Trail New Haven's grand Gothic architecture and Johnson's modernist marvel make for surprising architectural highlights.

31 Mainely Art With galleries and art walks galore, you can take home the local scenery in Belfast, Camden and Rockport.

History

From the moment the Pilgrims stepped ashore at Plymouth Rock, the region was on the map. Destinations here represent every aspect of history – Native American, Colonial, Revolutionary, maritime, literary and industrial.

2 Pilgrim Trail Chart the arrival and settlement of the New World's earliest incomers from Europe.

7 Rhode Island: East Bay Tour Pilgrims' houses and ancient burial grounds, and the grand mansions of pirates and privateers.

19 Southern Vermont Loop Learn about Bennington's role in the American Revolution, the Lincoln family home and Norman Rockwell's place in Vermont.

26 Maritime Maine Maine's coastal heritage, from shipbuilding to seafaring to fishing, is traced at museums along the coast.

Wildlife

The northern states are home to moose, bears, deer and other land mammals; dolphins, whales and seals frolic in the coastal waters; and the region's forests and marshes are full of migrating and resident birdlife.

3 Cape Cod & the Islands Onshore sanctuaries shelter abundant birdlife, while Stellwagen Bank attracts magnificent marine mammals.

11 Lower River Valley Cruise Connecticut's Lower River Valley and spot bald and golden eagles migrating from Canada for the winter.

21 Woodland Heritage Trail With a 95% success rate, odds are good you'll see a moose on the Gorham Moose Tour.

24 Lake Winnipesaukee Bobcats, mountain lions and loons inhabit the quieter nooks of Lake Winn.

NEED ^{TO} KNOW

CELL PHONES
The only foreign phones that work in the USA are GSM multiband models. Network coverage is poor in the White Mountains.

INTERNET ACCESS
Wireless internet access is available at most hotels and cafes, often free. Internet cafes aren't common, but hotels and libraries often provide computers for internet access.

FUEL
Gas stations are ubiquitous and many are open 24 hours a day. Small-town stations may only be open from 7am to 8pm or 9pm.

RENTAL CARS
Dollar (www.dollarcar.com)
Rent-A-Wreck (www.rentawreck.com)
Thrifty (www.thrifty.com)

IMPORTANT NUMBERS
AAA (☎800-222-4357)
Directory Assistance (☎411)
Emergency (☎911)

Climate

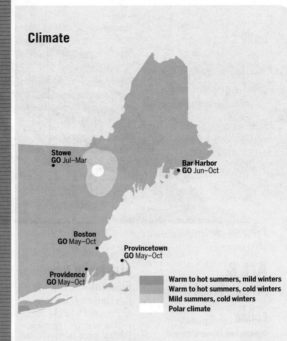

Stowe
GO Jul–Mar

Bar Harbor
• GO Jun–Oct

Boston
GO May–Oct

Provincetown
GO May–Oct

Providence
GO May–Oct

- Warm to hot summers, mild winters
- Warm to hot summers, cold winters
- Mild summers, cold winters
- Polar climate

When to Go

High Season (May–Aug, Oct)
» Accommodation prices increase by 50% to 100%; book well in advance.

» Expect temperate weather and blooming trees. July and August are hot and humid, except in mountain areas.

Shoulder Season (Apr, Sep)
» Accommodations are less likely to be booked in advance; lower prices may be negotiated (also applies to beach areas in May, early June and October).

» The air is crisp and cool, but blue skies prevail.

Low Season (Nov–Mar)
» Significantly lower prices for accommodations.

» Crowds thin out, but many sights are closed.

» November is chilly and gray, but real winter arrives with snowy skies and icy temperatures from December to March. Driving can be perilous.

Daily Costs

Budget: Less than $100
» Camping or hostel bed: $25–$45
» Meal at roadside diner: $5–$15
» State parks, walking tours: free

Midrange: $100–$250
» Double room in midrange hotel or B&B: $100–$200
» Meal at midrange restaurant: $20–$40
» Museum admission: $10–$20

Top End: More than $250
» Double room in top-end hotel: $200 or more
» Meal at the finest restaurants: $40–$60

Eating

Roadside diners Simple, cheap places with limited menus.

Seafood shacks No-frills seaside venues offering excellent seafood.

Farms Small farm cafes showing off the harvest.

Vegetarians Selections available at most restaurants and cafes.

Eating price indicators represent the cost of a main dish:

$	less than $10
$$	$10–$20
$$$	more than $20

Sleeping

B&Bs Quaint accommodations, often in historic houses, usually including an elaborate breakfast.

Motels Affordable roadside accommodations, usually on the outskirts of town.

Camping Facilities for tents, often at state and national parks. Some campgrounds also offer simple cabins.

Cottages, condos Multi-room units in a resort or complex, usually available for longer stays.

Sleeping price indicators represent the cost of a double room:

$	less than $100
$$	$100–$200
$$$	more than $200

Arriving in New England

Boston Logan International Airport

Rental cars Sumner or Ted Williams Tunnel toll is $3.50.

Silver-Line bus Travels downtown ($1.70 to $2).

Subway Free shuttle goes to blue-line Airport station; subway fares are $1.70 to $2.

Manchester International Airport

Rental cars Take the free shuttle bus to the rental-car offices.

Shared vans Rides (from $39) to southern New Hampshire and northern Massachusetts.

TF Green Airport (Warwick, RI)

Rental cars Take the free shuttle bus to the rental-car offices.

Trains Run to downtown Providence ($5, 20 minutes) and Boston ($8.25, 90 minutes).

Money

ATMs widely available. Credit cards accepted at most hotels and restaurants.

Tipping

Standard is 15% to 20% for waiters and bartenders, 10% to 15% for taxi drivers and $1 to $2 per bag for porters.

Opening Hours

State and national parks are open from dawn to dusk unless otherwise noted.

Bars 5pm–midnight, some places till 2am

Information 9am–5pm or 6pm Monday to Friday

Restaurants breakfast 6am–10am, lunch 11:30am–2:30pm, dinner 5pm–10pm

Shops 9am–7pm Monday to Saturday, some noon–5pm Sunday

Useful Websites

Boston Globe New England Guide (www.boston.com/travel/newengland) Travel tips and itineraries.

National Parks Service (www.nps.gov/parks) Fast facts about national parks, recreation areas and historic sites.

Visit New England (www.visitnewengland.com) Comprehensive listing of hotels and attractions.

For more, see the New England Driving Guide (p338).

CITY GUIDE

BOSTON

Narrow streets and stately architecture recall a history of revolution and transformation. Today, Boston is still forward-thinking and barrier-breaking. Follow the Freedom Trail to learn about the past; stroll along the Rose Kennedy Greenway to appreciate the present; and visit the galleries, clubs and student haunts to envision the future.

Getting Around

Park your car and explore the city by foot, bicycle or subway. The USA's oldest subway system, the **MBTA** (www.mbta. com; fare $1.70 to $2), is known on the ground as 'the T.' Boston's fabulous bike-share program, the **Hubway** (www. thehubway.com; registration $5, per hour $2), has 60 stations where you can borrow a bicycle for an hour or a day.

Parking

Street parking is scarce and meter readers are ruthless. Relatively affordable parking lots are located under the Boston Common and in the Seaport District.

Where to Eat

Boston's most famous eating area is the North End, packed with *salumeria* (delis),

Boston The harbor at night

pasticceria (pastry shops) and ristoranti. The Seaport District is the place to go for seafood, while Quincy Market is a giant food court that has something for everyone.

Where to Stay

Boston is small enough that almost all of its neighborhoods offer easy access to great sights, dining and entertainment. Beacon Hill and Back Bay are particularly charming. Although the West End is desolate, its hotels offer excellent value for their convenience to downtown Boston.

Useful Websites

Boston.com (www.boston.com) The online presence of the *Boston Globe*.

Universal Hub (www.universalhub.com) Bostonians talking to each other.

Sons of Sam Horn (www.sonsofsamhorn.net) Dedicated to discussion of all things Red Sox.

Lonely Planet (www.lonelyplanet.com/boston) Destination information, hotel bookings, traveler forum and more.

Trips Through Boston: 1 2 20

Massachusetts

CITY STREETS AND COW-DOTTED PASTURES, WINDSWEPT BEACHES AND FOREST-COVERED MOUNTAINS: Massachusetts offers an incredible diversity of landscapes. The state is small, but its scenery will satisfy your craving for eye candy (surely the foremost requirement for a rewarding road trip).

When you're ready for a pit stop, the Commonwealth has you covered, with a tantalizing spread of local specialties for you to choose from. And fuel up, because you have a lot to do. These trips show off four centuries of dramatic history, rich displays of artistry and creativity, and thrilling opportunities for outdoor adventure. Buckle up and enjoy the ride.

Berkshires Take the scenic route through the charming Berkshires (Trip 5)

Massachusetts

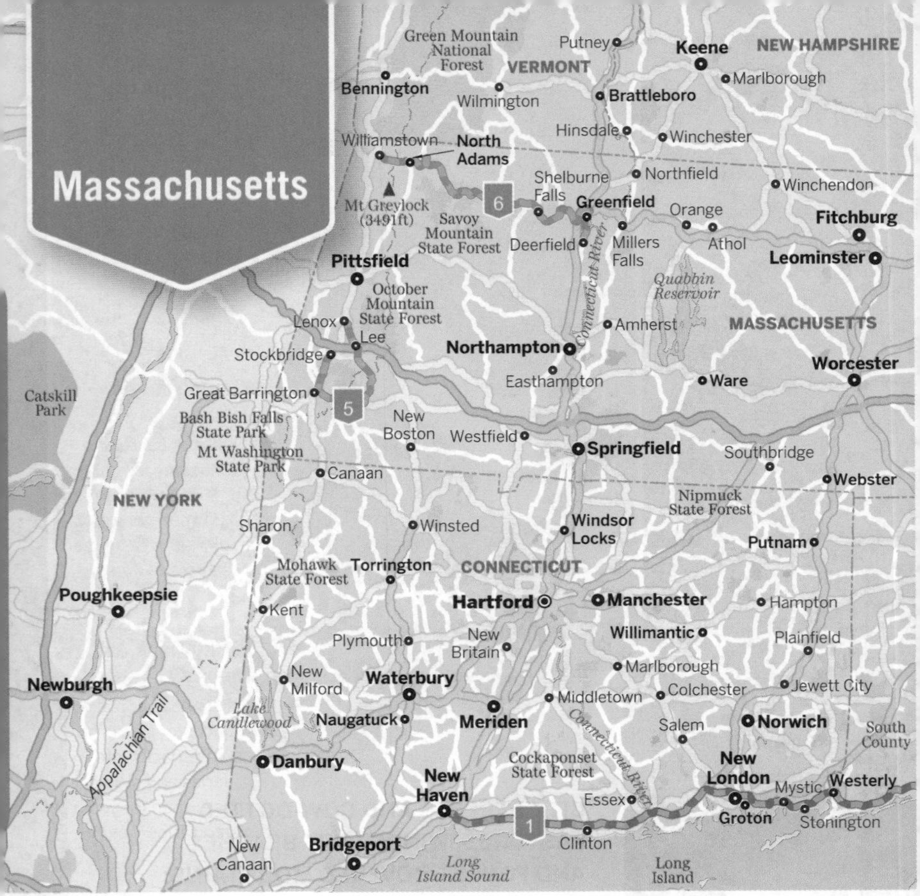
Green Mountain National Forest
VERMONT
Putney
Keene
NEW HAMPSHIRE
Marlborough
Bennington
Wilmington
Brattleboro
Hinsdale
Winchester
Williamstown
North Adams
Northfield
Winchendon
Shelburne Falls
Greenfield
Orange
Fitchburg
6
Mt Greylock (3491ft)
Savoy Mountain State Forest
Deerfield
Millers Falls
Athol
Leominster
Pittsfield
Connecticut River
Quabbin Reservoir
October Mountain State Forest
Lenox
Amherst
MASSACHUSETTS
Lee
Stockbridge
Northampton
Worcester
Easthampton
Catskill Park
Great Barrington
Ware
5
Bash Bish Falls State Park
New Boston
Westfield
Springfield
Southbridge
Mt Washington State Park
Canaan
Webster
NEW YORK
Nipmuck State Forest
Sharon
Winsted
Windsor Locks
Putnam
Mohawk State Forest
Torrington
CONNECTICUT
Poughkeepsie
Hartford
Manchester
Hampton
Kent
Plymouth
New Britain
Willimantic
Plainfield
Marlborough
New Milford
Waterbury
Jewett City
Newburgh
Middletown
Colchester
Lake Candlewood
Naugatuck
Meriden
Connecticut River
Salem
Norwich
South County
Appalachian Trail
Danbury
Cockaponset State Forest
New London
New Haven
Mystic
Westerly
Essex
Groton
Stonington
1
Clinton
New Canaan
Bridgeport
Long Island Sound
Long Island

Classic Trip

1 Coastal New England 6–8 Days

The ultimate coastal drive connects fishing villages, trading ports and naval centers. (p33)

2 Pilgrim Trail 4–5 Days

This trip for history buffs explores the New World's earliest settlements. (p43)

Classic Trip

3 Cape Cod & the Islands 5–7 Days

The slow, meandering route includes the cape's best beaches, oysters and art. (p51)

4 Around Cape Ann 2–3 Days

A cruise along the North Shore features clam shacks and coastal scenery. (p61)

5 Berkshire Back Roads 2–3 Days

This drive through the Berkshires offers inspired arts performances in splendid mountain settings. (p69)

6 Mohawk Trail 2–3 Days

The storied scenic highway is a conduit for history, art and adventure. (p77)

DON'T MISS

Stellwagen Bank

This National Marine Sanctuary is a rich feeding ground for humpback whales. See them on Trips **1** **3**

Gould's Sugar House

Fluffy pancakes and homemade ice cream show off delicious maple syrup, made at this family farm. Taste the goodness on Trip **6**

Rocky Neck Art Colony

Artists have converted Gloucester's colorful fishing shacks into galleries and studio space, open for your visit on Trips **1** **4**

Nauset Light

The iconic red-and-white beacon has been shining the light since 1877. Climb to the top on Trip **3**

Commercial Street

'Eclectic' doesn't begin to describe Provincetown's main drag, with art galleries, pet parades and gay cabaret. See the show on Trips **2** **3**

Provincetown (Trips 2 and 3)

31

Salem *At Derby Wharf, view the*
Friendship *and indulge your inner pirate*

Coastal New England

1

This drive follows the southern New England coast. A week of whale-watching, maritime museums and sailboats will leave you feeling pleasantly waterlogged.

TRIP HIGHLIGHTS

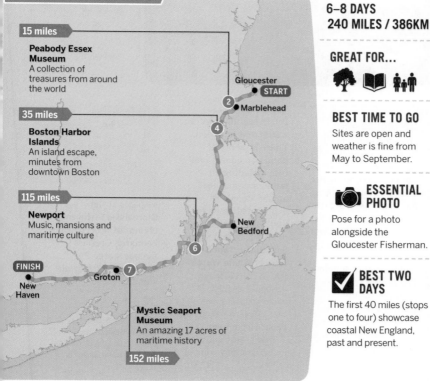

15 miles

Peabody Essex Museum
A collection of treasures from around the world

35 miles

Boston Harbor Islands
An island escape, minutes from downtown Boston

115 miles

Newport
Music, mansions and maritime culture

FINISH
New Haven

Groton

Mystic Seaport Museum
An amazing 17 acres of maritime history

152 miles

Gloucester **START**
Marblehead

New Bedford

6–8 DAYS
240 MILES / 386KM

GREAT FOR...

BEST TIME TO GO

Sites are open and weather is fine from May to September.

ESSENTIAL PHOTO

Pose for a photo alongside the Gloucester Fisherman.

BEST TWO DAYS

The first 40 miles (stops one to four) showcase coastal New England, past and present.

33

Classic Trip

1 Coastal New England

From a pirate's perspective, there was no better base in Colonial America than Newport, given the easy access to trade routes and friendly local merchants. Until 1723, that is, when the new governor ceremoniously hanged 26 sea bandits at Gravelly Point. This classic trip highlights the region's intrinsic connection to the sea, from upstart pirates to upper-crust merchants, from Gloucester fishermen to New Bedford whalers, from clipper ships to submarines.

1 Gloucester

Founded in 1623 by English fisherfolk, Gloucester is among New England's oldest towns. This port on Cape Ann has made its living from fishing for almost 400 years, and inspired works like Rudyard Kipling's *Captains Courageous* and Sebastian Junger's *The Perfect Storm*. Visit the **Marine Heritage Center** (www. gloucestermaritimecenter. org; Harbor Loop; adult/child/ senior/family $5/2/4/10;

⏱10am-5pm daily Jun-Oct) to see the working waterfront in action. There is plenty of hands-on educational fun, including an outdoor aquarium and an excellent exhibit dedicated to Stellwagen Bank, the nearby National Marine Sanctuary. **Capt Bill & Sons Whale Watch** (☎978-283-6995; www. captbillandsons.com; 24 Harbor Loop; adult/senior/ child $48/42/32) boats also depart from here.

Don't leave Gloucester before you pay your

respects at the **Gloucester Fishermen's Memorial**, where Leonarde Craske's famous statue *The Gloucester Fisherman* stands.

🍴 p41

The Drive » Head out of town on Western Ave (MA 127), cruising past the Gloucester Fisherman and Stage Fort Park.

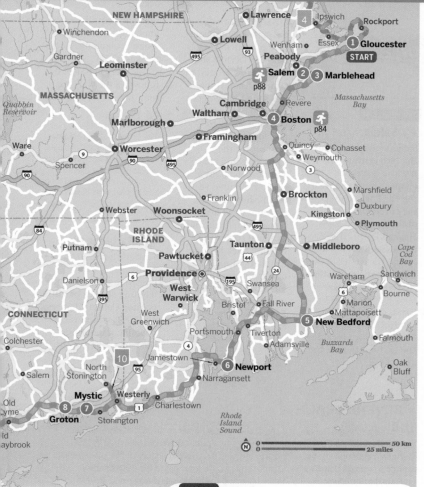

This winding road follows the coastline south through swanky seaside towns like Manchester-by-the-Sea and Beverly Farms, with occasional glimpses of the bay. After about 14 miles, cross the Essex Bridge and continue south into Salem. For a quicker trip, take MA 128 south to MA 114.

LINK YOUR TRIP

4 Around Cape Ann

Head north from Gloucester for more quaint coastal culture.

10 Connecticut Wine Trail

Continue south along the coast for a tasty tour through New England wine country.

35

TRIP HIGHLIGHT

2 Salem

Salem's glory dates to the 18th century, when it was a center for clipper-ship trade with the Far East, thanks to the enterprising efforts of the merchant Elias Haskell Derby. His namesake Derby Wharf is now the center of the **Salem Maritime National Historic Site** (www.nps.gov/sama; 193 Derby St; ⊘9am-5pm daily Apr-Nov, 1-5pm Mon-Fri & 9am-5pm Sat & Sun Dec-Mar), which includes the 1871 lighthouse, the tall ship *Friendship* and the state custom house.

Many Salem vessels followed Derby's ship *Grand Turk* around the Cape of Good Hope, and soon the owners founded the East India Marine Society to provide warehousing services for their ships' logs and charts. The new company's charter required the establishment of 'a museum in which to house the natural and artificial curiosities' brought back by members' ships. The collection was the basis for what is now the world-class **Peabody Essex Museum** (www.pem.org; Essex St Mall, New Liberty St; adult/child/student/senior $15/free/11/13; ⊘10am-5pm Tue-Sun). Still today, the museum contains an amazing collection of Asian art, amongst other treasures.

See more of Salem by following the walking tour, p88.

✕ ⊨ p41

The Drive » Take Lafayette St (MA 114) south out of Salem center, driving past the campus of Salem State College. After crossing an inlet, the road bends east and becomes Pleasant St as it enters Marblehead center.

3 Marblehead

First settled in 1629, Marblehead is a maritime village with winding streets, brightly painted Colonial houses, and 1000 sailing yachts bobbing at moorings in the harbor. This is the Boston area's premier

---

REVERE BEACH

Cruising through Revere, MA 1A parallels the wide sandy stretch of Revere Beach, which proudly proclaims itself America's first public beach, established in 1896. Scenic but soulless, the condo-fronted beach belies the history of this place, which was a raucous boardwalk and amusement park for most of the 20th century. Famous for roller coasters, dance halls and the Wonderland dog track, Revere Beach attracted hundreds of thousands of sunbathers and fun-seekers during summer months.

The area deteriorated in the 1970s due to crime and pollution. In 1978 a historic blizzard wiped out many of the remaining buildings and businesses and the 'Coney Island of New England' was relegated to the annals of history.

Revere Beach benefitted from a clean-up effort in the 1980s; nowadays, the beach itself is lovely to look at and safe to swim. Unfortunately, dominated by high-end condominium complexes, the area retains nothing of its former charm. Only one vestige of 'old' Revere Beach remains: the world-famous **Kelly's Roast Beef** (www.kellysroastbeef.com; 410 Revere Beach Blvd; sandwiches $6-10; ⊘lunch & dinner), which has been around since 1951, and still serves up the best roast-beef sandwiches and clam chowder in town. There's no indoor seating, so pull up some sand and enjoy the view. Beware of the seagulls: they're crazy for roast beef.

yachting port and one of New England's most prestigious addresses. Clustered around the harbor, Marblehead center is dotted with historic houses, art galleries and waterside parks.

The Drive ≫ Drive south on MA 129, exiting Marblehead and continuing through the seaside town of Swampscott. At the traffic circle, take the first exit onto MA 1A, which continues south through Lynn and Revere. Take the VFW Parkway (MA 1A) to the Revere Beach Parkway (MA 16) to the Northeast Expressway (US 1), which goes over the Tobin Bridge and into Boston.

TRIP HIGHLIGHT

④ Boston

Boston's seaside location has influenced every aspect of its history, but it's only in recent years that the waterfront has become an attractive and accessible destination for visitors. Now you can stroll along the **Rose Kennedy Greenway** (www.rosekennedygreenway. org), with the sea on one side and the city on the other. The focal point of the waterfront is the excellent **New England Aquarium** (www.neaq.org; Central Wharf; adult/child/senior $23/16/12; ☼9am-5pm Mon-Thu, to 6pm Fri-Sun; ℗), home to seals, penguins, turtles and oodles of fish. Parking is $18.

From Long Wharf, you can catch a ferry out to the **Boston**

PARKING IN BOSTON

Parking in downtown Boston is prohibitively expensive. For more affordable rates, cross the Fort Point Channel and park in the Seaport District. Park in lots on Northern Ave (near the Institute of Contemporary Art) for a flat rate of $12; the Necco Street Garage (further south, off A St) is only $6.

Harbor Islands (www. bostonislands.com; ferry adult/child $14/8; ☼hourly 9am-6pm May-Sep) for berry picking, beachcombing and sunbathing. Harbor cruises and trolley tours also depart from these docks. For another look at Boston, follow the walking tour, p26.

✕ 🛏 p41

The Drive ≫ Drive south out of Boston on I-93. You'll recognize the urban 'hood of Dorchester by pretty Savin Hill Cove and the landmark Rainbow Swash painted on the gas tank. At exit 4, take MA 24 south toward Brockton, then MA 140 south toward New Bedford. Take I-195 east for 2 miles, exiting onto MA 18 for New Bedford.

⑤ New Bedford

During its heyday as a whaling port (1765–1860), New Bedford commanded some 400 whaling ships – a vast fleet that brought in hundreds of thousands of barrels of whale oil for lighting lamps. Novelist Herman Melville worked on one of these ships for four years, and thus set his celebrated novel

Moby-Dick in New Bedford.

The excellent, hands-on **New Bedford Whaling Museum** (www. whalingmuseum.org; 18 Johnny Cake Hill; adult/child/senior & student $15/6/12/9; ☼9am-5pm Jun-Dec, 9am-4pm Tue-Sun Jan-May) celebrates this history. A 66ft skeleton of a blue whale welcomes you at the entrance. Inside, you can tramp the decks of the *Lagoda,* a fully rigged, half-size replica of an actual whaling bark.

The Drive ≫ Take I-195 west for about 10 miles. In Fall River, head south on MA 24, which becomes RI 24 as you cross into Rhode Island. Cross the bridge, with views of Mt Hope Bay to the north and Sakonnet River to the south, then merge onto RI 114, heading south into Newport.

TRIP HIGHLIGHT

⑥ Newport

Blessed with a deepwater harbor, Newport has been a shipbuilding base since 1646. Bowen's and Bannister's Wharf, once working wharves, now typify Newport's transformation from

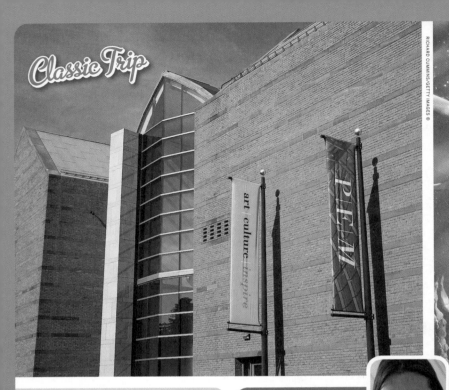

Classic Trip

WHY THIS IS A CLASSIC TRIP
MARA VORHEES, AUTHOR

Nothing evokes New England's salty air like driving along the old coastal roads. MA 127 winds through some of the state's prettiest seaside towns, giving glimpses of gracious mansions perched at the ocean's edge. Even better, I love cruising along MA 1A with the windows down, feeling the ocean breeze, hearing the seagulls' cries and recalling the glory days of Revere Beach.

Top: Peabody Essex Museum, Salem
Left: Mystic
Right: Observing marine life at a New England aquarium

a working city-by-the-sea to a resort town. Take a narrated cruise with **Classic Cruises of Newport** (www.cruisenewport.com; Bannister's Wharf; adult $18-27; ⊗ mid-May–mid-Oct) on *Rum Runner II,* a Prohibition-era bootlegging vessel, or *Madeleine,* a 72ft schooner. Or ogle the mansions on the walking tour on p152.

Although its pirate days are over, Newport's harbor remains one of the most active yachting centers in the country. Visit the **Museum of Yachting** (www.moy.org; Fort Adams State Park; adult/child $5/free; ⊗ noon-5pm Tue-Sat Jun-Oct) for a quick history in the America's Cup Gallery and to watch students at work in the restoration school. Looming beside the museum is **Fort Adams** (www.riparks.com/fortadams), one of the largest seacoast fortifications in the US. In August it is the venue for the **Newport Jazz Festival** (www.newportjazzfest.net) and the **Newport Folk Festival** (www.newportfolkfest.net).

✗ p41

The Drive » Head west out of Newport on RI 138, swooping over the Newport Bridge onto Conanicut Island and then over the Jamestown Bridge to pick up US 1 for the drive into Mystic. The views of the bay from both bridges are a highlight.

and light industrial areas. To hop across the Thames River to New London, head north along North St to pick up I-95 South.

8 Groton

Groton is home to the US Naval Submarine Base, the first and the largest in the country. It is off-limits to the public, but you can visit the **Historic Ship Nautilus & Submarine Force Museum** (www. ussnautilus.org; 1 Crystal Lake Rd; admission free; ⊙9am-4pm Wed-Mon; P), which is home to *Nautilus,* the world's first nuclear-powered submarine and the first sub to transit the North Pole.

Across the river, New London has a similarly illustrious seafaring history, although these days it's built a reputation for itself as a budding creative center. Each summer it hosts **Sailfest** (www.sailfest. org), a three-day festival with free entertainment topped off by the second-largest fireworks display in the Northeast. There's also a **Summer Concert Series**, organized by **Hygienic Art** (www.hygienic. org; 79 Bank St; ⊙11am-6pm Fri & Sat, noon-3pm Sun).

✗ p41

The Drive ≫ It's a 52-mile drive from Groton or New London to New Haven along I-95 South. The initial stages of the drive plough through the suburbs, but after that the interstate runs through old coastal towns such as Old Lyme, Old Saybrook and Guilford.

9 New Haven

Although most famous for its Ivy League university, Yale, New Haven also played an important role in the burgeoning anti-slavery movement when, in 1839, the trial of mutineering Mendi tribesmen was held in New Haven's District Court.

Following their illegal capture by Spanish slave traders, the tribesmen, led by Joseph Cinqué, seized the schooner *Amistad* and sailed to New Haven seeking refuge. Pending the successful outcome of the trial (for which former president John Quincy Adams came out of retirement to plead their case), the men were held in a jailhouse on the green, where a 14ft-high bronze memorial now stands. It was the first Civil Rights case held in the country.

Stretch your legs with a walking tour of New Haven's art galleries (p154). Or for a unique take on the New Haven shoreline take the 3-mile round trip on the **Shore Line Trolley** (www. shorelinetrolley.com; 17 River St, East Haven; adult/child under 15yr $6; ⊙10.30am-4.30pm daily Jun-Aug, Sat & Sun May, Sep & Oct; 🚻), the oldest operating suburban trolley in the country, which takes you from East Haven to Short Beach in Branford.

✗ p41

Classic Trip

TRIP HIGHLIGHT

7 Mystic

Many of Mystic's clipper ships launched from George Greenman & Co Shipyard, now the site of the **Mystic Seaport Museum** (www. mysticseaport.org; 75 Greenmanville Ave/CT 27; adult/6-17yr $24/15; ⊙9am-5pm Apr-Oct; 🚻). Today the museum covers 17 acres and includes more than 60 historic buildings, four tall ships and almost 500 smaller vessels. Interpreters staffing all the buildings are glad to discuss their crafts and trades. Most illuminating are the demonstrations on such topics as ship rescue, oystering and whaleboat launching. The museum's exhibits also include a replica of the 77ft slave ship *Amistad*.

If the call of the sea beckons, the **Sabino** (☎860-572-5351; adult/6-17yr $5.50/4.50), a 1908 steamboat, takes visitors on half-hour excursions up the Mystic River. The boat departs from the museum hourly from 11.30am to 4.30pm.

🛏 ✗ p41

The Drive ≫ The 7-mile drive from Mystic to Groton along US 1 South is through built-up suburbs

Eating & Sleeping

Gloucester ❶

✖ Two Sisters Coffee Shop   Diner $

(27 Washington St; meals $8-10; ⊙breakfast & lunch; 🖉) The fisherfolk go here for breakfast when they come in from their catch. They're early risers, so you may have to wait for a table. Corn beef hash, eggs in a hole and French toast all get rave reviews. Service is a little salty.

Salem ❷

✖ The Old Spot   Pub $$

(www.theoldspot.com; 121 Essex St; sandwiches $8-10, mains $15-18; ⊙lunch Fri-Sun, dinner daily) It's pub food, but so perfectly prepared that it becomes a dining experience. Dim lighting and plush pillows make the place extra comfortable and cozy.

Boston ❹

✖ Barking Crab   Seafood $$

(www.barkingcrab.com; 88 Sleeper St; mains $12-30; ⊙lunch & dinner) Big buckets of crabs, steamers dripping in lemon and butter, paper plates piled high with all things fried... The food is plentiful and affordable, and you eat it at communal picnic tables overlooking the water. Beer flows freely. Service is slack, but the atmosphere is jovial.

🛏 Harborside Inn   Boutique Hotel $$

(📞617-723-7500; www.harborsideinnboston. com; 185 State St; r from $199; 🅿 ❄ @ 🛜) Ensconced in a former warehouse, this waterfront hostelry strikes the right balance between historic digs and modern conveniences. Brick and granite walls and hardwood floors are offset perfectly by oriental carpets, sleigh beds and reproduction Federal-era furnishings.

Newport ❻

✖ White Horse Tavern   American $$$

(www.whitehorsetavern.us; 26 Marlborough St; mains $14-40; ⊙11.30am-9pm) If you'd like to eat at a tavern opened by a 17th-century pirate, then try this gambrel-roofed beauty. Menus for dinner (at which men should wear jackets) might include baked escargot or beef Wellington.

Mystic ❼

🛏 Whaler's Inn   Historic Hotel $$

(📞860-536-1506; www.whalersinnmystic. com; 20 E Main St; d $90-200, ste $199-260; 🅿🛜) Beside Mystic's historic drawbridge, this elegant hotel combines an 1865 Victorian house with a reconstructed luxury hotel and a modern motel. Rates include a continental breakfast as well as complimentary bicycles.

New London ❽

✖ Captain Scott's Lobster Dock   Seafood $$

(80 Hamilton St; meals $10-20; ⊙lunch & dinner May-Oct; 🖉) Captain Scott's is *the* place to go for seafood in summer. The setting's just picnic tables by the water, but you can feast on succulent (hot or cold) lobster rolls, followed by steamers, fried whole-belly clams, scallops or lobsters.

New Haven ❾

✖ Miya's Sushi   Sushi $$

(📞203-777-9760; miyassushi.com; 68 Howe St; meals $13-36; ⊙lunch & dinner) Superlative sushi – probably the best in the state – is prepared in this low-key spot by chef Bun Lai. Appetizers sport alluring names such as Concubine's Delight, but the true star is the kaiseki, a traditional multi-course Japanese dinner ($30).

Plymouth *Imagine life as a Pilgrim at Plimoth Plantation*

Pilgrim Trail **2**

Follow in the footsteps of the country's earliest European settlers, visiting the sites that remember their struggles and celebrate their successes in taming and claiming the New World.

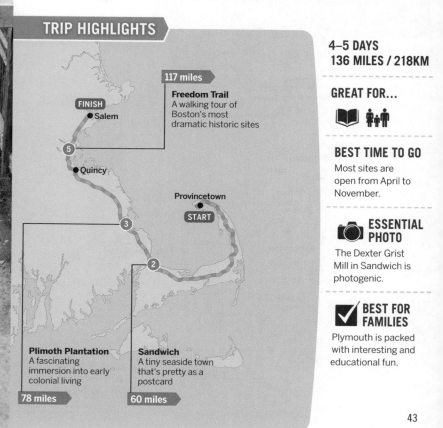

TRIP HIGHLIGHTS

117 miles

Freedom Trail
A walking tour of Boston's most dramatic historic sites

FINISH
● Salem

5

● Quincy

Provincetown ●
START

3

2

Plimoth Plantation
A fascinating immersion into early colonial living

78 miles

Sandwich
A tiny seaside town that's pretty as a postcard

60 miles

4–5 DAYS
136 MILES / 218KM

GREAT FOR...

BEST TIME TO GO
Most sites are open from April to November.

ESSENTIAL PHOTO
The Dexter Grist Mill in Sandwich is photogenic.

BEST FOR FAMILIES
Plymouth is packed with interesting and educational fun.

43

2 Pilgrim Trail

Your car is a time machine, transporting you back 400 years. The region's living museums allow you to experience firsthand what life was like for the colonists as they settled in the New World. Explore the sites and structures – churches and trading posts, homesteads and grist mills – that are still standing from those early days.

1 Provincetown

Most people don't know that months before the 'official' landing on Plymouth Rock, the Pilgrims arrived at the tip of Cape Cod. Despite the protected harbor and good fishing, they were unable to find a good source of reliable fresh water, so they headed off to Plymouth. But not before signing the Mayflower Compact, which is considered the first governing document of the Plymouth Colony. The **Pilgrim Monument**

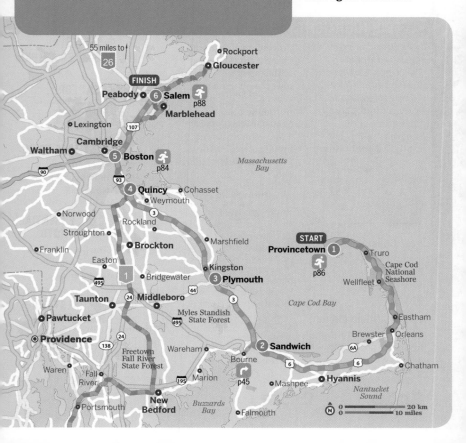

55 miles to
26

Rockport
Gloucester

FINISH
Peabody 6 Salem p88
Marblehead

Lexington
107
Cambridge
Waltham
90
5 Boston p84

Massachusetts Bay

93
4 Quincy   Cohasset
Weymouth

Norwood
3
Rockland
Stroughton
Marshfield
Franklin
Brockton
Easton
1
Bridgewater
24
Taunton   Middleboro
44
495
Myles Standish State Forest
Pawtucket
Providence
138
24
Freetown Fall River State Forest
Waren
Wareham
Bourne
195
Fall River
Marion
p45
New Bedford
Buzzards Bay
Falmouth

START
Provincetown 1 p86
Truro
Cape Cod National Seashore
Wellfleet

3 Plymouth
3
Cape Cod Bay

Eastham
Brewster   Orleans
6A
Chatham

2 Sandwich
6
6
Mashpee   Hyannis
Nantucket Sound

N 0   20 km
   0   10 miles

DETOUR:
BOURNE

Start ② Sandwich

Bourne is not as picturesque as nearby Sandwich, but it is historically significant, thanks to its strategic location at the northeast corner of Buzzards Bay, halfway between the Manomet and Scusset Rivers. Here, in 1627, the Pilgrims founded the Aptucxet Trading Post, which allowed easy access to the Dutch settlements to the south. The trading center would eventually lead to the construction of the Cape Cod Canal, which was built so traders could avoid the cape's hazardous eastern shore.

Nowadays, the **Aptucxet Trading Post Museum** (www.bournehistoricalsociety.org; 6 Aptucxet Rd; admission free; ☺10am-5pm Tue-Sat Jun-Aug) is an eclectic little museum, built on what is believed to be the oldest remains of a Pilgrim building ever found. Although the simple, unpainted clapboard structure standing today is a replica built on the original foundation, it's still possible to imagine Pilgrims, Wampanoag and Dutch coming here to barter goods, seeds, tools and food.

To reach the Aptucxet Trading Post, take MA 6A out of Sandwich and continue on Sandwich Rd for 7 miles along the Cape Cod Canal. Once in Bourne, turn right on Perry Rd and take the first left on Aptucxet Rd.

(www.pilgrim-monument.org; High Pole Hill Rd, Provincetown; adult/senior/student/child $10/7/7/4; ☺9am-5pm Apr-Dec, to 7pm Jun-Aug) commemorates the signing of the compact, as do a few exhibits at the on-site

LINK YOUR TRIP

1 Coastal New England

See more of maritime Massachusetts and Connecticut.

26 Maritime Maine

For a round of lighthouse photos and lobster feasts, take I-95 to Kittery.

Provincetown Museum. Climb 252ft (116 steps) to the top of the tall tower for magnificent views of Provincetown Harbor and the National Seashore. For a tour of more recent Provincetown history, follow the walking tour, p86.

 p49

The Drive » Head out of Provincetown on US 6, passing the picturesque East Harbor and the windblown beach shacks overlooking the ocean. You'll pass Pilgrim Heights, where the settlers found fresh water, and First Encounter Beach, site of the first violent clash with the native population. From Orleans, you can continue west on US 6, or take the slower, more scenic MA 6A, which shows off the cape's historic villages.

 TRIP HIGHLIGHT

2 Sandwich

With the waterwheel at the old mill, the white clapboard houses, and the swans on the pond, the center of Sandwich is as pretty as a Cape Cod town can be. The restored 17th-century **Dexter Grist Mill** (Water St; adult/child $3/2; ☺10am-5pm Mon-Sat, 1-5pm Sun) on the edge of Shawme Pond has centuries-old gears that still grind cornmeal. Nearby, **Hoxie House** (18 Water St; adult/child $3/2; ☺10am-5pm Mon-Sat, 1-5pm Sun) is one of the oldest houses on Cape Cod. The 1640 salt box-style structure has been faithfully restored, complete with antiques

EDUCATION IMAGES/UIG/GETTY IMAGES ©

and brick hearth, giving a good sense of early-settler home life.

The Drive » Hop on US 6 heading west over the Sagamore Bridge. Stay on MA 3 or branch off to MA 3A, which hugs the coast for the 14 miles north to Plymouth.

- - - - - - - - - - - -

TRIP HIGHLIGHT

❸ Plymouth

Plymouth is 'America's Home Town,' where the Pilgrims first settled in the winter of 1620. An innocuous, weathered ball of granite – the famous **Plymouth Rock** – marks the spot where they (might have) stepped ashore in this foreign land, while **Mayflower II** (www.plimoth. org; State Pier; adult/child/senior $10/7/9; ☺9am-5pm Apr-Nov) is a replica of the small ship in which they made the fateful voyage. Many museums and historic sites in the surrounding streets recall the Pilgrims' struggles, sacrifices and triumphs.

The best is **Plimoth Plantation** (www.plimoth. org; MA 3A; adult/child/senior $24/14/22; ☺9am-5:30pm Apr-Nov), a historically accurate recreation of the Pilgrims' settlement. Everything in the 1627 English Village –

46

Provincetown Take in the coastal scenery

costumes, implements, vocabulary, artistry, recipes and crops – has been painstakingly researched and remade. Costumed interpreters, acting in character, explain the details of daily life and answer your questions as you watch them work and play. The on-site Wampanoag Homesite replicates the life of a Native American community in the same area during that time.

✕ ➤ p49

The Drive >> Take MA 3 north for about 25 miles. In Quincy, take the Burgin Parkway 2 miles north into the center.

- - - - - - - - - - - -

4 Quincy

Quincy was first settled in 1625 by a handful of raucous colonists who could not stand the strict and stoic ways in Plymouth. History has it that this group went so far as to drink beer, dance around a maypole and engage in other festive Old English customs, which enraged the Pilgrims down the road. Nathaniel Hawthorne immortalized this history in his fictional account, *The*

Maypole of Merrimount. Eventually, Myles Standish arrived from Plymouth to restore order to the wayward colony.

What earns this town the nickname 'The City of Presidents' is that it is the birthplace of John Adams and John Quincy Adams. The collection of houses where the Adams family lived now comprises the **Adams National Historic Park** (www.nps.gov/adam; 1250 Hancock St; adult/child $5/free; 9am-5pm mid-Apr–mid-Nov, last tour 3:15pm). Besides the homes, you can also see where the presidents and their wives are interred in the crypt of the **United First Parish Church** (www.ufpc. org; 1306 Hancock St; adult/child/senior & student $4/free/3; 9am-5pm Mon-Sat, 1-5pm Sun mid-Apr–mid-Nov).

The Drive >> Take Newport Ave north out of town and merge onto I-93 heading north. Continue on the Central Artery straight through (and under) Boston, experiencing firsthand the benefits of the infamous Big Dig. Take exit 26 onto Storrow Dr for downtown Boston.

TRIP HIGHLIGHT

⑤ Boston

Ten years after the Pilgrims settled in Plymouth, they were followed by a group of Puritans – also fleeing the repressive Church of England – who founded the Massachusetts Bay Colony about 40 miles up the coast. The Puritans'

first seat of government was on the north shore of the River Charles, where excavations have uncovered the foundations of Governor John Winthrop's home, the so-called **Great House** (City Sq, Charlestown). Winthrop is buried alongside other early settlers in the **King's Chapel Burying Ground** (58 Tremont St).

Not too many physical structures remain from these earliest days of Boston settlement. The city's oldest house (1680) is the **Paul Revere House** (www.paulreverehouse.org; 19 North Sq; adult/child/senior & student $3.50/1/3; 9:30am-4:15pm), where the celebrated patriot lived. The oldest church (1723) is **Old North Church** (www.oldnorth.com; 193 Salem St; 9am-5pm), where two lanterns were hung in the steeple on the eve of the American Revolution. To see these and other sites from Boston's Revolutionary history, follow the **Freedom Trail** (www.thefreedomtrail. org), a 2.5-mile walking path that connects the most prominent historic landmarks. For a different perspective on this dynamic city, follow the walking tour, p84.

✗ ⮚ p49

The Drive >> As you exit Boston to the north, merge onto US 1 and cross the Tobin Bridge. The fastest route is to take MA 60 to MA 107, also known as the Salem

Parkway, which goes straight to Salem. Or hop on MA 16 over to MA 1A for a seaside route through Swampscott and Marblehead.

⑥ Salem

Founded by English fishermen in 1626, Salem was part of the Massachusetts Bay Colony. **Salem Pioneer Village** (www.pioneervillagesalem.com; Forest River Park; adult/student/senior $6/5/5; noon-4pm Jun-Oct) is an outdoor, interactive museum that gives visitors an idea of what daily life was like for settlers.

Salem is most famous – or infamous – as the site of the witch trials in 1692, when 19 people were hanged as a result of witch-hunt hysteria. Don't miss the **Witch Trials Memorial** (Charter St), a simple but dramatic monument that honors the innocent victims. To understand more about how this hysteria snowballed, visit the **Witch House** (www. salemweb.com/witchhouse; 310 Essex St; adult/child/senior $8.25/4.25/6.25; 10am-5pm May-Nov, longer hours Oct). This was the former home of Jonathan Corwin, a local magistrate who investigated witchcraft claims.

The town has dozens of other related sites, as well as a month-long Halloween extravaganza in October. To experience Salem beyond 'Witch City', follow the walking tour, p88.

✗ ⮚ p49

Eating & Sleeping

Provincetown ❶

✗ Purple Feather — Cafe $

(www.thepurplefeather.com; 334 Commercial St; snacks $2-10; ☺8am-midnight) Head to this stylish cafe for killer panini sandwiches, a rainbow of gelatos and decadent desserts all made from scratch. Lemon cupcakes have never looked so luscious. There's no better place in town for light eats and sweet treats.

Plymouth ❸

✗ All-American Diner — Diner $

(60 Court St; mains $6-12; ☺breakfast & lunch) You are here in America's Hometown; what better place to eat than the All-American Diner? It's a classic red-white-and-blue place, with a breakfast menu that reads like a novel. All of the breakfast items get rave reviews (especially the home fries). If you prefer lunch, try the Thanksgiving sandwich.

⌂ Pilgrim Sands — Hotel $$

(☎508-747-0900, 800-729-7263; www.pilgrimsands.com; 150 Warren Ave; d $155-195, apt $309; P @ ≋ ♿) This mini resort is a good option for families as it's right on a private beach and directly opposite Plimoth Plantation. Rooms with an ocean view are pricier, but the other rooms look out over Plimoth Plantation, which has its own charm. Rates decrease outside of summer months.

Boston ❺

✗ Warren Tavern — Pub $$

(www.warrentavern.com; 2 Pleasant St, Charlestown; ☺11am-1am) One of the oldest pubs in Boston, the Warren Tavern has been pouring pints for its customers since George Washington and Paul Revere drank here. It is named for General Joseph Warren, a fallen hero of the Battle of Bunker Hill (shortly after which – in 1780 – this pub was opened).

⌂ Ames Hotel — Boutique Hotel $$$

(☎617-979-8100; www.ameshotel.com; 1 Court St; r from $320; P ❄ ☎) It's easy to miss this understated hotel, tucked behind the granite facade of the historic Ames Building (Boston's first skyscraper). Starting in the lobby and extending to the guest rooms, the style is elegant but eclectic, artfully blending modern minimalism and old-fashioned ornamental details. The upper floors yield wonderful views over the city.

Salem ❻

✗ Red's Sandwich Shop — Diner $

(www.redssandwichshop.com; 15 Central St; dishes $3-9; ☺breakfast & lunch Mon-Sat, 6am-1pm Sun; ♿) This Salem institution has been serving eggs and sandwiches to faithful customers for over 50 years. The food is hearty and basic, but the real attraction is Red's old-school decor, complete with counter service and friendly faces. It's housed in the old London Coffee House building (1698).

✎ Morning Glory — B&B $$

(☎978-741-1703; www.morningglorybb.com; 22 Hardy St; d $165-190, ste $200-220; P ❄ @ ☎) To make his guests feel welcome, innkeeper and Salem native Bob Shea pulls out all the stops, not the least of which are the delectable homemade pastries prepared by his mother. Three frilly rooms and one sweet suite are named for Salem celebrities – that is, the witch-trial victims of 1692.

Provincetown *Enjoy quaint surrounds at Cape Cod's outermost point*

Classic Trip

Cape Cod & the Islands

3

A drive down the cape offers a beach for every mood. Besides sun, surf and sand, there are lighthouses to climb, oysters to eat, art and antiques to buy, and trails to hike.

TRIP HIGHLIGHTS

128 miles

Provincetown
A breeding ground for artistic, intellectual and alternative culture

FINISH 8

Wellfleet

6

105 miles

Cape Cod National Seashore
Hiking, biking, swimming and sunbathing amidst miles of pristine dunes and beaches

START
Sandwich

Yarmouth Port

5

Hyannis

96 miles

Brewster Tidal Flats
A spectacular seascape for a sunset

3

Nantucket
Cobblestone streets lined with blooming trees and 19th-century mansions

46 miles

5–7 DAYS
128 MILES / 206KM

GREAT FOR...

BEST TIME TO GO

Enjoy fine weather but avoid the crowds in May, June or September.

ESSENTIAL PHOTO

Brewster's otherworldly tidal flats are particularly photogenic at sunset.

BEST FOR FOOD & DRINK

Slurp oysters and devour classic pastries in Wellfleet.

Classic Trip

3 Cape Cod & the Islands

As the sun sets and the sky darkens, you slide your car into place alongside dozens of others facing the massive screen. Roll down the window, feel the salty breeze and recline your seat. After an exhilarating day of surf, sand and seafood, it's time to sit back and enjoy a double feature at the drive-in. Sounds like something out of a 1950s fantasy? It's summer on Cape Cod.

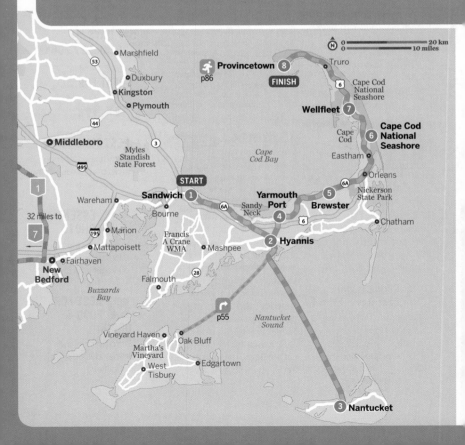

❶ Sandwich

Cape Cod's oldest town (founded in 1637) makes a perfect first impression as you cross over the canal from the mainland. In the village center, white-steepled churches, period homes and a working grist mill surround a picturesque swan pond.

Fun for kids and adults alike, the nearby 76-acre **Heritage Museums & Gardens** (www.heritage museumsandgardens.org; cnr Grove & Pine Sts; adult/child $15/7; ⏲10am-5pm Apr-Oct) sports a vintage automobile collection, an authentic 1912 carousel and unusual folk-art collections.

Before leaving town, take a stroll across the **Sandwich boardwalk**

LINK YOUR TRIP

1 Coastal New England

From Hyannis, take I-195 to New Bedford to intersect with this trip through maritime New England.

7 Rhode Island: East Bay

A longer trip on I-195 will zip you to Providence to take in the pleasures of picturesque Rhode Island.

(parking is $10 in summer), which extends 1350 scenic feet across an expansive marsh to **Town Neck Beach**. From MA 6A, head north onto Jarves St and bear left onto Boardwalk Rd.

The Drive » Heading east on MA 6A, also known as Old Kings Hwy, wind your way past cranberry bogs, wetlands and Shaker-shingle cottages. In Barnstable, take a right on MA 132 and head to the more commercial southern side of the cape. For a faster but less scenic version of this trip, take the Mid-Cape Hwy (US 6) instead of 6A.

❷ Hyannis

Most people traveling through Hyannis are here to catch a ferry to Nantucket or Martha's Vineyard (just like you). Fortunately, the village port has a few sights to keep you entertained while you wait for your boat – or even longer.

Take a walk through the harbor-side **HyArts District** (www.hyartsdistrict. com; 220 South St; ⏲11am-5pm Fri-Sun May-Jun, daily Jul-Sep), which includes the Guyer Barn, the colorful artist shanties nearby

and the art-strewn Walkway to the Sea.

Politicos will know that Hyannis has been the summer home of the Kennedy clan for generations. Back in the day, JFK spent his summers here – times that are documented with photographs and video at the **John F Kennedy Hyannis Museum** (http://jfkhyannis museum.org; 397 Main St; adult/child $8/3; ⏲9am-5pm Mon-Sat, noon-5pm Sun Apr-Oct, Sat & Sun only Nov & Mar). There is also a JFK Memorial at the family-friendly **Veterans Beach** (Ocean St), about a half-mile south of the Hy-Line Cruise dock.

🛏 p59

The Drive » Leave your car in Hyannis and take a one-hour catamaran trip or a much cheaper two-hour ferry trip to Nantucket (see p341). Don't miss the picturesque Brant Point Lighthouse as the ferry pulls into Nantucket harbor.

❸ Nantucket

Nantucket is New England at its most rose-covered,

cobblestoned, picture-postcard perfect. The island's only population center, Nantucket Town was once home port to the world's largest whaling fleet. Now a National Historic Landmark, the town boasts leafy streets lined with gracious period homes and public buildings. For the finest stroll, walk up cobbled **Main Street**, just past the c 1818 Pacific National Bank, where the grandest whaling-era mansions are lined up in a row.

While strolling the streets, pay a visit to the excellent **Nantucket Whaling Museum** (www.nha.org; 13 Broad St; adult/senior/student/child $17/15/15/8; ⏰10am-5pm daily May-Sep, Thu-Mon Oct-Dec, Sat & Sun Feb-Apr), which occupies a former spermaceti candle factory. The evocative exhibits relive Nantucket's 19th-century heyday as the whaling center of the world.

Close to town, there is a pair of family-friendly beaches to cool off. For wilder, less-frequented strands, you'll need to pedal a bike or hop on a bus to **Surfside** or **Nobadeer Beach**, 3 to 4 miles south of town.

✖ p59

The Drive ≫ Ferry back to Hyannis Port to pick up your car. From South St, turn north on Camp St and then turn right on Yarmouth Rd. Continue north for 3 miles, then turn right on MA 6A and continue into Yarmouth Port.

④ Yarmouth Port

Nearly 50 historic sea captains' homes are lined up along MA 6A in Yarmouth Port in a stretch known as **Captains' Mile**. Most of them are private homes; however, the Historical Society of Old Yarmouth maintains the 1840 **Captain Bangs Hallett House** (www.hsoy.org; 11 Strawberry Lane; adult/child $3/50¢; ⏰1-4pm Thu-Sun Jun-Oct). For more historic sites in Yarmouth Port, pick up the free self-guided Captains' Mile walking tour booklet.

Alternatively, stroll or walk 1 mile up Center St to **Grey's Beach**, also known as Bass Hole. A terrific quarter-mile-long boardwalk extends over a tidal marsh and creek, offering a unique vantage for viewing all sorts of sea life.

The Drive ≫ Continue east on MA 6A through the classy village of Dennis and on to Brewster. This section of road (between Barnstable and Brewster) is lined with old homes that have been converted into antique shops. Take the time to stop and browse, and come home with treasures ranging from nautical kitsch to art-deco cool.

TRIP HIGHLIGHT

⑤ Brewster

Brewster's best-known landmark is the **Brewster Store** (www.brewsterstore. com; 1935 MA 6A; ⏰6am-10pm), an old-fashioned country store that has been in operation since 1866. Penny candy is still sold alongside the local newspaper. Upstairs, you'll discover a stash of museum-quality memorabilia as old as the building.

When the tide goes out on Cape Cod Bay, the bayside beach becomes a giant sand bar, offering opportunities to commune with crabs, clams and gulls, and to take in brilliant sunsets. Best access to the tidal flats is via the **Point of Rocks** or **Ellis Landing Beaches** (parking is $15 in summer). Pick up a parking sticker and check the tide charts at the town hall.

✖ p59

The Drive ≫ Head east on MA 6A out of Brewster, then hop on US 6, lined with roadside motels and clam shacks. It's a quick trip through Orleans and Eastham to your next destination.

TRIP HIGHLIGHT

⑥ Cape Cod National Seashore

Extending some 40 miles around the curve of the Outer Cape, the Cape Cod National Seashore is a treasure trove of unspoiled beaches, dunes, salt marshes, nature trails and forests. Start your explorations at the **Salt Pond Visitor Center** (www.nps.gov/caco; cnr US 6 & Nauset Rd, Eastham; admission free; ⏱9am-5pm), which offers a wonderful view of the namesake salt pond. Numerous walking and cycling trails begin right at the visitor center; this is also the place to purchase a parking permit if you intend to spend time at any of the National Seashore beaches.

After this brief introduction, take Nauset Rd and Doane Rd to the picturesque **Coast Guard Beach** for swimming and bodysurfing; then drive along the aptly named Ocean View Dr to **Nauset Light** (www.nausetlight. org; admission by donation; ⏱1-4pm Sun), which has been shining on the cape since 1877.

The Drive » Take Nauset Rd back to the Mid-Cape Hwy and continue north to Main St in Wellfleet. For a scenic detour, turn right off the highway onto Le Count Hollow Rd, then left on

MASSACHUSETTS **3** CAPE COD & THE ISLANDS

DETOUR: MARTHA'S VINEYARD

Start ② Hyannis or ③ Nantucket

Your island destination is Oak Bluffs, the Vineyard's mecca for summer fun. Originally a retreat for a revivalist church group, it's now a retreat for beach-bound, ice-cream-eating party people.

In the mid-19th century, the members of the Methodist Camp Meeting Association (CMA) enjoyed a day at the beach as much as a good gospel service. They first camped out in tents, then built some 300 wooden cottages, each adorned with whimsical filigree trim. From bustling Circuit Ave, slip down the alley to discover the **Campgrounds**, a world of gingerbread houses adorned with Candyland colors. For a peek inside one, visit the **Cottage Museum** (www.mvcma.org; 1 Trinity Park; adult/ child $2/50¢; ⏱10am-4pm Mon-Sat, 1-4pm Sun), which contains exhibits on CMA history. The brightly painted cottages surround emerald-green **Trinity Park** and its open-air **Tabernacle** (1879), where the lucky descendants of the campers still gather for community sing-a-longs and concerts.

Further north on Circuit Ave, you can take a nostalgic ride on the **Flying Horses Carousel** (www.mvpreservation.org; cnr Lake & Circuit Aves; rides $2; ⏱10am-10pm), a National Historic Landmark that has been captivating kids of all ages since 1876. It's the country's oldest continuously operating merry-go-round, where the antique horses have manes of real horse hair.

Beginning just south of the Steamship Authority's ferry terminal a narrow strip of sandy **beach** runs unbroken for several miles. There is also a scenic **bike trail** (with plenty of places to rent) connecting Oak Bluffs with other parts of the Vineyard.

From Hyannis, **Hy-Line Cruises** (☎508-778-2600; www.hylinecruises.com) operates a slow ferry (adult/child $45/free, 1½ hours) once daily and a high-speed ferry (adult/child $71/48, 55 minutes) several times daily from late May to mid-October. Hy-Line also offers a once-daily ferry between Nantucket and Oak Bluffs from July to early September. Don't bother bringing your car unless you intend to stay a while, in which case you'll need to make arrangements well in advance.

LOCAL KNOWLEDGE
DIANNE LANGELAND,
EDITOR OF *EDIBLE CAPE COD*

The **Chatham Fish Pier** (54 Barcliff Ave Extension, Chatham) **is a great** place to watch the fishermen bring in their catch, especially on summer weekends, when the Cape Cod Commercial Hook Fishermen's Association sends seasoned fishermen to regale visitors with stories about the cape's past, present and future fishing industry.

Top: Fishermen off the coast of Chatham
Right: Wellfleet oysters

Ocean View Dr. From here, Long Pond Rd will cross the highway and deposit you on Main St in Wellfleet center.

- - - - - - - - - - - -

7 Wellfleet

Wellfleet is one of Cape Cod's unsung gems, offering some unspoiled beaches, a charming historic center and plenty of opportunities to slurp those glorious oysters.

By day, browse the 20-plus **art galleries** that are sprinkled around town. (Pick up the Wellfleet Art Galleries Association map, which has descriptive listings.) Or spy on the birdlife at Mass Audubon's 1100-acre **Wellfleet Bay Wildlife Sanctuary** (www.massaudubon.org; West Rd, off US 6; adult/child $5/3; ⊗8:30am-5pm), **where** trails cross tidal creeks, salt marshes and sandy beaches.

By night, park your car at the 1950s-era **Wellfleet Drive-In** (www.wellfleetcinemas.com; US 6, Wellfleet; 🅿), where everything except the feature flick is true to the era. Grab a bite to eat at the old-fashioned snack bar, hook the mono speaker over the car window and settle in for a double feature.

For a more raucous night, head to Cahoon Hallow Beach, where the cape's coolest summertime hangout is housed in the former lifeguard station, now known as the **Beachcomber** (www.thebeachcomber.com; 1120 Cahoon Hollow Rd).

✕ p59

The Drive » US 6 continues north through Truro, passing Truro Vineyards and Pilgrim Heights. On the right, the picturesque East Harbor is backed by pristine parabolic dunes; on the left, wind-blown beach shacks front Provincetown Harbor. Alternatively, take the slower-going Shore Rd (MA 6A), which branches off in North Truro and eventually becomes Commercial St in Provincetown.

TRIP HIGHLIGHT

8 Provincetown

Provincetown is far out. We're not just talking geographically (though it does occupy the outermost point on Cape Cod). We're also talking about the flamboyant street scenes, brilliant art galleries and unbridled nightlife. Once an outpost for fringe writers and artists, Provincetown has morphed into the hottest gay and lesbian destination in the Northeast. Even if you're only in town for a day, you'll want to spend part of it admiring the art and watching the local life on **Commercial Street**. For more attractions and oddities, follow the walking tour, p86.

Provincetown is also the perfect launching point for whale watching, since it's the closest port to Stellwagen Bank National Marine Sanctuary, the summer feeding ground for humpback whales. **Dolphin Fleet Whale Watch** (☎508-240-3636; www.whalewatch.com; MacMillan Wharf; adult/child $39/31; ☻Apr-Oct) offers up to nine tours daily, each lasting three to four hours.

✖ ⊨ p59

GLBTQ PROVINCETOWN

While other cities have their gay districts, in Provincetown the entire town is the gay district.

A-House (Atlantic House; www.ahouse.com; 4 Masonic Pl) P-town's gay scene got its start here and it's still the leading bar in town.

Boatslip Resort (www.boatslipresort.com; 161 Commercial St; admission $5; ☻4-7pm) Hosts wildly popular afternoon-tea dances.

Pied Bar (www.piedbar.com; 193 Commercial St; ☻6am-2am May-Oct) A popular waterfront lounge that attracts both lesbians and gay men. Particularly hot at sunset.

Eating & Sleeping

Hyannis ❷

🛏 Anchor-In   Hotel $$

(📞508-775-0357; www.anchorin.com; 1 South St; r incl breakfast $149-299; ❄@🛜🏊) Family run for 55 years, this boutique hotel offers a fine harbor-front location, with wonderful views from the heated pool and the sunny breakfast room. Bright rooms all have water-view balconies. Two-night minimum (and higher rates) on summer weekends.

Nantucket ❸

🍴 Black-Eyed Susan's   Modern American $$

(www.black-eyedsusans.com; 10 India St; mains $18-30; 🕐breakfast daily, dinner Mon-Sat) No reservations, no credit cards, and no alcohol (unless you bring it yourself). Yet islanders line up out the door to get one of a dozen tables at this understated gem. This is 'New American' at its finest: you've eaten these ingredients, but never before in these creative, decidedly delicious combinations.

Brewster ❺

🍴 Fish House   Seafood $$

(www.brewsterfish.com; 2208 MA 6A; lunch $10-16, dinner $18-28; 🕐lunch & dinner Tue-Sun) Once a retail fish market, this tiny, unassuming bistro has earned fiercely loyal patrons, thanks to artful presentations of classic seafood dishes. Start with the lobster bisque, naturally sweet with chunks of fresh lobster.

🛏 Nickerson State Park   Campground $

(www.mass.gov/dcr; 3488 MA 6A; tent & RV sites from $15) At the eastern end of town, this 2000-acre oasis has hundreds of woodsy campsites, offering access to eight ponds with sandy beaches ideal for swimming and boating, as well as miles of cycling and walking trails.

Wellfleet ❼

🍴 Bookstore & Restaurant   Seafood $$

(www.wellfleetoyster.com; 50 Kendrick Ave; mains $12-22; 🕐breakfast, lunch & dinner) This casual, family-run place raises its own oysters and littleneck clams, harvested at low tide in the waters right across the street. Sit out on the deck and enjoy a lovely view while you slurp.

🍴 PB Boulangerie & Bistro   Bakery, French $$

(📞508-349-1600; www.pbboulangeriebistro.com; 15 Lecount Hollow Rd; bakery items $3-8, dinner $24-36; 🕐bakery 7am-7pm Wed-Sun, bistro dinner Wed-Sun) Lines out the door are testament to the decadent delights available within. French-accented garçons serve up flaky pastries, scrumptious sandwiches and dark coffee for breakfast and lunch. Local seafood and classic French fare are on the dinner menu. You'll think you've died and gone to Paris.

Provincetown ❽

🍴 Mews Restaurant & Café   Bistro $$$

(📞508-487-1500, www.mews.com; 429 Commercial St; mains $12-33; 🕐dinner) A fantastic water view, a hot cocktail bar and superb food add up to Provincetown's finest dinner scene. Opt to dine gourmet downstairs, where you're right on the sand, or go casual from the cafe menu upstairs.

🛏 Carpe Diem   Inn $$$

(📞508-487-4242; www.carpediemguesthouse.com; 12 Johnson St; r incl breakfast $159-259; ❄@🛜) Sophisticated yet relaxed, this soothing inn blends smiling Buddhas, orchid sprays and artistic decor. The on-site spa facilities include a Finnish sauna, a hot tub and a menu of massage therapies.

Plum Island *Get back to nature amid acres of wildlife sanctuary*

Around Cape Ann

There's more to Cape Ann than widows' walks and sailing lore. This drive offers salt marshes and windswept beaches, oases of art and antiques, and more clam shacks than you can shake a shucker at.

TRIP HIGHLIGHTS

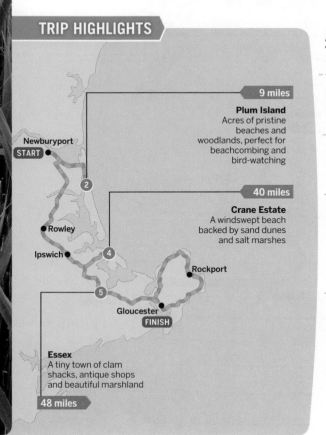

9 miles

Plum Island
Acres of pristine beaches and woodlands, perfect for beachcombing and bird-watching

Newburyport
START

40 miles

Crane Estate
A windswept beach backed by sand dunes and salt marshes

● Rowley

Ipswich ●

Rockport

Gloucester
FINISH

Essex
A tiny town of clam shacks, antique shops and beautiful marshland

48 miles

2–3 DAYS
54 MILES / 86KM

GREAT FOR...

BEST TIME TO GO

The water is warmest from July to September.

ESSENTIAL PHOTO

The red fishing shack at Rockport Harbor is called *Motif No 1* for its artistic appeal.

BEST FOR OUTDOORS

The Parker River Wildlife Refuge offers excellent hiking, swimming, kayaking and canoeing.

Around Cape Ann

Somebody once said that 'the humble clam… reaches its quintessence when coated and fried.' (A New Englander, no doubt.) The big-bellied bivalve – lightly battered and deeply fried – supposedly originated in Essex, Massachusetts, so Cape Ann is an ideal place to sample the New England specialty. This North Shore route takes you from clam shack to clam shack, with breaks in between eating for beachcombing, bird-watching, gallery-hopping and plenty of picture-taking.

❶ Newburyport

Situated at the mouth of the Merrimack River, the town of Newburyport prospered as a shipping port and silversmith center during the late 18th century.

Not too much has changed in the last 200 years, as Newburyport's brick buildings and graceful churches still show off the Federal style that was popular back then.

Today the center of this town is a model of historic preservation and

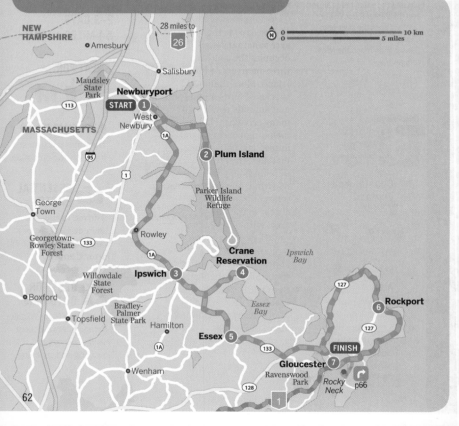

gentrification. Admire the public art as you take a stroll along the **Matthews Memorial Boardwalk**, which runs along the Merrimack and ends at the granite **Custom House Maritime Museum** (www.custom housemaritimemuseum.org; 25 Water St; adult/senior & child $7/5; 10am-4pm Tue-Sat, noon-4pm Sun May-Dec).

From here, you can browse in the boutiques along State St or admire the art galleries on Water St.

The Drive >> Go east on Water St, which follows the coastline out of town. It becomes the Plum Island Turnpike before passing the eponymous airport and the Parker River Visitor Center. Cross the river onto Plum Island and turn right on Sunset Dr to reach the wildlife refuge.

LINK YOUR TRIP

1 Coastal New England

Continue south from Gloucester and follow the coastline all the way through Connecticut.

26 Maritime Maine

From Newburyport, drive 26 miles north on I-95 to Kittery to experience the coastal culture of Maine.

- - - - - - - - - - -

TRIP HIGHLIGHT

2 Plum Island

A barrier island off the coast of Massachusetts, Plum Island has 9 miles of wide, sandy beaches surrounded by acres of wildlife sanctuary. These are among the nicest beaches on the North Shore, if you head to the furthest points on the island. **Sandy Point** (dawn-8pm), on the southern tip, is a state park that's popular for swimming, sunning and tide pooling.

Parker River Wildlife Refuge (www.parkerriver. fws.gov; Plum Island; per car/bike or pedestrian $5/2; dawn-dusk) is the 4662-acre sanctuary that occupies the southern three-quarters of Plum Island. More than 800 species of birds, plants and animals reside in its many ecological habitats, including beaches, sand dunes, salt pans, salt marshes, freshwater impoundments and maritime forests. Several miles of foot trails allow access to the inland area, with observation towers and platforms punctuating the trails at prime bird-watching spots. Stop at the **Visitor Center** (6 Plum Island Turnpike; 11am-4pm) for information and exhibits about the refuge.

p67

The Drive >> Depart the island on the Plum Island Turnpike. After about 2 miles, turn left on Ocean Ave, then left on High Rd (MA 1A). Continue south through picturesque farmland, stopping at farm stands for fresh eggs and produce. Go through the tiny town of Newbury, traversing beautiful forest and marshland, and picturesque Rowley, with the famous Sunday-morning Todd Farm Flea Market. Continue south into Ipswich.

- - - - - - - - - - -

3 Ipswich

Ipswich is one of those New England towns that is pretty today because it was poor in the past. It had no harbor and no source of water power for factories, so commercial and industrial development went elsewhere. As a result, Ipswich's 17th-century houses were not torn down to build grander residences. Nowadays, there are 58 existent 'first period' homes, including the 1677 **Whipple House** (www. ipswichmuseum.org; 1 South Village Green; adult/child $7/3; 10am-3pm Wed-Sun May-Oct), which is open to the public. For more historic homes, pick up a map from the **Visitor Center** (36 S Main St; 9am-5pm Jun-Oct).

p67

The Drive >> Head out of town on S Main St (MA 133) and turn left on Argilla Rd. Drive for about 4 miles through beautiful woods and marshland. The entrance to the Great House is on the left, while the beach is straight ahead.

TRIP HIGHLIGHT

4 Crane Estate

One of the longest, widest, sandiest beaches in the region is **Crane Beach** (www.thetrustees.org; Argilla Rd, Ipswich; admission $2; ☺8am-dusk; **P**), which has 4 miles of fine-sand barrier beach on Ipswich Bay (parking is $25/15/8 weekends/weekdays/low season; it's half-price after 3pm).

Crane Beach is set in the midst of the Crane Wildlife Refuge, so the entire surrounding area is pristinely beautiful. Five miles of trails traverse the dunes.

Above the beach, on Castle Hill, sits the 1920s estate of Chicago plumbing-fixture magnate Richard T Crane. The 59-room Stuart-style **Great House** (adult/child $10/free; ☺10am-4pm Thu, to 1pm Fri & Sat Jun-Sep) is sometimes open for tours. The lovely landscaped grounds, which are open daily, contain several miles of walking trails.

📖 p67

The Drive » Depart by way of Argilla Rd, but turn left on Northgate Rd, which will take you back to MA 133. Turn left and continue 2.6 miles east into Essex.

TRIP HIGHLIGHT

5 Essex

The meandering Essex River shares its name with this tiny town, home to only 3000 souls. The town's proud maritime history is on display at the **Essex Shipbuilding Museum** (www.essexshipbuilding museum.org; 66 Main St, Essex; adult/child $9/5; ☺noon-5pm Wed-Sun Jun-Oct, Sat-Sun Nov-May). Most of the collections of photos, tools and ship models came from local basements and attics, allowing Essex to truly preserve its local history. The collections are housed in the town's 1835 school house (check out the **Old Burying Ground** behind it). The historical society

Rockport

also operates a museum shipyard, a section of waterfront property where shipbuilding activities have taken place for hundreds of years.

Despite centuries of maritime history, nowadays the town is more famous for its ample antique shops and succulent clams. With plenty of picnic tables overlooking the namesake estuary, there is no better lunch stop.

✕ p67

The Drive ≫ Continue east on MA 133, then merge onto MA 128 heading north. At the traffic circle, take the third exit to Washington St (MA 127), which circles Cape Ann. Heading up the west side of the cape, the winding road follows the Annisquam River, with a long bridge over the inlet at Goose Cove. Rounding the tip of the cape, you'll pass through tiny Lanesville and Pigeon Cove, before coming down the east side into Rockport.

- - - - - - - - - - -

6 Rockport

Rockport takes its name from its 19th-century role as a shipping center for granite cut from the local quarries. The stone is still ubiquitous: monuments, building foundations,

DETOUR:
ROCKY NECK ART COLONY

Start **6** Rockport

The narrow peninsula of Rocky Neck jutting into Gloucester Harbor offers inspiring views of the ocean and the harbor. Between WWI and WWII, artists began renting the local fisherfolk's seaside shacks, which they used as studios. Today these same shanties, considerably gentrified, constitute the **Rocky Neck Art Colony** (www.rockyneckartcolony. org), home to dozens of studios and galleries. The centerpiece is the cooperative **Rocky Neck Gallery** (53 Rocky Neck Ave; ⊘11am-7pm Mon-Wed, 10am-8pm Thu-Sat, noon-6pm Sun mid-May–mid-Oct) in a beautiful space overlooking Smith Cove. Visit the first Thursday of the month, from June to October, for **Nights on the Neck**, when many galleries host receptions with refreshments, live performances and other entertainment.

From MA 127A (at the junction with MA 128), turn left onto E Main St and right onto Rocky Neck Ave.

pavements and piers remain as a testament to Rockport's past.

That's about all that's left of this industrial history, however. A century ago, Winslow Homer, Childe Hassam, Fitz Hugh Lane and other acclaimed artists came to Rockport's rugged shores, inspired by the hearty fisherfolk who wrested a hard but satisfying living from the sea. Today Rockport makes its living from tourists who come to look at the artists. The artists have long since given up looking for hearty fisherfolk because their descendants are all running boutiques and B&Bs.

The hub of Rockport is Dock Sq, recognizable by the oft-painted red fishing shack, decorated with colorful buoys. From here, **Bearskin Neck** juts into the harbor, lined with galleries, lobster shacks and souvenir shops.

🍴 p67

The Drive ›› Leave Rockport on South St (MA 127A), heading south past Delmater Sanctuary. Now Thatcher St, the road passes the lovely Good Harbor Beach, which is a fine spot for a cool-off. Merge onto Main St as you enter Gloucester center.

- - - - - - - - - - - - - - - -

7 Gloucester

Gritty Gloucester offers a remarkable contrast to the rest of Cape Ann. The working waterfront is dominated by marinas and shipyards, with a backdrop of fish-processing plants. This hardworking town has its own surprising charm, particularly visible in the brick buildings along Main St. Nearby, the tiny **Cape Ann Museum** (www. capeannhistoricalmuseum.org; 27 Pleasant St; adult/student & senior $8/6; ⊘1-5pm Tue-Sat, 1-4pm Sun Mar-Jan) is a gem – particularly for its impressive collection of paintings by Gloucester native Fitz Hugh Lane. Exhibits also showcase the region's granite-quarrying industry and – of course – its maritime history.

🛏 p67

Eating & Sleeping

Plum Island ②

🛏 Blue   Inn $$$

(☎978-465-7171; www.blueinn.com; 20
Fordham Way, Plum Island; d $365-465;
[P][❄][📶]) In a gorgeous beachfront location,
this sophisticated inn is quite a surprise on
unassuming Plum Island. Rooms feature high
ceilings, contemporary decor, fresh white linens
and streaming sunlight. Private decks and
in-room fireplaces are a few of the perks you'll
find, not to mention a bottle of wine chilling for
your arrival.

Ipswich ③

🍴 Clam Box   Seafood $$

(www.ipswichma.com/clambox; 246 High St/
MA 133; mains $15-25; 🕐lunch & dinner) You
can't miss this classic clam shack, located just
north of Ipswich center. Built in 1938, it actually
looks like a clam box, spruced up with striped
awnings. Folks line up out the door for crispy
fried clams and onion rings – arguably the best
in the land.

Crane Estate ④

🛏 Inn at Castle Hill   Inn $$$

(☎978-412-2555; http://innatcastlehill.
thetrustees.org; 280 Argilla Rd, Ipswich; r $195-
425; [P][❄][📶]) In the midst of acres of beautiful
grounds, the inn boasts 10 luxurious rooms,
each uniquely decorated with subtle elegance.
Instead of televisions (of which there are none),
guests enjoy a wraparound veranda and its
magnificent views of the surrounding sand
dunes and salt marshes.

Essex ⑤

🍴 JT Farnham's   Seafood $$

(88 Eastern Ave; mains $15-25; 🕐lunch & dinner;
[♿]) When the Food Network came to Essex to
weigh in on the fried-clam debate for the show
Food Feud, the winner was JT Farnham, thanks
to the crispiness of his clams. Pull up a picnic
table and enjoy the amazing estuary view.

🍴 Woodman's   Seafood $$

(www.woodmans.com; 121 Main St/MA 133;
mains $15-25; 🕐lunch & dinner; [♿]) This
roadhouse is the most famous spot in the
area to come for fried clams. In fact Chubby
Woodman supposedly invented this method of
preparation way back in 1916 (thus, 'Chubby's
Original' fried clams).

Rockport ⑥

🍴 Roy Moore Lobster Co   Seafood $$

(39 Bearskin Neck; mains $12-20; 🕐8am-6pm)
This takeout kitchen serves lobster-in-the-
rough, alongside melted butter, plastic fork and
wet wipe. Sit in the back on tables fashioned
from lobster traps, or head down the street to
the restaurant for a bit of refinement. Bring your
own beer or wine, as Rockport is a dry town.

Gloucester ⑦

🛏 Accommodations of
Rocky Neck   Apartments $$

(☎978-283-1625; www.
rockyneckaccommodations.com; 43 Rocky
Neck Ave; r Sun-Thu $135-145, Fri & Sat $145-
155; [P]) You don't have to be an artist to live
the bohemian life in Gloucester. The colony
association offers light-filled efficiencies – all
equipped with kitchenettes – at the Rocky Neck
Art Colony. The rooms are sweet and simple,
most with beautiful views of Smith Cove.

Massachusetts *Take your pick of farm-fresh fruit*

Berkshire Back Roads

5

These country roads offer a mix of cultural riches, sweet farmland and mountain scenery. In summer, enjoy music and dance in the open air; in autumn, indulge in apples straight from the orchard.

TRIP HIGHLIGHTS

2–3 DAYS
31 MILES / 50KM

1 mile

Tanglewood Music Festival
World-class music and an idyllic outdoor setting

1 **START**

● Lee

● Tyringham

30 miles

Norman Rockwell Museum
A wonderful collection of original paintings by everybody's favorite illustrator

FINISH **5**

4

23 miles

Great Barrington
The best small town in America, according to the experts

GREAT FOR...

BEST TIME TO GO

Cultural events are in full swing from June to September; fall foliage is best in October.

ESSENTIAL PHOTO

Compare your photo of Main St, Stockbridge, to the Rockwell painting.

BEST FOR FOODIES

Great Barrington practically invented the locavore movement.

OCEAN/CORBIS ©

5 Berkshire Back Roads

Pack a picnic of farm-fresh fruit and local cheese, spread your blanket on the lush green lawns, and settle in for an evening of world-class music under the stars. Or world-class dance. Or Shakespeare. Or experimental theater. Indeed, for every day you spend hiking the hills and photographing the scenery, you can spend an evening taking in a cultural master work.

TRIP HIGHLIGHT

❶ Lenox

Prized for its bucolic peace, this gracious town was a summer retreat for wealthy families with surnames like Carnegie, Vanderbilt and Westinghouse (who had made their fortunes by building factories in other towns). Lenox is the cultural heart of the Berkshires, and its illustrious past remains tangibly present today.

In the 19th century, writers such as Nathaniel

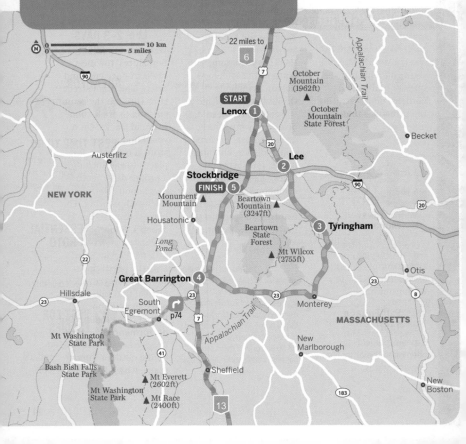

SUMMER FESTIVALS

The Berkshires are blessed with a world-class cultural calendar.

» **Aston Magna** (www.astonmagna.org) Listen to Bach, Brahms and Buxtehude and other early classical music in Great Barrington during June and July.

» **Bankside Festival** (www.shakespeare.org) Shakespearean plays are performed outdoors in a bucolic context in Lenox in July and August.

» **Berkshire Theatre Festival** (www.berkshiretheatre.org) Stop by for experimental summer theater in an old playhouse in Stockbridge from late July through October.

» **Jacob's Pillow** (www.jacobspillow.org) The best dance troupes of most cities can't top the stupefying and ground-breaking dance of Jacob's Pillow, which runs from mid-June through August near Lee.

» **Tanglewood Music Festival** (www.tanglewood.org) For many, the Berkshires' most famous festival and its outstanding orchestral music is reason enough to return to Lenox each summer.

Hawthorne and Edith Wharton set up shop here. Wharton's fabulous mansion, the **Mount** (www.edithwharton.org; 2 Plunkett St; adult/student/child $16/13/free; ⏲10am-5pm May-Oct), shows off a magnificent interior and formal gardens, demonstrating the principles that she

LINK YOUR TRIP

6 **Mohawk Trail**
For more beautiful Berkshire scenery and artistic offerings, drive north on US 7 to Williamstown.

13 **Fall Foliage Tour**
Expand your leaf-peeping to the other New England states.

describes in her book *The Decoration of Houses.*

About a mile west of Lenox center, **Tanglewood Estate** (www.bso.org; 297 West St/MA 183) is the summer home of the esteemed Boston Symphony Orchestra. From June to September, these beautifully manicured grounds host concerts of pop and rock, chamber music, folk, jazz and blues, in addition to the symphony. Traditionally, the July 4 extravaganza features Massachusetts native James Taylor.

✕ 🍽 p75

The Drive » Head out of Lenox on Walker St (MA 183), passing the historic Ventfort Hall, an impressive Jacobean Revival mansion that was a Morgan family home. One mile southeast of the center, turn right onto US 20 and drive 3 miles south, passing pretty Laurel Lake. Cross

the bridge over the Housatonic River as you enter Lee.

- - - - - - - - - - - - - - - -

2 **Lee**
Welcome to the Berkshires' towniest town, at once cute and gritty. The main street runs through the center, curving to cross some railroad tracks. On it you'll find a hardware store, a bar and a few places to eat, including a proper diner featured in a famous Norman Rockwell painting. The biggest draw to Lee is **Jacob's Pillow** (www.jacobspillow.org; 358 George Carter Rd, Becket; ⏲Jun-Aug), the prestigious summertime dance festival that takes place in neighboring Becket. Free **Inside/Out performances** (⏲6:15 Wed-Sun Jun-Aug) are held on the outdoor Simon Stage, which has an

amazing backdrop of the Berkshire hills.

✗ p75

The Drive » Continue east on US 20, crossing under the Turnpike. Turn right on MA 102, then make an immediate left on Tyringham Rd. Hugging the Housatonic River, this scenic road passes some pretty homesteads and woodsy hillsides, before entering Tyringham as Main St.

❸ Tyringham

Once the home of a Shaker community (1792–1874), this tiny village enjoys a gorgeous setting in the midst of the Tyringham Valley. To get some perspective on the pastoral splendor, take a 2-mile hike over the knobs of **Tyringham Cobble** (www.thetrustees.org; Jerusalem Rd; ☻dawn-dusk),

which offers wildflower-strewn hillsides and spectacular views.

You don't have to get out of your car to see the village's most famous attraction – the **Tyringham Gingerbread House** (www. santarella.us; 75 Main St), an architectural fantasy designed by sculptor Henry Hudson Kitson. This fairy-tale thatched-roofed cottage is readily

Stockbridge Main St

visible from the road, though the interior is not open to the general public.

The Drive » Depart Tyringham on Main St. Turn right on Monterey Rd, passing some woodsy places to hike and the inviting Monterey Town Beach. Look for the old-fashioned General Store in Monterey, then head west on MA 23. Pass Beartown State Forest and Butternut Mountain as you enter Great Barrington. Continue on State Rd, cross the bridge over

the Housatonic River and turn left onto Main St.

TRIP HIGHLIGHT

④ Great Barrington

Woolworths, diners and hardware stores have given way to art galleries, urbane boutiques and 'locavore' restaurants on Main St, Great Barrington, recently named the 'best

small town in America' by the Smithsonian Institution. The picturesque Housatonic River flows through the center of town, with the parallel **River Walk** (www.gbriverwalk.org) offering a perfect perch from which to admire it. Access the walking path from Main St (behind Rite-Aid) or from Bridge St.

DETOUR:
BASH BISH FALLS

Start ④ Great Barrington

In the very southwest corner of the state, near the New York state line, is **Bash Bish Falls** (www.mass.gov/dcr; admission free; ☺sunrise-sunset), the largest waterfall in Massachusetts. The water feeding the falls runs down a series of gorges before the torrent is sliced in two by a massive boulder perched directly above a pool. There it drops as a picture-perfect double waterfall. These 60ft-high falls are a popular spot for landscape painters to set up their easels.

To get there from Great Barrington, take MA 23 west to South Egremont. Turn right onto MA 41 south and then take the immediate right onto Mt Washington Rd (which becomes East St) and continue for 7.5 miles. Turn right onto Cross Rd, then right onto West St and continue 1 mile. Turn left onto Falls Rd and follow that for 1.5 miles.

There are two trailheads. The first is for a short, steep trail that descends 300ft over the course of a quarter-mile. For a more leisurely, level hike, continue another mile over the New York state line. This 0.75-mile trail takes about 20 minutes in each direction.

After a few hours' rest in small-town America, you might hanker for a hike in the hills. Head to **Monument Mountain** (www.thetrustees.org; US 7; ☺sunrise-sunset), 5 miles north of the center. In 1850, Nathaniel Hawthorne climbed this mountain with Oliver Wendell Holmes and Herman Melville, thus sealing a lifelong friendship. You can follow their footsteps on one of two hiking trails to the 1642ft summit of Squaw Peak. From the top you'll get fabulous views all the way to Mt Greylock in the northwestern corner of the state and to the Catskills in New York.

✗ ⊫ p75

The Drive 》 Head north out of town on Main St and turn right on State St to cross the Housatonic River. Drive north on US 7, passing the pretty Fountain Pond on the right and Monument Mountain on the left. Turn left on MA 102, which is Main St, Stockbridge.

- - - - - - - - - - - - - -

TRIP HIGHLIGHT

❺ Stockbridge

Main St, Stockbridge, is so postcard-perfect it looks like something out of a Norman Rockwell painting. In fact, it was depicted in the painting *Stockbridge Main Street at Christmas*. Stockbridge people and places inspired many of Rockwell's illustrations, as the artist lived here for 25 years. The **Norman Rockwell Museum** (www.nrm.org; MA 183; adult/child $15/free; ☺10am-5pm) displays the world's largest collection of Rockwell's original art, including the beloved *Four Freedoms* and a complete collection of *Saturday Evening Post* covers.

Norman Rockwell is the main draw, but Stockbridge was also home to Daniel Chester French in an earlier era. Sculptor of *Abraham Lincoln* at the Lincoln Memorial and *The Minuteman* in Concord, French spent his summers at **Chesterwood** (www.chesterwood.org; 4 Williamsville Rd; adult/child $15/free; ☺10am-5pm May-Oct), a 122-acre estate. His house and studio are substantially as they were when he lived here, with nearly 500 pieces of sculpture, finished and unfinished, in the studio.

✗ p75

Eating & Sleeping

Lenox ❶

✖ Haven Cafe & Bakery
Modern American $$

(www.havencafebakery.com; 8 Franklin St; ⏰ breakfast & lunch year-round, dinner Wed-Sat Jul & Aug; 📶) It looks like a cafe, but the sophisticated food evokes a more upscale experience. Try inventive egg dishes for breakfast or fancy salads and sandwiches for lunch – all highlighting local organic ingredients. Definitely save room for something sweet from the bakery counter.

🛏 Stonover Farm B&B
B&B $$$

(📞 413-637-9100; www.stonoverfarm.com; 169 Under Mountain Rd; ste incl breakfast $375-425; ❄ @ 🛜) A contemporary inn wrapped in a century-old farmhouse. The three suites in the main house and two stand-alone cottages ooze luxury, including oversized Jacuzzis, marble bathrooms and wine and cheese in the evening. This is pampering befitting its Tanglewood neighborhood setting.

Lee ❷

✖ Joe's Diner
Diner $

(63 Center St; mains $3-8; ⏰ 5:30am-9pm Mon-Sat, 7am-2pm Sun) There's no better slice of blue-collar Americana in the Berkshires than Joe's Diner. This spot inspired Norman Rockwell's painting *The Runaway* (1958), depicting a policeman sitting at a counter talking to a young boy. Take a look at the repro of it above the counter: Joe's has barely changed.

Great Barrington ❹

✖ Allium
Modern American $$

(📞 413-528-2118; www.alliumberkshires.com; 42/44 Railroad St; mains $12-28; ⏰ dinner) For

an atmospheric date, try the contemporary cuisine in this stylish restaurant, which manages to combine repurposed architectural elements and modern Scandinavian influences without being heavy-handed. Allium subscribes to the slow-food movement with a seasonal menu centered on fresh organic produce, cheeses and meats, with thoroughly satisfying results.

✖ Gypsy Joynt
Cafe $

(www.gypsyjoyntcafe.net; 293 Main St; ⏰ 8am-10pm Wed-Sun, to 4pm Mon; 📶) This is a family affair, with three generations pitching in to serve excellent, innovative pizzas, sandwiches and salads. To do that in Great Barrington, you must focus on local and organic. The Gypsy Joynt also throws in great coffee, live music and a super boho atmosphere.

🛏 Wainwright Inn
B&B $$

(📞 413-528-2062; www.wainwrightinn.com; 518 S Main St; r incl breakfast $139-199; ❄ 🛜) This c 1766 inn exudes historical appeal from its wraparound porches and spacious parlors to the period room decor. Most of the eight guest rooms come with working fireplaces. Breakfast is a decadent, delicious, three-course affair.

Stockbridge ❺

✖ Once Upon a Table
Bistro $$

(www.onceuponatablebistro.com; 36 Main St; lunch $12-15, dinner $25-40; ⏰ lunch & dinner) This bright spot in the Mews shopping arcade serves upscale fare in a sunny dining room. It's the best place in town for lunch, with choices like smoked-salmon-and-chevre omelets and seared-ahi salad Niçoise.

Near Charlemont *View the compelling* Hail to the Sunrise *statue on your way out of town*

Mohawk Trail

6

New England's oldest scenic highway offers invigorating art and architecture, stimulating action and adventure, and spectacular mountain scenery — everything you need for a weekend getaway.

TRIP HIGHLIGHTS

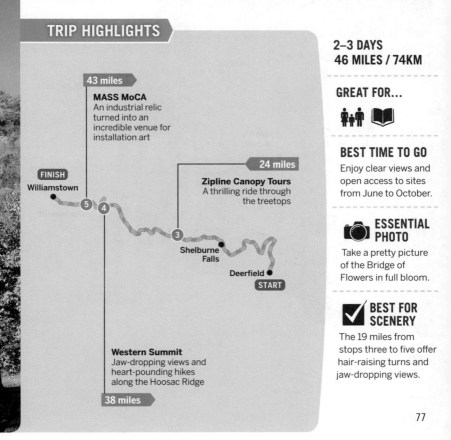

43 miles

MASS MoCA
An industrial relic turned into an incredible venue for installation art

24 miles

Zipline Canopy Tours
A thrilling ride through the treetops

FINISH
Williamstown

5 **4**

3

Shelburne Falls

Deerfield
START

Western Summit
Jaw-dropping views and heart-pounding hikes along the Hoosac Ridge

38 miles

2–3 DAYS
46 MILES / 74KM

GREAT FOR...

BEST TIME TO GO
Enjoy clear views and open access to sites from June to October.

ESSENTIAL PHOTO
Take a pretty picture of the Bridge of Flowers in full bloom.

BEST FOR SCENERY
The 19 miles from stops three to five offer hair-raising turns and jaw-dropping views.

6 Mohawk Trail

The road winds ever upward. Suddenly, around a bend, there is a clearing in the forest and the landscape sprawls out in a colorful tapestry, yielding views across the valley and into neighboring states. Welcome to the Western Summit of the Mohawk Trail, a 63-mile stretch of scenic byway, showing off raging rivers, idyllic farms and forest-covered mountains. Drivers, beware: it's practically impossible to keep your eyes on the road.

① Deerfield

Start your tour in **Historic Deerfield Village** (www.historic-deerfield.org; Old Main St; adult/child $12/5; ⏰9:30am-4:30pm Apr-Nov), an enchanting farming settlement that has escaped the ravages of time. Old Main St now presents a noble prospect: a dozen houses dating from the 1700s and 1800s, well preserved and open to the public. The homes have been restored and furnished according to actual historical records,

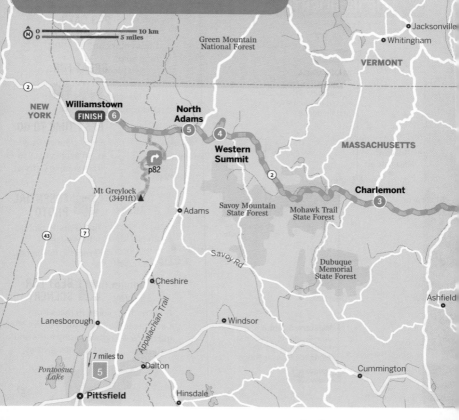

reflecting different periods in the village's history.

One block east of Old Main St, **Memorial Hall Museum** (www. americancenturies.mass. edu; Memorial St; adult/child $6/3; ☺11am-5pm May-Oct) contains lots of original artifacts from local homes, including the storied Indian House Door. This local farming family's front door was hacked through by attackers during the infamous 1704 raid, when Native Americans massacred or captured most of the village residents.

✕ 🛏 p85

The Drive ⟫ From Historic Deerfield Village, drive north on MA 10 (US 5) for about 3 miles and turn left to head west on MA 2A. At the traffic circle, take the second exit to continue west on the Mohawk Trail (MA 2). For souvenirs, look for the Native American—owned Mohawk Trading Post as you enter Shelburne. Turn left on Bridge St to continue into Shelburne Falls.

- - - - - - - - - - - - - -

❷ Shelburne Falls

The main drag in this artisan community is only three blocks long — a tiny but charming stretch of turn-of-the-20th-century buildings, housing art galleries and coffee shops alongside a barber shop, a general store and an old-fashioned pharmacy. Forming the background are the forested mountains, the Deerfield River and a pair of picturesque bridges that cross it — one made of iron, the other covered in flowers.

One paid gardener and a host of volunteers have been maintaining the **Bridge of Flowers** (Water St) since 1929. From April to October, more than 500 varieties of flowers, shrubs and vines flaunt their colors on the 400ft-long span.

Two blocks south, the swirling of rocks in the Deerfield River has created an impressive

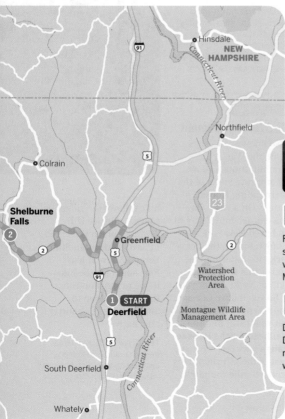

LINK YOUR TRIP

5 Berkshire Back Roads

From Williamstown, drive south on US 7 to hook up with this loop around the Massachusetts mountains.

23 Connecticut River Byway

Drive north or south from Deerfield to explore the mighty New England waterway.

collection of **glacial potholes** (Deerfield St) – near-perfect circular craters in the river bed. There are more than 50 potholes on display, including the world's largest, which has a 39ft diameter.

✕ p85

The Drive >> At the end of Bridge St, cross the metal bridge and turn right on State St, which runs parallel to the Deerfield River. Turn left on MA 2, saluting the Big Indian as you leave Shelburne Falls. The Mohawk Trail continues to follow the raging river, with Charlemont spread out along this road for several miles. Look for Zoar Outdoor near the intersection with MA 8A.

TRIP HIGHLIGHT

❸ Charlemont

Tucked in between the Deerfield River and the Hoosac hills, tiny Charlemont is worth a stop if you are craving an adrenaline rush. This is the home of **Zoar Outdoor** (📞800-532-7483; www.zaroutdoor. com; 7 Main St), offering canoeing, kayaking and whitewater rafting on the river rapids for all skill levels, including trips for children as young as seven years old. Come in spring for high-water adventure or in autumn for fall-foliage brilliance.

If you prefer to keep your feet dry, the **zip-line canopy tour** (www. deerfieldzipline.com; per person $94; ⊙Apr-Oct)

lets you unleash your inner Tarzan on a treetop glide above the Deerfield River Valley. All in all, the three-hour outing includes three rappels, two sky bridges and 11 zips that get progressively longer. The hardest part is stepping off the first platform – the rest is pure exhilaration!

The Drive >> Leaving Charlemont, you'll pass the *Hail to the Sunrise* statue honoring the Five Indian Nations of the Mohawk Trail. The next stretch is the highlight of the scenic byway, as it cuts across the eponymous state forest. Continue climbing through the town of Florida, which is punctuated by three rewarding lookouts: the unmarked Eastern Summit, the Whitcomb Summit (the highest along the Mohawk Trail) and finally the Western Summit.

TRIP HIGHLIGHT

❹ Western Summit

Also known as Perry's Peak, the Western Summit (2100ft) shows off amazing views of the surrounding Hoosac Range. On a clear day, you can see into Vermont and even New York. Unfortunately, the ticky-tacky tourist shop that marks this spot is now closed. No fudge for you!

So you'll have to bring your own sustenance; but you'll still find the trailhead for the **Hoosac Range** (www.bnrc.net) just east of the gift shop. This scenic 6-mile roundtrip

hike follows the ridgeline south to Spruce Hill summit, which is located in Savoy Mountain State Forest. Allow at least four hours for the hike; if you're short on time, the 1.5-mile loop to Sunset Rock is a shorter alternative.

The Drive >> Back in the car, the Mohawk Trail descends quickly, with an exhilarating spin around the Hairpin Turn to make

Fall foliage in Massachusetts Mt Greylock looms in the distance

your heart beat a little faster. Entering North Adams, the road follows the Hoosac River past vestiges of the industrial era.

TRIP HIGHLIGHT

5 North Adams

At first glance, North Adams' beautiful and bleak 19th-century downtown seems out of sync with the rest of the Berkshires. But nestled into this industrial-era assemblage is a contemporary-art museum of staggering proportions.

MASS MoCA (www. massmoca.org; 87 Marshall St; adult/child $15/5; ☺10am-6pm Jul & Aug, 11am-5pm Wed-Mon Sep-Jun) sprawls over 13 acres of downtown North Adams. After the Sprague Electric Company packed up in 1985, more than $31 million was spent to modernize the property into the country's biggest art gallery, which now encompasses 222,000 sq ft and over 25 buildings, including art-construction areas, performance centers and 19 galleries. One gallery is the size of a football field, giving installation

DETOUR:
MT GREYLOCK

Start ⑤ North Adams

Just west of downtown North Adams, look for the turn-off to Notch Rd, which will take you about 5 miles south to **Mt Greylock State Reservation** (parking is $2 at the summit). In summer (mid-May to mid-October) you can drive up; otherwise, park your car at the entrance and hike 5 miles to the summit, where you will be rewarded with 360 degrees of vistas, taking in five states and hundreds of miles.

At 3491ft, Mt Greylock is the state's highest peak. In the 19th century, Greylock was a favorite destination for New England's nature-loving writers, including Nathaniel Hawthorne and Henry David Thoreau. Herman Melville even dedicated a novel to 'Greylock's Most Excellent Majesty'. Nowadays, it is ceremoniously topped with a 92ft-high War Memorial Tower, which you can climb (making the mountain effectively 3583ft). From May to October, you can also eat and sleep at the magnificently sited Bascom Lodge (p151).

artists the opportunity to take things into a whole new dimension.

In addition to ever-changing, description-defying installations, there is a fascinating Sol LeWitt retrospective, which is on display until 2033. Little ones can always create and speculate in Kidspace, while on-site theater space hosts music festivals, dance parties, poetry recitals and every kind of performance art imaginable.

✕ ⊨ p85

The Drive » Exiting North Adams, the Mohawk Trail crosses the Hoosac River several times before becoming Main St, Williamstown.

- - - - - - - - - - - - -

⑥ Williamstown

Tiny Williamstown is nestled in the heart of the Purple Valley, so named because the surrounding mountains often seem shrouded in a lavender veil at dusk. It is the ultimate college town, dominated by the marble-and-brick buildings of elite Williams College.

In addition to welcoming green spaces and academic architecture, Williamstown is home to a pair of exceptional art museums. The **Sterling & Francine Clark Art Institute** (The Clark; www.clarkart.edu; 225 South St; admission Jun-Oct $15, Nov-May free; ◷10am-5pm, closed Mon Sep-Jun) is a gem, with wonderful collections of paintings by French Impressionists and their American contemporaries.

Down the road, the **Williams College Museum of Art** (www.wcma.org; Main St; admission free; ◷10am-5pm Tue-Sat, 1-5pm Sun) has an incredible collection of its own. The American Collection includes substantial works by notables such as Edward Hopper, Winslow Homer and Grant Wood, to name only a few. The photography collection is also noteworthy, with images by Man Ray and Alfred Stieglitz.

✕ ⊨ p85

Eating & Sleeping

Deerfield ❶

🛏 Deerfield Inn   Inn $$

(📞413-774-5587; www.deerfieldinn.com; the
Street; d incl breakfast $170-260; ❋🛜) For
historic New England atmosphere, spend the
night at this old-fashioned inn at the center of
Deerfield Village. Comfortable rooms evoke the
era, with floral wallpaper and patterned quilts,
though the modern conveniences are there
too. The on-site Champney's restaurant serves
traditional American fare, with an emphasis on
the local and sustainably grown.

Shelburne Falls ❷

✕ Gould's Sugar House   Breakfast $$

(www.goulds-sugarhouse.com; 270 Mohawk Trail;
⊙Mar-May & Sep-Nov) The standard order at
this family-run farm is fluffy pancake perfection,
drizzled with maple heaven. Other unexpected
highlights include the sugar pickles (yes, you
read that right) and maple ice cream. While you
wait (and you will wait), you can watch the syrup
being made.

North Adams ❺

✕ Public Eat & Drink   Pub $$

(www.publiceatanddrink.com; 34 Holden St;
sandwiches $9-11, mains $14-16; ⊙dinner Wed-
Mon) With exposed brick walls and big windows
overlooking the street, this cozy pub is a great
addition to North Adams. Come for an excellent
selection of craft beers and gourmet pub fare,
like brie burger or bistro steak.

🛏 Porches   Inn $$$

(📞413-664-0400; www.porches.com; 231 River
St; r incl breakfast $180-270, ste $250-320;

❋🛜🐾) Conveniently located across the
street from MASS MoCA, this 47-room inn
occupies a block of Victorian row houses,
renovated to reflect their working-class roots.
Period details include colorful wainscoting,
claw-foot tubs, French doors and – of course –
porches overlooking the activity of downtown
North Adams.

Williamstown ❻

✕ Mezze Bistro & Bar   Fusion $$$

(📞413-458-0123; www.mezzerestaurant.
com; 777 Cold Spring Rd/US 7; mains
$20-36; ⊙dinner) East meets West at this
chic restaurant that masterfully blends
contemporary American, Mediterranean and
Asian influences. Situated on three gorgeous
acres, Mezze's farm-to-table approach begins
with an edible garden right on-site. Also
features a selective wine list, a nice choice of
small plates and idyllic views through the big
windows.

🛏 Field Farm   Inn $$$

(📞413-458-3135; www.thetrustees.org/field
-farm; 554 Sloan Rd; r incl breakfast $175-295;
@🛜🐾) This one-of-a-kind inn offers an artful
blend of mid-20th-century modernity and
timeless mountain scenery. Six clean-lined
rooms are spacious and fitted with handcrafted
furnishings that reflect the modernist Bauhaus
style of the house. The sculpture-laden grounds
feature miles of lightly trodden walking trails.

🛏 Maple Terrace Motel   Motel $$

(📞413-458-9677; www.mapleterrace.com; 555
Main St; r incl breakfast $98-130; 🛜🐾) This
small, 15-room motel is a big old house on the
eastern outskirts of town, with rather elegant
units behind it. The Swedish innkeepers have
snazzed up the grounds with gardens that make
you want to linger.

STRETCH YOUR LEGS
BOSTON

Start/Finish Boston Common

Distance 2.5 miles

Duration Three hours

Everybody knows about the world-class museums and historical sites; but Boston also offers a network of verdant parks, welcoming waterways and delightful shopping streets, making it a wonderful walking city.

Take this walk on Trips

1 2

Boston Common

Welcome to the country's oldest public park (with a convenient underground parking facility below – what foresight!). A **bronze plaque** is emblazoned with the words of the treaty between Governor Winthrop and William Blaxton, who sold this land for £30 in 1634. The **Massachusetts State House** (www.sec. state.ma.us; cnr Beacon & Bowdoin Sts; admission free; ☉9am-5pm, tours 10am-3:30pm Mon-Fri) commands a prominent position in the park's northeast corner.

The Walk ≫ Follow the busy Bostonians crisscrossing the common. Exit the park from the western side, cross Charles St, and enter the tranquil Public Garden.

Public Garden

The Public Garden is a 24-acre botanical oasis of Victorian flowerbeds, verdant grass and weeping willows shading a tranquil lagoon. At any time of year, it is an island of loveliness, awash in seasonal blooms, gold-toned leaves or untrammeled snow. Taking a ride on the **Swan Boats** (www.swanboats. com; adult/senior/child $2.75/2/1.50; ☉10am-4pm mid-Apr–mid-Sep) in the lagoon has been a Boston tradition since 1877. And don't miss the famous statue **Make Way for Ducklings**, based on the beloved children's book by Robert McKloskey.

The Walk ≫ Cross the bridge and exit the garden through the southwestern gate to Arlington St. Stroll west on swanky Newbury St, perfect for window shopping and gallery hopping. Take a left on Clarendon St and continue to Boylston St.

Copley Square

Boston's most exquisite architecture is clustered around this stately Back Bay plaza. The centerpiece is the Romanesque **Trinity Church** (www. trinitychurchboston.org; 206 Clarendon St; adult/child/senior $7/free/5; ☉9am-5pm Mon-Sat, 1-6pm Sun), famed for its stained-glass windows. It's particularly lovely as reflected in the facade of the modern **John Hancock Tower**. This assemblage

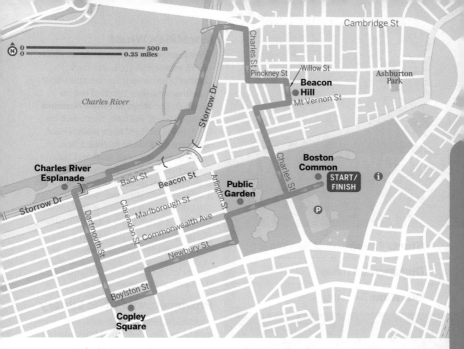

faces off against the elegant neo-Renaissance **Boston Public Library** (BPL; www.bpl.org; 700 Boylston St; admission free; ⊙9am-9pm Mon-Thu, to 5pm Fri & Sat), packed with sculpture, murals and other treasures.

The Walk ⟫ Head north on Dartmouth St, crossing the stately, dual-carriageway Commonwealth Ave, the grandest of Back Bay's grand avenues. Continue three more blocks to Back St, from where a pedestrian walkway crosses Storrow Dr to the esplanade.

Charles River Esplanade

The southern bank of the Charles River Basin is an enticing urban escape, with grassy knolls and cooling waterways, all designed by Frederick Law Olmsted. The park is dotted with public art, including an oversized bust of **Arthur Fiedler**, the long-time conductor of the Boston Pops. The **Hatch Memorial Shell** hosts free outdoor concerts and movies, including the famed Fourth of July concert by the Boston Pops.

The Walk ⟫ Walk east along the esplanade, enjoying the breezes and views of the Charles River. It's about a half-mile to the Longfellow Bridge, where you can climb the ramp and find yourself at the top of Charles St.

Beacon Hill

With an intriguing history and iconic architecture, Beacon Hill is Boston's most prestigious address. **Charles Street** is an enchanting spot for browsing boutiques and haggling over antiques. To explore further, wander down the residential streets lit with gas lanterns, admire the brick town houses decked with purple windowpanes and blooming flowerboxes, and discover streets such as stately **Louisburg Square** that capture the neighborhood's grandeur.

The Walk ⟫ Take your time strolling south along charming Charles St. For a glimpse of Louisburg Sq, walk two blocks east on Pinckney St. Then continue south to Boston Common.

STRETCH YOUR LEGS
PROVINCETOWN

Start/Finish MacMillan Wharf

Distance 1.3 miles

Duration Two hours

Ever since Charles Hawthorne opened the Cape Cod School of Art back in 1899, this little town at the tip of the cape has attracted artists, writers and other creative types exploring 'alternative' lifestyles.

Take this walk on Trips

[2] [3]

MacMillan Wharf

Start your walking tour at the central wharf, where fishing boats dock alongside passenger ferries and whale-watching cruisers. Perched out on the dock, the **Whydah Pirate Museum** (www.whydah.org; MacMillan Wharf; adult/child $10/8; ☼9:30am-7pm) is an unexpected curiosity. Captained by 'Black Sam' Bellamy, the *Whydah* sank in 1717 and to this day remains the only authenticated pirate ship ever salvaged. A local expedition recovered more than 100,000 items of booty – coins, jewelry, weapons – some of which are on display.

The Walk >> From MacMillan Wharf, stroll east on Commercial St. Take a quick detour to see an incredible, fantastical sculpture garden behind the wrought-iron fence on Center St. Then cross the street and enter the library.

Provincetown Public Library

Erected in 1860 as a church, this handsome belfry-topped building later became a museum, complete with a replica of Provincetown's famed race-winning schooner *Rose Dorothea*. When the museum went bust, the town converted the multifunctional building to the **Provincetown Public Library** (356 Commercial St; ☼10am-5pm Mon & Fri, noon-8pm Tue & Thu, 10am-8pm Wed, 10am-2pm Sat, 1-5pm Sun; 🛜). One catch: the boat was too big to remove, so it still occupies the upper deck, with bookshelves built around it.

The Walk >> Continue east on Commercial St. Grab a coffee at the ever-popular Wired Puppy, then turn left and walk up Pearl St. Cross Bradford St and continue to your next destination.

Fine Arts Work Center

The **Fine Arts Work Center** (www.fawc.org; 24 Pearl St) is one reason that this far-flung corner of Massachusetts continues to attract daring and creative minds. The progressive foundation supports emerging artists and writers, offering fellowships and facilities so they can immerse themselves in their creative endeavors. The on-site **Hudson D Walker Gallery** (🕘9am-5pm Mon-Fri) often hosts exhibits of work by past and present fellows, while readings, talks and presentations take place in the **Stanley Kunitz Common Room**.

The Walk » Return to Bradford St and turn left. Stroll for a few blocks along this backbone of Provincetown, which sees much less action than Commercial St. Bang a right on Bangs St and return to the main drag.

Provincetown Art Association & Museum

Founded in 1914, the **Provincetown Art Association & Museum** (PAAM; www. paam.org; 460 Commercial St; adult/child $7/ free; 🕘11am-8pm Mon-Thu, to 10pm Fri, to 5pm Sat & Sun) celebrates the town's thriving art community, displaying the works of hundreds of artists who have found their inspiration on the Lower Cape. Among the impressionist, modernist and contemporary works are pieces by Charles Hawthorne, who led the early Provincetown art movement, and Edward Hopper, who had a home and gallery in the Truro dunes.

The Walk » Walk west on Commercial St, passing through the eclectic East End.

East End

As you walk back along Commercial St toward MacMillan Wharf, you are traversing the **Provincetown East End Gallery District**. Between Bangs and Standish Sts, P-town's main drag is lined with galleries showcasing local and national (and some international) artists. Browse at your leisure, but don't miss the **Albert Merola Gallery** (www.albertmerolagallery.com; 424 Commercial St), which showcases works by both contemporary and notable past Provincetown artists. Pick up the free *Provincetown Art Guide* for a map and complete list of galleries.

The Walk » Continue walking west on Commercial St to return to MacMillan Wharf.

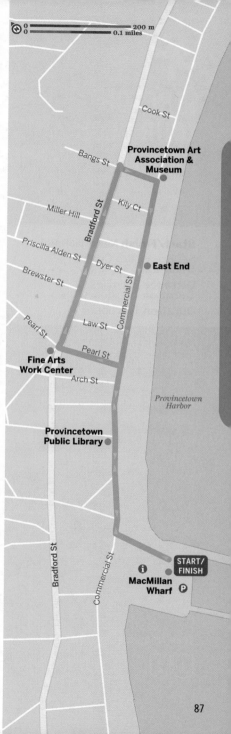

STRETCH YOUR LEGS
SALEM

Start/Finish National Park Service Visitor Center

Distance 2.4 miles

Duration Two hours

A lot of history is packed into this gritty city of witches and sailors – even more than you read in the textbooks. This walk highlights the architectural gems and little-known stories that are often overlooked.

Take this walk on Trips

National Park Service Visitor Center

Start your explorations at the **NPS Visitor Center** (www.nps.gov/sama; 2 Liberty St; ⊘9am-5pm), which offers information on Salem. For a good overview, catch a free screening of *Where Past Is Present*, a short film about Salem history. You can also pick up a map and description of several self-guided walking tours and other area attractions.

The Walk » From the visitor center, walk south on Liberty St for one block. The excellent Peabody Essex Museum sits at the corner of Essex St. Turn right and continue down Essex St.

Essex Street

The main drag in Salem is Essex St, a pedestrian mall that is lined with shops and cafes, a few historic buildings and several witch-themed attractions. The most prominent building is the **old Town Hall**, the red-brick beauty that was the seat of government in the 19th century. At the corner of Washington St stands a statue of Samantha Stephens, the spell-casting, nose-twitching beauty from the classic TV show *Bewitched*.

The Walk » Cross Washington St and continue west on Essex St. At Summer St, turn left and walk one block south to Chestnut St.

Chestnut Street

Lovers of old houses will revel in the grand antique homes on Chestnut St, which is among the most architecturally lovely streets in the country. One of these stately homes is the **Stephen Phillips Memorial Trust House** (www.phillipsmuseum.org; 34 Chestnut St; adult/child/senior & student $5/2.50/4; ⊘10am-4pm Tue-Sun Jun-Oct, Sat & Sun Nov-May), which displays the family furnishings of Salem sea captains, including a collection of antique carriages and cars.

The Walk » Retrace your steps on Chestnut St. Cross Summer St and continue walking on Norman St. Cross Washington St and continue

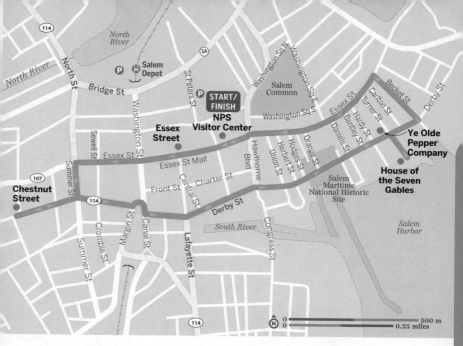

walking on Derby St, passing through the heart of the Salem National Maritime Historic Site.

Ye Olde Pepper Companie

In 1806, Englishwoman Mrs Spencer survived a shipwreck en route to the New World. She arrived in Salem all wet with nary a penny to her name. With a small loan, Mrs Spencer bought a barrel of sugar and created the 'Salem Gibraltar', a candy that sated the sweet teeth of sea captains and sailing merchants. Two centuries later, **Ye Olde Pepper Companie** (www. yeoldepeppercompanie.com; 122 Derby St; ⏱10am-6pm) still uses Mrs Spencer's recipes for old-fashioned delights such as Black Jacks (flavored with black strap molasses) and Gibraltars (lemon and peppermint treats). Sweet!

The Walk ≫ From Derby St, turn right on Turner St and stroll to the end of this lovely residential lane.

House of Seven Gables

'Halfway down a by-street of one of our New England towns stands a rusty wooden house, with seven acutely peaked gables facing towards various points of the compass, and a huge clustered chimney in their midst.' So wrote Nathaniel Hawthorne in his 1851 novel about the **House of the Seven Gables** (www.7gables.org; 54 Turner St; adult/ senior/child $12.50/7.50/11.50; ⏱10am-5pm Nov-Jun, to 7pm Jul-Oct). The admission fee allows entrance to the site's four historic buildings, as well as the luxurious gardens on the waterfront.

The Walk ≫ Continue east on Derby St. Peek inside the whimsical world of metal sculpture on the corner of Blaney St, before walking up Becket St. Turn left on Essex St and walk a half-mile back to the NPS Visitor Center.

Connecticut & Rhode Island

WITH LAKES, ORCHARDS, VINEYARDS AND COASTAL CLIFF WALKS, Connecticut and Rhode Island pack a big punch – even though they're two of the smallest states in the Union. Connecticut's pristine scenery has been luring artists, celebrities and moneyed Manhattanites since the 1900s and it's easy to see what drew them here: a historic rural landscape, genteel pre-Colonial towns, clam shacks and oyster harvests. Just down the road, tiny Rhode Island sports a jagged coastline trimmed with some of the best beaches in the northeast, while the cities of Providence and Newport brim with museums, galleries and gorgeous old cobbled neighborhoods. No wonder the Vanderbilts and their friends decamped here for summer balls and swimming. You'd be wise to follow suit.

Westerly, Rhode Island Bask on the sand or take to the water (Trip 8)

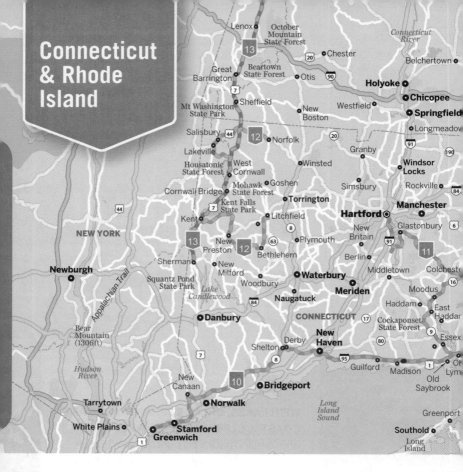

Connecticut & Rhode Island

DON'T MISS

Polo in Rhode Island

Enjoy polo in Portsmouth at the Glen Farm country estate on Trip 7

Golden Lamb Buttery

Mingle over drinks, head off for a hayride and then settle down for a gourmet dinner. Reserve ahead for Trip 9

Jonathan Edwards Winery

Those in the know pick up lunch along the way to this 48-acre estate overlooking the Atlantic. Perfect for afternoon picnics on Trip 10

Philip Johnson Glass House

Tour Connecticut's newest National Trust Historic Site and one of the world's most famous modern houses on Trip 10

Bantam Cinema

Watch stylish independent and foreign films in a converted red barn next to Lake Bantam on Trip 12

Block Island 'Gingerbread' house (Trip 8)

Newport *Stroll Cliff Walk and see how the wealthy vacationed in the 19th century*

Rhode Island: East Bay

7

East Bay is at the heart of Rhode Island's history. Tour the shoreline, and follow the trail from America's humble Colonial roots in Little Compton to the industrial boomtowns of Newport and Providence.

TRIP HIGHLIGHTS

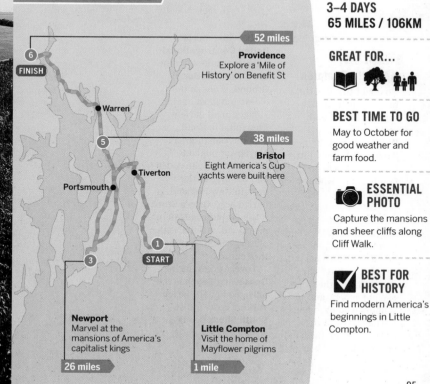

52 miles

6 FINISH

Providence
Explore a 'Mile of History' on Benefit St

● Warren

5

38 miles

Bristol
Eight America's Cup yachts were built here

● Tiverton

Portsmouth ●

3

1 START

Newport
Marvel at the mansions of America's capitalist kings

26 miles

Little Compton
Visit the home of Mayflower pilgrims

1 mile

3–4 DAYS
65 MILES / 106KM

GREAT FOR...

BEST TIME TO GO
May to October for good weather and farm food.

ESSENTIAL PHOTO
Capture the mansions and sheer cliffs along Cliff Walk.

BEST FOR HISTORY
Find modern America's beginnings in Little Compton.

Rhode Island's jagged East Bay tells the American story in microcosm. Start in Little Compton with the grave of Elizabeth Pabodie (1623–1717), the first European settler born in New England. Then meander through historic Tiverton and Bristol, where slave dealers and merchants grew rich. Prosperous as they were, their modest homes barely hold a candle to the mansions, museums and libraries of Newport's capitalist kings and Providence's intelligentsia.

Pawtucket

FINISH
Providence 6

Warwick

West Warwick

East Greenwich

8

Exeter

Wickford

North Kingston

Narragansett

South Kingston

TRIP HIGHLIGHT

1 Little Compton

No doubt tiring of the big-city bustle of 17th-century Portsmouth, early settler Samuel Wilbor crossed the Sakonnet River to Little Compton. His plain family home, **Wilbur House** (📞401-635-4035; 548 West Main Rd; adult/child $6/3; 🕐1-5pm Thu-Sun Apr-Oct, 9am-3pm Nov-Mar), built in 1690, still stands on a manicured lawn behind a traditional five-bar gate and tells the story of eight generations of Wilburs who lived here.

The rest of Little Compton, from the hand-hewn clapboard houses to the white-steepled **United Congregational Church**, overlooking the **Old Commons Burial Ground**, is one of the oldest and most quaint villages in all of New England. Elizabeth Pabodie, daughter of Mayflower pilgrims Priscilla and John Alden and the first settler born in New England, is buried here. **Gray's Store** (4 Main St), built in 1788 in nearby Adamsville, is the oldest general store in the country.

Lovely, ocean-facing **Goosewing Beach** is the only good public beach. Parking costs $10 at **South Shore Beach** (Little Compton; 🕐dawn-dusk),

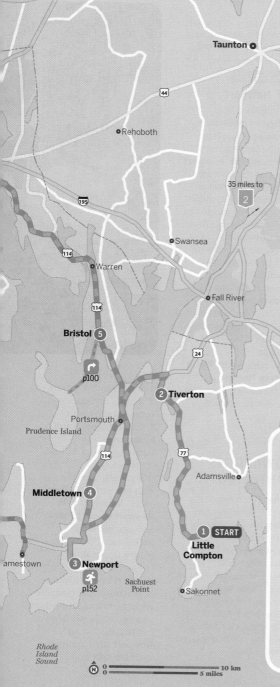

from where you can walk across a small tidal inlet.

🛏 p101

The Drive ›› Head north along RI 77 at a leisurely pace, enjoying the peaceful country scenery of rambling stone walls and clapboard farmhouses. To your left you'll occasionally get glimpses out to the water, which are particularly pretty in the late afternoon as the sun begins to set.

- - - - - - - - - - - - - -

② Tiverton

En route to Tiverton's historic Four Corners, stop in at **Sakonnet Vineyards** (☎1-800-919-4637; www.sakonnetwine.com; 162 West Main Rd; ⏲11am-5pm) for free daily wine tastings and guided tours. This will set you up nicely for the gourmet treats that await in Tiverton: **Gray's Ice Cream** (graysicecream.com; 16 East Rd; ⏲7am-7pm), where over 40 flavors are made on-site

§ LINK YOUR TRIP

8 Rhode Island: Coastal Culture

Explore Rhode Island's coastal culture, heading west along I-95 from Providence (p104).

2 Pilgrim Trail

Continue the historical journey in Plymouth with the Massachusetts Pilgrim Trail (p46).

daily; artisanal cheeses from the **Milk & Honey Bazaar** (milkandhoneybazaar. com; 3838 Main Rd; ☺10am-5pm Wed-Sat, noon-5pm Sun); and the gourmet deli bar at **Provender** (3883 Main Rd; ☺9am-5pm mid-Mar–Dec), where you can munch on giant cookies or forage for picnic fare.

Tiverton is an artists colony so it also offers some of the best shopping in the state, including handwoven Shaker-style rugs from **Amy C Lund** (www. amyclundhandweaver.com; 3964 Main Rd; ☺10am-5pm Wed-Sat, noon-5pm Sun) and museum-quality art from **Gallery 4** (www. gallery4tiverton.com; 3848 Main Rd; ☺11am-4:30pm Wed-Sat, noon-4:30pm Sun).

 p101

The Drive » Head north up Main St, leaving Tiverton and its green fields behind you, and merge onto the westbound RI 138/RI 24 south, which leads you directly into Newport.

TRIP HIGHLIGHT

③ Newport

Established by religious moderates fleeing persecution from Massachusetts Puritans, the 'new port' flourished to become the fourth richest city in the newly independent colony. Downtown, the Colonial-era architecture is beautifully preserved along with notable landmarks such as Washington Square's **Colony House**, where Rhode Island's declaration of independence was read in May 1776.

Just off the square, the gaslights of the **White Horse Tavern** (☎401-849-3600; www.whitehorsetavern. us; 26 Marlborough St),

America's oldest tavern, still burn, and on Touro St, America's first synagogue, **Touro Synagogue** (www. tourosynagogue.org; 85 Touro St; tours adult/child $12/free), still stands. Tour the past with our walk (p152) or on guided walks with **Newport History Tours** (www.newporthistorical. org; tours adult/child $12/5; ☺10am Thu-Sat May-Sep).

Fascinating as Newport's early history is, it struggles to compete with the town's latter-day success, when wealthy industrialists made Newport their summer vacation spot and

---

LOCAL KNOWLEDGE: POLO IN PORTSMOUTH

Drab though the urban environs of Portsmouth may seem, in-the-know locals rate Portsmouth as a family-friendly destination. Not least because the polo matches hosted at Glen Farm make for a great family day out. Home to the **Newport Polo Club** (www.nptpolo.com; 715 East Main Rd; adult/child $12/free; ☺gates open 1pm), the 700-acre 'farm' was assembled by New York businessman Henry Taylor, who sought to create a gentleman's country seat in the grand English tradition. In summer, the farm is host to the club's polo matches (check the website for dates), which are a perfect way to enjoy the property and get an authentic taste of Newport high life.

BOB ROWAN PROGRESSIVE IMAGE/CORBIS ©

Providence The library of Providence Athenaeum

built country 'cottages' down lantern-lined Bellevue Ave, modeled on Italianate palazzos, French chateaux and Elizabethan manor houses, and decorated with priceless furnishings and artworks. Tour the most outstanding with the **Preservation Society** (www.newportmansions.org; 424 Bellevue Ave; adult/child from $14.50/10).

✖ 🛏 p101

The Drive » Leave Newport by way of 10-mile Ocean Dr, which starts just south of Fort Adams and curls around the southern shore, past the grand mansions, and up Bellevue Ave before intersecting with Memorial Blvd. Turn right here for a straight shot into Middletown.

- - - - - - - - - - -

④ Middletown

Flo's (4 Wave Ave; mains $2.50-6; ⊙ closed Jan-Feb) jaunty red-and-white clam shack would be enough reason to visit Middletown, which now merges seamlessly with Newport. But the best fried clams in town taste better after a day on **Second Beach** (Sachuest Point Rd), the largest and most beautiful beach on Aquidneck Island. Curving around Sachuest Bay, it is backed by the 450-acre **Norman Bird Sanctuary** (www. normanbirdsanctuary.org; 583 Third Beach Rd; adult/child $6/3; ⊙9am-5pm), which teems with migrating birds.

The Drive » Leave Aquidneck Island via East Main Rd, which takes you north through the suburbs of Middletown and Portsmouth. After 6.5 miles, pick up the RI 114 and cross the bay via the scenic Mt Hope suspension bridge. From here it's a short 3-mile drive into Bristol.

- - - - - - - - - - -

TRIP HIGHLIGHT

⑤ Bristol

One-fifth of all slaves transported to America

DETOUR: PRUDENCE ISLAND

Start: ⑤ Bristol

Idyllic **Prudence Island** (www.prudenceferry.com; adult/child $6.60/2.90; ☺6am-6pm Mon-Fri, to 4pm Sat & Sun) sits in the middle of Narragansett Bay, an easy 25-minute ferry ride from Bristol. Originally used for farming and later as a summer vacation spot for families from Providence and New York, who travelled here on the Fall River Line Steamer, the island now has only 88 inhabitants. There are some fine Victorian and Beaux Arts houses near Stone Wharf, a lighthouse and a small store, but otherwise it's wild and unspoiled. Perfect for mountain biking, barbecues, fishing and paddling.

were brought in Bristol ships and by the 18th century the town was one of the country's major commercial ports. The world-class **Herreshoff Marine Museum** (www.herreshoff.org; 1 Burnside St; adult/child $10/free; ☺10am-5pm May-Oct) showcases some of America's finest yachts, including eight that were built for the America's Cup.

Local resident Augustus Van Wickle bought a 72ft Herreshoff yacht for his wife Bessie in 1895, but having nowhere suitable to moor it, he then had to build **Blithewold Mansion** (www.blithewold.org; 101 Ferry Rd; adult/child $11/3; ☺10am-4pm Tue-Sun mid-Apr–Oct). The Arts and Crafts mansion sits in a peerless position on Narragansett Bay and is particularly lovely in spring, when the daffodils line the shore.

Other local magnates included slave trader General George DeWolf who built **Linden Place** (☎401-253-0390; www.lindenplace.org; 500 Hope St; adult/child $8/6; ☺10am-4pm Thu-Sat May-Oct), famous as a film location for *The Great Gatsby*.

Bristol's **Colt State Park** (www.riparks.com; RI 114; ☺8:30am-4:30pm) is Rhode Island's most scenic park, with its entire western border fronting Narragansett Bay, fringed by 4 miles of cycling trails and shaded picnic tables.

🛏 p101

The Drive » From Bristol it's a straight drive north along RI 114, through the suburbs of Warren and Barrington, to Providence. After 17 miles, merge onto the I-195 W, which takes you the remaining 18 miles into the center of town.

TRIP HIGHLIGHT

⑥ Providence

Providence, the first town of religious liberal Roger Williams' new Rhode Island and Providence Plantation colony, was established so that 'no man should be molested for his conscience sake.' **Benefit Street's** 'Mile of History' gives a quick lesson in the city's architectural legacy with over 100 Colonial, Federal and Revival houses. Amid them you'll find William Strickland's 1838 **Providence Athenaeum** (www.providenceathenaeum.org; 251 Benefit St; admission free; ☺9am-7pm Mon-Thu, to 5pm Fri-Sun), inside which plaster busts of Greek gods and philosophers preside over a collection that dates to 1753.

Atop the hill sits **Brown University**, with its Gothic and Beaux Arts buildings arranged around the College Green. Nearby is **John Brown House** (www.rihs.org; 52 Power St; adult/child $8/4; ☺tours 1:30pm & 3pm Tue-Fri, 10:30am-3pm Sat Apr-Dec), which President John Quincy Adams thought to be 'the most magnificent and elegant mansion...on this continent.'

End the tour with a nod toward the bronze statue of *Independent Man*, which graces the pearly white dome of the **Rhode Island State House**.

🍴🛏 p101

Eating & Sleeping

Little Compton ❶

🛏 Stone House   Inn $$$

(📞401-635-2222; www.stonehouse1854.com; 122 Sakonnet Point; r $275-400; 🅿🛜) With its Italianate architecture, granite block and sandstone construction and frilly front porch, fabulous Stone House sits next to the best beaches in town and serves up lovely ocean views.

Tiverton ❷

✕ Evelyn's Drive-In   American $$

(www.evelynsdrivein.com; 2335 Main Rd; mains $5-18; 🕐lunch & dinner Apr-Sep; 🅿👪) Park on the crushed-shell driveway and eat mildly spiced lobster rolls and burgers on hot-dog buns. The gray clapboard building sits right next to the Nanaquaket Pond.

Newport ❸

✕ Fluke   Seafood $$$

(📞401-849-7778; flukewinebar.com; 41 Bowen's Wharf; mains $9-34; 🕐5-11pm Wed-Sat Nov-Apr, daily in summer) Fluke's Scandinavian-inspired dining room, with its blond wood and picture windows, offers an accomplished seafood menu featuring roasted monkfish, seasonal striped sea bass and plump scallops. Upstairs, the bar serves a rock-and-roll cocktail list.

✕ Mooring   Modern American $$

(📞401-846-2260; www.mooringrestaurant.com; Sayers Wharf; mains $6-36; 🕐lunch & dinner; 🅿👪) You can't get a better view of Narragansett Bay than from the mahogany deck of the Mooring. The grand dining room, with its nautical themed artwork and marble-topped bar, was once home to the New York Yacht Club.

🛏 Marshall Slocum Guesthouse   B&B $$

(📞401-841-5120; www.marshallslocuminn.com; 29 Kay St; r $79-275; 🅿✳🛜) This clapboard

Colonial house, a former parsonage, is situated between Historic Hill and downtown Newport. The period feel is preserved in the interiors, and rooms feature canopy beds, wide wooden floorboards and shuttered windows.

Bristol ❺

🛏 Governor Bradford Inn   Inn $$

(📞401-254-1745; www.mounthopefarm.org; 250 Metacom Ave; r $125-275; 🅿✳) Administered by the Mount Hope Trust, the Governor Bradford offers four individually styled rooms in a 300-year-old Georgian farmhouse. Once owned by the Haffenreffer family, of beer-brewing fortune, the house sits on 200 acres of pristine farmland.

Providence ❻

✕ Haven Brothers Diner   Diner $

(Washington St; meals $5-10; 🕐5pm-3am) This diner sits on the back of a truck. Legend has it that the business started as a horse-drawn lunch wagon in 1893. Climb up the rickety ladder to get basic diner fare alongside politicians and college kids.

✕ Local 121   Modern American $$

(www.local121.com; 121 Washington St; mains $16-32; 🕐lunch Tue-Sun, dinner daily) This old-school restaurant, housed in the former Dreyfus hotel, has an unpretentious grandeur. The menu is seasonal, including a local scallop po'boy and duck ham pizza. The tap room is a great place for a casual meal.

🛏 Providence Biltmore   Historic Hotel $$$

(📞401-421-0700; www.providencebiltmore.com; 11 Dorrance St; r $146-286; 🅿@) Make like an industrialist and check into the granddaddy of Providence's hotels. The Biltmore dates to the 1920s and retains the regal atmosphere in its dark wood details, curving staircases and heavy chandeliers.

Block Island Southeast Light is set dramatically atop 200ft cliffs

Rhode Island: Coastal Culture

8

After traveling this route along the state's jagged coastline and visiting the islands floating in Narragansett Bay, you will understand why Rhode Island earned the honor of being called the Ocean State.

TRIP HIGHLIGHTS

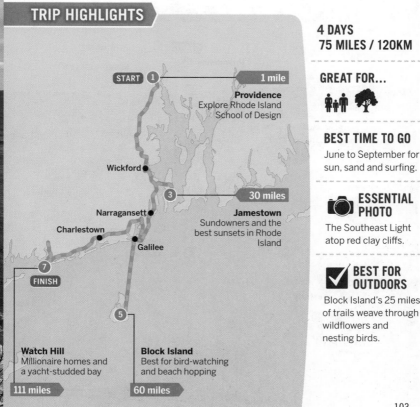

START 1 — 1 mile

Providence
Explore Rhode Island
School of Design

Wickford

3 — 30 miles

Jamestown
Sundowners and the
best sunsets in Rhode
Island

Narragansett

Charlestown

Galilee

7
FINISH

5

Watch Hill
Millionaire homes and
a yacht-studded bay

111 miles

Block Island
Best for bird-watching
and beach hopping

60 miles

**4 DAYS
75 MILES / 120KM**

GREAT FOR...

BEST TIME TO GO
June to September for
sun, sand and surfing.

ESSENTIAL PHOTO
The Southeast Light
atop red clay cliffs.

BEST FOR OUTDOORS
Block Island's 25 miles
of trails weave through
wildflowers and
nesting birds.

103

8 Rhode Island: Coastal Culture

Rhode Island might only take 45 minutes to drive across but it packs 400 miles of coastline into its tiny boundaries. Much of this takes the form of white sandy beaches, arguably the finest places for ocean swimming in the northeast. Then there are islands to explore, sea cliffs to walk along and isolated lighthouses to frame that perfect sunset shot.

TRIP HIGHLIGHT

1 Providence

Rhode Island's capital presents visitors with some fine urban strolling, from Brown University's campus on 18th-century **College Hill** to the city's **Riverwalk** and the historic downtown along Weybosset St. Along the way, visit the **Rhode Island School of Design** (RISD), the top art institution in the US and home to the **Museum of Art** (www.risdmuseum. org; 224 Benefit St; adult/child

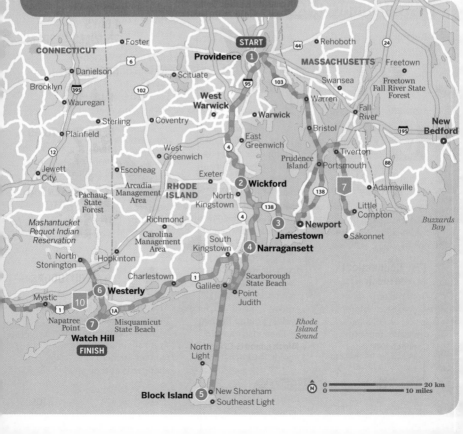

$10/3; ⏰10am-5pm Tue-Sun; ♿), with its collection of Roman and Etruscan artifacts, medieval and Renaissance works and 19th-century French paintings. RISD maintains several fine galleries. **Sol Koffler** (169 Weybosset St; ⏰noon-6pm) serves as the main exhibition space for graduate students, while **risd | works** (www.risdworks.com; 10 Westminster St; ⏰10am-5pm Tue-Sun) offers some of their work for sale.

If you're in town on the third Thursday of the month, you can catch **Gallery Night** (www.gallerynight.info; ⏰5-9pm Mar-Nov), when 23 galleries and museums open their doors for free viewings.

✕ ⛏ p109

LINK YOUR TRIP

7 Rhode Island: East Bay

Head east down RI 114 for a trip back in time to the earliest days of the colony (p95).

10 Connecticut Wine Trail

From Westerly, drive west to Stonington (p124) on US 1 for a gourmet tour of Connecticut's vineyards and farms.

LOCAL KNOWLEDGE: ALLIE'S

Poll a couple of Rhode Islander's for the state's best souvenir, and one of them will probably say a treat from **Allie's Donuts** (📞401-295-8036; 3661 Quaker Lane/RI 2; ⏰5am-3pm Mon-Fri, 6am-1pm Sat & Sun). Allie has been turning out hot-to-trot homemade doughnuts from her roadside shack on RI 2 for over 40 years and Rhode Islanders travel from across the state to take them away by the dozen ($7.20). Light as air, they are filled and topped with delectable condiments such as flaked coconut, chocolate and lemon cream and cherry jelly.

The Drive ≫ Leave Providence via Memorial Blvd and pick up the I-95 S. Meander through the suburbs for 1.5 miles and veer left onto RI 4 S toward North Kingstown. Exit at 7A–7B onto RI 403 east toward Quonset and after a couple of miles turn onto US 1 for Wickford.

② Wickford

Bypassed by the era of steamboats and train travel, Wickford's Main St and Pleasant St languished sleepily through the industrial revolution and are still lined with 18th-century Colonial and Federal homes, which lead down to the harbor where fishermen cast their lines off the pier. Rent kayaks from the **Kayak Centre** (www.kayakcentre.com; 9 Phillips St, Waterside; 2hr rental $28; ⏰10am-5pm Wed-Mon) for a paddle around the bay.

Then visit the **Old Narragansett Church** (📞401-294-4357; 60 Church Lane; ⏰11am-4pm Thu-Sun Jul-Aug or by appointment). It dates from 1707 and retains its box pews and upstairs gallery where plantation slaves were allowed to worship. Local artist Gilbert Scott (1755–1828), who painted the portrait of George Washington that graces the one-dollar bill, was baptized here in the silver baptismal font.

The Drive ≫ It is a short 4-mile drive along RI 1A S from Wickford to Conanicut Island. Once you're through the Wickford suburbs, take the RI 138 ramp over the Jamestown Bridge which affords expansive views of the bay. Once on the island, turn right down North Rd to Jamestown past the old smock windmill.

TRIP HIGHLIGHT

③ Jamestown

More rural than its prosperous neighbor, Newport, Jamestown's first inhabitants were Quaker farmers, shepherds and pirates.

Captain Kidd spent considerable time here and is said to have buried his treasure hereabouts.

These days, the real treasure in Jamestown is the peace and quiet. The waterfront is undeveloped and you can walk along **Conanicus Avenue** and take a bench overlooking the harbor. The **Jamestown ferry** (www.jamestownnewportferry. com; Conanicut Marina; adult/child return $18/8; 🕙May–Oct) sails to Newport with stops at Fort Adams and Rose Island. It is the best deal going for a harbor tour.

At the southernmost tip of Conanicut Island is **Beavertail State Park**, where you can enjoy one of the best vistas – and sunsets – in the Ocean State. Many vacationers bring lawn chairs, barbecues and picnics, and spend all day enjoying the walking trails and cliff-top views. At the point, picturesque **Beavertail Lighthouse** (1749), one of the oldest along the Atlantic coast, still signals ships into Narragansett Bay.

✗ p109

The Drive ❯❯ Leaving Conanicut Island, head south along the scenic route RI 1A, along which you'll enjoy woodsy roads around Saunderstown and glimpses of the bay as you skirt the shoreline south of Narragansett Pier.

SHERYL SAVAS/ALAMY ©

---

④ Narragansett

Scarborough State Beach, just south of Narragansett Pier, is one of the state's biggest beaches and is considered by many the best.

A few miles further south is **Galilee**, the departure point for **car ferries** (www.blockislandferry. com; round-trip adult/car/ bike $26.85/$103/$6.40; 🕙mid-Jun–early Sep) to Block Island. Sometimes called Point Judith in ferry schedules, Galilee is a workaday fishing town. Arrive in time and eat at dockside **Champlins** (📞401-783-3152; 256 Great Rd; mains $3-15; 🕙11am-9pm summer, shorter hr off-season), where they haul the fish right out of the bay onto your plate.

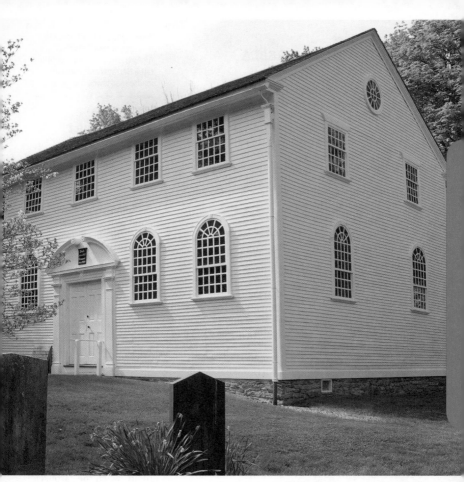

Wickford A picturesque church and cemetery

Further south still, the **Roger W Wheeler State Beach** is a good spot for families with small children. Not only does it have a playground and other facilities, it also has a very gradual drop-off and little surf. All-day parking in Galilee costs $10 in any of the several lots.

✕ ⛺ p109

The Drive >> Car-and-passenger ferries run from Galilee State Pier, Point Judith, to Old Harbor, Block Island (see p341).

- - - - - - - - - - -

TRIP HIGHLIGHT

5 Block Island

From the deck of the ferry you'll see a cluster of mansard roofs and gingerbread houses rising picturesquely from **Old Harbor**, Block Island's main centre of activity.

Beyond here, the island's attractions are simple. Stretching for several miles to the north of Old Harbor is the 3-mile **State Beach**, long enough to find a quiet spot even on a busy day. Otherwise, bike or hike around the island's rolling farmland,

FANTASTIC UMBRELLA FACTORY

A collection of 19th-century farm buildings and unkempt gardens, the **Fantastic Umbrella Factory** (☎401-364-6616; www.fantasticumbrellafactory.com; RI 1A, Charlestown; 🚗), a former commune, got its start as one of Rhode Island's strangest stores in 1968. You can find almost anything in a series of shacks filled with gift items, flowers, toys, handmade jewelry and authentic hippie hemp clothing. Exotic birds and farm animals walk all over the place, much to the delight of children.

pausing to admire the island's lighthouses: **Southeast Light**, set dramatically atop 200ft red clay cliffs, and **North Light**, which stands at the end of a long sandy lane lined with beach roses. In spring and fall, when migratory species fly south along the Atlantic Flyway, bird-watching opportunities abound.

Hire bikes from **Island Moped and Bike Rentals** (☎401-466-2700; Chapel St; per day bikes/mopeds $20/115; ⊙9am-8pm).

✖ ⎘ p109

**The Drive ›› **Take the ferry back to Galilee and follow the signs to the main interstate RI 1. This 20-mile stretch of highway to Westerly is pleasant enough, lined with thick woods and plenty of opportunities to detour to various beaches.

⑥ Westerly

Westerly sits on Rhode Island's western border, sharing the banks of the Pawcatuck River with Connecticut. In the 19th century it was a town of some wealth, thanks to its high-grade granite quarries. That heyday is long gone, although local **Misquamicut State Beach** still draws the weekending crowds who favor its scenic situation on Winnapaug Pond.

Nearby is the old-fashioned amusement resort of **Atlantic Beach Park** (www.atlanticbeachpark. com; Atlantic Ave, Misquamicut; 🚗), which offers miniature golf, wave rides, batting cages and the like.

✖ ⎘ p109

**The Drive ›› **It's a short and scenic 2-mile drive south down RI 1A from the centre of

Westerly to the heady heights of mansion-clad Watch Hill. Along the way, enjoy views over Little Narragansett Bay across landscaped lawns and gardens.

TRIP HIGHLIGHT

⑦ Watch Hill

The wealthy summer colony of Watch Hill, with its huge Queen Anne summerhouses, occupies a spit of land at the southwesternmost point of Rhode Island.

Visitors here spend their time at **East Beach**, which stretches for several miles from Watch Hill lighthouse all the way to Misquamicut. (The public access to the beach is located on Bluff Ave near Larkin Rd.) For children, an ice-cream cone and a twirl on the **Flying Horse Carousel** (Bay St; rides $1; ⊙11am-9pm) provide immediate gratification. The antique carousel dates from 1883 and its horses, suspended on chains, really do appear to 'fly' when the carousel spins.

For a leisurely beach walk, the half-mile stroll to **Napatree Point** is unbeatable with the Atlantic on one side and yacht-studded Little Narragansett Bay on the other.

Eating & Sleeping

Providence ❶

✕ Al Forno   Italian $$$

(📞401-273-9760; www.alforno.com; 577 S
Main St; mains $24-32; 🕐dinner Tue-Sat; 🅿)
This award-winning restaurant specializes in
wood-grilling. Favorites include plump scallops
wrapped in blackened bacon, and the wood-
grilled leg of lamb. The menu also features
handmade pastas as well as wood-fired pizzas.

🛏 Christopher Dodge House   Inn $$

(📞401-351-6111; www.providence-inn.com; 11
W Park St; r $120-180; 🅿) This 1858 Federal-
style house is furnished with early American
reproduction furniture and marble fireplaces.
Austere on the outside, it has elegant proportions,
large shuttered windows and wooden floors.

Jamestown ❸

✕ Village Hearth
Artisan Bakery   Bakery, Pizzeria $

(www.villagehearthbakerycafe.com; 2 Watson
Ave; mains $3.50-12; 🕐7am-4pm Fri & Sat,
7am-2pm & 4.30-7pm Sun) This low-slung
yellow shack is situated a block north of
the Jamestown village centre. It houses a
community bakery and, on Sundays only, a
pizzeria. It's a good pit stop for picnic fare,
selling excellent country loaves and pastries.

Narragansett ❹

✕ Aunt Carrie's   Seafood $$

(www.auntcarriesri.com; 1240 Ocean Rd, Point
Judith; mains $9-14; 🕐lunch daily late May-early
Sep, lunch Sat & Sun Sep, lunch Fri-Sun Apr-late
May) Open June through Labor Day, Aunt
Carrie's serves up fried clams and clam cakes
on its outdoor terrace. Eating here is a summer
ritual for Rhode Islanders.

🛏 Fisherman's Memorial
State Park   Campground $

(📞401-789-8374; www.riparks.com; 1011 Point
Judith Rd/RI 108; tent/RV sites residents $14/20,

nonresidents $20/35) This Galilee campground
is so popular that many families return year
after year to the same site. There are only 180
campsites, so it's wise to reserve early through
the RI State Parks website.

Block Island ❺

✕ Eli's   Modern American $$

(📞401-466-5230; www.elisblockisland.com;
456 Chapel St, Old Harbor; meals $12-28; 🕐from
6pm; 🅿) Serving 'Asian-inspired comfort food'
on two separate menus, one vegetarian and one
meat-loving, Eli's is a Block Island institution.
The locally caught sea bass special tastes so
fresh, mildly salty and sweet that the flavor will
haunt you for weeks.

🛏 Atlantic Inn   Historic Inn $$$

(📞401-466-5883; www.atlanticinn.com; High
St, Old Harbor; d $175-300; 🕐late Apr-Oct) This
gracefully appointed Victorian house overlooks
the town center from its perch on a grassy
hilltop. The views over ocean and town are
beautiful, the wide porch features Adirondack
chairs, and a well-stocked bar serves cocktails
to accompany the sunset.

Westerly ❻

✕ Shelter Harbor Inn   Historic Inn $$

(📞401-322-8883; www.shelterharborinn.com; 10
Wagner Rd; mains $14-26; 🅿) Work up an appetite
with a stroll along the inn's private beach, then
order homey fare such as chicken pie or finnan
haddie (smoked haddock). Traditional Rhode
Island johnnycakes are always on the menu, too.

🛏 Langworthy Farm   B&B $$

(📞401-322-7791; www.langworthyfarm.com;
308 Shore Rd; r $130-185; 🅿) Sitting at the head
of the beach road to Misquamicut, handsome
Langworthy Farm offers comfortable rooms,
ocean views and wine tasting in the winery. A
full country breakfast is included.

Woodstock Take to the roads in fall, when leaves are ablaze in reds and yellows

Quiet Corner

9

Connecticut's Quiet Corner is known locally as 'the last green valley' between Boston and Washington. With its stone walls and red barns, it offers some of the loveliest rural scenery in New England.

TRIP HIGHLIGHTS

72 miles

Woodstock
Enjoy 4000 blooms at Roseland Cottage

FINISH 7
6

53 miles

Pomfret
Brunch at 'The Bean' and enjoy the local scene

START
Coventry

Brooklyn

Willimantic

2

Lisbon

13 miles

Lebanon
Walk the green where Rochambeau's revolutionary troops camped

3

Norwich
Admire plaster casts of the Parthenon marbles and more

25 miles

---

3 DAYS
72 MILES / 116KM

GREAT FOR...

BEST TIME TO GO
June to October for historic home openings.

ESSENTIAL PHOTO
Trumbull's house on Lebanon's village green.

BEST FOR FOODIES
Dinner and wine tasting at Sharpe Hill vineyard.

Quiet Corner

The Quiet Corner has the distinction of nurturing state hero Nathan Hale, the patriot-spy from Coventry whose only regret was that he had 'but one life to lose for his country,' and state heroine, abolitionist and Canterbury school teacher Prudence Crandall. Take this trip for a glimpse of New England long ago, when Washington plotted revolution on Lebanon's Green, and where local farms still welcome visitors with small-town friendliness.

① Coventry

Begin at the beginning at the **Nathan Hale Homestead** (www.ctlandmarks.org; 2299 South St; adult/under 6yr $7/free; ⊙11am-4pm Wed & Fri-Sun mid-May–Oct) on the edge of the **Nathan Hale State Forest** (www.stateparks.com). Nathan, whose five brothers also served in the Revolutionary War, was already in the Continental army when his father built this rather fine red clapboard farmhouse in 1776. Inside, period

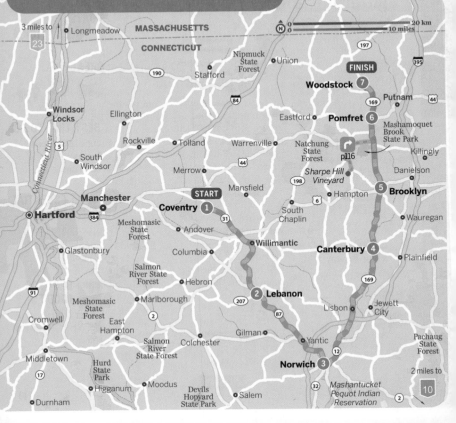

furnishings re-create the domestic life of the early colony, along with a display of memorabilia of the schoolteacher turned patriot who was eventually pegged as a spy by the British and hanged at the age of 21. There are also tours of the heirloom gardens, guided walks around the 450-acre estate, Colonial cooking demonstrations and fall lantern tours.

 p117

The Drive » Sweep round Lake Wangumbaug, past the Nathan Hale Cemetery and onto CT 31, which soon merges with CT 32 southwards. Loop through industrial Willimantic, once home to the American Thread Company and known as 'Thread City,' and stop for barbecued ribs if you're hungry (p117).

LINK YOUR TRIP

10 Connecticut Wine Trail

Meander south down CT 2 to the Jonathan Edwards Winery in North Stonington and join the Connecticut Wine Trail (p124).

23 Connecticut River Byway

From hills and meadows to the banks of the Connecticut River, pick up the Byway at Springfield (p252) and travel north along its course.

Cross the bridge, adorned with its giant bullfrogs, and pick up CT 289 south to Lebanon.

- - - - - - - - - - - -

TRIP HIGHLIGHT

② Lebanon

The best way to get acquainted with Lebanon's mile-long historic **Green** is to take a stroll around it on the walking path. On the eastern side, the butter-yellow **Jonathan Trumbull Jr House** (780 Trumbull Hwy; admission free; ◷noon-4pm Sat & Sun mid-May–mid-Oct) was home to Washington's military secretary, who hosted the great general in front of its eight fireplaces in March 1781. On the southwestern side of the Green you'll find **Jonathan Trumbull House** (169 West Town St; admission free; ◷1-6pm Fri, 11-5pm Sat & Sun mid-May–mid-Oct), the home of Trumbull's father, governor of Connecticut and the only Colonial governor to defy the Crown and support the War of Independence.

Next door, the strange little Palladian clapboard is actually the **Wadsworth Stable**, where Washington's horse overnighted. A little beyond that is the two-room **Revolutionary War Office** (149 West Town St), where Washington met with Trumbull and the Comte de Rochambeau to coordinate military strategy.

The Drive » Pick up CT 87 and head south along its leafy route, straight into Norwich. It's a short 11-mile drive.

- - - - - - - - - - - -

TRIP HIGHLIGHT

③ Norwich

Money from the Quiet Corner's mills flowed into Norwich, accounting for the handsome Victorian houses set around the **Norwichtown Green**, the gorgeous Second Empire **City Hall** and the unique Romanesque Revival **Slater Memorial Museum** (www.norwichfreeacademy. com; adult/under 12yr $3/free; ◷9am-4pm Tue-Fri, 1-4pm Sat & Sun), designed by Stephen Earle in 1886.

The museum was commissioned by William Slater, an educated and well-travelled man who aspired to make the great art of the Classical and Renaissance periods accessible to Norwich's citizens. With this in mind, he commissioned the 227 plaster casts that fill the museum's Beaux Arts interior on his grand tour in 1894–95. Ranging from the Parthenon Marbles to Michelangelo's *Pieta,* the casts were created via a now-illegal process from molds of the original. Visit the exhibit of Slater's grand tour before heading into the museum, which still forms part of the Norwich Free Academy.

 p117

The Drive » From the Norwichtown Green, head down Washington St and Broadway, past grand Victorian mansions and the architecturally noteworthy City Hall, before picking up N Main St and heading out of town in a northwesterly direction to pick up the National Scenic Byway CT 169. Once en route, the scenery quickly becomes picturesque following low stone walls into deeply rural Canterbury.

- - - - - - - - - - -

④ Canterbury

Tiny Canterbury was at the forefront of the abolitionist cause some 30 years before the Civil War, thanks to Baptist schoolmistress Prudence Crandall. The **Prudence Crandall House Museum** (www.cultureandtourism.org; 1 South Canterbury Rd; adult/child $3/2; 10am-4pm Wed-Sun May-Nov) was the site of the academy, which Crandall opened in 1831.

When Crandall later accepted Sarah Harris, the daughter of a free African American farmer, among her students in the fall of 1832, many prominent townspeople withdrew their daughters from the school in protest. Rather than give in, Crandall changed her admissions policy and offered schooling to the free African American community. By April 1833, some 20 girls from Boston, Providence, New York and Philadelphia had enrolled. This caused an angry backlash; the

MIRA/ALAMY ©

school was vandalized, its well poisoned and, in July, Prudence was arrested. When the case against her was finally dismissed on September 9, 1834, the school was set on fire and Prudence reluctantly closed its doors.

The Drive » Leaving Canterbury's clapboard homesteads behind you, continue north on CT 169

to Brooklyn. To your right, sweeping views across paddocks and the distant valley open up and the country road is lined with farmyards and historic Dutch barns.

- - - - - - - - - - -

⑤ Brooklyn

By the time you hit Brooklyn, you're in the heart of the Quiet Corner, where admiring the scenery and stopping in

Woodstock Roseland Cottage-Bowen House

at local farms and ice-cream stalls is the main activity.

First stop is the **Creamery Brook Bison Farm** (☎860-779-0837; www.creamerybrookbison.net; 19 Purvis Rd; wagon tours adult/child $8.50/7; ⏰10am-2pm Sat or by appointment; 🚻), where you can take the equivalent of a Quiet Corner safari among the bison herd before

stocking up at the farm shop. Then move on to **Meadow Stone Farm Shoppe** (☎860-792-1651; www.meadowstonefarm.com; 199 Hartford Rd; ⏰by appointment; 🚻), where everything, from the goat's milk and cheeses to the specialty skin care products, is produced on the farm or with produce from the farm. If you want to see the soaps and

cheeses being made, call ahead to find out about production times.

🍴 p117

The Drive » On your way out of Brooklyn, you'll pass the access road to the Golden Lamb Buttery (see p117) on your left. Continue along CT 169, beneath the leafy canopy that creates the impression of driving through a verdant green tunnel. You'll pass fruit orchards on your right, which

DETOUR: SHARPE HILL VINEYARD

Start: ⑥ Pomfret

In nearby **Abington**, up a winding country road buried deep in the forest, you'll find the Quiet Corner's most scenic vineyard, **Sharpe Hill** (☎860-974-3549; sharpehill.com; 649 108 Wade Rd; tastings $12, mains $26-35; ⊙11am-5pm Fri-Sun). It's also arguably Connecticut's finest vineyard, with over 250 medals for its signature Chardonnay Ballet of Angels and its St Croix Cabernet Franc. To appreciate the beautiful setting, consider spending the day here, walking up through the vineyard for spectacular views, tasting wine on the patio and then sitting down to a gourmet farm-to-table lunch or dinner in the gracious Fireside Tavern.

belong to Lapsley Orchard farm, where you can PYO in season.

TRIP HIGHLIGHT

⑥ Pomfret

With its expansive Colonial homes and hearty restaurants, Pomfret is considered the heart of the Quiet Corner, and is where many visitors choose to base themselves. Farming lives on in the vineyards, nurseries and orchards that surround it, while legends live on in **Mashamoquet Brook State Park** (www.ct.gov; 147 Wolf Den Dr, Pomfret Center). Here, local hero Israel Putnam, who led the troops at Bunker Hill in

Boston, is said to have crawled into the den of a she-wolf that was ravaging local sheep, and shot it.

To follow in his footsteps, take the trail past the campground to Wolf Den. You can then continue on a 5-mile loop through thick woodland. Take a swimming costume along if you fancy bathing in the shallow pond.

✕ ⊨ p117

The Drive » The final stretch of CT 169 from Pomfret to Woodstock continues past farmland and the Roseland Lake, up through the modern buildings and grassy playing fields of South Woodstock, before arriving in Woodstock proper.

TRIP HIGHLIGHT

⑦ Woodstock

The **Roseland Cottage-Bowen House** (www.historicnewengland.org; 556 Rte 169; adult/student $8/4; ⊙11am-5pm Wed-Sun Jun-Oct) is proof that wealthy Americans had fancy summer homes even in the mid-1800s. Beautifully preserved, this lovely Gothic Revival house sports pointed arches, crockets and stained-glass windows.

The garden is also a historic treasure, laid out according to the 1850 plan with some 4000 blooms bordered by formal boxwood parterres. Other follies include an aviary, a summerhouse, an icehouse and a vintage bowling alley.

After a stroll around the garden, head down to **Woodstock Orchards** (www.woodstockorchardsllc.com; 494 Rte 169; ⊙9am-5pm; ⊞) for a glass of fresh cider and to stock up on apples and berries before heading home. You'll also find them at the enormous **Woodstock Fair** (www.woodstockfair.com; 281 Rte 169; adult/child $12/free; ⊙9am-10pm Fri-Sun, to 8pm Mon Labor Day weekend; P ⊞).

✕ ⊨ p117

Eating & Sleeping

Coventry ①

🛏 Daniel Rust House B&B $$
(☎860-742-0032; www.thedanielrusthouse.com; 2011 Main St; d $120-185; P) Serving travelers since 1800, the four period rooms brim with history. The finest is the Anna White room with its antique canopy bed, although the Mary Rose has a secret closet that was used to hide slaves traveling to freedom on the Underground Railroad.

Willimantic

✗ Yellow Rose BBQ Barbecue $
(81 Main St; sandwiches $4.49; ⏰11am-12:30am) There's no electric smoker here, just a trailer, a wood-fired charcoal grill and a man with an axe. The baby-back ribs and brisket melt in your hands and there's Hosmer Mountain Soda to accompany them. Prices are by the half-pound ($5.49 to $6.99).

Norwich ③

🛏 Spa at Norwich Inn Historic Inn $$$
(☎860-425-3500; www.thespaatnorwichinn.com; 607 West Thames St; d $200-250, ste $295-325; P🛜♨) Set in 42 acres of woodland near the Public Golf Course, Norwich's elegant Georgian spa offers 36 treatment rooms, indoor and outdoor pools, tennis and golf. Be sure to book a room in the main house overlooking the flowering gardens.

Brooklyn ⑤

✗ Golden Lamb Buttery Modern American $$$
(☎860-774-4423; www.thegoldenlamb.com; 499 Wolf Den Rd; lunch mains $10-15, dinner $75; ⏰lunch Tue-Sat, dinner Fri & Sat) Dinner here isn't just a meal – it's an experience. Guests mingle over drinks, head off for a hayride and then settle into an award-winning prix-fixe meal.

Pomfret ⑥

✗ Vanilla Bean Cafe Modern American $$
(www.thevanillabeancafe.com; cnr Rtes 44, 169 & 97; mains $6.50-16; ⏰7am-3pm Mon-Tue, to 8pm Wed-Sun; 🖴) Families, cyclists and Sunday drivers regularly make the pilgrimage to 'The Bean' for creative casual dining, live music and artful surroundings.

✗ We-Li-Kit Farm Ice Cream $
(www.welikit.com; 728 Hampton Rd; scoops from $3.50; ⏰11am-8pm Mon-Thu, to 9pm Fri & Sat; 🖴) Sit at trestle tables and slurp sundaes and homemade ice cream with holidaymakers and locals. The 'Road Kill' cup is particularly delicious: vanilla topped with walnuts, white chocolate chips and cherry swirls.

🛏 Chickadee Cottage B&B $$
(☎806-963-0587; 70 Averill Rd; cottages $175-210; P🛜) The spacious Carriage House here has its own deck, kitchenette and separate entrance, while the Lower Nest sleeps four. It also sits on the edge of the 500-acre Audubon preserve and neighbors the Air Line State Park scenic hiking and biking path.

Woodstock ⑦

✗ Mrs Bridge's Pantry Tearoom $
(www.mrsbridgespantry.com; 292 Rte 169, South Woodstock; meals $3-8.25; ⏰10am-6pm Wed-Mon; 🖴) Sit down to English tea with crumpets, scones and clotted cream in this quaint wooden teashop. Tea comes served in china cups and there's a light menu of British classics such as beans on toast and ploughman's lunch.

🛏 Taylor's Corner B&B $$
(☎888-974-0490; www.taylorsbb.com; 880 Rte 171; r $115-170, ste $100-145; P❄🛜) Taylor's Corner has just three antique-filled rooms overlooking lovely perennial-planted gardens. Features include real wood-burning fireplaces, wide-plank floorboards and curious beehive ovens.

Connecticut *Top-notch wines and pretty vistas make for a heady mix*

Connecticut Wine Trail

10

Connecticut has established itself as a serious wine-growing region. Combine this vineyard tour of some of the best producers with gourmet dining in Greenwich and New Haven's stellar galleries.

40 miles

Shelton
Experience 150 years of agriculture at the Jones farm

47 miles

New Haven
Tour the Gothic campus of previous presidents

North Stonington
FINISH
● Westerly
6

● Guilford

3 **4**

2

Greenwich
START

New Canaan
Admire an iconic modern house set amid the forest

15 miles

Stonington
Go antiquing among 18th-century sea captains' homes

103 miles

5 DAYS
132 MILES / 212KM

GREAT FOR...

BEST TIME TO GO
August to October for the grape harvest.

ESSENTIAL PHOTO

Philip Johnson's glass cube amid the trees.

BEST FOR OUTDOORS

Picnicking at the Jonathan Edwards Winery.

119

GÜNTER GRÄFENHAIN/HUBER/4CORNERS ©

10 Connecticut Wine Trail

Starting on Connecticut's moneyed Gold Coast, this tour wends its way between vineyards to encompass the compact downtown of Greenwich, with its high-end shops and notable museums; Philip Johnson's radical mid-century modern Glass House in New Canaan; and New Haven's neo-Gothic turrets. At its northern reaches Stonington's 19th-century sea captains' homes cluster amid maritime vineyards, which produce some of the state's finest drops.

1 Greenwich

In the early days, Greenwich was home to farmers and fishermen who shipped oysters and potatoes to nearby New York. But with the advent of passenger trains and the first cashed-up commuters, the town became a haven for Manhattanites in search of country exclusivity. Along **Greenwich Avenue**, high-end boutiques and gourmet restaurants line the route where the town's trolley once traveled.

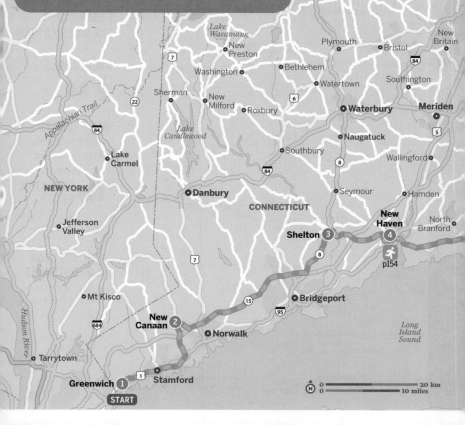

One of Greenwich's wealthiest 19th-century inhabitants was Robert Moffat Bruce, a textile tycoon who lived in what is now the **Bruce Museum** (www.brucemuseum.org; 1 Museum Dr; adult/student $7/6; ☺10am-5pm Tue-Sat, 1-5pm Sun). Now a variety of galleries house a natural science collection and a permanent display of Impressionist works by the Cos Cob art colony, as well as hosting more than a dozen art exhibits a year.

✕ p125

The Drive » Head northeast along I-95, paralleling US 1, the old Boston–New York post road, until you come to the steel-and-glass towers of metropolitan Stamford. Then take exit 9 onto CT 106 and head inland through the suburbs to New Canaan.

TRIP HIGHLIGHT

② New Canaan

The only Gold Coast town without a shoreline, New Canaan

LINK YOUR TRIP

1 Coastal New England

From Stonington, continue north along I-95 across the Jamestown Bridge to Newport for more salty coastal scenery.

9 Quiet Corner

Continue north along scenic CT 169 to Canterbury for a laid-back tour of the Quiet Corner.

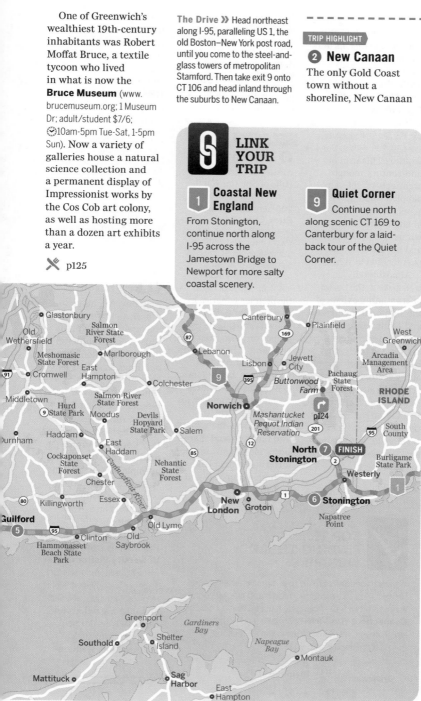

is characterized by large clapboard houses, grand Georgian mansions and, unusually, one of the most famous modern houses in the world: the 1949 **Philip Johnson Glass House** (☎866-811-4111; philipjohnsonglasshouse.org; 199 Elm St; house/site tour $30/$45; ⏰Wed-Mon May-Nov). This icon of mid-century modern architecture, set in a dappled wood on 47 acres, was the home of late Pritzker Prize winner Philip Johnson, and his art collector partner, David Whitney.

Almost totally transparent, the house offers stunning views of the autumnal countryside and Johnson's intriguing collection of contemporary art. Guided tours must be reserved; visitors assemble at the visitors centre across the street from the New Canaan train station. In addition to the house, the tour includes a look at Da Monsta, the concrete-and-Styrofoam gatehouse to the property.

✗ p125

The Drive ≫ Leave bucolic New Canaan via CT 123 S and after 2 miles merge with the CT 15. Head north toward New Haven, skirting the suburbs of Norwalk, Westport and Trumbull, then take exit 8 onto CT 8 toward Waterbury. After 6 miles you'll arrive in Shelton.

- - - - - - - - - - - -

TRIP HIGHLIGHT

❸ Shelton

Nestled in the White Hills of Shelton you'll find the 150-year-old, 400-acre **Jones Family Farm** (☎203-929-8425; www.jonesfamilyfarms.com; 606 Walnut Tree Hill Rd; ⏰10am-5.30pm Mon-Sat, 11am-5.30pm Sun mid-Dec–mid-Nov, noon-5pm Mon-Fri mid-Nov–mid-Dec), home of one of the premier wineries in the state. Jones Winery is known for using its own grapes or those from local vineyards. The vineyard's founder and resident winemaker, Jamie Jones, is now the sixth generational family member to operate the farm.

Aside from the winery and tasting room there's berry picking in summer, a Heritage Farm Hike in June, pumpkins and hayrides in fall and,

of course, Christmas trees in November and December. You can also sign up for cooking classes and wine-education suppers at the Harvest Kitchen studio. Check the website for details.

The Drive ≫ Rejoin CT 8 and cross the Housatonic River before taking exit 15 onto CT 34. After less than a mile, take the ramp onto CT 15 N, which weaves through New Haven's exclusive golf greens for 4 miles. Then take exit 59 onto CT 69 S, which takes you right into the center of New Haven.

- - - - - - - - - - - -

TRIP HIGHLIGHT

❹ New Haven

New Haven is home to America's third oldest university, Yale, and its leafy green is bordered by graceful Colonial buildings, statehouses and churches. The 1816 **Trinity Church** resembles England's Gothic York Minster, while the Georgian-style, 1812 **Center Church on the Green** is a fine example of New England Palladian. But nowhere is the city's history more palpable than at **Yale University**.

Pick up a free map of the campus from **Yale University Visitor Center** (www.yale.edu/visitor; cnr Elm & Temple Sts; ⏰9am-4:30pm Mon-Fri, 11am-4pm Sat & Sun) and take a stroll around the stately buildings, where alumni such as Presidents William

TOP TIP:
FINDING THOSE WINERIES

It's worth bearing in mind that most wineries are tucked away down country roads, and finding your way can often be a challenge. A useful resource is the **Connecticut Wine Trail** (www.ctwine.com) brochure, which covers all the wineries in the state along with detailed driving directions.

North Stonington Jonathan Edwards Winery

H Taft, George HW Bush and Bill Clinton once studied.

In more recent years, New Haven has also built a reputation for itself as an arts mecca. Take a tour of the art galleries with our walking tour on p154.

✖ ⊫ p125

The Drive ›› The 14-mile drive east from New Haven to Guilford is easy but uneventful. The highlight is crossing the New Haven harbor bridge before rejoining I-95 through the conurbations of East Haven and Branford before reaching Guilford.

- - - - - - - - - - - -

⑤ Guilford

In the historic seaside town of Guilford, **Bishop's Orchards Winery** (☎203-453-2338; www.bishopsorchards.com; 1355 Boston Post Rd; ⊘10am-7pm Mon-Sat, 11am-6pm Sun; 🖪) has been serving shoreline communities with fresh produce since 1871. Much more than just a winery, Bishop's is also a pick-your-own farm, where berries, peaches, pears, apples and pumpkins can be picked from June through October. The rich variety of produce means the Bishop's

market (open year-round) is one of the best in the area. If you have kids, they'll get a kick out of the llamas, alpacas and grazing goats.

The coastline around Guilford is wonderful, but much of it is built up. However, the nearby **Hammonasset Beach State Park** (www.ct.gov/dep/hammonasset; exit 62 off I-95) provides a 1100-acre oasis, with a 2-mile pine-backed beach, boardwalk trails and excellent facilities for camping, picnicking and swimming.

✖ p125

123

↱ DETOUR: BUTTONWOOD FARM

Start: **7** North Stonington

Beginning as early as mid-July, an astonishing number of interactive corn mazes begin cropping up on farms throughout New England. Travel north up CT 201 and you can get lost in the themed maze at **Buttonwood Farm** (www.buttonwoodfarmicecream. com; 471 Shetucket Turnpike, Griswold; ⊘noon-9pm Mar-Oct; 🚻), pick pumpkins from their patches, take hayrides and finish up with some of the farm's delicious homemade ice cream. In October, the maze is also open for nighttime adventures – if you dare!

The Drive ≫ Leave I-95 and pick up the old post road, US 1. This takes you through genteel Madison to the marshy doorstep of Hammonasset Beach State Park. Stop for a stroll or a picnic, then continue on US 1 for another 6 miles before rejoining I-95 for the remaining 28 miles to Stonington.

TRIP HIGHLIGHT

6 Stonington

Stonington is one of the most appealing towns on the Connecticut coast. Compactly laid out on a peninsula, the town offers complete streetscapes of 18th- and 19th-century houses, many of which were once sea captains' homes.

The main thoroughfare, **Water Street**, features shops selling antiques and Quimper porcelain, colorfully painted dinnerware handmade in France since the 17th-century. At the southern end is the 'point,' with a park, a lighthouse and a tiny beach.

Situated on Stonington's south-facing slopes, **Stonington Vineyards** (☎860-535-1222; 523 Taugwonk Rd; tasting/tour $12/free; ⊘noon-4pm Mon-Fri, 11am-5pm Sat & Sun Jan-May, 11am-5pm daily May-Nov) produces some of the state's finest table wines, thanks to its glacial soils and maritime climate not unlike that of Bordeaux in France. As a result, you can expect creamy Chardonnays and award-winning Cabernet Franc.

✕ 🛏 p125

The Drive ≫ Exit Stonington on US 1, which takes you through some very pretty rural countryside lightly dotted with handsome country homes. At Westerly, turn northward on US 2 for a further 5 miles, before turning right on Main St and heading into North Stonington.

- - - - - - - - - - - - - -

7 North Stonington

Heading northward away from the coast, you arrive at one of the most picturesque and scenically situated vineyards on the tour, the **Jonathan Edwards Winery** (☎860-535-0202; www.jedwardswinery.com; 74 Chester Maine Rd; ⊘11am-5pm daily May-Dec, Wed-Sun Jan-Apr) in North Stonington. Housed in a lovingly renovated dairy barn on a hilltop overlooking the Atlantic, it is the perfect spot for a late-afternoon BYO picnic and wine tasting.

In winter, oenophiles warm themselves around the stone fireplace in the wood-paneled tasting room, while the knowledgeable and enthusiastic staff talk through a variety of wines, both from the Connecticut coast and the Edwards vineyards in Napa, CA.

Eating & Sleeping

Greenwich ❶

✖ Meli-Melo　　　　　　Creperie $

(362 Greenwich Ave; crepes $3-15; ☺lunch & dinner) Meaning hodgepodge in French, Meli-Melo serves salads, soups and sandwiches, but its specialty is undoubtedly the buckwheat crepes. Try the exotic smoked salmon, chive sauce, lemon and daikon.

✖ Restaurant Jean-Louis　　French $$$

(☏203-622-8450; www.restaurantjeanlouis. com; 61 Lewis St; mains $38, prix-fixe lunch $29; ☺lunch & dinner Mon-Fri, dinner Sat) Few Connecticut towns are as associated with fine dining as Greenwich. Head to Jean-Louis for award-winning *'nouvelle classique'* cuisine, which includes pan-seared ostrich with polenta and cognac.

New Canaan ❷

✖ Sole　　　　　　　　Italian $$

(☏203-972-8887; 105 Elm St; mains $14-24; ☺lunch & dinner Mon-Sat, dinner Sun) Sit at the marble-topped bar with a glass of Pinot Grigio and watch the chef prepare wood-fired pizzas and northern Italian dishes such as Tuscan bread salad or handmade potato gnocchi with sausage, mushrooms and basil.

New Haven ❹

✖ Union League Cafe　　French $$$

(☏203-562-4299; www.unionleaguecafe.com; 1032 Chapel St; mains $17-34, prix fixe before 6pm $35; ☺lunch & dinner Mon-Fri, dinner Sat) Situated in the vintage Sherman Building, the Union League Cafe is a serious French restaurant serving classics such as organic veal cheeks with sautéed wild mushrooms, paired with a serious Burgundy from the extensive wine list.

✖ ZINC　　　　　Modern American $$

(☏203-624-0507; zincfood.com; 964 Chapel St; mains $7-15; ☺dinner Mon & Sat, lunch & dinner Tue-Fri) Organic ingredients provide the basis for inventive Asian and Southwestern dishes. For the most rewarding experience, sample small plates including duck nachos, spicy shrimp paella or the eggplant and pepper wrap.

🛏 Study at Yale Hotel　　　　Boutique Hotel $$

(☏203-503-3900; www.studyhotels.com; 1157 Chapel St; r $189-359; P🅿🛜) This boutique hotel evokes a mid-century modern sense of sophistication ('Mad Men' chic) without being overtly pretentious, while rooms enjoy contemporary touches such as iPod docking stations and cardio machines with built-in TVs.

Guilford ❺

✖ Place　　　　　　　Seafood $

(www.theplaceguilford.com; 901 Boston Post Rd/US 1; mains $5-12; ☺5-9pm Mon-Fri, 1-10pm Sat & Sun Apr-Oct) Drive in, snag a tree stump for a stool, crack open the cold beer or wine you've brought with you and order up a feast of littleneck clams, lobsters and charred corn on the cob from the open-air fire pit.

Stonington ❻

✖ Noah's Cafe　　　　American $$

(☏860-535-3925; www.noahsfinefood.com; 115 Water St; meals $14-24; ☺Tue-Sun) A popular place with two small rooms with original stamped-tin ceilings. It's famous for its seafood (especially chowder and scallops) and pastries like the apple spice and sour cream coffee cake.

🛏 Orchard Street Inn　　　B&B $$

(☏860-535-2681; www.orchardstreetinn. com; 41 Orchard St; d $175-235; P🅿🛜) This atmospheric five-room inn enjoys glimpses of Long Island Sound from the bedroom windows. Rooms are furnished in comfortable period style, and you have free use of bicycles to get around town.

East Haddam Gillette Castle boasts spectacular views of the Connecticut River

Lower River Valley

11

The Connecticut River surfaces in a spring-fed pond near the Canadian border and cuts a 410-mile trail southeast. Tour the valley for a glimpse of the state's first settlers and holidaying industrialists.

TRIP HIGHLIGHTS

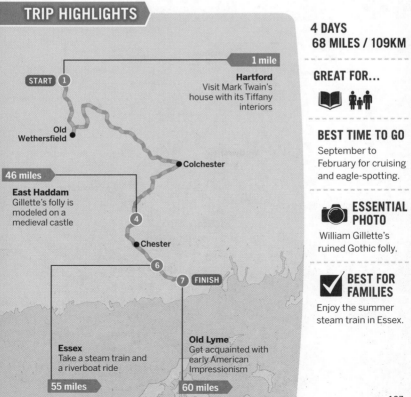

START ① **1 mile**

Hartford
Visit Mark Twain's house with its Tiffany interiors

Old Wethersfield

Colchester

46 miles

East Haddam
Gillette's folly is modeled on a medieval castle

④

Chester

⑥

⑦ **FINISH**

Essex
Take a steam train and a riverboat ride

55 miles

Old Lyme
Get acquainted with early American Impressionism

60 miles

4 DAYS
68 MILES / 109KM

GREAT FOR...

BEST TIME TO GO
September to February for cruising and eagle-spotting.

ESSENTIAL PHOTO
William Gillette's ruined Gothic folly.

BEST FOR FAMILIES
Enjoy the summer steam train in Essex.

127

11 Lower River Valley

Once the engine of 19th-century commerce, the Connecticut River – New England's longest waterway – now enchants visitors with its historic towns, artist colonies, nature conservancies and gracious country inns. River cruises and steam train rides allow for authentic glimpses into provincial Connecticut life. Even Hartford, the state capital, is rediscovering the river these days with new parks and walkways landscaped along its banks.

TRIP HIGHLIGHT

❶ Hartford

Despite the exodus of the insurance companies that earned Hartford its reputation as the 'filing cabinet of America,' those passing through will be surprised at how much the city has to offer. The standout **Wadsworth Atheneum** (www.wadsworthatheneum. org; 600 Main St; adult/child $10/5; ⏰11am-5pm Wed-Fri, 10am-5pm Sat & Sun) houses 40,000 pieces of art in a castle-like Gothic

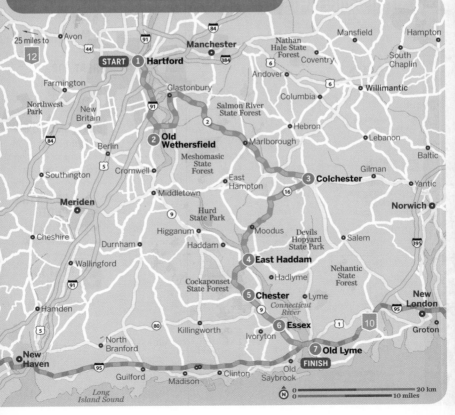

Revival building. These include some by Hartford native Frederic Church, alongside 19th-century Impressionist works and a small but outstanding collection of surrealist art.

Other notable sites include **Mark Twain House** (www.marktwainhouse.org; 351 Farmington Ave; adult/6-16yr $15/9; ☺9:30am-5:30pm Mon-Sat, noon-5:30pm Sun), where novelist Samuel Langhorne Clemens (1835–1910) spent 17 years of his life writing the *Adventures of Tom Sawyer* and *Huckleberry Finn*. Architect Edward Tuckerman Potter embellished the house with turrets and gables, and some of the interiors were styled by Louis Comfort Tiffany. Next door to the Twain house is **Harriet Beecher Stowe House** (www.

LINK YOUR TRIP

10 Connecticut Wine Trail

Travel west to Guilford (p123) along I-95 for a taste of Connecticut's Cabernet Sauvignon and New Haven culture.

12 Litchfield Hills Loop

Head into the hills on US 44 for bucolic rural views, market towns and gourmet eats (p135).

LOCAL KNOWLEDGE: RICK'S SUGAR SHACK

Follow the hand-painted sign deep into the maple forest surrounding East Hampton to arrive at **Rick's Sugar Shack** (☎860-267-7117; www.rickssugarshack.com; 69 Collie Brook Rd, East Hampton; ☺10am-3pm Sat & Sun). Here you'll find Rick standing over his stove, boiling down the next batches of maple syrup or making his locally renowned maple sweets. Between July and October you will also find him at the East Hampton Farmers Market on Saturday and at Christmas he holds a special mapling shindig.

harrietbeecherstowe.org; 73 Forest St; adult/5-16yr $9/6; ☺9:30am-4:30pm Wed-Sat, noon-4:30pm Sun). Built in 1871, the house reflects Stowe's ideas about decorating and domestic efficiency, which she expressed in her bestseller *American Woman's Home*. Stowe is most famous for her antislavery book, *Uncle Tom's Cabin*.

✗ p133

The Drive 》 Exit Hartford along Capitol Ave and Hudson, and merge onto the Colin Whitehead Hwy. Join I-91 S for a short 3.5-mile drive through Hartford's suburbs before taking exit 26 for Old Wethersfield.

- - - - - - - - - - - - - -

2 Old Wethersfield

A quick jaunt down I-91 will bring you to the historic district of Old Wethersfield. Despite sitting in the larger Hartford suburbs, Old Wethersfield is a living monument to the past, perfectly preserved for over 375 years. Wander around and you'll find hundreds of historic homes, as well as a number of interesting museums. The best way to get your bearings, however, is to start at the **Wethersfield Museum** (www.wethhist.org; 200 Main St; adult/child $3/free; ☺10am-4pm Mon-Sat, 1-4pm Sun).

The Drive 》 Accommodation in Hartford and Old Wethersfield tends to be underwhelming, expensive and business oriented. It's far better to push on across the river, via CT 3 N. The pretty, historic town of Glastonbury has some great B&B options (p133). From there, continue along CT 2 toward Colchester.

- - - - - - - - - - - - - -

TRIP HIGHLIGHT

3 Colchester

Rural Colchester, with its grazing fields and serried ranks of vines, is a certified Community Wildlife Habitat and listed on the National Register of Historic

J SCHULTES/DREAMSTIME.COM ©

Places. However, the real reason to come to Colchester is so you can visit **Cato Corner Farm** (catocornerfarm.com; 178 Cato Corner Rd; ⊙11am-4pm Sat & Sun), where mother-and-son cheese makers Elizabeth and Mark craft dozens of aged farmhouse cheeses with raw milk from their herd of Jersey cows. Many of the cheeses, such as the Dairyere (a firm washed-rind cheese), are prizewinners.

Near the cheese shop is the notable **Priam Vineyards** (priamvineyards. com; 11 Shailor Hill Rd; ⊙11am-5pm Fri-Sun mid-Mar–Dec), a

24-acre, solar-powered, sustainable vineyard growing French and American varieties such as Cabernet Sauvignon, Riesling, Merlot, Cayuga and St Croix. In summer, visitors can take self-guided tours of the vineyards, picnic amid the vines and even enjoy live music concerts.

The Drive » Leaving the interstate, turn southwest along Middletown Rd (CT 16) through farmland and alongside Babcock Pond until you reach CT 149, where you turn left and head directly south back toward the river. This part of the drive passes pleasantly through rural communities and historic towns along tree-lined roads.

TRIP HIGHLIGHT

4 East Haddam

Looming on one of the Seven Sisters hills just above East Haddam is **Gillette Castle** (www. ct.gov/dep/gillettecastle; 67 River Rd; adult/6-12yr $10/4; ⊙10am-4:30pm), a turreted mansion made of fieldstone. Built in 1919 by eccentric actor William Gillette, who made his fortune in the role of Sherlock Holmes, the folly is modeled on the medieval castles of Germany's Rhineland and the views from its terraces are spectacular.

Hartford Mark Twain House

The surrounding 125 acres are a designated state park and open year-round but the interior is only open for tours from late May through mid-October.

With residents such as Gillette and banker William Goodspeed, East Haddam became a regular stopover on the summer circuit for New Yorkers, who traveled up on Goodspeed's steamship. To entertain them, he built the **Goodspeed Opera House** (☎860-873-8668; www.goodspeed. org; 6 Main St; tickets $45-70; ☺performances Wed-Sun Apr-Dec) in 1876. It's now dedicated to preserving and developing American musicals, and you can still enjoy your intermission drinks on the balcony overhanging the river.

The Drive » From East Haddam, cross the Connecticut River via the steel swing bridge and meander southeast through rural countryside for about 5 miles before merging with I-9 S toward Old Saybrook. After 1.5 miles, take exit 6 for Chester.

- - - - - - - - - - - -

TRIP HIGHLIGHT

⑤ Chester

Cupped in the valley of Pattaconk Brook, Chester is one of the most charming river towns along the Connecticut. Its quaint Main St is lined with good restaurants and thriving galleries and workshops, and most visitors come to simply browse the antique shops and indulge in some fine dining.

The **Connecticut River Artisans** (www. ctriverartisans.com; 5 W Main St; ☺noon-6pm) co-operative offers one-of-a-kind craft pieces including jewelry, pottery, folk art as well as clothing. Otherwise, drop in to have a coffee at local provender **Simon's**

TOP TIP:
CHESTER–HADLYME
FERRY

In summer you can cross the Connecticut River on the **Chester–Hadlyme Ferry** (car/walk-on $3/1; ⏰7am-6:45pm Mon-Fri, 10:30am-5pm Sat & Sun Apr-Nov). The five-minute river crossing on the *Selden III* is the second oldest ferry service in America, beginning in 1769. The ferry ride affords great views of Gillette Castle and is a fun way to link up with the Essex Steam Train, which runs between Chester and Essex.

Marketplace (www.simonsmarketplacechester.com; 17 Main St; ⏰lunch) and pick up some tasty deli treats.

🍴 p133

The Drive » Rejoin I-9 for the short 6-mile hop to Essex.

TRIP HIGHLIGHT

6 Essex

Handsome, tree-lined Essex, established in 1635, features well-preserved Federal-period homes, legacies of rum and tobacco fortunes made in the 19th century. Today the town prides itself on the oldest-known continuously operating waterfront in the country. That, and the **Connecticut River Museum** (www.ctrivermuseum.org; adult/6-12yr $8/5; ⏰10am-5pm Tue-Sun late May-early Sep), next to the Steamboat Dock, where exhibits recount the area's history, including a replica of the world's first submarine, the American Turtle,

built by Yale student David Bushnell in 1776.

The best way to experience the river is to take the **Essex Steam Train & Riverboat Ride** (www.essexsteamtrain.com; 1 Railroad Ave; train only adult/child $17/9, train & riverboat $26/17; ⏰3 times daily May-Oct), which transports you to Deep River on a steam train and then runs you up to the Goodspeed Opera House at East Haddam in a riverboat. The train trip takes about an hour; with the riverboat ride, the excursion takes 2½ hours. In February look out for eagle-watching cruises, as bald eagles migrate to winter in the river valley.

🛏 p133

The Drive » For the final leg of the trip, rejoin I-9 for an uneventful drive south. Just the other side of the highway, Ivoryton offers some good accommodation options (p133). Leave I-9 at exit 70 onto CT 156 E, which will loop round onto Shore Rd. Then follow the signs into Old Lyme.

TRIP HIGHLIGHT

7 Old Lyme

Since the early 20th century, Old Lyme has been the center of the Lyme Art Colony, which embraced and cultivated the nascent American Impressionist movement. Numerous artists, including William Chadwick, Childe Hassam, Willard Metcalfe and Henry Ward Ranger, came here to paint, staying in the mansion of local art patron Florence Griswold.

Her house, which her artist friends decorated with murals (often in lieu of paying rent), is now the **Florence Griswold Museum** (www.flogris.org; 96 Lyme St; adult/child $8/free; ⏰10am-5pm Tue-Sat, 1-5pm Sun) and contains a fine selection of both Impressionist and Barbizon paintings. The estate consists of her Georgian-style house, the Krieble Gallery, the Chadwick studio and Griswold's beloved gardens. The neighboring **Lyme Academy of Fine Arts** (lymeacademy.edu; 84 Lyme St; admission free; ⏰10am-4pm Tue-Sat) features rotating drawing, painting and sculpture exhibits by students.

🛏 p133

Eating & Sleeping

Hartford ❶

🍴 Max Downtown   American $$$

(☎860-522-2530; www.maxrestaurantgroup.
com/downtown; 185 Asylum St; mains $27-37;
🕑lunch & dinner Mon-Fri, dinner Sat & Sun) With
its retro-luxe look, 'pre-Prohibition' cocktails,
curved wooden bar and massive wrought-iron
chandeliers, this is where the professional
and political classes come to dine on classic
chophouse fare.

Glastonbury

🍴 Plan B   Burgers $$

(☎860-430-9737; www.planbtavern.com; 120
Hebron Ave; mains $7-14) A rowdy joint with a
cabinet of bourbons behind the bar, televised
football games and red-leather booths. The
burgers are 100% organic beef and come in a
bewildering array of options. For the full blow-
out, try one with truffle chips.

🛏 Connecticut River
Valley Inn   B&B $$$

(☎860-633-7374; www.connecticutrivervalley
inn.com; 2195 Main St; d $185-250; P ✳ 🛜)
This large Colonial clapboard sits proudly on
Glastonbury's Main St and offers four handsome
bedrooms, artfully decorated by host Pat
Brubaker. But the best bit is the sumptuous
homemade breakfast, which features baked
muffins and lavender scones straight out of the
oven, pancakes and hot salmon quiche.

Chester ❺

🍴 Restaurant L&E   French $$

(☎860-526-5301; restaurantfrench75bar.com;
59 Main St; mains $16-29; 🕑dinner Tue-Sun)
This intimate French bistro with its cutlery
chandelier is a romantic setting for classic
French dining, including well-executed versions
of coquille St Jacques and braised oxtail. The
small bar opens at 4pm.

River Tavern   American $$

(☎860-526-9417; www.rivertavernchester.net;
23 Main St; mains $17-30; 🕑lunch & dinner)
There's invariably a crowd waiting for tables
at this New York–style bistro with its wood-
accented bar and dining room. They're here for
the seasonal menu, which includes shad from
the Connecticut River.

Essex ❻

🛏 Griswold Inn   Historic Inn $$

(☎806-767-1776; www.griswoldinn.com; 36
Main St; d $110-190, ste $190-305; P 🛜) The
Griswold has been Essex's social centerpiece
since 1776. The Hunt Breakfast (served 11am to
1pm Sunday) has been a tradition since the War
of 1812, when British soldiers occupying Essex
demanded to be fed. The 30 guest rooms have
modern conveniences and its suites have wood-
burning fireplaces.

Ivoryton

🛏 Copper Beech Inn   Historic Inn $$$

(☎806-767-0330; www.copperbeechinn.com;
46 Main St; d $179-279, ste $329-379; P 🛜)
Yankee charm meets European sophistication
at Copper Beech, where rooms brim with
sumptuous touches such as fluffy bathrobes,
oriental rugs and fresh flowers. For dinner, head
to one of two restaurants, each serving versions
of contemporary French-country and New
American dishes (mains $18 to $27).

Old Lyme ❼

🛏 Bee & Thistle Inn   Historic Inn $$

(☎860-434-1667; beeandthistleinn.com; 100
Lyme St; d $135-275; P) A butter-yellow Dutch
colonial farmhouse, the Bee & Thistle dates
to 1756 and is furnished with period beds
and wing-backed armchairs. Its dining room
(open to nonguests) is a romantic setting for a
gourmet experience (meals $25 to $42, open
Wednesday to Sunday).

Kent Amble among hickory forests in this lovely part of the Litchfield Hills

Litchfield Hills Loop

12

Litchfield Hills is often described as 'the Hamptons for people who like privacy.' We like the area for its gently forested hills and lakes, resident artists and Colonial farmhouses with their PYO policies.

TRIP HIGHLIGHTS

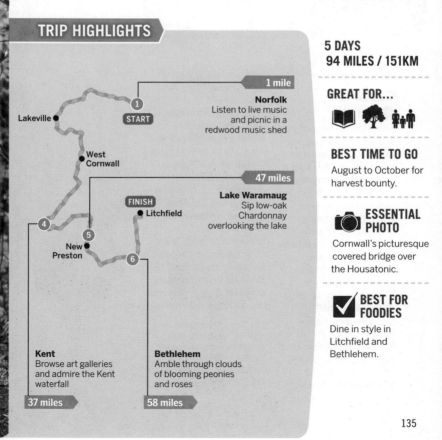

1 mile

Norfolk
Listen to live music and picnic in a redwood music shed

47 miles

Lake Waramaug
Sip low-oak Chardonnay overlooking the lake

Lakeville

West Cornwall

START
1

FINISH
Litchfield

4

5

New Preston

6

Kent
Browse art galleries and admire the Kent waterfall

37 miles

Bethlehem
Amble through clouds of blooming peonies and roses

58 miles

5 DAYS
94 MILES / 151KM

GREAT FOR...

BEST TIME TO GO
August to October for harvest bounty.

ESSENTIAL PHOTO
Cornwall's picturesque covered bridge over the Housatonic.

BEST FOR FOODIES
Dine in style in Litchfield and Bethlehem.

135

With scenery to match the Green Mountains of Vermont, pre-Colonial villages worthy of any movie set, and the finest food, culture and music in Connecticut, the Litchfield Hills attracts a sophisticated crowd of weekending Manhattanites. But its hardwood forests, dappled river valleys and lakes, and abundant autumn fairs offer endless possibilities for intrepid walkers, anglers, antiquers and history buffs.

TRIP HIGHLIGHT

1 Norfolk

Norfolk's bucolic scenery and cool summers have long attracted prosperous New Yorkers. They built many of the town's fine mansions, its well-endowed Romanesque Revival library and its Arts and Crafts–style town hall, now the **Infinity Music Hall & Bistro** (www.infinityhall.com; 20 Greenwoods Rd W; ☺dinner Wed-Sun).

Most opulent of all was **Whitehall**, the summer estate of Ellen and Carl Battell Stoeckel, passionate (and moneyed) music-lovers who established the **Norfolk Music Festival** (www.norfolkmusic.org; Ellen Battell Stoeckel Estate, US 44; tickets $25-100; ☺Jul-Aug). These extravagant affairs – the couple thought nothing of recruiting and paying for a special train to transport a 70-piece New York philharmonic orchestra to their festival – were among the most popular summer events in New England. On her death in 1939, Ellen Stoeckel bequeathed the redwood 'Music Shed' to Yale University Summer School of Music, ensuring the tradition continues.

The Drive » Head west along the main, forest-lined route US 44 for Lakeville's twin town of Salisbury. From here it's a short, 1-mile drive along historic Main St to Lakeville's town center.

❷ Lakeville

The rolling farmland in this quiet and remote corner of the Litchfield Hills is home to millionaires and movie luminaries such as Meryl Streep. The Rockefellers favored the famous Hotchkiss preparatory school, and in Lakeville, Paul Newman raced the **Lime Rock Race Track** (www.limerock.com; 497 Lime Rock Rd; ⏱Apr-Nov), which he thought was the most beautiful racing track in America. Today the seven-turn, 1.5-mile circuit hosts vintage and historic automobile races, along with regular stock-car races.

Otherwise, head to the peaks of **Bear Mountain** or **Lion's Head** for eye-popping panoramas. Part of the **Appalachian**

🔗 LINK YOUR TRIP

11 Lower River Valley

From Woodbury, take CT 84 for Mark Twain's hometown of Hartford (p128) and a leisurely drive down the Connecticut River Valley.

13 Fall Foliage Tour

Head north on CT 7 for leaf-peeping, walking and zip-lining in Massachusetts, Vermont and New Hampshire (p143).

137

National Scenic Trail (www.appalachiantrail.com), you'll find the trailheads leading off Rte 41.

📖 p141

The Drive » Exit Lakeville south on Sharon Rd before picking up the CT 112 E past the Lime Rock Race Track. From here, the drive swoops south through rolling farmland, dotted with big red-and-white barns and stables. After 5 miles, turn south on US 7 into West Cornwall.

- - - - - - - - - -

3 West Cornwall

The village of West Cornwall is just one of six Cornwall villages in Connecticut, but it is the most famous thanks to its picturesque **covered bridge**. The bridge was known as the 'Kissing Bridge,' because horse-drawn carriages were able to slow down to a steady trot inside, thus allowing their passengers a brief bit of alone time.

Otherwise, the area attracts nature-lovers,

birders and hikers who come to hike, fish and boat on the lazy Housatonic River. In winter the nearby **Mohawk Mountain Ski Area** (www.mohawkmtn.com; 42 Great Hollow Rd, Cornwall) is the largest ski resort in the state, with 24 slopes and trails.

The Drive » The 14-mile drive south along US 7 to Kent from West Cornwall is the most scenic stretch of the trip, especially in fall, when the thickly forested hillsides are ablaze. The road runs parallel to the Appalachian Trail and Housatonic River for most of the way, offering lots of opportunities to stop and stretch your legs along the river.

- - - - - - - - - -

TRIP HIGHLIGHT

4 Kent

During summer, weekenders throng to Kent's small but respected clutch of art galleries to enjoy the **Litchfield Jazz Festival** (http://litchfieldjazzfest.com), held here each August.

JON ARNOLD IMAGES LTD/ALAMY ©

The area around Kent presents some of the loveliest rural scenery in the hills. At **Kent Falls State Park**, a waterfall tumbles 250ft over the rocky hillside. Hike the easy trail to the top, or just settle into a sunny picnic spot. Nearby, the **Sloane-Stanley Museum** (www.cultureandtourism. org; US 7; adult/child $8/5; ⏲10am-4pm Wed-Sun May-Oct) houses a barn full of early American tools, collected by artist and author Eric Sloane, who painted the cloud-filled sky mural at the Smithsonian Air and Space Museum in

---

💬 **LOCAL KNOWLEDGE:**
BANTAM CINEMA

Locals know that one of the best things to do on rainy days is book in to see a film at the **Bantam Cinema** (www.bantamcinema.com; 115 Bantam Lake Rd, Bantam). Housed in a converted red barn on the shores of Lake Bantam, it's the oldest continuously operating movie theater in Connecticut and is a real Litchfield experience. The well-curated screenings focus on independent and foreign films, and the 'Meet the Filmmaker' series features guest directors, actors and producers, many of whom live here.

Lake Waramaug

Washington, DC. In autumn, the adjacent **Connecticut Antique Machinery Association** (www.ctamachinery.com; US 7; adult/child $3/1.50; ⏰10am-4pm Wed-Sun May-Oct; ♿) is a fabulous child-friendly attraction with all manner of steam-powered locomotives.

✕ ⌯ p141

The Drive » Take the CT 341 eastward out of Kent, climbing up out of the valley through more forested hills. After 10 miles, turn south toward Warren along CT 45. After a further 1.6 miles, Lake Waramaug will peek between the trees on your left.

- - - - - - - - - - -

TRIP HIGHLIGHT

⑤ Lake Waramaug

Of the dozens of lakes and ponds in the Litchfield Hills, Lake Waramaug stands out. As you make your way around the northern shore of the lake on North Shore Rd, you'll come to the **Hopkins Vineyard** (☎860-868-7954; www.hopkinsvineyard.com; 25 Hopkins Rd, New Preston; ⏰10am-5pm May-Dec). The wines here are made mostly from French-American hybrids and the low-oak Chardonnay frequently wins awards.

The vineyard hosts wine tastings, and the view from the bar is worth the trip, particularly when the foliage changes in the fall. Be sure to arrive well before closing time for a tasting, and call ahead during the low season.

✕ ⌯ p141

The Drive » Leaving Lake Waramaug along North and East Shore Rd, turn left onto US 202 toward Bantam. At Lake Bantam, take CT 209 and 109 around the western and southern edges of the lake and after 3.5 miles turn right onto CT 61 S into Bethlehem.

DETOUR: WOODBURY

Start: **6** Bethlehem

At the southern border of the Litchfield Hills, Woodbury is justifiably famous as the 'antiques capital' of Connecticut, boasting over 30 dealerships and 20 stores along historic Main St. **Woodbury Antiques Dealers Association** (www.antiqueswoodbury.com) publishes an online guide.

While you're in Woodbury, don't forget to stop by the **Good News Cafe** (☏203-266-4663; www.good-news-cafe.com; 649 Main St S/US 6; mains $7-29; ☺Wed-Mon). Run by Carole Peck, considered the Alice Waters of the East Coast, the cafe is a magnet for celebrities and lovers of fine food who come for the locally sourced farm produce and inventive, seasonal menus.

TRIP HIGHLIGHT

6 Bethlehem

Bethlehem is Connecticut's 'Christmas Town' and every year thousands of visitors come for the **Christmas Fair** (www.ci.bethlehem.ct.us) and to have their Christmas mail hand-stamped in the village post office.

The town's religious history extends to the founding of the first theological seminary in America by local resident Reverend Joseph Bellamy. His home, the **Bellamy-Ferriday House & Garden** (☏203-266-7596; 9 Main St N; adult/child $7/4; ☺11am-4pm Thu-Sun May-Sep, Sat & Sun Oct), a 1750s clapboard mansion, is open to the public and is a treasure trove of delftware, Asian art and period furnishings. Equally exquisite is the garden, the design of latter-day owner Caroline Ferriday, who designed it to resemble an Aubusson Persian carpet. Its geometrical box hedges are in-filled with frothing peonies, lilacs and heirloom roses.

✗ p141

The Drive » The final drive north to Litchfield passes through more bucolic scenery, dotted with country farmhouses and past the shores of Lake Bantam. Head north out of Bethlehem along CT 61, past the Bellamy-Ferriday House & Garden, then connect to CT 63 via Old Litchfield Rd, for a straight run into town.

7 Litchfield

The centerpiece of the region is Connecticut's best-preserved late-18th-century town. Founded in 1719, Litchfield prospered as a main thoroughfare between New York and Boston. The town itself converges on a long oval green, and is surrounded by swaths of protected land.

Walk down **North Street** and **South Street** (with a free walking tour sheet from the information kiosk) and admire the great mansions. Washington slept at the **Sheldon Tavern** on North St on his way to confer with General Rochambeau. Down the street, **Bull House** was home to Ludlow Bull, the American Egyptologist who participated in the discovery of Tutankhamen's gold-filled tomb. On South St, New Jersey judge Tapping Reeve founded America's first law school, the **Tapping-Reeve House & Law School** (www.litchfieldhistoricalsociety.org/lawschool.html; 82 South St; adult/child $5/free; ☺11am-5pm Tue-Sat, 1-5pm Sun mid-May–Nov) in 1775. Admission to the small **Litchfield History Museum** (☺11am-5pm Tue-Sat, 1-5pm Sun mid-May–Nov) is included in the ticket.

✗ 🛏 p141

Eating & Sleeping

Lakeville ②

🛏 Inn at Iron Masters   Motel $$

(☎860-435-9844; www.innatironmasters.com;
229 Main St/US 44; r $109-206; P🛜) At first
glance this single-story inn looks suspiciously
like a Florida motel, but the interior is all New
England quilts and cutesy flower motifs. The
grounds feature gardens and gazebos, and
there's a large common fireplace for chilly
evenings.

Kent ④

✕ Belgique Salon de Thé   Tearoom $

(☎860-927-3681; www.belgiqueonline.com;
1 Bridge St; pastries $3-8; ⊙lunch Thu-Sun,
dinner Fri & Sat) Susan and Pierre Gilissen have
brought a little slice of Belgium to Kent with
their chocolatier and tea salon. You can drop in
for lunch, tea or a savory dinner. Reservations
are recommended.

🛏 Inn at Kent Falls   Historic Inn $$$

(☎860-927-3197; www.theinnatkentfalls.
com; 107 Kent-Cornwall Rd/US 7; r $215-350;
P🛜✉) This historic inn dates back to
the early 1900s. Original floorboards, three
generous lounges with open fireplaces and a
grand piano make for a home-away-from-home
atmosphere. Breakfast is a communal affair,
with homemade pancakes and fresh baked
croissants.

Lake Waramaug ⑤

✕ Community
Table   Modern American $$

(☎860-868-9354; communitytablect.com;
223 Litchfield Turnpike/US 202; brunch $10-14;
⊙brunch Sun, dinner Thu-Mon) The name of
this Scandinavian-inspired restaurant comes
from the 300-year-old black walnut table, where
you can sit down to Sunday brunch. The modern
American menu is locally sourced.

🛏 Hopkins Inn   B&B $$

(☎806-868-7295; www.thehopkinsinn.com;
22 Hopkins Rd; r $120-135, apt $150-240;
P❄🛜🐾) Across the road from Hopkins
Vineyard, this homely B&B has a variety of
rooms and an apartment. The restaurant
(meals $15 to $20, open April to December),
with its wonderful views over Lake Waramaug,
specializes in Austrian cuisine.

Bethlehem ⑥

✕ Woodward
House   Modern American $$$

(☎203-266-6902; www.thewoodwardhouse.
com; 4 The Green; mains $19-36; ⊙dinner Wed-
Sun) Housed in a 1740s saltbox, the Woodward
retains its original wainscoting and hand-hewn
beams. The walls are hung with contemporary
artworks, and the modern American menu
includes Long Island duck and grass-fed beef
tenderloin.

Litchfield ⑦

✕ West Street
Grill   Modern American $$

(☎860-567-3885; weststreetgrill.com; 43
West St; mains $15-25) A Parisian-style bistro
on Litchfield's historic green, this is one of the
state's top restaurants. Over the years, its
inventive modern American cooking has earned
it nods from *Gourmet* magazine and the *New
York Times*. The shrimp salad with orange and
fennel is delightful.

🛏 Tollgate Hill Inn   Historic Inn $$

(☎860-567-1233; www.tollgatehill.com; 571
Torrington Rd/US 202; r $95-170, ste $160-195;
P❄🛜) Two miles east of Litchfield, this 1745
property used to be the main way station for
travelers between Albany and Hartford. Divided
between three buildings, including one of the
oldest schoolhouses in Connecticut, rooms
have a private deck and pull-out couch.

Connecticut *Break from your tour with a slice of pumpkin pie*

Classic Trip

Fall Foliage Tour

13

Touring New England in search of autumn's changing colors has become so popular that it has sprouted its own subculture of 'leaf-peepers.' Immerse yourself in the fall harvest spirit.

TRIP HIGHLIGHTS

212 miles

Lake Champlain
Cruise the lake on a 43ft schooner for the best views

316 miles

Bretton Woods
Zip-line 1000ft through a golden leaf canopy

47 miles

Berkshires
Pack a picnic in the Berkshires' gourmet shops

10 miles

Kent
Autumn foliage framing the Housatonic River

St Johnsbury

North Conway **FINISH**

Manchester

Sherman **START**

5–7 DAYS
424 MILES / 682KM

GREAT FOR...

BEST TIME TO GO
August to November for the harvest and autumn leaves.

ESSENTIAL PHOTO
Kent Falls set against a backdrop of autumnal colors.

BEST FOR OUTDOORS
Zip-lining through the tree canopy in Bretton Woods.

143

Classic Trip

13 Fall Foliage Tour

The brilliance of fall in New England is legendary. Scarlet and sugar maples, ash, birch, beech, dogwood, tulip tree, oak and sassafras all contribute to the carnival of autumn color. But this trip is about much more than just flora and fauna: the harvest spirit makes for family outings to PYO farms, leisurely walks along dappled trails and tables groaning beneath delicious seasonal produce.

➊ Lake Candlewood

With a surface area of 8.4 sq miles, Candlewood is the largest lake in Connecticut. On the western shore, the **Squantz Pond State Park** (www.ct.gov; 178 Shortwoods Rd, New Fairfield) is popular with leaf-peepers, who come to amble the pretty shoreline. In Brookfield and Sherman, quiet vineyards with acres of gnarled grapevines line the hillsides. Visitors can tour the award-winning **DiGrazia Vineyards** (www.

digrazia.com; 131 Tower Rd, Brookfield; ⏰11am-5pm daily May-Dec, Sat & Sun Jan-Apr) or opt for something more intimate at **White Silo Farm Winery** (www.whitesilowinery.com; 32 CT 37; tastings $7; ⏰11am-6pm Fri-Sun Apr-Dec), where the focus is on specialty wines made from farm-grown fruit.

For the ultimate bird's-eye view of the foliage, consider a late-afternoon hot-air-balloon ride with **GONE Ballooning** (www.flygoneballooning.com; 88 Sylvan Crest Dr; adult/under

12yr $250/125) in nearby Southbury.

✗ p151

The Drive ›› From Danbury, at the southern tip of the lake, you have a choice of heading north via US 7, taking in Brookfield and New Milford (or trailing the scenic eastern shoreline along Candlewood Lake Rd S); or heading north along CT 37 and CT 39 via New Fairfield, Squantz Pond and Sherman, before reconnecting with US 7 to Kent.

TRIP HIGHLIGHT

2 Kent

Kent has previously been voted *the* spot in all of New England (yes, even beating Vermont) for fall foliage viewing. Situated prettily in the Litchfield Hills on the banks of the Housatonic River, it is surrounded by dense woodlands. For a

LINK YOUR TRIP

6 **Mohawk Trail**
Pick up the Mohawk Trail at Williamstown (p82) for more spectacular mountain vistas and rural New England charm.

17 **Robert Frost Country**
Join this tour of the Green Mountains at Middlebury (p188) and experience the poet's words embodied in verdant forests and Vermont's most famous mountains.

Classic Trip

LOCAL KNOWLEDGE
ANNE MCANDREW & DAVE FAIRTY, BACKCOUNTRY OUTFITTERS

Kent is beautiful in the fall. The best hiking trail during the season leads up to Caleb's Peak from Skiff Mountain Rd, hooking up with the Appalachian Trail. At the summit you have the most fantastic views of the Housatonic Valley. If you like, you can camp at any of the shelters on the trail or try Macedonia Brook State Park, which is private and rustic with over 80 miles of hiking trails.

Top: Cornwall Bridge, Housatonic Meadows State Park
Right: Venturing up Mt Equinox, near Manchester

sweeping view of them, hike up Cobble Mountain in **Macedonia Brook State Park** (www.ct.gov; 159 Macedonia Brook Rd), a wooded oasis 2 miles north of town. The steep climb to the rocky ridge affords panoramic views of the foliage against a backdrop of the Taconic and Catskill mountain ranges.

NORMAN EGGERT/ALAMY ©

DAVID LYONS/ALAMY ©

The 2175-mile Georgia-to-Maine **Appalachian National Scenic Trail** (www.appalachiantrail.org) also runs through Kent and up to Salisbury on the Massachusetts border. Unlike much of the trail, the Kent section offers a mostly flat 5-mile river walk alongside the Housatonic, the longest river walk along the entire length of the trail.

The trailhead is accessed on River Rd, off CT 341.

The Drive » The 15-mile drive from Kent to Housatonic Meadows State Park along US 7 is one of the most scenic drives in Connecticut. The single-lane road dips and weaves between thick forests, past Kent Falls State Park with its tumbling waterfall (visible from the road), and through West Cornwall's picturesque covered bridge, which spans the Housatonic River.

3 Housatonic Meadows State Park

During the spring thaw, the churning waters of the Housatonic challenge kayakers and canoeists. By summer the scenic waterway transforms into a lazy, flat river perfect for fly-fishing. In the **Housatonic Meadows State Park** (☎806-672-6772; US 7; tent

Classic Trip

sites residents/nonresidents $17/27; ⊘mid-Apr–mid-Oct), campers vie for a spot on the banks of the river while hikers take to the hills on the Appalachian Trail. **Housatonic River Outfitters** (www.dryflies. com; 24 Kent Rd, Cornwall Bridge) runs guided fishing trips with gourmet picnics.

Popular with artists and photographers, one of the most photographed fall scenes is the **Cornwall Bridge** (West Cornwall), an antique covered bridge that stretches across the broad river, framed by vibrantly colored foliage.

On Labor Day weekend, in the nearby town of Goshen, you can visit the **Goshen Fair** (www.goshenfair.org), one of Connecticut's best old-fashioned fairs, with ox-pulling and wood-cutting contests. Also in Goshen is **Nodine's Smokehouse** (www.nodinesmokehouse.com;

39 North St; ⊘9am-5pm Mon-Sat, 10am-4pm Sun), a major supplier to New York gourmet food stores.

The Drive » Continue north along US 7 toward the Massachusetts border and Great Barrington. After a few miles you leave the forested slopes of the park behind you and enter expansive rolling countryside dotted with large red-and-white barns. Look out for hand-painted signs advertising farm produce and consider stopping overnight in Falls Village, which has an excellent B&B (p151).

- - - - - - - - - - -
TRIP HIGHLIGHT

④ Berkshires

Blanketing the westernmost part of Massachusetts, the rounded mountains of the Berkshires turn crimson and gold as early as mid-September. The effective capital of the Berkshires is **Great Barrington**, a formerly industrial town whose streets are now lined with art galleries and upscale restaurants. It's the perfect place to pack your picnic or rest your legs before or after a hike in nearby **Beartown**

State Forest (www.mass. gov/dcr; 69 Blue Hill Rd, Monterey). Crisscrossing some 12,000 acres, hiking trails yield spectacular views of wooded hillsides and pretty Benedict Pond.

Further north, **October Mountain State Forest** (www.mass.gov/dcr; 256 Woodland Rd, Lee) is the state's largest tract of green space (16,127 acres), also interwoven with hiking trails. The name – attributed to Herman Melville – gives a good indication of when this park is at its loveliest, with its multicolored tapestry of hemlocks, birches and oaks.

✗ p151

The Drive » Drive north on US 7, the spine of the Berkshires, cruising through Great Barrington and Stockbridge. In Lee, the highway merges with scenic US 20, from where you can access October Mountain. Continue 16 miles north through Lenox and Pittsfield to Lanesborough. Turn right on N Main St and follow the signs to the park entrance.

- - - - - - - - - - -
TRIP HIGHLIGHT

⑤ Mt Greylock State Forest

Massachusetts' highest peak is not so high, at 3491ft, but a climb up the 92ft-high **War Veterans Memorial Tower** rewards you with a panorama stretching up to 100 verdant miles, across the Taconic, Housatonic and Catskill ranges, and

---

✓ **TOP TIP:**
NORTHERN BERKSHIRE FALL FOLIAGE PARADE

If your timing is right, you can stop in North Adams for the **Fall Foliage Parade** (www.fallfoliageparade.com), held in late September or early October. Now in its 57th year, the event follows a changing theme, but it always features music, food and fun – and, of course, foliage.

over five states. Even if the weather seems drab from the foot, driving up to the summit may well lift you above the gray blanket, and the view with a layer of cloud floating between tree line and sky is simply magical.

Mt Greylock State Reservation (www.mass. gov/dcr; park free, summit $2; ⌚visitors center 9am-4:30pm, auto road late May-Oct) has some 45 miles of hiking trails, including a portion of the Appalachian Trail. Frequent trail pull-offs on the road up – including some that lead to waterfalls – make it easy to get at least a little hike in before reaching the top of Mt Greylock.

🍴 📛 p151

The Drive 》 Return to US 7 and continue north through the quintessential college town of Williamstown. Cross the Vermont border and continue north through the historic village of Bennington. Just north of Bennington, turn left on Rte 7A and continue north to Manchester.

- - - - - - - - - - - - - -

6 Manchester

Stylish Manchester is known for its magnificent New England architecture. For fall foliage views, head south of the center to 3828ft-high **Mt Equinox** (📞802-362-1114; www.equinoxmountain. com; car & driver $12, each additional passenger $2;

⌚9am-dusk May-Oct), the highest mountain accessible by car in the Taconic Range. Wind up the 5.2 miles – with gasp-inducing scenery at every hairpin turn – seemingly to the top of the world, where the 360-degree panorama unfolds, offering views of the Adirondacks, the lush Battenkill Valley and Montreal's Mt Royal.

If early snow makes Mt Equinox inaccessible, visit 412-acre **Hildene** (📞802-362-1788; www. hildene.org; Rte 7A; museum & grounds adult/child $13/5, grounds only $5/3; ⌚9:30am-4:30pm), a Georgian Revival mansion that was once home to the Lincoln family. It's filled with presidential memorabilia and sits nestled at the edge of the Green Mountains, with access to 8 miles of wooded walking trails.

📛 p151

The Drive 》 Take Rte 7 north to Burlington. Three miles past Middlebury in New Haven, stop off at Lincoln Peak Vineyard for wine tasting or a picnic lunch on the wraparound porch.

- - - - - - - - - - - - - -

TRIP HIGHLIGHT

7 Lake Champlain

With a surface area of 490 sq miles, straddling New York, Vermont and Quebec, Lake Champlain is the largest freshwater lake in the US after the Great Lakes.

On its northeastern side, **Burlington** is a gorgeous base to enjoy the lake. Explore it by foot on our walking tour (p212). Then scoot down to the wooden promenade, take a swing on the four-person rocking benches and consider a bike ride along the 7.5-mile lakeside bike path.

For the best offshore foliage views we love the *Friend Ship* sailboat at **Whistling Man Schooner Company** (📞802-598-6504; www.whistlingman. com; Boathouse, College St; 2hr cruise adult/child $35/20; ⌚May-Oct), a 43ft sloop that accommodates a mere 17 passengers. Next door, **ECHO Lake Aquarium & Science Center** (www.echovermont. org; 1 College St; adult/child $12.50/9.50; ⌚10am-5pm) explores the history and ecosystem of the lake, including a famous snapshot of Champy, Lake Champlain's mythical sea creature.

🍴 p151

The Drive 》 Take I-89 southeast to Montpelier through swooping valleys, passing Camels Hump State Park and CC Putnam State Forest. At Montpelier, pick up the I-93 northeast and pass through St Johnsbury and Littleton, before taking a left onto US 302 into the Crawford Notch State Park, where you'll find Bretton Woods.

DETOUR:
KANCAMAGUS SCENIC BYWAY

Start: ❾ **North Conway**

From North Conway, the 34.5-mile Kancamagus Scenic Byway, otherwise known as NH 112, passes through the White Mountains from Conway to Lincoln in New Hampshire. You'll drive alongside the Saco River and enjoy sweeping views of the Presidential Range from Kancamagus pass. Inviting trailheads and pull-offs line the road. From Lincoln, a short drive north on I-93 leads to Franconia Notch State Park, where the foliage in September and October is simply spectacular.

TRIP HIGHLIGHT

❽ Bretton Woods

Unbuckle your seat belts and step away from the car. You're not just peeping at leaves today, you're swooping past them on zip lines that drop 1000ft at 30mph. The four-season **Bretton Woods Canopy Tour** (☎603-278-4947; www.brettonwoods.com; US 302; per person $110; ⏰tours 10am & 2pm) includes a hike through the woods, a stroll over sky bridges and a swoosh down 10 cables to tree platforms.

If this leaves you craving even higher views, cross US 302 and drive 6 miles on Base Rd to the coal-burning, steam-powered **Mount Washington Cog Railway** (☎603-278-5404; www.thecog.com; adult/child/senior $62/39/57; ⏰ 8:30am-4:30pm late May-Nov) at the western base of Mt Washington, the highest peak in New England. This historic railway has been hauling sightseers to the mountain's 6288ft

summit since 1869. For details about attractions at the summit, see (p241).

The Drive » From Crawford Notch, drive 20 miles east on US 302, a route that parallels the Saco River and the Conway Scenic Railroad. At the junction of NH 16 and US 302, continue east on US 302 into North Conway.

❾ North Conway

Many of the best restaurants, pubs and inns in North Conway come with expansive views of the nearby mountains, making it an ideal place to wrap up a fall foliage road trip. If you're traveling with kids or you skipped the cog railway ride up Mt

Washington, consider an excursion on the antique steam Valley Train with the **Conway Scenic Railroad** (☎603-356-5251; www.conwayscenic.com; 38 Norcross Circle; adult/child 4-12yr/child 1-3yr from $15/11/free; ⏰mid-Jun–mid-Oct); it's a short but sweet round-trip ride through the Mt Washington Valley from North Conway to Conway, 11 miles south. The Moat Mountains and the Saco River will be your scenic backdrop. First-class seats are usually in a restored Pullman observation car. For details about the Notch Train to Crawford Notch, see p242.

🛏 p151

Eating & Sleeping

Lake Candlewood ❶

✗ American Pie — Bakery $$

(www.americanpiecompany.com; 29 Sherman Rd/CT 37, Sherman; mains $9-20; ⊙7am-9pm Tue-Sun, to 3pm Mon) A local favorite serving up 20 varieties of homemade pie, including pumpkin and blueberry crumb, alongside burgers, steaks and salads.

Falls Village

🛏 Falls Village Inn — Historic Inn $$$

(☎860-824-0033; www.thefallsvillageinn.com; 33 Railroad St; d/ste $209/299; P🐾) The heart and soul of one of the smallest villages in Connecticut, this inn originally served the Housatonic Railroad. Now the six rooms are styled by interior decorator Bunny Williams, and the Tap Room is a hangout for Lime Rock's racers.

Berkshires ❹

✗ Castle Street Café — Modern American $$$

(☎413-528-5244; www.castlestreetcafe.com; 10 Castle St; mains $21-29; ⊙dinner Wed-Mon, brunch Sat & Sun; 🎵) The menu reads like a who's who of local farms: Ioka Valley Farm grass-fed beef, Rawson Brook chevre and Equinox Farm mesclun greens. Prime time to dine is Friday or Saturday, when there's live jazz.

Mt Greylock State Forest ❺

🛏 Bascom Lodge — Lodge $$

(☎413-743-1591; www.bascomlodge.net; 1 Summit Rd, Adams; dm/r $35/125, breakfast & lunch $5-10, dinner $28-32; ⊙breakfast, lunch & dinner Jun-Oct) At the summit of Mt Greylock, this rustic mountain lodge boasts – arguably – the most scenic setting in the state. Come for basic accommodations, unexpectedly gourmet meals and jaw-dropping views.

Manchester ❻

🛏 Equinox — Resort $$$

(☎802-362-4700, 800-362-4747; www.equinoxresort.com; 3567 Main St/Rte 7A; r $280-600, ste $490-1500; @🐾🛰) One of Vermont's most famous resorts, this grand white-pillared property – with its own library and front porch – sits in vast grounds with tennis courts and an 18-hole golf course.

Lake Champlain ❼

✗ Shanty on the Shore — Seafood $$

(☎802-864-0238; 181 Battery St, Burlington; meals $11-24; ⊙lunch & dinner) With its superb lake views, this seafood joint serves fresh lobster, fish and shellfish in an unfussy, down-to-earth fashion with local touches such as salmon broiled in Vermont maple syrup.

North Conway ❾

🛏 Red Elephant Inn — B&B $$

(☎603-356-3548; www.redelephantinn.com; 28 Locust Lane; r $135-225; ❄🛰) Perched on a hill with views of the Moat Mountains, this stylish 8-room property also has a sense of fun – rooms include the Domestic Cat and Neiman Marcus. Coffee, fruit and cookies are available all day.

STRETCH YOUR LEGS
NEWPORT

Start/Finish Memorial Blvd

Distance 4 miles

Duration 3.5 hours

Newport's status as a summer resort stretches back to the 19th century, when America's wealthiest industrialists erected mansions along Bellevue Ave. Admire their extravagant summer 'cottages,' which still line Newport's cliff tops, on this walk.

Take this walk on Trips

International Tennis Hall of Fame

To experience something of the 19th-century American aristocracy's approach to leisure, visit the **International Tennis Hall of Fame** (www. tennisfame.com; 194 Bellevue Ave; adult/child $12/free; ☺9:30am-5pm). It lies inside the Newport Casino building (1880), which served as a summer club for Newport's wealthiest residents. If you've brought your whites, playing on one of its 13 grass courts ($130 for one or two people per 90 minutes) is a delightful throwback to earlier times; otherwise, have a drink lawnside at the **La Forge Casino Restaurant**.

The Walk » Stroll along lantern-lined Bellevue Ave past Newport's first 'cottage,' the Elizabethan folly of Kingscote on the right. Further on you'll pass the National Museum of American Illustration on the left, before arriving at Rosecliff.

Rosecliff

Further down Bellevue Ave stands the impressive **Rosecliff** (www.newport mansions.org; 548 Bellevue Ave; adult/child $14.50/5.50; ☺10am-6pm mid-Mar–mid-Nov), built for Mrs Hermann Oelrichs, an heiress of the Comstock Lode silver discovery. Designed to look like the Grand Trianon at Versailles, its palatial ballroom and landscaped grounds quickly became the setting for some enormous parties. In June the **Newport Flower Festival** is held here.

The Walk » Continue straight along Bellevue Ave to reach Rough Point. In quick succession you'll pass the Astor's stucco mansion, Beechwood, on the left, along with William Vanderbilt's garishly opulent Marble House, with its white marble driveway and grand porte cochere.

Rough Point

While the splendor of the grounds alone is worth the price of admission to **Rough Point** (www.newportrestoration. com; 680 Bellevue Ave; adult/child $25/free; ☺10:30am-1:30pm Apr-Oct), this faux-English manor house also contains

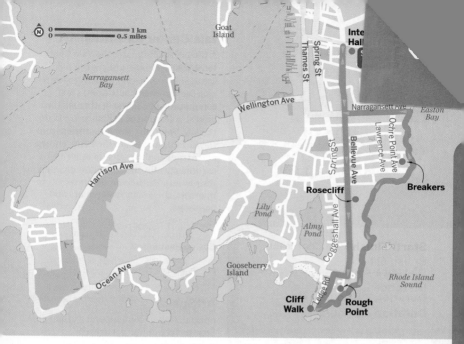

Doris Duke's impressive art holdings, including medieval tapestries, furniture owned by French emperors, Ming-dynasty ceramics, and paintings by Renoir and Van Dyck. The house sits in a peerless location right on the point.

The Walk ≫ To access the start of the Cliff Walk at Bailey's (Reject's) Beach, head right down to the end of Bellevue Ave. Before the avenue starts to merge with Ocean Ave, take a left down Ledge Rd to the trailhead.

Cliff Walk

In 1975, eager to protect their privacy, Newport's mansion owners sought to close **Cliff Walk** (www.cliffwalk.org), the public footpath that snakes along the cliff top overlooking their front lawns. The move was prevented by local fishermen and the 3.5-mile path was designated a National Recreation Trail. The best section runs from Ledge Rd near Rough Point to the Forty Steps (each one named for someone lost at sea) on Narragansett Ave.

The Walk ≫ Head down Ledge Rd, from Bellevue Ave, and pick up the Cliff Walk trail. The views are spectacular, with white surf pounding the rocks to your right and robber baron mansions to your left. The stretch between Ruggles Ave and Narragansett Ave is the most scenic, passing the Breakers, Vineland and French Gothic Ochre Court.

Breakers

Built at the behest of Cornelius Vanderbilt II, the **Breakers** (www. newportmansions.org; 44 Ochre Point Ave; adult/child $19.50/5.50; ⊙9am-6pm mid-Mar–Dec) is the most magnificent of the Newport mansions. A 70-room Italian Renaissance mega-palace, it was inspired by 16th-century Genoese palazzos, and over 200 craftsmen were engaged to complete the lavish marquetry, mosaics and ornate sculptural details.

The Walk ≫ Exit Cliff Walk up the Forty Steps, which will bring you up to Narragansett Ave. From here, it's a short walk back to Bellevue Ave. Turn right to return to the start and the International Tennis Hall of Fame for a drink.

STRETCH YOUR LEGS
NEW HAVEN

Start/Finish Yale Center for British Art

Distance 1.8 miles

Duration 2.5 hours

White-steepled churches, Colonial Revival buildings and neo-Gothic turrets form the stage-set for this exploration of New Haven's thriving arts scene, which includes Revolutionary canvases, rare manuscripts, community craftwork and avant-garde visual arts.

Take this walk on Trips

1 10 20

Yale Center for British Art

A Chapel St landmark, the **Yale Center for British Art** (www.ycba.yale.edu; 1080 Chapel St; admission free; ◷10am-5pm Tue-Sat, noon-5pm Sun) was Louis Kahn's last commission and is the setting for the largest collection of British art outside the UK. Spanning three centuries from the Elizabethan era to the 19th century, and arranged thematically as well as chronologically, the collection gives an insight into British art, life and culture in prints, drawings, watercolors and paintings.

The Walk ≫ This half-mile walk takes you past the New Haven Green. The white spire of Center Church will be visible above the trees and the Gothic Revival Trinity Church will be on your left. After Temple St, take the second right onto Orange St.

ArtSpace

Specializing in contemporary visual arts and community outreach, nonprofit **ArtSpace** (www.artspacenh.org; 50 Orange St; ◷noon-6pm Tue-Thu, to 8pm Fri & Sat) organizes the annual **City-Wide Open Studios** each fall. During the event it is possible to take a peek inside the workspaces of some of New Haven's up-and-coming artists. Check out the website for exact details.

The Walk ≫ Retrace your steps to Church St and stroll northeast beside the green. On your right you'll pass the Federal Courthouse, the turreted City Hall and the Amistad Memorial. Continue onto Whitney Ave and then turn right on Audubon St.

Creative Arts Workshop

New Haven's Audubon Arts District is located between Church and Orange Sts. In its midst is the **Creative Arts Workshop** (www.creativeartsworkshop.org; 80 Audubon St; ◷9:30am-5:30pm Mon-Fri, 9am-noon Sat), a visual arts studio that operates both as a cultural resource center and an art school. Classes are available.

In June, the workshop and the art district are abuzz with activity,

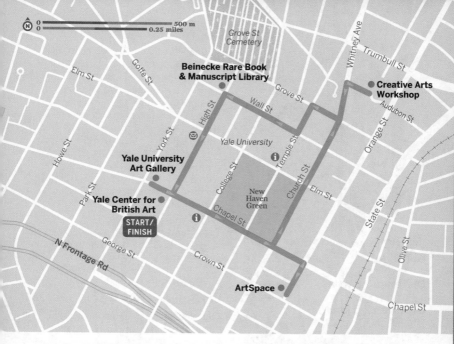

hosting events for the two-week-long **International Festival of Arts & Ideas** (www.artidea.org).

The Walk ≫ Retrace your steps to Whitney Ave, walk south and turn right on Grove St. Walk one block beside the redbrick Timothy Dwight College, take a left down Temple St and then a right down Wall St. From here it's a pleasant tree-lined walk to picture-worthy Beinecke Plaza.

Beinecke Rare Book & Manuscript Library

On your stroll back, swing past the **Beinecke Rare Book & Manuscript Library** (www.library.yale.edu/beinecke; 121 Wall St; admission free; ☺9am-7pm Mon-Thu, to 5pm Fri). This extraordinary piece of architecture is the largest building in the world designed for the preservation of rare manuscripts. The windowless cube has walls of Danby marble, which subdue the effects of light, while inside glass towers display sculptural shelves of books, including one of only 48 surviving Gutenberg Bibles (1455).

The Walk ≫ Exit Beinecke Plaza westward onto historic High St. Walk southwest, passing the grand Sterling Memorial Library on your right, and towering Dwight Hall on your left. When you hit Chapel St, turn right and you'll find the modern exterior of the art gallery on your right.

Yale University Art Gallery

The oldest university art museum in the country, **Yale University Art Gallery** (www.artgallery.yale.edu; 1111 Chapel St; admission free; ☺10am-5pm Tue-Sat, 1-6pm Sun) was opened in 1832 with Colonel John Trumbull's collection of paintings depicting the American Revolution. Now it is home to 185,000 objects, including paintings, sculpture, silverware and artifacts from as far afield as Asia, South America and Africa.

The Walk ≫ From the Yale University Art Gallery you can see the Yale Center for British Art across the street, where you started your walk.

Vermont

FOR ANYONE WHO APPRECIATES SLOW-PACED MEANDERING and nonstop scenic beauty, Vermont is paradise. The Green Mountain State has an eclectic allure offering outdoor adventure, vibrant local arts, photogenic villages, great locavore eating and the USA's highest per-capita concentration of microbreweries and covered bridges. Throughout the state, stubborn mountain ridges ensure an ever-present sense of adventure and discovery as you zigzag through one of America's most uniformly bucolic landscapes. Vermont also provides fertile ground for creative thinkers, whose passions are reinvigorating the state's traditional small-town culture.

Stowe Maple trees sparkle with brilliant bursts of color (Trip 14)

Weston Vermont Country Store (Trip 14)

Vermont's Spine: Route 100 3–4 Days
14 Cross the state from south to north along the Green Mountains. (p161)

Cider Season Sampler 3–4 Days
15 Sample Vermont's bounty during its most colorful season. (p171)

Vermont Back-Roads Ramble 3–4 Days
16 Head into the most rural corners and see why this is the true Vermont. (p179)

Robert Frost Country 1–2 Days
17 Venture through Robert Frost's stomping grounds and see what inspired his poetry. (p187)

Lake Champlain Byway 2–3 Days
18 Discover the scenic road spanning the mainland to the Lake Champlain Islands. (p195)

Southern Vermont Loop 2–3 Days
19 Explore the major landmarks and history paired with culinary and shopping highlights. (p203)

✓ DON'T MISS

Ben & Jerry's Factory Tour
Find out how two high-school pals created America's most celebrated ice cream on Trip 14

Magic Hat Brewery
Take an 'Artifactory' tour at Vermont's most famous microbrewery. Taste your favorite on Trip 18

Shelburne Museum
Learn about Vermont farm life and admire Americana in a village-like setting on Trip 18

Boyden Valley Winery
Visit the award-winning winery and sip fruit wine with maple or traditional varietals. Go wine tasting on Trip 15

Stowe
Vermont's most stunning mountain village is a mix of traditional New England architecture and awe-inducing peaks. Visit Stowe on Trip 14

Waterbury *The ultimate thirs*
quencher: fresh cider at Cold Hollow

COLD
HOLLOW
CIDER MILL

Legendary Cider Donuts

eal Vermont "Agri"-tainment

Vermont's Spine: Route 100

14

Yodeling pickles (yes, really), peaceful villages, otherworldly gondola rides and scoops of America's most famous ice cream keep you dazzled and dreamy along Rte 100.

TRIP HIGHLIGHTS

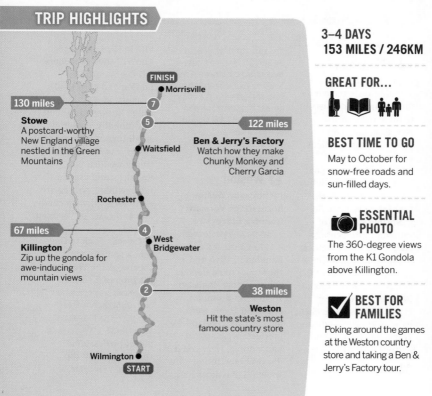

130 miles — 7

Stowe
A postcard-worthy New England village nestled in the Green Mountains

● Morrisville **FINISH**

5 — 122 miles

Ben & Jerry's Factory
Watch how they make Chunky Monkey and Cherry Garcia

● Waitsfield

Rochester ●

67 miles — 4

Killington
Zip up the gondola for awe-inducing mountain views

● West Bridgewater

2 — 38 miles

Weston
Hit the state's most famous country store

Wilmington ●
START

3–4 DAYS
153 MILES / 246KM

GREAT FOR...

BEST TIME TO GO

May to October for snow-free roads and sun-filled days.

ESSENTIAL PHOTO

The 360-degree views from the K1 Gondola above Killington.

BEST FOR FAMILIES

Poking around the games at the Weston country store and taking a Ben & Jerry's Factory tour.

Classic Trip

14 Vermont's Spine: Route 100

Spanning Vermont from bottom to top, Vermont's revered Rte 100 cuts through the state's most legendary ski resorts, past its best-known and kooky general stores with the verdant Green Mountains always at its side. This drive takes you on a slow meander through the state, though you might speed up in anticipation of the Ben & Jerry's Factory tour looming on the final stretch of road.

1 Wilmington

Chartered in 1751, Wilmington is the winter and summer gateway to Mt Snow, one of New England's best ski resorts and an excellent summertime mountain-biking and golfing spot. There are no main sights per se but the **Historic District** on W Main St is a prime example of 18th- and 19th-century architecture and is chock full of restaurants and boutiques; the bulk of the village is on the National Register of Historic Places. This is an excellent base to stay overnight and grab a bite before your journey up north.

✕ ﹏ p169

The Drive >> Driving north on Rte 100, first you'll pass through ski country (look for Mt Snow on your left) and sleepy hamlets – Jamaica is a prime dose of rural Vermont, with a country store and several antique shops.

TRIP HIGHLIGHT

2 Weston

Picturesque Weston is home to the **Vermont Country Store** (www.vermontcountrystore.com; Rte 100; ⊙9am-5:30pm), founded in 1946 and the state's most famous country store. It's a time warp from a simpler era when goods were made to last, and quirky products with appeal had a home. Here you'll discover electronic yodeling plastic pickles, taffeta slips and three kinds of shoe stretchers with customizable bunion and corn knobs – in short, everything you didn't know you needed. Additionally, it carries small toys and games of yesteryear Americana (think wooden pick-up-sticks and vintage tiddlywinks), plus entire sections filled with candy jars and cases of Vermont cheese.

Crowds flock to the renowned summer theater at the **Weston Playhouse** (☎802-824-5288; www.westonplayhouse.org; 703 Main St; tickets $25-50; ⊙performances late Jun-early Sep), Vermont's oldest professional theater, just off the gazeboed circular

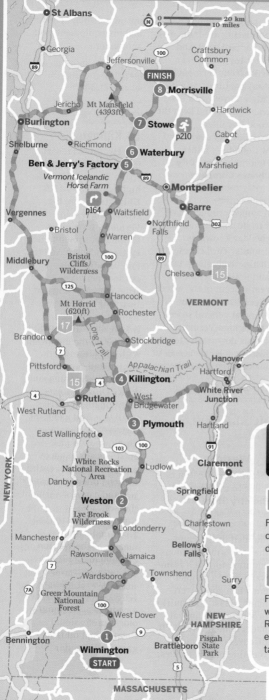

town green. The views upstream to Weston's waterfall and 19th-century mill are the stuff of tourist legend. Recent shows include Arthur Miller's *Death of a Salesman* (starring Christopher Lloyd of *Back to the Future* fame), *Fiddler on the Roof* and child-friendly *You're a Good Man, Charlie Brown*.

The Drive » Continue north on Rte 100. At Plymouth Union, veer off to the right onto Rte 100A for a few miles until you reach Plymouth Center.

❸ Plymouth

Gazing across the high pastures of Plymouth, you feel a bit like Rip Van Winkle – only it's the past you've woken up to. President Calvin Coolidge's boyhood home looks much as it

LINK YOUR TRIP

15 Cider Season Sampler

From Killington, head west on Rte 4 to enjoy fall's delicious delights.

17 Robert Frost Country

From Rochester, head west on Rte 73 to embrace Robert Frost's legacy and enjoy some wine and mead tasting.

did a century ago, with homes, barns, a church, a one-room schoolhouse and a general store gracefully arrayed among old maples on a bucolic hillside. At Plymouth's heart is the preserved **President Calvin Coolidge State Historic Site** (www.historicvermont. org/coolidge; 3780 Rte 100A; adult/child/family $7.50/2/20; ☻9:30am-5pm late May–mid-Oct). The village's streets seem sleepy today, but the museum tells a tale of an earlier America filled with elbow grease and perseverance. Tools for blacksmithing, woodworking, butter

making and hand-laundering are indicative of the hard work and grit it took to wrest a living from Vermont's stony pastures. As a boy, Calvin hayed with his grandfather and kept the wood box filled.

Originally cofounded by Coolidge's father, Plymouth's **Frog City Cheese Company** (www. frogcitycheese.com; 106 Messer Hill Rd; ☻9am-5pm) recently resumed production of a traditional farmhouse cheddar known as granular curd cheese. Its distinctively sharp tang and grainy texture are reminiscent of the wheel cheese traditionally found at general stores throughout Vermont. Panels downstairs tell the history of local cheese making, while a museum

upstairs displays cheese-making equipment from another era.

The Drive » Drive back along Rte 100A and turn right to return to Rte 100 N.

TRIP HIGHLIGHT

④ Killington

The largest ski resort in the east, Killington spans seven mountains, highlighted by 4241ft Killington Peak, the second highest in Vermont. It operates the largest snowmaking system in North America and its numerous outdoor activities – from winter skiing and boarding to summer mountain biking and hiking – are all centrally located on the mountain. Killington Resort, the East Coast's answer to Vail, runs the efficient **K1-Express Gondola** (☎802-422-3261; www. killington.com; round-trip $15; ☻10am-5pm late Jun-early Sep & Oct 1-8, Sat & Sun only early-late Sep), which in winter transports up to 3000 skiers per hour in heated cars along a 2.5-mile cable and is the highest lift in Vermont. In summer and fall it whisks you to impeccable vantage points above the mountains: leaf-peeping atop the cascade rainbow of copper, red and gold in foliage season is truly magical.

Note that, outside the winter peak,

DETOUR: VERMONT ICELANDIC HORSE FARM

Start: ④ **Killington**

Icelandic horses are one of the oldest, and some say most versatile, breeds in the world. They're also friendly and unbelievably affectionate beasts, and are fairly easy to ride even for novices – they tend to stop and think (rather than panic) if something frightens them. The **Vermont Icelandic Horse Farm** (☎802-496-7141; www.icelandichorses.com; N Basin Rd, Waitsfield; rides 1-3hr $50-100, full day incl lunch $195; ☻riding tours by appointment), 3 miles west of Rte 100 (the tarmac ends and becomes a dirt road), takes folks on one- to three-hour or full-day jaunts year-round; it also offers two- to five-day inn-to-inn treks (some riding experience required). The farm also runs **Mad River Inn** (www.madriverinn.com; r incl breakfast $125-175), a pleasant inn a short trot away.

establishments restrict their opening times. Be sure to call in advance to confirm hours.

✕ ⨿ p169

The Drive ›› Continue on Rte 100 N. Roughly 10 miles past Rochester, the road enters a narrow and wild corridor of protected land. A little pullout on the left provides viewing access to pretty Moss Glen Falls. A mile or so later, the small ponds of Granville Gulf comprise one of the state's most accessible moose-watching spots (the best chance of seeing these big critters is at dawn or dusk).

- - - - - - - - - - - - - - -

TRIP HIGHLIGHT

❺ Ben & Jerry's Factory

No trip to Vermont would be complete without a visit to the **Ben & Jerry's Factory** (www.benjerry.com; 1281 Waterbury-Stowe Rd/Rte 100, Waterbury; tours $4; ⊙9am-9pm late Jun–mid-Aug, to 7pm mid-Aug–late Oct, 10am-6pm late Oct–late Jun), the biggest production center for America's most famous ice cream. Yeah, the ice-cream making is interesting but a visit to the factory also explains how school pals Ben and Jerry went from a $5 ice-cream-making correspondence course to a global enterprise and offers a glimpse of the fun in-your-face culture that made these ice-cream pioneers so successful. You're treated to a (very) small free

VERMONT FRESH NETWORK

Fresh local food is never far away in the Green Mountain State, thanks to the **Vermont Fresh Network** (www.vermontfresh.net), a partnership between the state's restaurants and farmers. Restaurants commit to supporting local producers by buying direct from the farm, while 'farmers dinners' throughout the year allow diners to meet the people who put the food on their table. For a full list of participating restaurants and upcoming events, see the website.

taste at the end, but if you need a larger dose beeline for the on-site scoop shop.

Quaintly perched on a knoll overlooking the parking lot, the Ben & Jerry's Flavor Graveyard's neat rows of headstones pay silent tribute to flavors that flopped, like Makin' Whoopie Pie and Dastardly Mash. Each memorial is lovingly inscribed with the flavor's brief life span on the grocery store of this earth and a poem in tribute. Rest in Peace Holy Cannoli, 1997–1998! Adieu Miss Jelena's Sweet Potato Pie, 1992–1993!

The Drive ›› Continue along Rte 100 for a few miles and you'll start to enter the commercial end of Waterbury – your next stop is on your right.

- - - - - - - - - - - - - - -

❻ Waterbury

The waft of fresh pressed cider hits you before you reach the door: see how it's made at **Cold Hollow**

Cider Mill (www.coldhollow. com; ⊙8am-7pm Jul–late Oct, to 6pm late Oct-Jun), which features a working cider press to make its cloudy nonalcoholic cider and famous cider doughnuts (guaranteed love at first bite). The cider itself tastes so crisp and fresh you'd swear there was a spigot coming right out of the apple. The gift shop is packed with the most inventive gourmet goodies in town, including corn relish, horseradish jam and piccalilli.

Afterward, walk across the parking lot to the **Grand View Winery** (www. grandviewwinery.com; 4 tastes $2; ⊙11am-5pm) for sips of its award-winning wines. Options vary by season but on our visit we sampled the delicate non-oaky Riesling, strawberry rhubarb fruit wine and, for the first time, dandelion wine. Our verdict? Aromatic, slightly sweet and grin-inducing yumminess.

Classic Trip

ASSEMBLY/GETTY IMAGES ©

HILARY MCHONE/GETTY IMAGES ©

LOCAL KNOWLEDGE
WILL WIQUIST, GREEN MOUNTAIN CLUB

One of the easiest walking trails in the area is the Short Trail, right behind the **Green Mountain Club visitor center** (www.greenmountainclub. org; 4711 Waterbury-Stowe Rd, Waterbury; ⊘9am-5pm mid-May–mid-Oct, 10am-5pm Mon-Fri mid-Oct–mid-May). **It's a fairly flat loop with picnic areas, and boasts views of Mt Worcester and Stowe Pinnacle on the way back. Another option is the Kirchner Woods Trail** (www.stowelandtrust.org), **where you enjoy fine mountain views while roaming among hardwoods, maple trees and a working sugar house.**

Top: Soak up the sun at a resort in Stowe
Left: Hiker takes in Vermont views
Right: Stowe

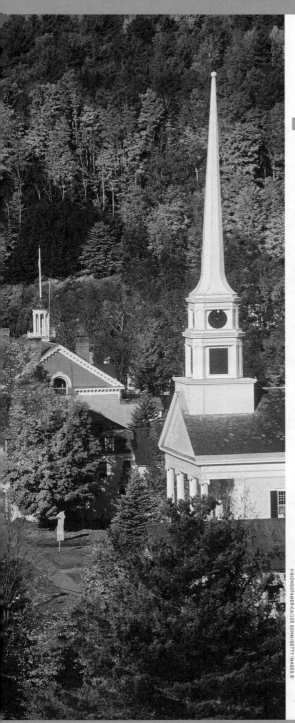

The Drive » Wipe that ice-cream smile off your face and replace it with an ear-to-ear grin as you ascend Rte 100 to the magnificent Vermont ski village of Stowe.

TRIP HIGHLIGHT

⑦ Stowe

In a cozy valley where the West Branch River flows into the Little River and mountains rise to the sky in all directions, the quintessential Vermont village of Stowe (founded in 1794) bustles quietly; see our walk on p210. Nestled in the Green Mountain National Forest, the highest point in Vermont, Mt Mansfield (4393ft) towers in the background, juxtaposed against the town, making this *the* classic Vermont picture-postcard scene. With more than 200 miles of cross-country ski trails, some of the finest mountain biking and downhill skiing in the east, and world-class hiking, this is a natural mecca for adrenaline junkies and active families.

In addition to winter snow sports, **Stowe Mountain Resort** (www. stowe.com; Mountain Rd) opens from spring through to fall with **gondola sky rides** (adult/child $25/17; ☺10am-4:30pm late Jun–mid-Oct), **an alpine slide** (adult/child $17/15; ☺10:30am-4:30pm late Jun–mid-Oct, Sat & Sun only Sep-Oct) **and a scenic**

VISIONSOFAMERICA/JOE SOHM/GETTY IMAGES ©

Classic Trip

auto **toll road** (per car $27; ⊙ late May–mid-Oct) that zigzags to the top of Mt Mansfield.

If *The Sound of Music* is one of your favorite things, the hilltop **Trapp Family Lodge** (www. trappfamily.com; 700 Trapp Hill Rd) boasts sprawling views and oodles of activities, such as hiking, horse-drawn sleigh and carriage rides, lodge tours detailing the family history (often led by a member of the Trapp family), summer concerts on their meadow and frothy goodness at the on-site Trapp Family Brewery.

✕ 🛏 p169

THE VERMONT REPUBLIC 1777–91

Vermont held its ground as an independent republic for 14 years (eat your heart out, Texas!) before joining the union. In July 1777, Vermonters drafted the first constitution to outlaw slavery, authorize a public school system and give every man (regardless of property ownership) the right to vote. In recent years, the Second Vermont Republic movement has begun clamoring for secession. Vermont's independent spirit lives on!

The Drive » Continue along Rte 100 – you'll pass pretty Christmas-tree farms on either side before reaching your final stop.

- - - - - - - - - -

❽ Morrisville

When you see the logo bearing a Kokopelli flute-player off to the left, you know you've arrived at **Rock Art Brewery** (www. rockartbrewery.com; 632 Laporte Rd/Rte 100; 4-5 tastes in souvenir glass $4; ⊙10am-5:30pm Mon-Sat, free tours Fri & Sat 2pm & 4pm). Pop into the friendly tasting room and brewery for samples, including the signature American Red, a malty pale ale that also goes by the nickname 'Super Glide,' because, you know, it glides down oh-so-easily.

Eating & Sleeping

Wilmington ❶

✖ Wahoo's Eatery — American $

(☎802-464-0110; VT 9; burgers, sandwiches & wraps $5-7.25; ⏰ lunch & dinner May-Oct) This local institution is a mere roadside snack shack, less than a mile west of VT 100, but it whips up quality burgers (made with grass-fed Vermont beef), hand-cut fries and handmade conch fritters, plus wraps, sandwiches, hot dogs, salads and ice cream.

🛏 Old Red Mill Inn & Restaurant — Inn $

(☎802-464-3700; www.oldredmill.com; Rte 100 N; s $55-65, d $70-80; ⏰ closed Apr–mid-Jun & Nov; 📶) This converted former sawmill overlooking the Deerfield River offers simple rooms (chunky wood furnishings, checkered bedspreads). Original millworks occupy common areas and on-site food ($10 to $25) varies by season: summer picnic fare is served at Jerry's Deck Bar & Grill; in winter, the rustic interior dining room takes over with hearty New England favorites.

Killington ❹

✖ Vermont Inn — American $$$

(☎802-775-0708; US 4; meals $17-28; ⏰ dinner) One of the mountain's best-value dining options, the inn offers rack of lamb, local veal and variations on the steak theme. The menu changes nightly and is served next to a cozy fireplace in winter.

🛏 Inn at Long Trail — Inn $$

(☎802-775-7181; www.innatlongtrail.com; 709 US 4; r incl breakfast $120-140, ste $150; 📶) The first hotel expressly built (in 1938) as a ski lodge, the rustic decor makes use of tree trunks (the bar is fashioned from a single log). The rooms are cozy and suites include fireplaces.

Stowe ❼

✖ Blue Moon Café — International $$$

(☎802-253-7006; www.bluemoonstowe.com; 35 School St; meals $18-31; ⏰ dinner Wed-Sun) In a converted house with a little sun porch, this intimate bistro is one of New England's top restaurants. Mains change monthly, but the contemporary cuisine usually includes something like crab cakes, salmon dishes, steak with chipotle and jicama or dishes utilizing locally foraged mushrooms.

✖ Depot Street Malt Shoppe — Diner $

(☎802-253-4269; 57 Depot St; dishes $4-10; ⏰11:30am-9pm) Burgers, chocolate sundaes and old-fashioned malteds reign at this fun, 1950s-themed restaurant. The egg creams hit the spot in any season.

🛏 Brass Lantern Inn B&B — B&B $$

(☎802-253-2229; www.brasslanterninn.com; 71 Maple St, Rte 100; r incl breakfast $105-235; 📶) Just north of the village, this beautiful inn has spacious, antique-laden rooms with handmade quilts, some featuring fireplaces and views of Mt Mansfield.

🛏 Trapp Family Lodge — Lodge $$$

(☎802-253-8511; www.trappfamily.com; 700 Trapp Hill Rd; r from $270; @📶🏊) This is *the* spot for taking a twirl and pretending you're Julie Andrews. The Austrian-style chalet, built by Maria von Trapp of *The Sound of Music* fame, houses traditional lodge rooms, or you can rent one of the modern villas or cozy guesthouses (prices are highly variable; call to inquire) scattered across the property.

Woodstock *A picture-perfect Autumn landscape*

Cider Season Sampler

15

Vermont is radiant in harvest season, its farm stands overflowing with fresh produce and leaves just showing the first hints of color.

TRIP HIGHLIGHTS

Cambridge

Burlington

4

93 miles

Shelburne
Hop in a wagon and
take a farm tour

Barre

Middlebury

East
Thetford
FINISH

START
1

Rutland

3

Bridgewater Corners
Decide if Long Trail is
your favorite Vermont
craft beer

15 miles

Quechee
Stare down at
Vermont's version of
the Grand Canyon

1 mile

3–4 DAYS
225 MILES / 363KM

GREAT FOR...

BEST TIME TO GO
August to October,
when apple-picking is
at its prime.

 **ESSENTIAL
PHOTO**

Capture the orchards
at Shelburne Farms in
the early evening light.

 **BEST FOR
FOODIES**

Crisp apples from
Shelburne Farms and
dinner at Simon Pearce,
a divine meal with a view.

171

15 Cider Season Sampler

When most people think Vermont food and drink, beer or maple syrup come to mind. But these days, vineyards are brimming with excitement and locavore restaurants are sprouting like mushrooms around the state. Chefs, farmers and communities have begun to work together in mutually supportive ways and autumn is the best time to embrace the bounty in a blaze of colors.

TRIP HIGHLIGHT

1 Quechee

Vermont's answer to the Grand Canyon, the **Quechee Gorge** is a 163ft-deep scar that cuts about 3000ft along a stream. View it from the bridge or work off those pancake breakfasts with a hike to the bottom – the 15-minute descent through pine forest is beautiful, following a trail on the south side of Hwy 4.

Drop by the **Charlotte Village Winery's** tasting

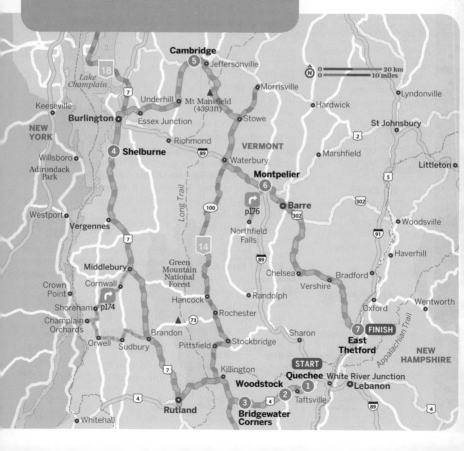

room (3968 Greenbush Rd; ⊙ 11am-5pm), at the gorge parking lot, for free samples of its grape and fruit varietals, such as peach Chardonnay or dry blueberry wine – a remarkably complex, spicy tipple that packs a punch.

In downtown Quechee Village, beeline to **Simon Pearce** (www.simonpearce. com; 1760 Main St; ⊙ store 9am-4pm, glassblowing 9am-9pm), in the old woolen mill cantilevered out over the Ottauquechee River. Pearce, an Irish glassblower, immigrated to Quechee in 1981, drawn by a vision of running his entire operation self-sufficiently with hydro power. Three decades later, he's built a small empire. His flagship Quechee store displays pottery and glassware

LINK YOUR TRIP

14 **Vermont's Spine: Route 100**

Connect to Rte 100 after Cambridge to explore Vermont's mountain-hugging road.

18 **Lake Champlain Byway**

In Shelburne you can connect with this scenic journey up through Vermont's Champlain Islands.

DON'T MISS: MORE THAN HOT AIR

While the Quechee-Woodstock general area affords no end of outdoor activities, none is likely to prove as memorable as a balloon ride. **Balloons Over New England** (📞 800-788-5562; www.balloonsovernewengland. com) does it in style, with 'champagne' trips that last 2½ to three hours and cost from $350 per person.

and offers glassblowing demonstrations daily.

✕ p177

The Drive » Follow Rte 4 west to Woodstock.

- - - - - - - - - - - - - -

❷ Woodstock

Chartered in 1761, Woodstock has been the highly dignified seat of scenic Windsor County since 1766. The townspeople built grand Federal and Greek Revival homes surrounding the oval village green, and four of Woodstock's churches can claim bells cast by Paul Revere. Senator Jacob Collamer, a friend of Abraham Lincoln's, once observed, 'The good people of Woodstock have less incentive than others to yearn for heaven.'

Billings Farm & Museum (www.billingsfarm. org; VT 12; adult/child/student/senior $12/3/6/11, incl Marsh-Billings-Rockefeller National Historical Park adult/child 16-17yr/senior $17/15/13; ⊙10am-5pm daily May-Oct, 10am-3:30pm Sat & Sun Nov-Feb, closed Mar-Apr) employs

a mix of 19th- and 20th-century methods. Visitor activities vary with the seasons, from horse and sleigh rides to the afternoon milking of the cows to demonstrations of strawberry shortcake made in the cast-iron stove.

The **Marsh-Billings-Rockefeller National Historical Park** (www. nps.gov/mabi; Elm St; mansion tours adult/child/senior $8/free/$4; ⊙10am-5pm May-Oct, tours every 30min) contains a mansion with exhibits on environmental conservation and 20 miles of trails. Combined tickets with Billings Farm & Museum are available.

🛏 p177

The Drive » Drive west on Rte 4 to Bridgewater Corners, following the curve of the Ottauquechee a few miles upstream.

- - - - - - - - - - - - - -

TRIP HIGHLIGHT

❸ Bridgewater Corners

Located in an unassuming spot right

off the road on the left, **Long Trail Brewery** (www. longtrail.com; cnr Rtes 4 & 100A; ⊙brewery 10am-6pm, pub food 11am-5pm) is what many consider to be Vermont's number one producer of craft beer. On a sunny day, it's delightful to sit in its riverside beer garden, modeled after Munich's Hofbrauhaus. Inside is a cozy beer hall that's great for sampling brews. Check out the self-guided brewery tour on the 2nd floor – the small platform explaining the process is worth visiting if you want to know how that frothy goodness is produced. The brewpub serves snacks and meals, but we prefer to stick to the drinks.

DETOUR: CHAMPLAIN ORCHARDS

Start: ❸ **Bridgewater Corners**

After passing through Rutland on Rte 7, hop onto Rte 73 west in Brandon and follow the lazy curves of Otter Creek for a couple of miles before breaking into wide open farm country cascading toward Lake Champlain. Just shy of the lakeshore, double back east on Rte 74 to **Champlain Orchards** (www.champlainorchards.com; 2955 Rte 74 W, Shoreham; ⊙8am-6pm Jul-Oct; 🏕), where you can pick two-dozen varieties of apples (including many New England heirlooms) or watch the pressing and bottling of ultra-fresh cider. The orchard is famous for its free 'while-you-pick' acoustic concerts and an annual October harvest celebration. After, continue on Rte 74 west until it hits Rte 7 in Middlebury and head north.

The Drive » Continue on Rte 4 west through Killington; you'll cut straight across the Green Mountains. In Rutland, take Rte 7 north to Shelburne.

TRIP HIGHLIGHT

❹ Shelburne

In 1886 William Seward Webb and Lila Vanderbilt Webb built a little place for themselves on Lake Champlain. The 1400-acre farm, designed by landscape architect Frederick Law Olmsted (who also designed New York's Central Park), was both a country house for the Webbs and a working farm. These days, the century-old estate and National Historic Landmark exists as **Shelburne Farms** (www.shelburnefarms.org; off US 7; adult/child 3-17yr/senior with tour $11/7/9, without tour $8/5/6; ⊙cheese making, tours, inn & farmyard 9am-5:30pm mid-May–mid-Oct, walking trails 10am-4pm year-round, 1½hr tours 9:30am, 11:30am, 1:30pm & 3:30pm; 🏕), a working farm and environmental education center.

Tours, in a truck-pulled open wagon, are a barrel of fun: you can admire the buildings (inspired by European Romanticism), observe cheese making, and learn about maple syrup and mustard production. Hikers can meander the walking trails and kids love the animals in the children's farmyard. In mid-September, drop by and celebrate autumn traditions at the annual Harvest Festival, featuring hay rides, a hay-bale maze, music and antique farm machines.

✕ 🛏 p177

The Drive » Head north on Rte 7 through Burlington (p212). Hop on Rte 15, then Rte 128, then Rte 104.

❺ Cambridge

Even fermented berries have a place in Vermont's food culture. When harvest season is over, some of them go into the dessert wines at **Boyden Valley Winery** (www.boydenvalley.com; cnr Rtes 15 & 104; ⊙10am-5pm, closed Mon-Thu Jan-Apr), **20 miles north in the stunningly beautiful Lamoille River**

Farm-fresh pumpkins

175

DETOUR: COVERED BRIDGE CENTRAL

Start: ⑥ Montpelier

Vermont is rich in these classic beauties, but you generally don't get two (and almost three) for the price of one. From Montpelier, take VT 12 southwest to Northfield Falls to the intersection of Cox Brook Rd, where two covered bridges are within walking distance of each other. **Station Bridge** and **Newell Bridge** both span a section of the river that's about 100ft across. **Upper Bridge** is a bit further up Cox Brook Rd.

valley at the foot of Mt Mansfield. Savor the views and check out the award-winning Gold Leaf, a Vermont-inspired concoction that uses maple syrup straight from the farm combined with local apples.

The Drive ≫ Continue on Rte 104 east to Rte 15 to Rte 100 south. In Waterbury hop on I-89 east.

- - - - - - - - - - -

⑥ Montpelier

With 9000 residents, Montpelier is America's smallest capital city and the only one without a McDonald's. It's home to the prestigious New England Culinary Institute (NECI), so stop here for a dose of Vermont history paired with fine food.

Adjacent to the gold-domed **State House** (www.vtstatehouse.org; State St; admission & tours free; ⊘8am-

4pm Mon-Sat, tours every 30min 10am-3:30pm Mon-Fri, 11am-2:30pm Sat Jul–mid-Oct), whose front doors are guarded by a massive statue of American Revolutionary hero Ethan Allen, is the **Vermont Historical Society** (http://vermonthistory.org; State St; adult/student/senior $12/3/5; ⊘10am-4pm Tue-Sat, noon-4pm Sun May-Oct). Its award-winning 'Freedom and Unity' exhibit walks you through 400 years of Vermont history. From your first few steps into an Abenaki wigwam, you're asked to consider the true meaning of this state motto. Controversies aren't brushed under the rug, either: a short film presents the early-20th-century debate over women's suffrage alongside footage from the 1999 statehouse hearings where citizens

voiced their support or opposition to civil unions. In a very Vermontish way, you're invited to ponder issues on your own (versus assent to someone else's party line). The panoply of voices and imaginative presentation keep this exhibit fun and lively.

✕ ⊨ p177

The Drive ≫ Next, head southeast along Rtes 110 and 113 to the Connecticut River in East Thetford.

- - - - - - - - - - -

⑦ East Thetford

Like a roadside farm stand on organic steroids, **Cedar Circle Farm** (www.cedarcirclefarm.org; Pavilion Rd; ⊘10am-6pm Mon-Sat, to 5pm Sun; ♣) offers endless opportunities to appreciate Vermont's summer bounty: pick-your-own strawberries, blueberries, flowers and pumpkins and the opportunity to wander through lush fields of produce or lounge in an Adirondack chair by the river. Summer and fall events include dinners in the field, workshops on canning and freezing, and strawberry (June) and pumpkin (October) festivals.

The Drive ≫ Hop on I-91 south, then I-89 north to return to Quechee.

Eating & Sleeping

Quechee ❶

✕ Simon Pearce Restaurant
International $$

(📞802-295-1470; The Mill, Main St; meals $15-35; 🕑lunch & dinner) Angle for a window seat overlooking the waterfall and covered bridge, where you can drink from Pearce-made stemware blown by hand in the adjacent glass workshops. Enjoy specialties such as sesame-seared chicken or field-greens salad with Vermont blue or goat cheese.

Woodstock ❷

🛏 Ardmore Inn
Inn $$

(📞802-457-3887, 800-497-5692; www.ardmoreinn.com; 23 Pleasant St; r incl breakfast $135-215; 📶) In a stately 1867 Victorian–Greek Revival building, this congenial, centrally located inn features five antique-laden rooms with oriental rugs and private marble bathrooms. Breakfasts are seemingly never-ending.

Shelburne ❹

✕ Bistro Sauce
International $$

(📞802-985-2830; 97 Falls Rd; meals $15-30; 🕑lunch & dinner daily, brunch Sun) Expect anything from market fish with preserved-lemon risotto to vegetable tart with curried quinoa at this relaxed and casual farmhouse bistro. It takes the locavore movement a step further than most: butter comes from nearby farms and wild-foraged mushrooms appear seasonally. A stellar wine list and local, live music rounds out a meal; the bar is also a prime hangout.

🛏 Inn at Shelburne Farms
Inn $$

(📞802-985-8498; www.shelburnefarms.org; 1611 Harbor Rd; r from $220, with shared bathroom $170-200; 🕑mid-May–mid-Oct; 📶) One of the top 10 places to stay in New England, here you can indulge in a decadent lifestyle by taking tea (served every afternoon), or chill out playing billiards in one of the common areas, complete with elegant, original furnishings. Four cottages (scattered across the property) with full kitchens are also available from $320 per night.

Montpelier ❻

✕ NECI on Main
American $$

(📞802-223-3188; 118 Main St; brunch $18, meals $16-25; 🕑lunch & dinner Tue-Sat, brunch Sun) The New England Culinary Institute's signature restaurant is a multilevel spot boasting an open window to the kitchen – this allows you to watch first-year student chefs at work. The fare features locavore produce and Sunday brunch is an excellent all-you-can-eat affair.

✕ La Brioche
Cafe, Bakery $

(📞802-229-0443; 89 Main St; sandwiches $5-8; 🕑6:30am-7pm Mon-Fri, 7:30am-5pm Sat & Sun) NECI's first restaurant is a casual bakery and cafe offering soups and sandwiches on homemade bread, among other things. It starts running out of items at about 2pm, so time it right if you're hungry.

🛏 Inn at Montpelier
Inn $$$

(📞802-223-2727; www.innatmontpelier.com; 147 Main St; r incl continental breakfast $165-250; 📶) This first-rate inn made up of two refurbished Federal houses right in the heart of town boasts luxurious rooms with fireplaces. Coffee in wicker rocking chairs on the wraparound veranda is the perfect tonic for a lazy afternoon.

Montgomery Pick your favorite covered bridge in this bucolic village

Vermont Back-Roads Ramble

16

Proudly rural, sometimes bizarre, always an adventure: the pace slows off the beaten path, but Vermont is never dull. Discover why the most rewarding journeys often lurk down the curve of a dirt road.

TRIP HIGHLIGHTS

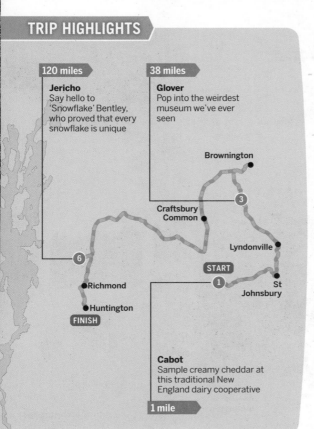

120 miles

Jericho
Say hello to 'Snowflake' Bentley, who proved that every snowflake is unique

38 miles

Glover
Pop into the weirdest museum we've ever seen

Brownington

Craftsbury Common

Lyndonville

START
1

St Johnsbury

6

Richmond

Huntington

FINISH

Cabot
Sample creamy cheddar at this traditional New England dairy cooperative

1 mile

3–4 DAYS
144 MILES / 232KM

GREAT FOR...

BEST TIME TO GO
May to October for warmish weather and snow-free roads.

ESSENTIAL PHOTO
Snap the papier-mâché creatures at the Bread & Puppet Museum.

BEST FOR OUTDOORS
Enjoy stunning vistas of bucolic rolling hills and peaceful, sparsely populated countryside.

16 | Vermont Back-Roads Ramble

Some say this is the real Vermont: historic villages frozen in time, narrow mountain passes crossed by dirt roads, expanses of farmland stretching out to lush maple-covered mountains and swimming holes at the foot of waterfalls. Warning: this trip is full of curves, backtracking and dirt roads without phone service. Promise: oodles of fun capturing the spirit of meandering back roads that makes Vermont so addictive to spontaneous explorers.

TRIP HIGHLIGHT

1 Cabot

Despite its nationwide distribution network, **Cabot Creamery** (www.cabotcheese.com; 2878 Main St; ⏱9am-5pm Jun-Oct, 9am-4pm Nov-Dec & Feb-May, 10am-4pm Jan; tours $2) remains basically true to its roots as a New England dairy cooperative. Its half-hour tour gives you a look at the cheese-making process (not to mention high-tech machinery painted like Holsteins), after which you can pig

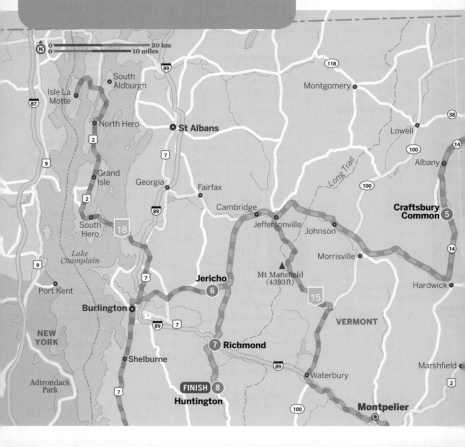

out to your heart's content in the sample room.

The Drive » Chart a zigzag course along Rte 232, Rte 15 and Hwy 2 to St Johnsbury and then I-91 into Lyndonville.

❷ St Johnsbury & Lyndonville

Home to the country's oldest art gallery (founded in 1871) still in its original form, the **St Johnsbury Athenaeum** (www.stjathenaeum.org; 1171 Main St; admission $8; ⏱10am-5pm) is built around its crown jewel, Albert Bierstadt's 10ft-

COVERED BRIDGES OF MONTGOMERY

A 20-mile drive north from Johnson via Rtes 100C and 118 takes you to the covered-bridge capital of Vermont. In an idyllic valley at the confluence of multiple watersheds, the twin villages of Montgomery and Montgomery Center share seven spans crisscrossing the local rivers. Especially beautiful – though challenging to find – is remote **Creamery Bridge** just off Hill West Rd, which straddles a waterfall with a swimming hole at its base.

by-15ft painting *Domes of the Yosemite*. The rest of the collection consists of works by such Hudson River School painters as Asher B Durand, Worthington Whittredge and Jasper Crospey.

It's tough to label the **Lyndonville Freighthouse** (☏802-626-1174; www.thelyndonfreighthouse.com; 1000 Braid St; ⏱6:30am-2:30pm, extended hours Apr-Oct). The authentic 1870 railroad freight house consists of a country store (selling Vermont staples and trinkets), a local art gallery, and a family restaurant and

ice-cream counter, but most of all, head upstairs for its **tiny railroad museum** and check out the miniature train whistling its way along the track.

✕ ⊨ p185

The Drive » Hop on Rte 122 west. After 14.5 miles, look for a bright turquoise school bus on your left.

TRIP HIGHLIGHT

❸ Glover

You'll encounter the bus first, parked across from the barn with painted letters proclaiming

LINK YOUR TRIP

15 Cider Season Sampler

After Craftsbury Common, join the Cider Season Sampler trip in Cambridge for a taste of Vermont harvest season.

18 Lake Champlain Byway

After Richmond hop on I-89 north to Burlington for a trip along pristine islands and jagged shorelines.

'Cheap Art Store.' Get ready for the super wacky – you've stumbled upon the **Bread & Puppet Museum** (www.breadandpuppet.org; 753 Heights Rd; admission free; ⏲10am-6pm Mon-Sat), a tour de force of avant-garde art. For nearly 50 years, the internationally renowned theater has been staging politically charged, satirical spectacles. It tours nationally and internationally outside of summer; Vermont performances take place on weekends in July through August, starring gigantic puppets (some up to 20ft tall) borne through the fields on the company's hilltop farm. When no show is going on, visit the museum in the cavernous old barn and admire freakishly frightening but impressive papier-mâché angels, devils, horses and other fantastic creatures from past performances, hauntingly crammed across two stories. Oh, and the name? The director bakes bread and shares it with the audience at each performance to create a sense of community.

🛏 p185

DETOUR:
HILL FARMSTEAD BREWERY

Start: ❸ Glover

You know you're getting close when the asphalt disappears and you haven't had a phone signal for 30 minutes. Down two dirt roads in the middle of nowhere (town population roughly 600), **Hill Farmstead Brewery** (📞802-533-7450; www.hillfarmstead.com; 403 Hill Rd, Greensboro Bend; 4 tastes $5; ⏲12-5pm Wed-Sat but call to confirm, tours by appointment) is, well, a farm on a hill, with a garage that holds a brewery and tasting nook. It produces a mere 300 to 400 gallons per week, and the output rarely leaves the state, yet Hill Farmstead has a cult following for its small-batch brews.

Produced by Shaun Hill, known for his creative concoctions and uncompromising adherence to quality, many of the beers have names based on the Hill family: Damon, a bourbon barrel–aged Russian Imperial Stout, is the namesake of Shaun's childhood dog; the hoppy IPA, Edward, is named after Shaun's grandfather. Bitter, malty, spicy – friendly staff will guide you to your favorite at the tiny bar. Sips of this stuff guarantee a satisfied smile.

The Drive ≫ Continue west along Rte 122 and turn right onto Rte 16 north. Merge with Rte 5 and in Orleans turn east (right) onto Rte 58 to reach another sleeping beauty, Brownington.

- - - - - - - - - - -

❹ Brownington

Brownington's well preserved but little visited **Old Stone House Museum** (www.oldstonehousemuseum.org; 109 Old Stone House Rd; adult/child $8/3; ⏲11am-5pm Wed-Sun mid-May–mid-Oct) is just one of many lovely 19th-century buildings reposing under the shade of equally ancient maple trees. The museum pays tribute to educational trailblazer Alexander Twilight, the USA's first African American college graduate, who built Brownington's boarding school and ran it for decades.

The Drive ≫ Take Rte 14 south. After Albany, veer left onto Wylie Hill Rd, which becomes North Craftsbury Rd, Craftsbury Common's main street.

- - - - - - - - - - -

❺ Craftsbury Common

A short jaunt off the main road takes you through Craftsbury Common, where you'll find what may be Vermont's most spectacular village green. White clapboard buildings surround a rectangular lawn that hasn't changed one

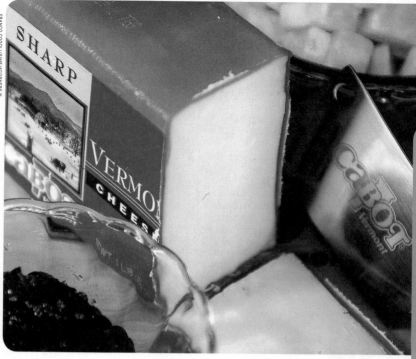

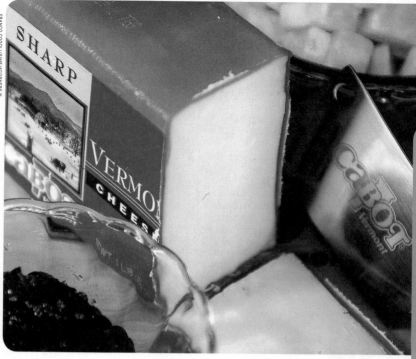

FRANCO COGOLI/SIME/4CORNERS ©

Cabot Taste-test the cheese at Cabot Creamery

iota since the mid-19th century.

✕ 🛏 p185

The Drive » Continue on North Craftsbury Rd and turn left on Rte 14 and continue south. At Hardwick segue with Rte 15 – look for the Fisher Covered Railroad Bridge on your left. This century-old span, with its cupola designed as an outlet for steam locomotives' smoke, is among the last covered railroad bridges in America still in regular use.

TRIP HIGHLIGHT

❻ Jericho

The ultra-photogenic **Old Red Mill** (www.jerichohistoricalsociety.org/mill.htm; Rte 15; admission free; ⊙10am-5pm Mon-Sat, 1-5pm Sun) sits astride the Browns River gorge. Inside the mill, a nice display of Vermont crafts shares space with a free museum showcasing the captivating microphotography of native son 'Snowflake' Bentley, who provided groundbreaking evidence that no two snowflakes are created equal. Out back, the Browns River Trail traverses a soft carpet of evergreen needles to a little sandy beach with big boulders and a deep pool for swimming.

The Drive » Continue south on Browns Trace Rd to Rte 117, then continue on Rte 2 east into Richmond.

❼ Richmond

Richmond is a small town that has done a remarkable job of preserving its village feel, despite the encroachment of Burlington's suburbs and a major interstate highway just west. Visit the early-19th-century **Old Round Church** (www.oldroundchurch.com; Bridge St; admission free; ⊙Jun-Oct), one of Vermont's most unique structures. The graceful 16-sided

LOCAL KNOWLEDGE:
COMMUNITY + LOCAL FARE = SUCCESS

The locavore movement, promoting the idea of seasonal food obtained from local sources, is the norm in Vermont, but **Claire's** (www.clairesvt.com; 41 South Main St, Hardwick; dishes $12-30; ⊙5-9pm Mon-Sat, 11-2pm & 5-8pm Sun, closed Wed winter) takes it one step further and is a poster child for how a community can make a difference. It was launched in 2008 by business leaders as a community-supported enterprise, and neighbors invested $1000 up front in return for discounts on meals. The result? A thriving restaurant that supports the local community. Produce is largely sourced from within 15 miles of the restaurant and 80% of every dollar the restaurant spends on food goes directly to the farmers. It also features the country's first corn syrup–free bar, with natural sodas and mixers. The wine list features Vermont wines (oddly, most Vermont restaurant wine lists seem to favor Californian and foreign wines). It's also a local hangout and features live music every Thursday evening. Food is international with odes to Vermont, such as cocktails sweetened with maple syrup and local-ale-infused sauces.

Jim Flint, Northeast Kingdom resident

edifice, used by multiple congregations over the years, is as elegant inside as outside and sits tranquilly by the Winooski River.

In July and August, it's well worth checking in at **Owl's Head Blueberry Farm** (www.owlsheadfarm.com; 263 Blueberry Farm Rd; ⊙9am-4pm Fri-Sun, 5pm-sunset Tue & Thu, 10am-sunset Wed mid-July–late Aug), a scenic spot to pick your own berries.

✕ p185

The Drive » The main road curves south of the Old Round Church toward Huntington.

- - - - - - - - - - - - - - -

⑧ Huntington

Huntington's gorgeous valley is presided over by Vermont's most distinctively shaped peak, the **Camel's Hump** (it actually looked like a sleeping lion to early French explorers). It remains one of the state's wildest spots, the only significant Vermont peak not developed for skiing, and the summit is a hiker's dream: from Huntington Center, head east 3 miles, dead-ending at the trailhead for the 6-mile Burrows to Forest City loop. After climbing through forest, the final ascent skirts rock faces above the tree line, affording magnificent views.

Eating & Sleeping

St Johnsbury & Lyndonville ❷

✗ Anthony's Diner
Diner $

(📞802-748-3613; 50 Railroad St; dishes $3-15; 🕐breakfast, lunch & dinner Mon-Sat, breakfast & lunch Sun) This is a local institution with a large counter. Try the mountain-size Vermont woodsman burger or sample the homemade soups, chowders and desserts – a deserved source of pride.

✗ Trout River Brewery
American $$

(📞802-626-9396; www.troutriverbrewing. com; Hwy 5; pizzas from $11; 🕐4-9pm Fri & Sat) Sample a few beers and try the sourdough pizza on Friday and Saturday nights.

🛏 Wildflower Inn
Inn $$

(📞800-627-8310, 802-626-8310; www. wildflowerinn.com; 2059 Darling Hill Rd; r $135-475; 🐾) With a 500-acre backyard and views that won't quit, the Wildflower rates among New England's family-friendliest inns. Feast your eyes on the amazing vistas from the farm surrounding the inn. Amenities include a petting barn, an outdoor hot tub and swimming pool, and miles of hiking trails.

Glover ❸

🛏 Rodgers Country Inn
Inn $$

(📞802-525-6677, 800-729-1704; http:// virtualvermont.com/rodgers; 582 Rodgers Rd; r per person incl breakfast per day from $80, cabins per week from $600) Not far from the shores of Shadow Lake, Jim and Nancy Rodgers offer five guest rooms in their 1840s farmhouse and two cabins for longer stays. Hang out on the front porch and read, or take a stroll on the

350-acre former dairy farm. The inn will appeal to those who really want to feel what it's like to live in rural Vermont. Three-course, home-cooked dinners are available to guests for $15 per person.

Craftsbury Common ❺

✗ Craftsbury General Store
American $

(📞802-586-2811; http://craftsburygeneralstore. com; 118 S Craftsbury Rd; 🕐7am-8pm, reduced hours in winter) The community-owned Craftsbury General Store serves tasty deli treats and a killer mac 'n' cheese. It showcases everything from local honey to handmade clothing and furniture in its Vermont Local Products section.

🛏 Craftsbury Inn
Inn $$

(📞802-586-2848, 800-336-2848; www. craftsburyinn.com; s/d incl breakfast from $90/100, with shared bathroom $60/90; 📶) This charming B&B sits across from the general store, half a mile east of Craftsbury Common. Breakfasts on the back porch are hearty affairs, enlivened by the occasional sighting of one of the llamas the owners keep on their farm.

Richmond ❼

✗ On the Rise Bakery
American $

(📞802-434-7787; www.ontherisebakery.net; Bridge St; 🕐7am-3pm Sun-Mon, to 8pm Tue, to 10pm Wed-Sat) Beyond the delectable baked goods, On the Rise wins points for its wood-fired pizzas and local microbrews. It's a good place to soak up some community spirit over a sandwich.

Rochester *Get a taste of small-town, rural Vermont life*

Robert Frost Country

17

Robert Frost's poetry drew on New England's rural life and settings. Embrace his prose and imagery at the Robert Frost Interpretive Trail, followed by tastes of Vermont wine and mead.

TRIP HIGHLIGHTS

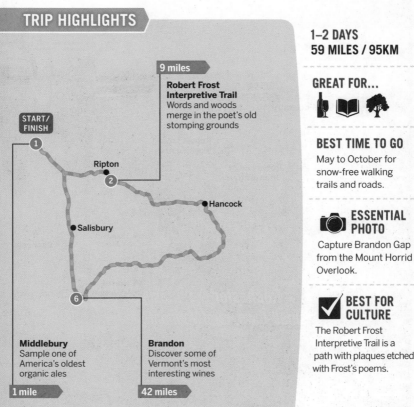

9 miles

Robert Frost Interpretive Trail
Words and woods merge in the poet's old stomping grounds

START/ FINISH

1

Ripton
2

● **Hancock**

● **Salisbury**

6

Middlebury
Sample one of America's oldest organic ales

1 mile

Brandon
Discover some of Vermont's most interesting wines

42 miles

1–2 DAYS
59 MILES / 95KM

GREAT FOR...

BEST TIME TO GO
May to October for snow-free walking trails and roads.

ESSENTIAL PHOTO
Capture Brandon Gap from the Mount Horrid Overlook.

BEST FOR CULTURE
The Robert Frost Interpretive Trail is a path with plaques etched with Frost's poems.

17 Robert Frost Country

This loop through Robert Frost country will take you deep into the Green Mountains and rural two-lane roads that cut up and over the mountain range. You'll start in hip college town Middlebury to sample one of Vermont's most popular microbrews, absorb Robert Frost poetry in the woods that inspired him and experience small-town Vermont life in Rochester. Last, you'll finish by tasting mead, the forefather of fermented drinks.

TRIP HIGHLIGHT

❶ Middlebury

Prosperity resides at the crossroads, and Middlebury obviously has its share. Aptly named, the town stands at the nexus of eight highways – as a result, it's always busy with traffic and the main square is lively and bustling.

A must-see for microbrew fans is **Otter Creek Brewery** (www.ottercreekbrewing.com; 793 Exchange St; ⊙10am-6pm

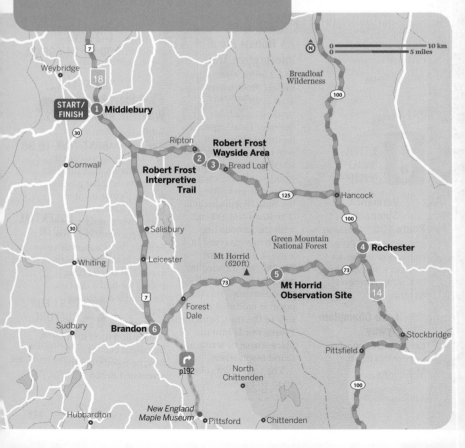

ROBERT FROST'S VERMONT

In 1920 Robert Frost (1874–1963) moved from New Hampshire to Vermont seeking 'a better place to farm and especially grow apples.' For almost four decades, Frost lived in the Green Mountain State, growing apples and writing much of his poetry in a log cabin in Ripton, a beautiful hamlet set in the Vermont mountains 10 miles southeast of Middlebury on Rte 125, where he kept a summer home. Today, tiny Ripton and the surrounding area in the Green Mountain National Forest have been officially designated **Robert Frost Country**.

Mon-Sat, 11am-4pm Sun), north of town. Tours three times daily (except Sunday) give you a chance to clamber amid vats of barley and hops, and taste samples afterwards to your heart's content. In addition to its many fine namesake brews, Otter Creek brews Wolaver's, one of America's oldest certified organic ales.

🍴 🛏 p193

The Drive » Drive east along Rte 125 through East

LINK YOUR TRIP

14 Vermont's Spine: Route 100

Connect to Rte 100 in Hancock or Rochester to explore the northern or southern portion of this trip.

18 Lake Champlain Byway

Connect to the starting point of this trip in Middlebury.

Middlebury, a lengthy linear village (set along a road instead of around a grassy square in the traditional Vermont manner) that's home to the Waybury Inn, famous as the inn in the 1980s hit TV show *Newhart*. Afterwards, wind your way up the mountain as you enter Robert Frost country.

- - - - - - - - - - - - -

2 Robert Frost Interpretive Trail

At 1.2 miles, the circular Robert Frost Interpretive Trail is an easy hike marked by half a dozen of Frost's poems mounted on wooden posts along the way, while the surrounding woods and meadows are highly evocative of his work. Poems include 'The Road Not Taken,' with the famous line 'Two roads diverged in a wood, and I/I took the one less traveled by/ and that has made all the difference.' Yes, this poem is mounted at a fork in the trail, bringing Frost's words into the place where he wrote and found inspiration.

The trail takes roughly 30 to 40 minutes,

depending on how often you stop. Look for wild blueberry bushes growing at the far end of the trail (the tiny berries usually ripen in summer, and nothing's more New England than eating them straight from the bush – mmmm).

The Drive » Drive less than a mile further east until you see the sign for the Robert Frost Wayside Area on the left.

- - - - - - - - - - - - -

3 Robert Frost Wayside Area

While the interpretive trail is an excellent way to embrace Frost's poetry in the woods, this turnoff contains detailed plaques with information about the poet and the time he spent living and teaching in the surrounding area. Beyond the plaques are several excellent picnic areas and the starting points for half a dozen well-marked walking trails.

Frost owned a farm nearby and used it when he taught classes – in fact, he cofounded the renowned Bread Loaf

School of English at Middlebury College. The farm is owned by the college (it is part of the Bread Loaf School), but you can take a peek at its exterior if you venture down Frost Rd, a dirt road just past the parking area.

The Drive » Continue east on Rte 125 to Hancock and turn right onto Rte 100 south.

4 Rochester

This unassuming blink-and-you'll-miss-it town, with a simple village green lined by well-maintained, historic New England homes, is worth a stop to experience rural Vermont life minus the masses of tourists in other towns.

The not-so-aptly-named **Big Town Gallery** (www.bigtowngallery. com; 99 North Main St; ☺10am-5pm Wed-Sat, 11am-4pm Sun) showcases small but excellent art exhibits; it also hosts a summer-long reading series and the popular BigTent festival, with poetry, music and performance art, each July. Also drop by **Sandy's Books & Bakery** (www.seasonedbooks. com; 30 North Main St; ☺7:30am-6pm Mon-Sat, to 2pm Sun; 🤙), a cafe and bookstore that serves as a local hangout. With homemade everything – granola, biscuits, bagels, whole-wheat bread – Sandy's serves up mean dishes such as spinach and egg-filled biscuits, spanakopita, salads and soups. Tables are scattered between bookshelves, so it's a great spot for a java break and a browse of the new and used books (or the locally made Vermont Soap). We dare you to resist the cookies.

 p193

The Drive » Drive west on Rte 73.

5 Mount Horrid Observation Site

The 'gap roads' that run east–west over the Green Mountains offer some of the most picturesque views of the region. Rte 73 from Rochester to Brandon crosses the Brandon Gap (2170ft), starting with a gentle climb up the spine of the mountain. Pull over at the Mount Horrid Observation Site, which overlooks a pretty little beaver pond and boasts views of the not-at-all-horrid 800ft Mount Horrid Cliff and the spectacular rolling mountains. Also keep an eye out for the resident white-bellied, grey- and black-colored peregrine falcons (also known as duck hawks), known for their high-speed hunting dives of over 200mph.

The Drive » Continue west on Rte 73.

🔵 LOCAL KNOWLEDGE: MOOSALAMOO NATIONAL RECREATION AREA

Straddling the area between Brandon, Rochester and Middlebury and accessible from all three towns, **Moosalamoo National Recreation Area** (www.moosalamoo. org) is packed with over 70 miles of trails great for walking, mountain biking and snowshoeing. You can also go horseback riding, or take advantage of the excellent berry-picking spots (there are wild strawberries, blackberries and raspberries). We use the website as it is chock-full of resources, including downloadable maps of trails. It's updated with recommendations according to season – for example, which trails are best for spring hiking or winter snowshoeing.

Rick Gottesman and Kathleen Byrne, owners of the Gathering Inn in Hancock

Blueberries Pick your own at many spots in Vermont

DETOUR:
NEW ENGLAND MAPLE MUSEUM

Start: **6** Brandon

Worth a jaunt south is the tiny but fascinating **New England Maple Museum** (www.maplemuseum.com; 45 Rte 7, Pittsford; adult/child $2.50/0.75; ⊙10am-4pm mid-Mar–late May & Nov-late Dec, 8:30am-5:30pm late May-Oct), which traces the history of maple syrup sugaring in Vermont. Read about how Native Americans discovered that maple sap cooked on an open fire produced what we know as maple syrup; ponder the antique photos of Vermont's maple sugarers; and inspect antique and modern sugaring utensils and equipment. You'll also learn how maple syrup is made today, from tapping trees to placing syrup into the bottles that appear on the table at pancake breakfasts. The visits include tastings, so you can find out if your favorite grade is fancy, medium or dark.

TRIP HIGHLIGHT

6 Brandon

Brandon is packed with antique shops, restaurants and galleries. But the best reason to stop is to indulge your inner oenophile at **Tastes of the Valley** (www.neshoberiverwinery.com; 8 Park St; ⊙10am-6pm Tue-Sat Nov-Apr, to 9pm Fri May-Oct), a friendly tasting room run by the Neshobe River Winery. Start with a sample of the off-dry white Traminette; the balanced Frontenac red, affably named Purple Haze; or the fruit wine Cassis (made with blackcurrants). It also pours Vermont tipples for wineries and distillers that don't have their own tasting rooms, such as Eden Ice Cider, the award-winning dessert wine made from apples (fruit is pressed when ice-cold from the Vermont winter, producing a concentrated, high-sugar liquid heaven), and the small-batch Vermont Artesano Meads. Made from honey and fruit, mead is supple and sometimes more dry than sweet, depending on the variety. When we stopped by, Tastes had just received a license to serve beer, so look for samples of local microbrews when you pop in.

✕ p193

The Drive ⟫ Drive north on Rte 7 back to Middlebury. On the outskirts of Brandon keep your eye out on the right side for Queen Connie, the 19ft-tall concrete gorilla holding up a life-sized gold Volkswagen Beetle in her right hand. She stands in front of Pioneer Auto Sales and was commissioned in the 1980s (by the female car-dealership owner) as a fun way to lure customers in.

Eating & Sleeping

Middlebury ❶

✕ 51 Main   International $$

(☎802-388-8209; www.go51main.com; 51
Main St; meals $8-22; ☉11:30am-midnight;
☎) Overlooking Otter Creek, this restaurant,
lounge, bar and live-music venue was started by
a few Middlebury College students who wanted
to create a fun, social space where people could
dine, perform and generally hang out. It stocks
board games (entire families often come in to
play), holds live concerts, features a convivial,
casual bar and serves up international fare
(from savory crepes and quiche to Bunny chow
(a South African curry served in a bread bowl)
and mac-and-fromage, made with Vermont
cheddar, of course. It's an airy, high-ceilinged
place that never seems to feel crowded even
when it's packed with loyal patrons.

🛏 Inn on the Green   Inn $$$

(☎802-388-7512, 888-244-7512; www.
innonthegreen.com; 19 S Pleasant St; r incl
continental breakfast $200-240, ste $300-
340; @☎) Lovingly restored to its original
stateliness, this 1803 Federal-style home offers
spacious rooms and suites across the main
house and in an adjoining carriage house (the
latter's rooms are more modern). One of its
signature treats is breakfast served in bed each
morning.

🛏 Waybury Inn   Inn $$

(☎802-388-4015, 800-348-1810; www.
wayburyinn.com; Rte 125; r/ste incl breakfast
from $180/220; ☎) A favorite of Robert Frost,
this former stagecoach stop in the neighboring
town of East Middlebury has a popular pub and
sumptuous guest rooms. The inn's exterior was
used in the 1980s TV show *Newhart* to evoke the
traditional New England inn (though Bob's never
actually been here). In summer, laze away an
afternoon in the swimming hole underneath the
nearby bridge; in winter, warm yourself in the
pub. There's also an on-site restaurant serving
New England–focused dinners ($15 to $25) in a
cozy, wood-paneled space or out on the porch
and terrace in summer.

Rochester ❹

🛏 Liberty Hill Farm   B&B $$

(☎802-767-3926; www.libertyhillfarm.com; 511
Liberty Hill Rd; r incl dinner & breakfast per adult/
teen/child $110/70/55; 🐎) With its magnificent
red barn and White River Valley panoramas, this
working farm is a Vermont classic.

Brandon ❻

✕ Café Provence   French $$

(☎802-247-9997; http://cafeprovencevt.
com; 11 Center St; ☉11:30am-9pm Mon-Sat,
9am-9pm Sun, closed Mon late Oct-late May;
🐎) While the focus is on Provencal and French
specialties such as moules marinières and
bouillabaisse-inspired seafood stew, this elegant
bistro also serves up non-French fare such
as succulent burgers (made from beef from a
nearby farm) and vegetarian lasagna for dinner
or clam chowder and southwestern barbecue
pulled-pork wraps for lunch. Parents, take note:
kids eat free (from the children's menu) all day
every Sunday. For bites on the go, check out its
sister property, Gourmet Provence, a bakery,
sandwich, wine and cheese shop around the
corner at 37 Center St.

South Hero Greet sunrise with postcard-perfect marina views

Lake Champlain Byway

18

Traditional Vermont life meets foodie hub Burlington with sips of Magic Hat beer. Add a spin around islands hugging the Canadian border and your snap-happy self won't be able to stop smiling.

TRIP HIGHLIGHTS

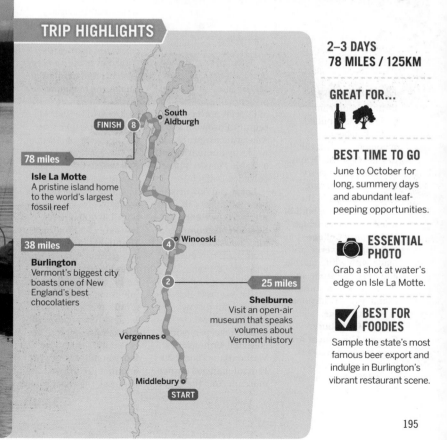

FINISH 8 — South Aldburgh

78 miles

Isle La Motte
A pristine island home to the world's largest fossil reef

38 miles

Burlington
Vermont's biggest city boasts one of New England's best chocolatiers

4 — Winooski

2

25 miles

Shelburne
Visit an open-air museum that speaks volumes about Vermont history

Vergennes

Middlebury
START

**2–3 DAYS
78 MILES / 125KM**

GREAT FOR...

BEST TIME TO GO
June to October for long, summery days and abundant leaf-peeping opportunities.

ESSENTIAL PHOTO
Grab a shot at water's edge on Isle La Motte.

BEST FOR FOODIES
Sample the state's most famous beer export and indulge in Burlington's vibrant restaurant scene.

195

18 Lake Champlain Byway

Vermont's vibrant college towns and the state's most fascinating museum begin this official scenic byway. Then, unfolding like a forgotten ribbon just north of Burlington, you encounter the desolate Champlain Islands, a 27-mile stretch of four largely undeveloped isles – all connected by US 2 and a series of bridges and causeways filled with history and a touch of wine tasting.

1 Middlebury

In 1800 Middlebury College was founded, and it has been synonymous with the town ever since. Despite Middlebury's history of marble quarrying, most buildings in the town's center are built of brick, wood and schist. **Middlebury College buildings**, however, are made with white marble and gray limestone and the campus is a stunning example of a traditional Vermont college.

The **Middlebury College Museum of Art** (www.middlebury.edu/arts/museum; S Main St, VT 30; admission free; ⊙10am-5pm Mon-Fri, noon-5pm Sat & Sun, closed Mon mid-Aug–early Sep & mid-Dec–early Jan) presents fine collections of Cypriot pottery, 19th-century European and American sculpture, and works by luminaries such as Pablo Picasso and Salvador Dalí.

Local and downright peculiar objects sit pretty at the **Henry Sheldon Museum** (www.henrysheldonmuseum.org; 1 Park St; adult/child under 6yr/child 6-18yr/senior $5/free/3/4.50; ⊙10am-5pm Tue-Sat year-round, 11am-4pm Sun fall, winter & spring). Sheldon, a town clerk and storekeeper, avidly collected 19th-century Vermontiana. The 1829 Federal mansion-turned-museum runs the gamut from folk art to bric-a-brac to an upstairs room devoted to curios such as a cigar holder made of chicken claws and Sheldon's own teeth.

✗ ⊨ p201

The Drive » Head north along Rte 7. Three miles past Middlebury, stop off at New Haven's Lincoln Peak Vineyard (www.lincolnpeakvineyard.com) for wine tasting or a picnic lunch on its wraparound porch.

TRIP HIGHLIGHT

2 Shelburne

Feast your eyes on the stunning array of 17th- to 20th-century American artifacts – folk art, textiles, toys, tools, carriages, furniture – spread over the 45-acre grounds and gardens at **Shelburne Museum** (www.shelburnemuseum.org; Rte 7; adult/child under 6yr/child 6-14yr $20/free/10, tickets valid for 2 consecutive days; ⊙10am-5pm, from noon Sun early May-late Oct, to 7:30pm Thu mid-Jun–mid-Aug; ⊕). This remarkable place is set up as a mock village, with 150,000 objects housed in 39 buildings. Highlights include a full-size covered bridge, a classic round barn, an 1871 lighthouse, a one-room schoolhouse, a railway station with a locomotive and a working blacksmith's forge. The collection's sheer size lets you tailor your visit. Families are drawn to the carousel, the Owl Cottage

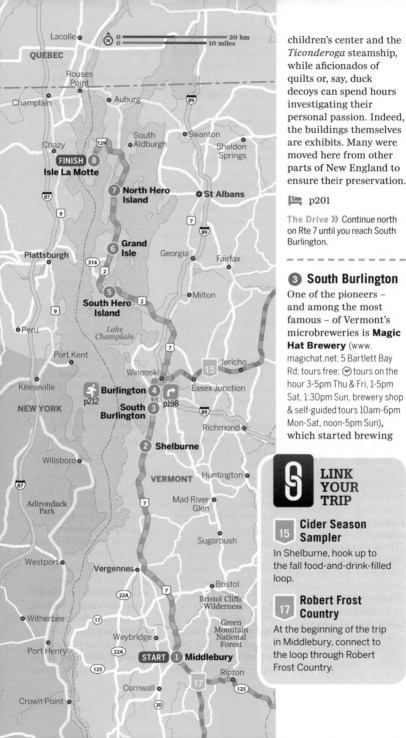

children's center and the *Ticonderoga* steamship, while aficionados of quilts or, say, duck decoys can spend hours investigating their personal passion. Indeed, the buildings themselves are exhibits. Many were moved here from other parts of New England to ensure their preservation.

🛏 p201

The Drive ≫ Continue north on Rte 7 until you reach South Burlington.

❸ South Burlington

One of the pioneers – and among the most famous – of Vermont's microbreweries is **Magic Hat Brewery** (www.magichat.net; 5 Bartlett Bay Rd; tours free; ☺ tours on the hour 3-5pm Thu & Fri, 1-5pm Sat, 1:30pm Sun, brewery shop & self-guided tours 10am-6pm Mon-Sat, noon-5pm Sun), which started brewing

§ LINK YOUR TRIP

15 Cider Season Sampler

In Shelburne, hook up to the fall food-and-drink-filled loop.

17 Robert Frost Country

At the beginning of the trip in Middlebury, connect to the loop through Robert Frost Country.

in 1995. The 'Artifactory' exudes an infectious creative energy, with over 20 varieties flowing from four dozen taps. Half-hour tours take you through the history of Vermont breweries and Magic Hat's role, how it makes its beer and keeps environmental impact as low as possible, and its involvement in the community (such as the annual Magic Hat Mardi Gras and its support of the performing arts). Guides happily answer any question you have, such as who writes the sayings on the inside of each bottle cap. You can enjoy free tastes both before and after the tour. Must-trys are the trademark No 9 (pale ale with a hint of apricot); the Orlio organic brews;

and Odd Notion, a whimsically changing seasonal creation.

The Drive » Continue north on Rte 7 to Burlington.

TRIP HIGHLIGHT

④ Burlington

Perched overlooking the glistening Lake Champlain, Vermont's largest city would be a small city in most other states, but Burlington's size is one of its charms. With the University of Vermont (UVM) swelling the city by 13,400 students, and a vibrant cultural and social life, Burlington has a spirited, youthful character. And when it comes to nightlife, this is Vermont's epicenter.

Just before you reach the city center,

a chocolate stop is in order. The aroma of rich melted cocoa is intoxicating as you enter the gift shop next to the glass wall overlooking the small factory at **Lake Champlain Chocolates** (www. lakechamplainchocolates.com; 750 Pine St; tours free; ⊙ tours on the hour 9am-2pm Mon-Fri, shop 9am-6pm Mon-Sat, 11am-5pm Sun). Take the tour to get the history of the chocolatier and ample samples to taste test the gooey goodness. Oh, and this shop is the only one with factory-seconds shelves containing stacks of chocolate at a discount. It tastes the same as the pretty stuff but for cosmetic reasons can't be sold at regular price. The cafe serves coffee drinks and its own luscious ice cream.

For a walking tour of Burlington, see p212.

🛏 ✕ p201

The Drive » Cast off for the Champlain Islands, cruising 10 miles north of Burlington on I-89 to exit 17, then west on Hwy 2. After Sand Bar State Park – a great picnic and swimming spot – cross the causeway and look for the photo-perfect parking island halfway across.

⑤ South Hero Island

Vermont's first vineyard, **Snow Farm Winery** (www. snowfarm.com; 190 West Shore Rd; ⊙10am-5pm May-Dec) boasts a sweet tasting

**DETOUR:
INTERVALE & ADAM'S BERRY FARM**

Start: ④ **Burlington**

Here, in the midst of Vermont's most urban corridor, you'd scarcely expect to discover pristine farmland. Surprise! Five miles north on Hwy 7, tucked between the urban hubs of Burlington and Winooski, the **Intervale Center** is a positively bucolic complex of community gardens and farms hugging the fringes of the Winooski River. Descending from Hwy 7, Intervale Rd turns to dirt and passes through a lush tunnel of trees to **Adam's Berry Farm** (📞802-578-9093; http://adamsberryfarm.com; Intervale Rd, Burlington), where pick-your-own strawberry, blueberry and raspberry operations run from late May till the first frost (daily hours vary; call to confirm).

Grand Isle Pear harvest

LOCAL KNOWLEDGE:
ALLENHOLM ORCHARDS

Just outside the town of South Hero, grab a Creemee (that's Vermont-speak for soft-serve ice cream) at **Allenholm Orchards** (www.allen holm.com; 150 South St; ☺9am-5pm late May-Christmas Eve; 🚻), or pick a few apples for the road ahead. This perennially popular orchard sponsors Vermont's largest apple festival (South Hero Applefest) every October.

room tucked away down a dirt road (look for the signs off Hwy 2). Sample its award-winning whites or have a sip of Ice Wine in the rustic barn (three tastes are free), or drop by on Thursday evening for the free **concert series** (☺6:30-8:30pm Jun-Sep) on the lawn next to the vines – you can expect anything from jazz to folk to light rock-and-roll.

The Drive » Continue north on Hwy 2.

6 Grand Isle

The **Hyde Log Cabin** (www.historicvermont.org; 228 Hwy 2; adult/child under 14yr $2/free; ☺11am-5pm Sat & Sun Jul–mid-Oct), the oldest (1783) log cabin in Vermont and one of the oldest in the US, is worth a short stop to see how settlers lived in the 18th century and to examine traditional household artifacts from Vermont.

The Drive » Continue north on Hwy 2.

7 North Hero Island

Boaters for miles around cast anchor at popular general store **Hero's Welcome** (www. heroswelcome.com; 3537 Hwy 2; ☺6:30am-6:30pm Mon-Sat, 7am-6pm Sun). The store's amusing wall display of 'World Time Zones' – four clocks showing identical hours for Lake Champlain's North Hero, South Hero, Grand Isle, and Isle La Motte – reflects the prevailing island-centric attitude. Pick up a souvenir, grab a sandwich or coffee and snap some pics on the outdoor terrace overlooking the boat landing.

✕ 🛏 p201

The Drive » From Hwy 2, head west 4 miles on Rte 129 to historic Isle La Motte.

TRIP HIGHLIGHT

8 Isle La Motte

Pristine Isle La Motte is one of the most historic of all the Champlain Islands. Signs along its western shore signal its traditional importance as a crossroads for Native Americans, and French explorer Samuel de Champlain landed here in 1609.

Tool around the loop road hugging the coast, stopping at **St Anne's Shrine** (www.saintannesshrine. org; 92 St Anne's Rd; ☺shrine mid-May–mid-Oct, grounds year-round), on the site of Fort St Anne, Vermont's oldest settlement. Though it is welcoming to all, this is a religious place, so be respectful of those who come to pray. The site features a striking granite statue of Samuel de Champlain, and its waterfront has spectacular views and a large picnic area.

Isle La Motte is also home to the 20-acre **Fisk Quarry Preserve** (www. ilmpt.org; West Rd; ☺dawn-dusk), the world's largest fossil reef, 4 miles south of St Anne's Shrine. Half a million years old, the reef once provided limestone for Radio City Music Hall and Washington's National Gallery. Interpretive trails explain the history of the quarry.

Eating & Sleeping

Middlebury ❶

✗ Otter Creek Bakery   Bakery $

(📞802-388-3371; www.ottercreekbakery.com; 14 College St; sandwiches $4-5; ⏰7am-6pm Mon-Sat, to 3pm Sun) This bakery, with some outdoor seating, is popular for takeout pastries, strong coffee and creative sandwiches.

🛏 Middlebury Inn   Inn $$

(📞802-388-4961, 800-842-4666; www. middleburyinn.com; 14 Court House Sq, Rte 7; r $120-275; 📶) This inn's fine old main building (1827) has beautifully restored formal public rooms and charming guest rooms. The adjacent Porter Mansion, with Victorian-style rooms, is full of architectural details. Lower-priced guest rooms are in the less interesting modern motel units (basic spaces, no antiques).

Shelburne ❷

🛏 Northstar Motel   Motel $

(📞802-863-3421; www.northstarmotelvt.com; 2427 Shelburne Rd; s/d incl breakfast $50/90; 📶) These plain, tidy rooms are neat as a pin and the staff are wonderful. This is a no-fuss option for budget travelers or those who prefer to allocate their money toward the culinary delights nearby (which we highly recommend).

Burlington ❹

✗ August First Bakery & Cafe   Bakery, Pizzeria $

(📞802-540-0064; 149 South Champlain St; meals $9-14; ⏰11:30am-5pm Mon-Thu, 11:30am-5pm & 6-9pm Fri, 8am-3pm Sat) Most days this bakery-cafe is a hot spot for a cup of coffee, sandwiches and its famous breads. Flatbread Friday is a huge hit – the tables are pushed together and there is pizza and beer, with unlimited flatbread (pizza on a flat crust) and salads for $12 ($8 for kids 10 and under). Expect anything from traditional pepperoni to more exotic gorgonzola and pear pizzas and everything in between.

✗ Blue Bird Tavern   International $$

(📞802-540-1786; http://bluebirdvermont. com; 86 Paul St; meals $9-25; ⏰ lunch & dinner) Nominated for a James Beard award within its first year of operation, Burlington's most experimental locavore eatery features a seasonal menu with small and large plates – expect anything from hot oysters with seaweed aioli and maple sugar to mac 'n' cheese with peas, morel mushrooms and snails. Fries come with homemade ketchup and mayonnaise. Be sure to book.

🛏 Sunset House B&B   B&B $$

(📞802-864-3790; www.sunsethousebb.com; 78 Main St; r $120-170; 📶) This sweet B&B features four tidy guest rooms. Bathrooms are shared, and there's a small common kitchen. This is the only B&B smack in the center of downtown.

North Hero Island ❼

🛏 North Hero House   B&B $$

(📞802-372-4732; Hwy 2; www.northherohouse. com; r from $140; 📶) This country inn sits right across from the water, with quilt-filled rooms, many with private porch and four-poster bed, and offers two appealing eating options. The cozy restaurant serves New American cuisine (meals $18 to $28; open for dinner) and boasts water views. The fantastic outdoor Steamship Pier Bar & Grill (sandwiches $10 to $18; open for lunch and dinner June to September) feeds you kabobs, burgers and lobster rolls with a fresh cocktail smack on the pier, the water glistening beside you.

Hildene Visit the stately former home of the Lincoln family

Southern Vermont Loop

19

Southern Vermont's serene towns burst to life with vibrant art scenes, historic districts and shopping nirvana for both cheese and clothes addicts. Crisscross the Green Mountains for a taste of it all.

TRIP HIGHLIGHTS

56 miles

Mt Equinox
You'll think you're on the top of the world

60 miles

Manchester
Shop your heart out in a quintessential Vermont town

Jamaica

Townshend

Wilmington

Brattleboro

Bennington
Find out why Bennington was crucial to the American Revolution

44 miles

2–3 DAYS
111 MILES / 178KM

GREAT FOR...

BEST TIME TO GO
May to October for great weather and autumnal colors.

 ESSENTIAL PHOTO
Capture views of farms, valleys and the Green Mountains from the top of Mt Equinox.

 BEST FOR OUTDOORS
Roam the trails on the grounds of Hildene, the Lincoln family estate.

203

Southern Vermont Loop

Tidy white churches and inns surround village greens throughout historic southern Vermont, a region that's home to several towns that predate the American Revolution — one contains the former home of the Lincoln family. Combine with community art centers, scenic byways, one of Vermont's most famous cheese makers and the peak of Mt Equinox for a mix of history and culture in brilliant surrounds.

❶ Brattleboro

Perched at the confluence of the Connecticut and West Rivers, Brattleboro is a little gem that reveals its facets to those who stroll the streets and prowl the dozens of independent shops and eateries. An energetic mix of aging hippies and the latest crop of pierced and tattooed hipsters fuels the town's sophisticated eclecticism, keeping the downtown scene percolating and skewing its politics decidedly leftward.

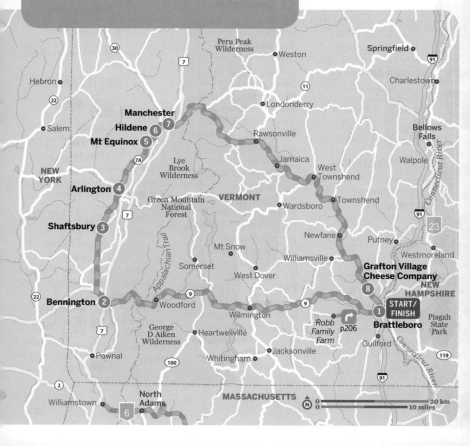

The Whetstone Brook runs through the south end of town, where a wooden stockade dubbed Fort Dummer was built to defend Vermont's first Colonial settlement (1724) against Native Americans. The town received its royal charter a year later, named for Colonel William Brattle Jr of the King's Militia.

Housed in a 1915 former railway station, the **Brattleboro Museum & Art Center** (www. brattleboromuseum.org; 10 Vernon St; adult/child under 6yr/student/senior $6/free/3/4; ⏰11am-5pm Thu-Mon) has a wealth of inventive exhibits by local artists in a variety of media, and the contemporary crafts shop and art space **Vermont Artisans Gallery**

LINK YOUR TRIP

6 Mohawk Trail
Explore New England's oldest scenic highway in Massachusetts. From Bennington, drive 13 miles south on Rte 7 to Williamstown.

23 Connecticut River Byway
Follow the river and visit college towns in New Hampshire. From Brattleboro drive 23 miles north on I-91 to Walpole.

(☎802-257-7044; www. vtartisans.com; 106 Main St) has outstanding creations by Vermont artists. The gallery's hours are seasonal.

✖️ 🛏️ p209

The Drive » Take Rte 9 west along the Molly Stark scenic byway. Look for the covered bridges just after Brattleboro and then climb uphill (your ears will pop!). Pause at the Hogback Mountain viewpoint and take in the three-state overlook (you'll see Massachusetts, New Hampshire and Vermont countryside).

- - - - - - - - - - - - -

TRIP HIGHLIGHT

2 Bennington

Bennington is divided into three sections: workaday town (Bennington proper), college town (North Bennington) and **Old Bennington**; the latter holds the main sights. The charming hilltop Colonial site is studded with 80 Georgian and Federal houses and the **Old First Church** (1 Monument Circle), built in 1806 in Palladian style. Its churchyard holds the remains of five Vermont governors, numerous American Revolution soldiers and poet Robert Frost (1874–1963), the best-known, and perhaps best-loved, American poet of the 20th century.

Up the hill to the north, the **Bennington Monument** (www. historicvermont.org/bennington; 15 Monument Circle; adult/child $3/1; ⏰9am-5pm mid-Apr–Oct) commemorates the crucial Battle of Bennington during the American Revolution. Had Colonel Seth Warner and the local 'Green Mountain Boys' not helped weaken British defenses during this battle, the colonies might well have been split. The obelisk built between 1887 and 1891 offers impressive views – an elevator whisks you two-thirds of the way up the 306ft tower.

✖️ 🛏️ p209

The Drive » Head out of town along scenic Rte 7A and drive 4 miles north to Shaftsbury. As the road winds along the valley the southernmost section of the Green Mountains emerges on your left.

- - - - - - - - - - - - -

3 Shaftsbury

When he moved his family to Shaftsbury, Robert Frost was 46 years old and at the height of his career. The **Robert Frost Stone House Museum** (www. frostfriends.org; 121 Rte 7A; adult/child under 18yr $5/2.50; ⏰10am-5pm Tue-Sun May-Dec) opens a window into the life of the poet, with one entire room dedicated to his most famous work, 'Stopping by Woods on a Snowy Evening,' which he penned here in the 1920s.

DETOUR: ROBB FAMILY FARM

Start: ① Brattleboro

Run by the same family for about a century, the 400-acre **Robb Family Farm** (www.robbfamilyfarm. com; 827 Ames Hill Rd; ◷10am-5pm Mon, Tue & Thu-Sat, 1-5pm Sun late Feb-early Apr) features maple-sugaring demonstrations and hay or sleigh rides ($7/5 per adult/child, reservations essential), which usually end with a hot chocolate and doughnuts. From Rte 9 in Brattleboro, pass I-91 and then turn left on Greenleaf St (which becomes Ames Hill Rd); head 3 miles and look to the right.

The Drive ›› Continue north along scenic Rte 7A for 6 miles past bucolic farmland and wooded hollows to Arlington.

④ Arlington

Arlington's tiny maple-syrup shop (the sweet stuff is made on site) houses the **Norman Rockwell Exhibition** (☎802-375-6747; Rte 7A; admission $2; ◷9am-5pm May-Oct), a homage to the artist who lived in Arlington from 1939 to 1953. A section of the shop displays 500 of Rockwell's *Saturday Evening Post* covers and shows a short film about his life. Exhibition hours vary; call to confirm.

The Drive ›› Continue north along scenic Rte 7A. Mt Equinox, your next stop, will start to loom in the distance.

TRIP HIGHLIGHT

⑤ Mt Equinox

The private **Mt Equinox Skyline Drive** (www.

equinoxmountain.com; car & driver $12, each additional passenger $2; ◷9am-dusk May-Oct) toll road winds via hairpin turns seemingly up to the top of the world. It's believed that the mountain's name is a corrupted Native American phrase meaning 'place where the very top is.' Rather than drive, you can undertake the five-plus-hour hike (2918ft elevation gain) on Burr and Burton and Lookout Rock Trails, which will take you to the summit and back. Hiking information is available at the Equinox hotel and resort (p209), where the trail begins.

The Drive ›› Continue north along Rte 7A 5 miles to Hildene, on the outskirts of Manchester. The area is an excellent place for an overnight stay – oodles of B&Bs and hotels congregate in Manchester proper and along Rte 7A as you approach town.

⑥ Hildene

Abraham Lincoln's wife, Mary Todd Lincoln (1818–82), and their son, Robert Todd Lincoln (1843–1926), came here during the Civil War; as an adult Robert built **Hildene** (www.hildene.org; Rte 7A; museum & grounds adult/child $13/5, grounds only $5/3; ◷9:30am-4:30pm), a 24-room Georgian Revival mansion. Robert enjoyed the house until his death in 1926, and his great-granddaughter lived here until her death in 1975. Soon after, it was converted into a museum filled with Lincoln family personal effects and furnishings, including the hat Abraham Lincoln probably wore when he delivered the Gettysburg Address, and a brass cast of his hands, the right one swollen from shaking hands while campaigning for presidency. The 1000-pipe Aeolian organ springs to life during the free tours (they run every 30 minutes).

Tickets include access to the surrounding grounds, with 8 miles of walking trails; the Hoyt Formal Garden, an exquisite flower garden designed to resemble a stained-glass Romanesque cathedral window; and a solar-powered barn where you can watch Hildene goat cheese being produced.

Grafton Village Cheese Company A cheese maker cuts slabs of curd

The Drive >> Continue north on Rte 7A to central Manchester.

- - - - - - - - - - -

TRIP HIGHLIGHT

❼ Manchester

Manchester has been a fashionable resort town for almost two centuries. These days, the draws are the nearby skiing and hiking, the relaxed New England town vibe and the upscale outlet shopping (Manchester contains more than 100 shops, from Armani to Banana Republic).

Two families put the place on the map – the Lincolns (see p206) and the Orvises. Franklin Orvis (1824–1900) established the Equinox House Hotel; his brother, Charles, founded the Orvis Company, makers of fly-fishing equipment with a worldwide following. Orvis Company products are showcased in the **American Museum of Fly Fishing & Orvis** (www.amff. com; 4070 Rte 7A; adult/child $5/3; ☺10am-4pm Tue-Sun),

which reputedly holds the world's best display of equipment, with fly collections and rods used by Ernest Hemingway, Bing Crosby and several US presidents, including Herbert Hoover. If you can believe it, the latter penned the tome *Fishing for Fun & to Wash Your Soul.*

If art is more your thing, check out the **Southern Vermont Arts Center** (www.svac. org; West Rd; adult/child $8/3; ☺galleries 10am-5pm Tue-Sat, noon-5pm Sun) for its excellent outdoor sculpture, 10 galleries of classic and contemporary art and changing exhibits.

🍴 🛏 p209

The Drive >> Take Rte 30 south toward Brattleboro. Wind your way along the curvy road straight over the Green Mountains. Just after Townshend Dam Recreation Area, look for Scott Bridge, Vermont's longest covered bridge, on the right. Finally, pass through postcard-worthy Newfane and admire its

Georgian and Greek Revival architecture.

- - - - - - - - - - -

❽ Grafton Village Cheese Company

Just before Brattleboro lies the cheese-making facility for **Grafton Village Cheese Company** (www.graftonvillagecheese. com; 400 Linden St/VT30; ☺10am-6pm). Watch sublime cheddars being made, taste and discover your favorite and pick up a chunk to take with you. The shop also sells wine and local beer. Next door is the **Retreat Petting Farm**, where you can say hello to farm animals (May through October only) and bask in the stunning setting. The farm also gives out information about local trails on its doorstep. Look for the large cluster of red barns (or listen for the goats).

The Drive >> Continue south along Rte 30 to Brattleboro.

Eating & Sleeping

Brattleboro ❶

✗ TJ Buckley's   American $$$

(☎802-257-4922; 132 Elliot St; meals $32-39; ⏰dinner Thu-Sun) This upscale but authentic 1927 diner seats just 18 lucky souls. The menu of four mains changes nightly. Reservations strongly recommended; cash only.

🛏 Latchis Hotel   Hotel $$

(☎802-254-6300; www.latchis.com; 50 Main St; r $90-170, ste $170-200; 🛜) Located in the epicenter of downtown, the hotel's art deco overtones are refreshing and wonderfully surprising for New England.

Bennington ❷

✗ Pangea   International $$

(☎802-442-7171; 1 Prospect St, North Bennington; meals $13-25; ⏰dinner Tue-Sun) One of the finer restaurants in Vermont, Pangea feels like a stylish living room and serves locally sourced ingredients with an international twist, such as shrimp on organic udon noodles in a curry peanut sauce or herbes-de-Provence-rubbed Delmonico steak (a boneless top sirloin cut of meat) topped with gorgonzola.

🛏 South Shire Inn   Inn $$

(☎802-447-3839; www.southshire.com; 124 Elm St; r incl breakfast $175-255, ste $265; 🛜) An extremely plush, antique-filled Victorian inn, the centrally located South Shire offers high-ceilinged rooms (scattered across a main house and carriage house) with raised plastic moldings; some rooms have fireplaces.

Manchester ❼

✗ Little Rooster Cafe   Cafe $$

(☎802-362-3496; Rte 7A; dishes $7-11; ⏰breakfast & lunch Thu-Tue, dinner Fri & Sat

Jun-Oct) This colorful spot serves dishes such as Asian vegetables with noodles, and chicken or grilled portobello focaccia. In summer it serves a bistro dinner menu (ranging from burgers with locally sourced beef to lentil and sweet-potato curry; mains are $14 to $22) on weekends. It's cash only, and be prepared to wait for a table.

✗ Perfect Wife   International, Pub $$

(☎802-362-2817; 2595 Depot St; tavern menu $5-9, restaurant menu $12-21; ⏰dinner Tue-Sat) In addition to serving international fare such as sesame-crusted salmon and filet mignon in its cobblestone-walled restaurant, the Perfect Wife's tavern serves pub staples and is an excellent evening hangout, with live music most nights (mainly rock, blues and folk).

🛏 Equinox   Resort $$$

(☎802-362-4700, 800-362-4747; www.equinoxresort.com; 3567 Main St/Rte 7A; r $280-600, ste $490-1500; @🛜🐾) One of Vermont's most famous resorts, this grand property – with its own library and front porch – occupies one main house plus four separate buildings and includes vast grounds with tennis courts and an 18-hole golf course. Choice is wide, from modern, elegant rooms to cottages with canopied beds and wood-burning fireplaces to luxury town houses with kitchens.

🛏 Weathervane Motel   Motel $$

(☎802-362-2444; www.weathervanemotel.com; Rte 7A; r incl breakfast $95-175; 🛜🐾) This fantastic, tidy stretch of simple, no-frills rooms arches across six gorgeous acres of land – this is one of the best values in the area. The congenial owners have peppered the comfy, laid-back lounge with antiques and the grounds with wagons and pumpkins for a relaxed New Englandy feel.

STRETCH YOUR LEGS
STOWE

Start/Finish Quiet Path

Distance 2.5 miles

Duration Two to three hours

This walk takes you along the Quiet Path, a circular walk across bucolic farmland, and then through the center of Stowe village. You'll cross a pedestrian covered bridge, visit local galleries and shops, and learn about Stowe's skiing and snowboarding history.

Take this walk on Trip

14

Quiet Path

The Quiet Path is a delightful, easy 1.8-mile walk that features mountain views and takes you past bucolic farmlands along the west branch of the Little River. Along the way, special plaques explain the ecosystem of the area. The loop is blissfully devoid of cyclists or anything else that moves quickly.

The Walk >> Access the walk from the parking lot beneath the church on Main St. Follow the signs to the recreation path and veer right after the second bridge. The path loops around and returns to the start. Walk up the hill, turn right at the church, then right onto Mountain Rd.

Stowe Walkway

A pedestrian covered bridge (1972), the Stowe Walkway hugs the road across the Waterbury River. One of Stowe's most photographed spots, it's a mini, skinny version of the covered bridges you see across the state and features a sweet Stowe sign at the entrance.

The Walk >> Cross the pedestrian bridge. At the other end, cross the street and turn left; your next stop is on your right.

Straw Corner Shops

Stowe has no shortage of galleries and craft shops displaying work by artists of local and international renown. Within the **Straw Corner Shops** (Mountain Rd), offerings are traditional, contemplative, sometimes prankish and always finely hewn. Look for the **Straw Corner Mercantile** (☏802-253-3700; 57 Mountain Rd; ☺10am-6pm), featuring folk art, Americana, prints and artsy home accessories; and **Stowe Craft Gallery & Design Center** (☏802-253-4693; www.stowecraft.com; 55 Mountain Rd; ☺10am-6pm, to 8pm Thu-Sat Jul & Aug), with adventurous, eclectic and surreal works of art and craft.

The Walk >> Turn right out of the parking lot and cross Main St to the next stop, which is right across the street.

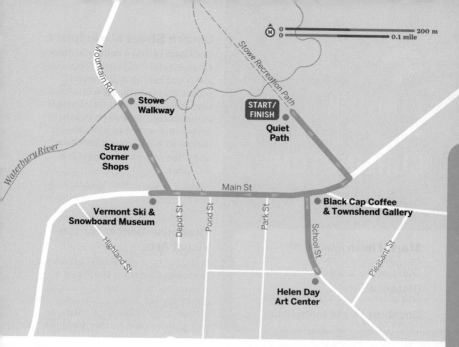

Vermont Ski & Snowboard Museum

Located in an 1818 meeting house that was rolled to its present spot by oxen in the 1860s, the **Vermont Ski & Snowboard Museum** (☏802-253-9911; www.vtssm.com; 1 S Main St; suggested donation $3-5; ☻noon-5pm Thu-Tue, closed Apr-late May) is a tribute to skiing and boarding, with over 7500 cataloged items. It tells the tale of the famous 10th Mountain Division of skiing troops from WWII history, traces the evolution of equipment (75 years of Vermont ski lifts!) and gives you a chance to chuckle at 1970s slope-side fashion.

The Walk » Turn right out of the museum and walk down Main St — you'll pass oodles of shops and restaurants. Turn right onto School St and walk three blocks until you see your next stop on the right.

Helen Day Art Center

This gently provocative **community art center** (☏802-253-8358; www.helenday.com; School St; ☻noon-5pm Thu-Tue Jun–mid-Oct & Dec, Tue-Sat mid-Oct–Nov & Jan-May) hosts rotating traditional and avant-garde exhibits. It also sponsors 'Exposed,' an annual town-wide outdoor sculptural show from mid-July to mid-October.

The Walk » Walk back down School St the way you came. At Main St, the next stop is on your right at the corner.

Black Cap Coffee & Townshend Gallery

What's art without coffee? After a browse through the Townshend Gallery (featuring rotating exhibits by mainly local artists), drop into **Black Cap Coffee** (☏802-253-2123; 144 Main St; dishes $5-7; ☻7am-6pm Mon-Sat, from 8am Sun; ☏) for a cuppa and a bite. It's located in an old house with a small but delightful front porch.

The Walk » To return to the beginning of the Quiet Path, cross Main St and walk down the hill (the church will be on your right) to the parking lot.

STRETCH YOUR LEGS
BURLINGTON

Start/Finish Pearl & Church Sts

Distance 3 miles

Duration Two to three hours

This walk takes you along Burlington's main drag and pedestrian hangout strip, ending with a stroll along the city's finest asset, Lake Champlain. You'll learn about the history of the city and the lake's ecosystem, and see where Burlington's outdoorsy residents sail, cycle and run a few steps from the center of town.

Take this walk on Trips

13 | 15 | 18

Church Street Marketplace

Get a dose of urban culture at Church St Marketplace, the city's commercial and social hub. This attractive pedestrian zone is lined with shops, food carts, restaurants, cafes, street musicians and climbing rocks that are popular with young children. It's packed with locals any time of day and is the epicenter of nightlife on weekends.

The Walk » Walk along the pedestrian mall. After College St, you will see your next stop on the right.

Firehouse Center for the Visual Arts

At Burlington's community art center, **Firehouse Center for the Visual Arts** (www.burlingtoncityarts.com; 135 Church St; ⊙noon-5pm Tue-Thu & Sun, noon-8pm Fri, 9am-8pm Sat) features Vermont artists, as well as those from further afield, with a focus on contemporary art.

The Walk » From Church St, turn right onto Main St. You'll immediately see the lake looming in front of you. Walk downhill; the road dead-ends at your next stop.

Union Station

The brick Beaux Arts–style structure (built in 1915) is **Union Station** (1 Main St), the former station for the Central Vermont railway; look for the quirky steel-winged monkeys looming on top of the building. Inside, admire the revolving local art; head downstairs to see murals detailing the history and development of Burlington, and a local artist sculpture entitled *Train Ball*.

The Walk » Exit on the bottom floor and turn right. You'll pass the old platform, which looks like it could receive passengers anytime. Walk on the path following the tracks.

ECHO Lake Aquarium & Science Center

Nature-lovers, or those interested in green architecture, will definitely want to explore the **ECHO Lake Aquarium &**

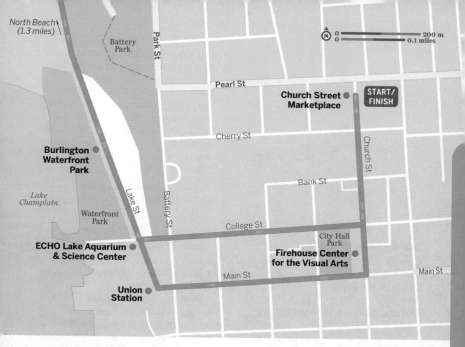

Science Center (www.echovermont.org; 1 College St; adult/child $12.50/9.50; ⏱10am–5pm; 🐾), a waterfront science museum that is LEED-certified for its state-of-the-art environmentally friendly design. Focusing on Lake Champlain's ecosystem, it features a moderate-sized aquarium with local fish and hands-on touch tanks. Don't miss the stand devoted to the lake's mythical sea creature, Champy.

The Walk ❯❯ Cross the roundabout and you'll see the boathouse off to the left and the boardwalk up ahead, both part of your next stop.

Burlington Waterfront Park

Refreshingly unencumbered by the souvenir stands that crowd the more developed waterfronts, the park has a low-key promenade with swinging four-person benches and swaths of grassy spots. Its marina contains **Splash at the Boathouse** (www.splashattheboathouse.

com; College St; ⏱11am–10pm mid-May–Sep), an outdoor restaurant and bar on a floating dock that's perfect for watching the sun set over the lake and the Adirondack Mountains beyond with a cocktail (best for the drinks and views, not the food).

The Walk ❯❯ Walk down the boardwalk and continue past the sailing club to the Burlington Recreation Path, a paved path that takes you along the lake. The elevation increases slightly to give you excellent views from above.

North Beach

This wide stretch makes you feel like you've landed on a small ocean. Wriggle your feet in the sand, breathe in the crisp air and, if it's summer, dive in.

The Walk ❯❯ Return to the Burlington Recreation Path and walk back to the waterfront park. Then walk east along College St and north up Church St until you return to the Church St Marketplace.

New Hampshire

THE BEST THING ABOUT A TRIP THROUGH THE GRANITE STATE? The whole place is one big scenic attraction. You don't have to drive through miles of suburbia to get to the good stuff because most of it is the good stuff: lofty peaks, shimmering lakes, crashing waterfalls and powerful rivers. After crossing the state line, it's all within a half-day's travel.

In the north, the word presidential best describes the drive. Mt Washington anchors the magnificent Presidential Range, filled with trails. It's all about lake views and water fun at Lake Winnipesaukee, where wildlife roams in nearby hills. Vistas are gentler along the Connecticut River and in towns near Mt Monadnock, regions that draw artists and families with their museums, mountains and covered bridges.

Crawford Notch State Park Take in views of Mt Washington (Trip 22)
DANITA DELIMONT/GETTY IMAGES ©

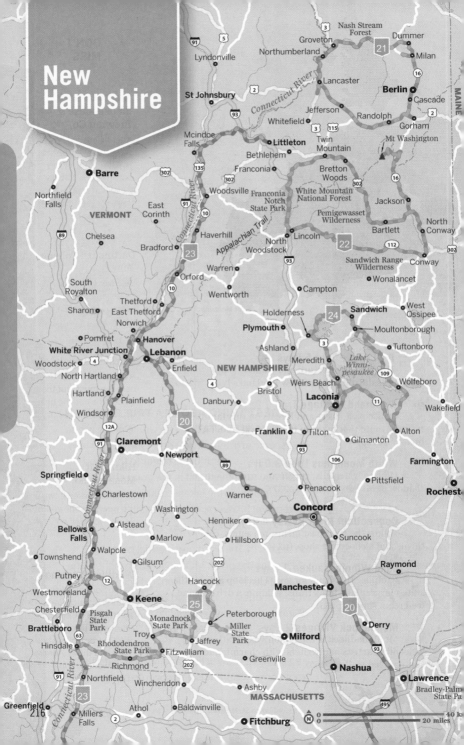

New Hampshire

MAINE

Nash Stream Forest
Dummer
Milan
Groveton
Northumberland
Lancaster
Berlin
Cascade
Jefferson
Whitefield
Randolph
Gorham
Mt Washington
Littleton
Twin Mountain
Bethlehem
Bretton Woods
Franconia
White Mountain National Forest
Woodsville
Franconia Notch State Park
Pemigewasset Wilderness
Jackson
North Conway
Lincoln
Bartlett
North Woodstock
Sandwich Range Wilderness
Conway
Wonalancet
Warren
Campton
Wentworth
Holderness
Sandwich
West Ossipee
Plymouth
Moultonborough
Ashland
Tuftonboro
Meredith
Lake Winnipesaukee
Wolfeboro
Bristol
Weirs Beach
Danbury
Laconia
Wakefield
Franklin
Tilton
Alton
Gilmanton
Farmington
Warner
Penacook
Pittsfield
Rochest
Washington
Henniker
Concord
Hillsboro
Suncook
Raymond
Hancock
Manchester
Peterborough
Miller State Park
Milford
Derry
Monadnock State Park
Troy
Jaffrey
Greenville
Rhododendron State Park
Fitzwilliam
Nashua
Lawrence
Richmond
Winchendon
Ashby
Bradley-Palm State Pa
Northfield
MASSACHUSETTS
Greenfield
Millers Falls
Athol
Baldwinville
Fitchburg

VERMONT

Lyndonville
St Johnsbury
Barre
Northfield Falls
Mcindoe Falls
East Corinth
Chelsea
Bradford
Haverhill
South Royalton
Sharon
Thetford
East Thetford
Norwich
Pomfret
Hanover
White River Junction
Lebanon
Woodstock
Enfield
North Hartland
Hartland
Plainfield
Windsor
Claremont
Newport
Springfield
Charlestown
Bellows Falls
Alstead
Townshend
Walpole
Putney
Marlow
Gilsum
Westmoreland
Chesterfield
Keene
Brattleboro
Hinsdale
Pisgah State Park

Connecticut River

Appalachian Trail

216

0   40 km
0   20 miles

Mt Monadnock (Trip 25)

Classic Trip

20 Ivy League Tour 5 Days
History, architecture and traditions are highlights during tours of New England's Ivies. (p219)

21 Woodland Heritage Trail 2 Days
Cruise past rivers and forests on this family-friendly route that takes in theme parks and logging history. (p229)

22 White Mountains Loop 3 Days
Hike to waterfalls, gorges and summits in the shadow of Mt Washington. (p237)

Classic Trip

23 Connecticut River Byway 4 Days
Follow the river past farms, museums, college towns and a chocolate shop. (p245)

24 Lake Winnipesaukee 2 Days
Families, this trip's for you. This loop around the state's largest lake links trails, wildlife, a drive-in and ice-cream shops. (p255)

25 Monadnock Villages 2 Days
Mt Monadnock is the region's captivating host, welcoming artists and writers with charming towns and sun-dappled trails. (p263)

☑ **DON'T MISS**

Moat Mountain Smokehouse & Brewing Co
After hiking up Mt Washington, swap lies about the trail at this pub in North Conway, the region's top outdoor town. For brews and views tackle Trip **22**

Dartmouth College Tour
Discover Orozco's riveting mural in the campus library. Enjoy it on Trips **20** **23**

Burdick Chocolate
A decadent dessert here is a must, but the quiche may be the best you've ever tasted. Try it on Trip **23**

Hiking Mt Monadnock
If Thoreau hiked it twice, the view must be good. See for yourself on Trip **25**

Wildlife Watching
At the Squam Lakes Natural Science Center and the Loon Center, learn about local wildlife from folks who want it to thrive. Admire their work on Trip **24**

Dartmouth College *Hallowed halls and tradition await at this campus*

Classic Trip

Ivy League Tour

20

This trip celebrates history and education as it rolls between New England's Ivies, where campus tours sneak behind the gates for an up-close look at the USA's greatest universities.

TRIP HIGHLIGHTS

START 1 — 1 mile

Hanover
Follow the Appalachian Trail to the Dartmouth Green

Concord, NH

Manchester

127 miles — **5** **6** — Boston

Concord, MA
Get Transcendental with Emerson and Thoreau

140 miles

Cambridge
Study the 'statue of three lies' on Harvard Yard

7

FINISH
8

New Haven
From the Tomb to the cemetery, sites are a bit macabre

296 miles

Providence
Get acquainted with Brown, the most rambunctious of the Ivies

199 miles

5 DAYS
296 MILES / 476KM

GREAT FOR...

BEST TIME TO GO
Catch student-filled campuses September to November.

ESSENTIAL PHOTO
Stand beside the statue of John Harvard, the man who didn't found Harvard.

BEST HISTORY
Learn about the USA's oldest university during a Harvard tour.

20 Ivy League Tour

What's most surprising about a tour of the Ivy League? The distinct personalities of the different campuses, which are symbiotically fused with their surrounding landscapes. Compare fresh-faced Dartmouth, with its breezy embrace of New Hampshire's outdoors, to enclaved Yale, its Gothic buildings fortressed against the urban wilds of New Haven. But the schools all share one trait – vibrant, diverse and engaged students who dispel any notions that they're out-of-touch elites.

TRIP HIGHLIGHT

1 Hanover, New Hampshire

When the first big snowfall hits **Dartmouth College**, an email blasts across campus, calling everyone to the central Green for a midnight snowball fight. The Green is also the site of elaborate ice sculptures during Dartmouth's **Winter Carnival**, a weeklong celebration that's been held annually for more than 100 years.

North of the Green is **Baker Berry Library**, which holds an impressive mural called the *Epic of American Civilization*. Painted by Jose Clemente Orozco, it traces the course of civilization in the Americas from the Aztec era to modern times. At 4pm, stop by the adjacent **Sanborn Library**, where tea is served during the academic year for 10¢. This tradition honors a 19th-century English professor who invited students for chats and afternoon tea. For a free

student-led **walking tour** (☎603-646-2875; www. dartmouth.edu/admissions/ visit/plan) of the campus, stop by the admissions office on the 2nd floor of McNutt Hall on the west side of the Green. Call or check online to confirm departure times.

The collection at Dartmouth's **Hood Museum of Art** (www. hoodmuseum.dartmouth. edu; 6034 E Wheelock St; admission free; ⊙10am-5pm Tue & Thu-Sat, 10am-9pm Wed, noon-5pm Sun) includes nearly 70,000 items. The collection is particularly strong in American pieces, including Native American art. One highlight is a set of Assyrian reliefs dating to the 9th century BC. From the museum, turn left onto E Wheelock St and walk toward the Hanover Inn. You'll soon cross the **Appalachian Trail**, which runs through downtown.

LINK YOUR TRIP

23 Connecticut River Byway

From Hanover, drive south on NE 10 for riverside history.

10 Connecticut Wine Trail

Jump from grades to grapes in New Haven by heading north along US 1.

From here, it's 431 miles to Mt Katahdin in Maine.

✗ p227

The Drive >> From Hanover, follow NH 120 east to I-89 south. Take exit 117 to NH 4 east, following it to NH 4A. Turn right and follow NH 4A 3.5 miles to the museum.

---

② Enfield Shaker Museum

The Enfield Shaker site sits in stark contrast to today's college campuses. In fact, the two couldn't be more different – except for the required communal housing with a bunch of non-relatives. But a trip here is illuminating. Set in a valley overlooking Mascoma Lake, the Enfield Shaker site dates to the late 18th century. At its peak, some 300 members lived in Enfield. Farmers and craftspeople, they built impressive wood and brick buildings and took in converts, orphans and children of the poor – essential for the Shaker future since sex was not allowed in the pacifist, rule-abiding community. By the early 1900s the community had gone into decline and the last family left in 1917.

The **museum** (📞603-632-4346; www. shakermuseum.org; 447 NH 4A; adult/child $8.50/4; 🕙10am-5pm Mon-Sat, noon-5pm Sun) centers on the Great Stone Dwelling, the largest Shaker dwelling house ever built. You can also explore the gardens and grounds. If you're nice, the guide might let you ring the rooftop bell. Spend the night on the 3rd and 4th floor of the building. **Accommodations** (r $95-135; 🖥) feature traditional Shaker furniture, but not phones or TVs, although there is wi-fi.

The Drive >> Return to I-89 south. After 54 miles, take I-93 north 3 miles to exit 15E for I-393 east. From there, take exit 1 and follow the signs.

---

③ Concord, New Hampshire

New Hampshire's capital is a trim and tidy city with a wide Main St dominated by the striking **State House**, a granite-hewed 19th-century edifice topped with a glittering dome. New Hampshire schoolteacher Christa McAuliffe, chosen to be America's first teacher-astronaut, is honored at the **McAuliffe-Shepard Discovery Center** (📞603-271-7827; www.starhop.com; 2 Institute Dr; adult/child $9/6; 🕙10am-5pm Thu, Sat & Sun, 10am-5pm & 6:30-9pm Fri, daily 15 Jun-Aug; 🚼). She died in

the *Challenger* explosion on January 28, 1986. The museum also honors New Hampshire native Alan B Shepard, a member of NASA's elite Mercury corps who became America's first astronaut in 1961. Intriguing exhibits chronicle their lives and spotlight aviation, and earth and space sciences. There's also a planetarium.

The Drive >> Return to I-93 south, passing through Manchester before entering Massachusetts. Follow I-495 south toward Lowell.

---

④ Lowell, Massachusetts

In the early 19th century, textile mills in Lowell churned out cloth by the mile, driven by the abundant waterpower of Pawtucket Falls. Today, the historic buildings in the city center – connected by the trolley and canal boats – comprise the Lowell National Historic Park, which gives a fascinating peek at the workings of a 19th-century industrial town. Stop first at the **Market Mills Visitors Center** (www.nps.gov/lowe; 246 Market St, Market Mills; 🕙9am-5pm) to pick up a map and check out the general exhibits. Five blocks northeast along the river, the **Boott Cotton Mills Museum** (www.nps.gov/lowe; 115 John St; adult/child/student

$6/3/4; ⏱9:30am-5pm) has exhibits that chronicle the rise and fall of the industrial revolution in Lowell, including technological changes, labor movements and immigration. The highlight is a working weave room, with 88 power looms. A special exhibit on **Mill Girls & Immigrants** (40 French St; admission free; ⏱1:30-5pm) examines the lives of working people, while seasonal exhibits are sometimes on display in other historic buildings around town.

The Drive ≫ Take the Lowell Connector to US 3 heading south. In Billerica, exit to Concord Rd. Continue south on Concord Rd (MA 62) through Bedford. This road becomes Monument St and terminates at Monument Sq in Concord center. Walden Pond is about 3 miles south of Monument Sq, along Walden St (MA 126) south of MA 2.

TRIP HIGHLIGHT

⑤ Concord, Massachusetts

Tall, white church steeples rise above ancient oaks in Colonial Concord, giving the town a stateliness that belies the American Revolution drama that occurred centuries ago. It is easy to see how so many writers found their inspiration here in the 1800s.

Ralph Waldo Emerson was the paterfamilias of literary Concord and the founder of the Transcendentalist movement (and, incidentally, a graduate of Harvard College). His home of nearly 50 years, the **Ralph Waldo Emerson Memorial House** (www.rwe.org/emersonhouse; 28 Cambridge Turnpike; adult/child/senior & student $7/free/5; ⏱10am-4:30pm Thu-Sat, 1-4:30pm Sun mid-Apr–Oct), often hosted his renowned circle of friends.

One of them was Henry David Thoreau (another Harvard grad), who put Transcendentalist beliefs into practice when he spent two years in a rustic cabin on the shores of **Walden Pond** (www.mass.gov/dcr; 915 Walden St). The glacial pond is now a state park, surrounded by acres of forest. A footpath circles the pond, leading to the site of Thoreau's cabin on the northeast side. Parking is $5.

✖ p227

The Drive ≫ Take MA 2 east to its terminus in Cambridge. Go left on the Alewife Brook Pkwy (MA 16), then right on Massachusetts Ave and into Harvard Sq. Parking spaces are in short supply, but you can usually find one on the street around the Cambridge Common.

TRIP HIGHLIGHT

⑥ Cambridge, Massachusetts

Founded in 1636 to educate men for the ministry, Harvard is America's oldest college. The geographic heart of the university – where red-brick buildings and leaf-covered paths exude academia – is **Harvard Yard**. For maximum visual impact, enter the yard through the wrought-iron Johnston Gate, which is flanked by the two oldest buildings on campus, **Harvard Hall** and **Massachusetts Hall**.

The focal point of the yard is the **John Harvard statue**, by Daniel Chester French. Inscribed 'John Harvard, Founder of Harvard College, 1638,' it is commonly known as the 'statue of three lies': John Harvard was *not* the college's founder but its first benefactor; Harvard was actually founded in 1636; and the man depicted isn't even Mr Harvard himself! This symbol hardly lives up to the university's motto, *Veritas* (truth).

ALL ABOUT HAAAHHHVAAAHHHD

Want to know more? Get the inside scoop from savvy students on the unofficial **Harvard Tour** (www.trademarktours.com; per person $10).

Classic Trip

LOCAL KNOWLEDGE
EDDIE HORGAN, HARVARD '14; STUDENT MANAGER & GUIDE, THE HAHVAHD TOUR

In the northeast corner of Harvard's campus you'll find the Divinity School. One of our favorite secret spots at the school is the **Harvard Labyrinth**, used for contemplation, meditation and exercise. It's somewhat remote, but easy to find as it sits next to Andover Hall, the main Harvard Divinity School building. The labyrinth takes about 15 minutes to complete.

Top: Connecticut River, near Dartmouth College
Left: Harvard University
Right: Lofty heights at Harvard University

Most Harvard hopefuls rub the statue's shiny foot for good luck; little do they know that campus pranksters regularly use the foot like dogs use a fire hydrant.

So, what's the best thing about Harvard University? The architecture? The history? Arguably, it's the location. Overflowing with coffeehouses and pubs, bookstores and record stores, street musicians and sidewalk artists, panhandlers and professors, **Harvard Square** exudes energy, creativity and nonconformity – and it's all packed into a handful of streets between the university and the river. Spend an afternoon browsing bookstores, riffling through records and trying on vintage clothing; then camp out in a local cafe.

✕ ⨆ p227

The Drive ❯❯ Hop on Memorial Dr and drive east along the Charles River. At Western Ave, cross the river and follow the signs to I-90 heading east ($1.25 toll). Cruise through the tunnel (product of the notorious Big Dig) and merge with I-93 south. Follow I-93 south to I-95 south. Take I-95 south to Providence.

- - - - - - - - - -

TRIP HIGHLIGHT

❼ Providence, Rhode Island

College Hill rises east of the Providence River, and atop it sits **Brown**

University (www.brown. edu), the rambunctious younger child of an uptight New England household. Big brothers Harvard and Yale carefully manicure their public image, while the little black sheep of the family prides itself on staunch liberalism. Founded in 1764, Brown was the first American college to accept students regardless of religious affiliation, and the first to appoint an African American woman, Ruth Simmons, as president in 2001. Of its small 700-strong faculty, five Brown professors and two alumni have been honored as Nobel laureates.

The campus, consisting of 235 buildings, is divided into the Main Green and Lincoln Field. Enter through the wrought-iron **Van Wickle Gates** on College St. The oldest building on the campus is **University Hall**, a 1770 brick edifice, which was used as a barracks during the Revolutionary War. Free tours of the campus begin from

the **Brown University Admissions Office** (401-863-2378; Corliss Brackett House, 45 Prospect St). Call for times.

✕ p227

The Drive » Take Memorial Blvd out of Providence and merge with I-95 south. The generally pleasant tree-lined interstate will take you around the periphery of Groton, Old Lyme, Guilford and Madison, where you may want to stop for a coffee or snack. Exit at junction 47 for downtown New Haven.

- - - - - - - - - - -

TRIP HIGHLIGHT

8 New Haven, Connecticut

Gorgeous, Gothic Yale University is America's third-oldest university. Head to the **Yale University Visitor Center** (www.yale.edu/visitor; cnr Elm & Temple Sts; 9am-4:30pm Mon-Fri, 11am-4pm Sat & Sun) to pick up a free map or take a free one-hour **tour** (10:30am & 2pm Mon-Fri, 1:30pm Sat).

The tour does a good job of fusing historical and academic facts and passes by several standout monuments, including Yale's tallest building, **Harkness Tower**. Guides refrain, however, from mentioning the tombs scattered around the

campus. No, these aren't filled with corpses; they're secret hangouts for senior students. The most notorious **Tomb** (64 High St) is the HQ for the Skull & Bones Club, founded in 1832. Its list of members reads like a who's who of high-powered politicos and financiers over the last two centuries.

The original burial ground for alumni, such as Yale's founder, the Reverend James Pierpont (1659–1714), is New Haven's pleasant **Green**, where an estimated 5000 to 10,000 people were buried before the cemetery was moved to **Grove Street Cemetery** (www.grovestreetcemetery. org; 227 Grove St; 9am-4pm). The first chartered cemetery in the country, Grove St's geometric pattern echoes the nine squares of the city, and the elaborate sarcophagi, obelisks and headstones are arranged by family group. Around the turn of the century, Yale medical students would sneak in here at night to dig up bodies for dissection. You can simply join the free guided **tour** (11am Sat May-Nov).

✕ 🛏 p227

Eating & Sleeping

Hanover ❶

✖ Lou's
Diner $

(http://lousrestaurant.net; 30 S Main St; breakfast $7-11, lunch $8-10; ☺breakfast & lunch) A Dartmouth institution since 1947, this is Hanover's oldest restaurant and it's always packed with students. From the retro tables or Formica-topped counter, order diner fare that has a bit of panache. The baked goods are highly recommended.

Concord ❺

✖ Country Kitchen
Sandwiches $

(181 Sudbury Ave; sandwiches $5-10; ☺breakfast & lunch Mon-Fri) At lunchtime, this little yellow house often has a line out the door, which is testament to its tiny size and amazing sandwiches. The Thanksgiving sandwich, with carved turkey, is the hands-down favorite. No credit cards and no seating, save the picnic table out front.

Cambridge ❻

✖ Cafe Pamplona
Cafe $

(12 Bow St; mains $8-15; ☺11am-midnight) In a cozy cellar on a backstreet, this no-frills European cafe is the choice among old-time Cantabrigians. In addition to tea and coffee drinks, Pamplona has light snacks, such as gazpacho, sandwiches and biscotti.

🛏 Irving House
Guesthouse $$

(☎617-547-4600; www.irvinghouse.com; 24 Irving St; r with shared bath $135-190, with private bath $165-255; P❄@☎) The 44 rooms at this property behind Harvard Yard vary, but every bed is covered with a quilt, and big windows let in plenty of light. Museum passes are a nice perk.

Providence ❼

✖ Louis Family Restaurant
Diner $

(www.louisrestaurant.org; 286 Brook St; mains $2-9; ☺daily; 🚸) Bleary-eyed students eat strawberry-banana pancakes and drink drip coffee at their favorite greasy spoon. The place is loaded with bad art and faded pictures, and prices are stuck in the 1960s, with spaghetti dinners for $5.

New Haven ❽

✖ Frank Pepe's Pizzeria
Pizzeria $

(157 Wooster St; pizzas $5-20; ☺4-10pm Mon, Wed & Thu, 11:30am-11pm Fri & Sat, 2:30-10pm Sun) Pepe's serves immaculate pizzas fired in a coal oven in frenetic surroundings, just as it has since 1925 when Frank Pepe got off the boat from Naples. His signature dish is the white-clam pizza, and it's well worth the wait.

🛏 Farnam Guesthouse
B&B $$

(☎203-562-7121; www.farnamguesthouse.com; 616 Prospect St; r $149-199; P❄☎) The Farnams have a long association with Yale as alums, donors and professors, and you can stay in their grand Georgian Colonial mansion in the best neighborhood in town. Expect old-world ambience, with Chippendale sofas, wingback chairs, Victorian antiques and plush oriental carpets.

Milan Hill State Park Fancy
spending the night in a yurt?

Woodland Heritage Trail

21

Embrace the solitude on this loop through the North Woods, where the stories of entrepreneurs, immigrants, lumberjacks and one very effective conservationist are as fascinating as the scenery.

TRIP HIGHLIGHTS

2 DAYS
75 MILES / 121KM

GREAT FOR...

BEST TIME TO GO

June to October for warm weather, fall foliage and open-for-business attractions.

ESSENTIAL PHOTO

Stark Covered Bridge, which anchors a picturesque village.

BEST FOR HISTORY

Learn about logging at Northern Forest Heritage Park.

3 miles

Jefferson
Hunt for elves and St Nick at Santa's Village

43 miles

Milan Hill State Park
Sleep in a yurt and climb a fire tower

Groveton

6

52 miles

Berlin
Legends of the loggermen still thrill today

8

4

2

START/ FINISH

9

Weeks State Park
Visit the hilltop home of a famous conservationist

13 miles

Gorham
If you don't see a moose then your eyes aren't open

75 miles

21 Woodland Heritage Trail

Why is northern New Hampshire so wild? Because a forward-thinking US senator from the Granite State, John W Weeks, introduced a bill in 1909 that birthed the modern national forest system. This trip makes the most of Weeks' vision by circling the White Mountain National Forest's rugged Kilkenny District, plunked dramatically between the Connecticut and Androscoggin Rivers and the Presidential Range. But it's not all lumberjacks and moose – Santa himself has somehow muscled onto the landscape.

❶ Six Gun City & Fort Splash

This trip starts with guns a' blazin' at **Six Gun City & Fort Splash** (☎603-586-4592; www.sixguncity.com; 1492 Presidential Hwy/US 2; adult & child/senior $23/18; ◷10am-5pm late May-early Sep), an Old West theme park east of Jefferson that, well, doesn't have much to do with New Hampshire's logging past. But, hey, everybody likes cowboys, right? Younger kids will most enjoy the low-key

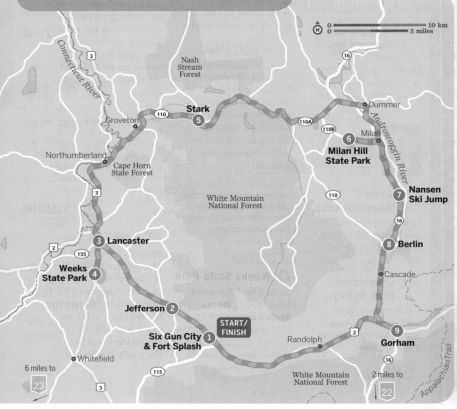

rides, which include a roller-coaster, a raft coaster, go-karts and some waterslides. Stop by the appropriately named Water Wheel (see p235) for maple syrup, New Hampshire gifts and a hearty meal.

The Drive » From the Water Wheel, look both ways for logging trucks, then turn right on US 2 and head to Jefferson.

TRIP HIGHLIGHT

② Jefferson

Just west of mountain-ringed Jefferson is another theme park, **Santa's Village** (📞603-586-4445; www.santasvillage.com; 528 Presidential Hwy/US 2; adult & child/senior $27/25; ⏱9:30am-6pm daily late Jun-Aug, to 5pm Sat & Sun late May-late Jun, Sep & Oct). Look for Santa's 26 elves as you enjoy the kiddie-focused rides, a Ferris

LINK YOUR TRIP

22 White Mountains Loop

From Gorham drive south to Mt Washington, New England's highest peak.

23 Connecticut River Byway

Vistas are bucolic on the Connecticut River Byway, which rolls south from Lancaster.

wheel and the *Jingle Bell Express* train. Kids can even visit Santa himself, usually found relaxing at home. The attached splash park, Ho Ho H2O, is open on warm days. The park opens weekends in December for holiday visits.

🍴 🛏 p235

The Drive » Continue west 7 miles from Santa's Village to Lancaster, passing clapboard homes, logging trucks and commanding views of the Presidential Range.

③ Lancaster

Photo op! Substitute your face for Paul Bunyan's at the **Great North Woods Welcome Center** (📞603-788-3212; www.northerngatewaychamber.org; 25 Park St; ⏱10am-4pm Mon-Sat) in downtown Lancaster. Here you can pick up maps and brochures before wandering past the boutiques and antique stores lining nearby Main St.

The Drive » Follow US 3 for 3 miles south out of downtown Lancaster. The park entrance is on the left, across the street from a scenic pull-off.

TRIP HIGHLIGHT

④ Weeks State Park

Named for US senator John Weeks, **Weeks State Park** (📞603-788-4004; www.nhstateparks.org; US 3; adult/child $5/3; ⏱10am-5pm Sat & Sun late-

May–mid-Jun & early Sep-early Oct, 10am-5pm Wed-Sun mid-Jun–early Sep) sits atop Mt Prospect. Weeks was a Lancaster native who introduced legislation in 1909 that helped to stem the degradation of local lands caused by unregulated logging. This legislation became known as the Weeks Act. By authorizing the federal government to purchase land at the head of navigable streams, the Act kick-started the national forest system by adding more than 19 million acres of land to the nation's holdings.

The park encompasses the 420-acre Weeks estate, where you can explore the Weeks home and enjoy 360-degree mountain views from the property's stone fire tower.

The Drive » From Lancaster, drive north on US 3, also known as the Daniel Webster Hwy, through Coos Junction, passing bogs and paralleling the railroad tracks. In Groveton, 10 miles north, snap a photo of the covered bridge before continuing east on NH 110.

⑤ Stark

Fans of George RR Martin's novel *Game of Thrones* can't be blamed if they ask directions to Winterfell, the northern holdfast of the Stark family that sits on the fringes of the lonely Wolfswood.

But there aren't any wildling or wargs in this roadside village (that we saw, anyway), just the impossibly picturesque **Stark Covered Bridge**. This white, 134ft Paddleford truss bridge – constructed in 1862 and subsequently rebuilt and strengthened – spans the Upper Ammonoosuc River. It's flanked by the white 1850 Union Church and a white schoolhouse, making for an eye-catching photo. General John Stark was a famous commander during the American Revolution (see the box, p234).

Two miles east, pull over for the **Camp Stark Roadside Marker**, which describes the WWII prisoner-of-war camp located nearby, where prisoners were put to work cutting pulpwood. It was the only war camp in New Hampshire.

The Drive >> Continue east 2.7 miles. Make a sharp left onto NH 110A at the junction of NH 110 and NH 110A. Drive just over 3.5 miles (you'll pass 110B, a cut-through) to NH 16 and a view of

the mighty Androscoggin River. Turn right and follow NH 16 south towards Berlin. Turn right at 110B for a short drive to Milan Hill State Park.

TRIP HIGHLIGHT

6 Milan Hill State Park

How often do you get to spend the night in a purple yurt? Yep, that's an option at **Milan Hill State Park** (☏603-449-2429; www.nhstateparks.org; 427 Milan Hill Rd; day-use fee adult/child $4/2; ☼year-round, camping mid-May–mid-Oct), also known for its cross-country skiing and snowshoe trails. The 45ft fire tower provides expansive views of New Hampshire's mountains as well as mountain ranges in Vermont, Maine and Canada. The park is pet friendly, so bring Fido for a walk or picnic. The park is open year-round but only staffed seasonally. No day-use fee is collected in the low season. The park is just south of New Hampshire's

GAVIN HELLIER/GETTY IMAGES ©

13 Mile Woods Scenic Area, which stretches along NH 16 and the Androscoggin River a few miles north and is known to be a popular strip for free-ranging moose.

🛏 p235

The Drive >> Continue south on NH 16, keeping your eyes open for moose, particularly in the morning and early evening. The road hugs the western side of the birch-lined Androscoggin River, a log-carrying highway in the first half of the 20th century.

7 Nansen Ski Jump

Four miles south of Milan, on the way into Berlin, pull over

BOOM PIERS

Driving south on NH 16 from Milan to Berlin, it's hard to miss the compact clusters of wood that rise from the middle of the river. Are they beaver dams? Small islands? Nope, those eye-catching clusters are boom piers, human-made islands that were used by lumbermen to separate logs by owner during the annual log drives. (Stamps that identified the owners were hammered into the end of the logs.) The log drives ended in 1963.

Stark Traverse the delightful Stark Covered Bridge

at the historic marker describing the **Nansen Ski Jump**, which is visible on the adjacent hill as you look north. This 171ft ski jump, first used in 1936, was the site of Olympic ski-jump trials in 1938. It was last used in 1982.

TRIP HIGHLIGHT

8 Berlin

On the western bank of the river in Berlin, take a self-guided tour through a recreated logging camp and learn about the region's logging past at the **Northern Forest Heritage Park**

(☎603-752-7202; www. northernforestheritage.org; 961 Main St; adult/child $6/4; ☯10am-4pm Mon-Fri late May-early Oct, hours vary Sat & Sun). Berlin was the site of numerous successful sawmills and papermaking operations, which were dependent on timber driven downstream from the North Woods.

For more history, step inside the park's **Brown House Museum** (admission free; ☯9am-4pm Mon-Fri, seasonally Sat); it once served as a boarding house for sawmill workers. Here you'll learn about the town's

history as a logging center between the 1860s and 1930s. Spiked boots, a crosscut saw and other tools are on display. Lumbermen who lost their lives on the river were memorialized by nailing their boots to a tree near where they perished. Guides share stories about the lumbermen during **river boat tours** (adult/child $15/8; ☯6pm Jun-Oct) that leave from the park.

✖ p235

The Drive ≫ From Berlin follow NH 16 – and the Androscoggin River – 6 miles south to Gorham.

LIVE FREE OR DIE

New Hampshire is the most politically conservative state in New England, with a libertarian streak that runs deep. It's tough and rugged, and its citizens still cling with pride to the famous words uttered by General John Stark, victor at the crucial Battle of Bennington: 'Live Free or Die!' The famous saying graces local license plates and appears all over the state.

TRIP HIGHLIGHT

9 Gorham

Gorham is a regional crossroads, linking roads flowing in from the North Woods, from Mt Washington and North Conway, and from the Rangeley Lakes region of northwestern Maine. Stop here for one of the area's best restaurants, Libby's Bistro. Housed in an old bank building, it has a relaxed speakeasy feel and uses local produce, in-season vegetables and New Hampshire seafood. Original wall safes speak of the building's banking past.

By this point, you've probably seen several moose-crossing signs dotting the route. If you still haven't seen an actual moose, join a moose safari with **Gorham Moose Tours** (☎603-466-3103; www.gorhamnh.org; information booth at 69 Main St; ⏱6:30pm Mon & Wed-Sat late May-Sep, plus Tue Jul). These determined folks know where the moose are and have a 95% moose-spotting success rate (and, yes, they've done the math!).

The Drive ≫ Complete the loop by returning to Six Gun City & Fort Splash, just west of the junction of US 2 and NH 115.

Eating & Sleeping

Jefferson ②

✕ Water Wheel
American $

(www.waterwheelnh.com; 1955 Presidential Hwy/US 2; mains $6-11; ⏰6am-2pm Jun-Aug, closed Tue & Wed Sep-May) A red water wheel marks the spot at this down-home eatery where decorative bears hang from the wooden rafters. Portions are hearty, and breakfast is served all day.

🛏 Jefferson Inn
B&B $$

(📞603-586-7998; http://jeffersoninn.com; 6 Renaissance Lane; r incl breakfast $135-195; ❄🔊🐾) Eleven homespun rooms – think quilts, old brooms and washboards on the wall – fill this attractive Victorian house perched on a hill above the Presidential Hwy. Four rooms have air-con and two rooms are pet friendly.

🛏 Evergreen Motel
Motel $

(📞603-586-4449; www.evergreenmotelnh.com; 537 Presidential Hwy/US 2; r incl breakfast $89; 🔊🐾♿) This 18-room mom-and-pop establishment is across the street from Santa's Village. There's also a complimentary 18-hole golf course on site. Snowmobilers can ride to their doors from the Corridor 5 route.

Milan Hill State Park ⑥

🛏 Milan Hill State Park
Campground $

(📞603-449-2429; www.nhstateparks.org; 427 Milan Hill Rd; tent & RV sites/yurts from $23/50; ⏰mid-May–mid-Oct) Four furnished yurts, each sleeping four people, are on offer. There are also six campsites, three of them available by reservation.

Berlin ⑧

✕ Sweet Mama's Bakery
Bakery $

(751 Main St; pastries & bread under $10; ⏰8am-6pm Wed-Fri, to 2pm Sat) Whoopee pies, baked doughnuts, cupcakes and a sign reading 'Sweet Mama's' – how could you not pull over? Friendly, delicious; get there early for the snowballs.

Gorham ⑨

✕ La Bottega Saladino's
Italian $

(www.saladinoitalianmarket.com; 152 Main St; mains $7-13; ⏰10am-6pm Tue-Thu, to 9pm Fri & Sat) The sandwiches at Saladino's, which includes a restaurant, market and deli, are tasty, filling and perfect for packing in a cooler for a picnic. The small restaurant serves salads, panini and pasta dishes.

✕ Libby's Bistro & Saalt Pub
American $$$

(📞603-466-5330; www.libbysbistro.net; 111 Main St; mains $11-28; ⏰bistro from 4:30pm Fri & Sat, pub 4:30-10:30pm Wed-Sat, to 8:30pm Sun) After a complete revamp of the interior and the menu, this 15-year-old bistro now serves globally inspired cuisine that incorporates local ingredients. In the pub, look for more casual fare, from New England seafood stew to French country baguettes and Moroccan tuna salad. In 2012, chef Liz Jackson was a James Beard semi-finalist for best chef in the Northeast – although she downplays such accolades, hoping to keep the dining experience fun.

🛏 Mt Madison Inn
Motel $$

(📞603-466-3622; www.mtmadisonmotel.com; 365 Main St; r $98-102, ste $132; ❄🔊🐾) King and queen rooms at this 32-room motel were getting an upgrade at press time. All rooms were recently re-carpeted and come with microwaves and refrigerators. A few rooms are pet friendly; pets are $5 per pet per night.

🛏 Top Notch Inn
Motel $$

(📞603-466-5496; www.topnotchinn.com; 265 Main St; r $89-119, house $189; ⏰mid-May–late Oct; ❄🔊🐾) A brown moose stands guard outside the Top Notch. In addition to standard motel rooms, the inn has five 'no-kids' rooms (aka Country Rooms) that are also pet free. The three-room Pinkham House, a restored farmhouse, sleeps up to eight people. Laundry facilities are available.

White Mountains Heed adventure's call with world-class hiking and stellar views

White Mountains Loop

22

Adventure calls from every trailhead on this notch-linking loop that swoops along the Kancamagus Hwy, climbs the slopes of Mt Washington and passes the mighty flumes of Franconia Notch.

TRIP HIGHLIGHTS

3 DAYS
135 MILES / 217KM

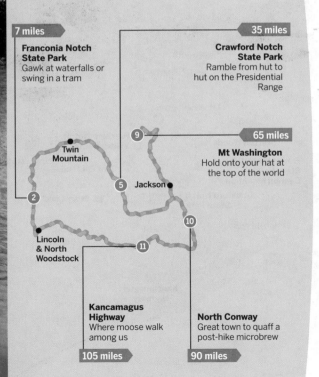

7 miles

Franconia Notch State Park
Gawk at waterfalls or swing in a tram

35 miles

Crawford Notch State Park
Ramble from hut to hut on the Presidential Range

65 miles

Mt Washington
Hold onto your hat at the top of the world

Twin Mountain

Jackson

Lincoln & North Woodstock

Kancamagus Highway
Where moose walk among us

105 miles

North Conway
Great town to quaff a post-hike microbrew

90 miles

GREAT FOR...

BEST TIME TO GO
Visit from May to October for warm days and full foliage.

ESSENTIAL PHOTO
Capture Presidential peaks from the CL Graham overlook.

BEST FOR HISTORY
Bretton Woods, where the World Bank was created.

237

22 | White Mountains Loop

Hikers, lace up your boots and grab your walking sticks. The White Mountain National Forest, with an assist from the Appalachian Mountain Club, is home to one of the most impressive trail networks in the nation. What will you experience? Waterfalls crashing through gorges, streams rippling past an abandoned settlement and mountain huts serving up meals and beds for weary ramblers. Not a hiker? Locomotive rides through leafy terrain, and a fairy-tale theme park bring the adventure to you.

1 Lincoln & North Woodstock

Outdoor shops, an adventure outfitter and a gob-smacking array of pancake houses line the Kancamagus Hwy on its run through Lincoln and nearby North Woodstock. Start at the **White Mountains Visitor Center** (☏ 603-745-8720; www.visitwhitemountains. com; 200 Kancamagus Hwy, North Woodstock; ☺ 8:30am-5pm), where a life-size stuffed moose and free cups of Keurig coffee set

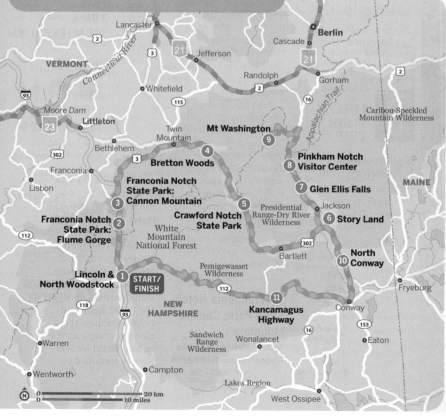

the mood for adventure. This is also the place to grab brochures and trail maps and purchase a White Mountain National Forest Recreation Pass ($3/5 per day/week), which is required for extended stops at national forest trailheads. Want to leave the planning to others? Try **Alpine Adventures** (☏603-745-9911; www. alpinezipline.com; 41 Main St, Lincoln; tours $79-109) a few doors down. These knowledgeable folks lead backwoods safaris and zip-line tours.

 p243

The Drive ≫ Drive north on I-93. US 3 joins I-93 near Flume Gorge for an 8-mile stretch that's flanked by the Kinsman and Franconia Mountain ranges in Franconia Notch State Park.

 LINK YOUR TRIP

21 Woodland Heritage Trail

From the Mt Washington Auto Rd, drive north 8 miles to Gorham for a trip into New Hampshire's logging past.

23 Connecticut River Byway

Drive toward Littleton on I-93 north from Franconia Notch to start a pastoral drive along the Connecticut River.

 TRIP HIGHLIGHT

2 Franconia Notch State Park: Flume Gorge

Expect crowds at **Flume Gorge** (☏603-745-8391; www.nhstateparks.org; I-93, exit 34A; adult/child $15/13; ⏱9am-5pm mid-May–mid-Oct), a natural granite sluice with 90ft walls in Franconia Notch State Park. But don't let elbow jostling keep you away – the verdant, moss-covered cliffs and rushing stream are worth it. The trail has a sturdy walkway, making it accessible for everyone. If you're going to ride the Cannon Mountain Aerial Tramway, buy the Discovery Pass (adult/child $28/22). It covers the flume and the tram at a reduced rate.

Take a walk or a bike ride on the 8-mile **Recreation Trail** beside the Pemigewasset River or stroll 500ft to the **Basin**, the first of several waterfalls accessed from the Basin parking lot north of the Flume Gorge Visitor Center.

The Drive ≫ From the visitor center, drive north on I-93 to exit 34B.

3 Franconia Notch State Park: Cannon Mountain

A short drive north, the **Cannon Mountain Aerial Tramway** (☏603-823-8800; www.cannonmt.com; I-93, exit 34B; round-trip adult/child $15/12; ⏱9am-5pm late May–mid-Oct) whisks you to a lookout point so lofty that you'll feel you've sprouted wings.

Everybody mourns the **Old Man of the Mountain**, a rock formation that remains the state symbol despite its collapse in May 2003. Inside the Tramway Valley Station, the departure point for the tram, you'll find the **Old Man of the Mountain Museum** (admission free; ⏱9am-5pm late May–mid-Oct), where there are forensically accurate diagrams of 'the Profile's' collapse, and tributes to this beloved symbol.

The Drive ≫ Follow I-93 north to exit 35, taking US 3 north to Twin Mountain, where you'll pass a prison-striped moose at the police station. Fill up the tank at Foster's Crossroads, then follow US 302 east.

TRIP HIGHLIGHT

4 Bretton Woods

From July 1–22, 1944, the **Mount Washington Hotel** (www.brettonwoods. com; 310 Mt Washington Hotel Rd) hosted the Bretton Woods International Monetary Conference. This history-making summit established the World Bank and helped stabilize the global economy as WWII ended. World leaders were determined to avoid the disastrous economic fallout that occurred after WWI. Today, spend a sumptuous night in one of the resort's 200 rooms or simply stop by to wander past the historic photographs beside the lobby.

For details of the Mount Washington Cog Railway, see p150.

🛏 p243

The Drive » Follow US 302 south 4 miles to the park.

TRIP HIGHLIGHT

5 Crawford Notch State Park

The Pond Loop and Sam Tilley trails are two easy riverside hikes in this **state park** (☎603-374-2272; www.nhstateparks.org; 2057 US 302) at the base of the White Mountains. For details about local trails, stop by the **Appalachian Mountain Club Highland Center** (☎front desk 603-278-4453, reservations 603-466-2727; www.outdoors.org/highland; US 302), one of the country's best

launch pads for outdoor exploration. There's an information desk, a dining room and a small outdoor retail shop. Overnight lodging is also available, and hikers can link to the AMC's popular hut-to-hut trail system from here. The huts are lodge-like dorms offering meals, bunks and stellar views. The Highland Center is just north of the park.

The Conway Scenic Railroad's Notch Train (see p242) stops at the nearby 1891 **Crawford Depot & Visitor Center** (www.outdoors.org; ⏱9am-5pm Jun–mid-Oct), which contains a small but good collection of train-related history.

🛏 p243

The Drive » Continue east on US 302, passing Dry River Campground and the Crawford Notch General Store. Turn left at NH 16, and continue 0.25 miles to Story Land.

6 Story Land

With its bright, off-kilter facade, **Story Land**

(☎603-383-4186; www.storylandnh.com; 850 NH 16; adult & child/senior $29/27; ⏱daily mid-Jun–Aug, Sat & Sun late May–mid-Jun & Sep), 0.25 miles north of US 302, is like a Venus flytrap, luring families in for a closer look, then preventing escape with scenes of kiddie-minded fun just beyond its protective wall. What's inside this roadside theme park? Shows, games and 21 rides based on fairy tales and make-believe. This popular place gets a thumbs-up from kids and parents alike.

✓ **TOP TIP: HIKER SHUTTLE**

Need transportation before or after a strenuous one-way hike? Use the **AMC hiker shuttle** (www.outdoors.org/lodging/lodging-shuttle.cfm) system for your pick-up or drop-off. These shuttles run daily from June to mid-September, then on weekends to mid-October. Prices range from $10 to $22 per ride.

Crawford Notch State Park

The Drive >> Drive north on NH 16. In 2 miles, take a photo break at the covered bridge in tiny Jackson. Continue 8 miles to the trailhead for Glen Ellis Falls.

7 Glen Ellis Falls

Only a stone's throw off NH 16, stop at Glen Ellis Falls for a few snapshots. This easy walk brings you 0.3 miles to a 60ft waterfall, one of the prettiest in the region. Most can make the hike without breaking a sweat.

The Drive >> Continue north almost 1 mile to the visitor center.

8 Pinkham Notch Visitor Center

Hikers tackling Mt Washington should stop by the **Pinkham Notch Visitor Center** (☑front desk 603-466-2721, reservations 603-466-2727; www.outdoors. org; NH 16) for information, maps and a diorama that spotlights area trails. The 4.2-mile **Tuckerman Ravine Trail** to the summit starts behind the visitor center. Appropriate preparation for this brutal climb – which can be deadly in bad weather – is imperative.

p243

The Drive >> Drive 3 miles north to the entrance to the Auto Rd.

TRIP HIGHLIGHT

9 Mt Washington

Welcome to Mt Washington, New England's highest peak and the site of the world's second-highest recorded wind gust: 231mph (and the highest ever observed by man). The heavy chains wrapped around the **Auto Road Stage Office** at the summit attest that winter here is no laughing matter.

The **Sherman Adams Summit Building** (state park 603-466-3347, general info 603-356-2137; www.mountwashington.org; 8:30am-6pm late May-early Sep), run by the state-park system, has souvenirs, refreshments and a lookout tower. It also holds the nonprofit **Mount Washington Observatory & Museum** (800-706-0432; www.mountwashington.org; museum adult/child $3/1), which was raising funds for a complete remodeling at press time. If you time it right, the winding **Mt Washington Auto Road** (603-466-3988; www.mountwashingtonautoroad.com; Rte 16, Pinkham Notch; car & driver/child 5-12yr/extra adult $25/6/8; 8am-5pm May-Oct) will be open, but there will still be snow and ice at the summit. Two runners reached the top, a 7.6-mile climb, in less than one hour (!) during the annual Mt Washington Road Race.

The Drive >> Backtrack to the junction of NH 16 and US 302. Follow US 302/NH 16 southeast to North Conway, stopping at the Intervale Scenic Vista for views, brochures and restrooms.

TRIP HIGHLIGHT

10 North Conway

North Conway is the perfect mountain town: lively pubs, a top-notch breakfast joint and numerous quaint inns. Shopaholics can pop into one of the 60-plus outlet stores, including LL Bean. North Conway is also home to the **Conway Scenic Railroad** (603-356-5251; www.conwayscenic.com; 38 Norcross Circle; adult/child from $50/35; mid-Jun–mid-Oct), which runs half-day train trips up into Crawford Notch on the Notch Train. On sunny days they may attach the open-air coach car, a restored Pullman with no glass in the windows that's perfect for shutterbugs.

What happens when you push the red button inside the mock observatory building at the **Mount Washington Weather Discovery Center** (603-356-2137; www.mountwashington.org; 2779 White Mountain Hwy/NH 16; admission free; 10am-5pm)? We won't spoil the surprise, but you might want to hold on tight. This small but fascinating museum examines wild weather events and explains the unique weather conditions atop Mt Washington.

🍴 🛏 p243

The Drive >> US 302 splits from NH 16 south of downtown. Follow NH 16 heading south for 2.5 miles, taking it through Conway, then hop onto NH 112, which is better known as the Kancamagus Hwy.

TRIP HIGHLIGHT

11 Kancamagus Highway

Roll down the windows and slip on your shades. It's time to drive. This 34.5-mile byway, named for a peace-seeking Sagamon chief, rolls through the White Mountain National Forest unhampered by commercial distractions or pesky stoplights – although you do need to gauge your speed and watch for wildlife. Stop by the **Saco Ranger District Office** (603-447-5448; www.fs.usda.gov/whitemountain; 33 Kancamagus Hwy; 8am-4:30pm) for maps, information and a recreation pass ($3/5 per day/week) if you plan to park and explore.

Fifteen miles west, pull over at **Sabbaday Falls** for an easy climb to flumes cascading through granite channels and small pools. After the falls, the road starts rising and leafy maples are replaced by dark conifers. At **Kancamagus Pass** (elevation 2855ft) only Mt Washington can beat the serene view. For camera-ready panoramas, stop at the **CL Graham Wangan Grounds Overlook** just east of the pass or the **Pemi Overlook** just west.

The **Lincoln Trail** at the Lincoln Woods parking area further west follows the Pemigewasset River for 2.9 miles. Kids enjoy the suspension bridge beside the visitor center.

The Drive >> From here, drive west on NH 112 to return to Lincoln and North Woodstock.

Eating & Sleeping

Lincoln & North Woodstock ❶

✕ Cascade Coffee House
Cafe $

(115 Main St, North Woodstock; sandwiches $3-9; ⏱7am-7pm; 📶) Comfy couches, welcoming staff and locally roasted coffee make this a great spot for hanging out. Also sells breakfast sandwiches and panini. Hours vary seasonally.

Bretton Woods ❹

🛏 Omni Mt Washington Hotel & Resort
Hotel $$$

(📞603-278-1000; www.brettonwoods.com; 310 Mt Washington Hotel Rd; r $289-449, ste $549; ❄@📶🏊) Open since 1902, this grand hotel maintains a sense of fun – note the moose's head overlooking the lobby and the framed local wildflowers in many of the guest rooms. Also offers 27 holes of golf, red-clay tennis courts, an equestrian center and a spa. There's a $25 daily resort fee.

Crawford Notch State Park ❺

🛏 AMC Highland Center
Lodge $$

(📞603-466-2727; www.outdoors.org; US 302, Crawford Notch; r adult/child/youth 13-17yr $95/35/80, per person s/d incl breakfast & dinner from $137; 📶) This four-season lodge, run by the Appalachian Mountain Club (AMC), is an ideal base for hikers. Rooms are basic but comfortable and come in several configurations. Most packages include hearty breakfasts and dinners, and gear rentals. Rates vary depending on room type and age; 10% to 20% discounts are available for AMC members. The dining room is open to the public.

Pinkham Notch Visitor Center ❽

🛏 Joe Dodge Lodge
Lodge $

(📞603-466-2727; www.outdoors.org; NH 16, Pinkham Notch; r with shared bathroom adult/child/youth 13-17yr $47/20/40, incl breakfast & dinner $67/57/30; 📶) Part of the AMC camp at Pinkham Notch, the lodge has 103 rooms in a variety of configurations. Most packages include breakfast and dinner. There are discounts for AMC members; the dining room is open to the public.

North Conway ❿

✕ May Kelly's Cottage
American, Irish $$

(www.maykellys.com; 3002 White Mountain Hwy; mains $10-22; ⏱from 4pm Tue-Thu, from noon Fri-Sun) Irish conviviality and friendliness? May Kelly's is the real deal. Local-attic decor, helpful waitresses, mountain views and hearty mains make it a top choice.

✕ Moat Mountain Smokehouse & Brewing Co
American $$

(www.moatmountain.com; 3378 White Mountain Hwy; sandwiches $9-11, mains $14-25; ⏱11:30am-11pm Sun-Thu, to 11:30pm Fri & Sat) The modern-day equivalent of the travelers' inns of frontier days, Moat Mountain serves good beer and great eats.

✕ Peaches
American $

(www.peachesnorthconway.com; 2506 White Mountain Hwy; mains $6-9; ⏱7am-2:30pm) Tempting breakfasts include apple and cinnamon crepes, California omelets and strawberry French toast stuffed with cream cheese. Sandwiches and salads are available for lunch.

🛏 Colonial Motel
Motel $$

(📞603-356-5178; www.thecolonialmotel.com; 2431 White Mountain Hwy; r $95-150, ste $240; ❄📶🏊🐾) Rooms are traditional but inviting at this 26-room family-run property set back slightly from the main drag. There's a $10 fee per dog per night.

🛏 Golden Gables
Motel $$

(📞603-356-2878; www.goldengablesinn.com; 1814 White Mountain Hwy; r $108-199, ste $152; ❄📶🏊) The balconies with mountain views close the deal at this stylish motel. It has a back lawn perfect for letting the kids run free.

Northampton *Explore Smith College's eclectic buildings and verdant grounds*

Classic Trip

Connecticut River Byway

23

This drive links mill towns, white-clapboard villages and colleges as it unfurls beside farms, forests and the Connecticut River, which roars then ripples through New Hampshire and Massachusetts.

TRIP HIGHLIGHTS

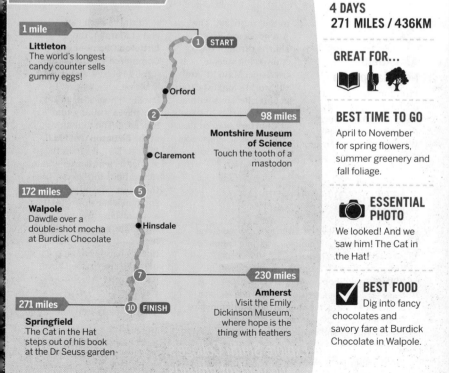

1 mile

Littleton
The world's longest candy counter sells gummy eggs!

● Orford

2 ——— **98 miles**

Montshire Museum of Science
Touch the tooth of a mastodon

● Claremont

172 miles ——— **5**

Walpole
Dawdle over a double-shot mocha at Burdick Chocolate

● Hinsdale

7 ——— **230 miles**

Amherst
Visit the Emily Dickinson Museum, where hope is the thing with feathers

271 miles ——— **10** FINISH

Springfield
The Cat in the Hat steps out of his book at the Dr Seuss garden

1 START

4 DAYS
271 MILES / 436KM

GREAT FOR...

BEST TIME TO GO

April to November for spring flowers, summer greenery and fall foliage.

ESSENTIAL PHOTO

We looked! And we saw him! The Cat in the Hat!

BEST FOOD

Dig into fancy chocolates and savory fare at Burdick Chocolate in Walpole.

Classic Trip

23 Connecticut River Byway

Taking a road trip beside the Connecticut River is like earning a liberal arts degree in one weekend. There's Fort at No 4's Colonial history; natural sciences and wildlife at the Montshire; poetry from Emily Dickinson in Amherst; and a mini session in the arts among the sculpture-dotted grounds of Saint-Gaudens. And you'll surely feel like one of the students while strolling the lively campuses of Amherst, Smith and Mt Holyoke.

TRIP HIGHLIGHT

❶ Littleton, New Hampshire

Littleton may be off the beaten path, but it's an inspirational place to start this trip. The White Mountains hover to the southeast. The Ammonoosuc River churns through town. A towering steeple overlooks Main St. And the world's longest candy counter beckons with a rainbow's array of sweets at **Chutters** (www.chutters.com; 43 Main St; ⏰9am-6pm Mon-Sat, 10am-6pm Sun).

LITTLETON: SHOPPING ON MAIN STREET

Littleton's Main St is lined with indie-owned stores. For outdoor gear and clothing, step into **Lahout's** (www.lahouts.com; 99 Main St; ⏰9:30am-5:30pm), America's oldest ski shop. A few doors down is **Village Book Shop** (www.booksmusictoys.com; 81 Main St; ⏰9am-5pm), with lots of local and regional books. Downstairs, the **League of New Hampshire Craftsmen** (⏰10am-5pm) runs a gallery that sells jewelry, pottery and other arts and crafts made in New Hampshire.

At the eastern end of Main St, the **Littleton Chamber of Commerce Visitor Center** (☎603-444-6561; www.littletonareachamber.com; 2 Union St; ⏰9am-5pm Mon-Fri) provides a walking-tour brochure. The tour stops at the **Littleton Grist Mill**. Built in 1797, it's back in service as a mill after renovations initiated in the 1990s. The adjacent Ammonoosuc drops 144ft as it crashes through town. The **covered bridge** here, built in 2004, looks like it's barely hanging onto the riverbank – but it's perfectly safe for walking.

✕ ⛏ p253

The Drive ≫ Take I-93 north to exit 44 and NH 135 south. This bucolic road passes fields,

red barns and cattle-crossing signs as it hugs the river. Snap a photo of the covered bridge in Woodstock, then continue south on NH 10. In Orford, look left for the Seven Ridge Houses. Built by local craftspeople between 1773 and 1839 in the Bullfinch style, they're impressive. Continue south on NH 10 into Hanover, following it past the Dartmouth green. Take NH 10A/W Wheelock St over the Connecticut River, then take the first left onto Montshire Rd.

TRIP HIGHLIGHT

2 Montshire Museum of Science, Norwich, Vermont

Rub the tooth of a mastodon. View current images from the Hubble telescope. Watch leafcutter ants at work. But whatever you do at the **Montshire** (📞802-649-2200; www.montshire.org; 1 Montshire Rd; adult/child $12/10; ⏲10am-5pm; 👶), don't park your car near the planet Neptune – it's part of the model solar system that stretches the

LINK YOUR TRIP

20 Ivy League Tour
Cross the river near the Montshire museum to tour Dartmouth College.

25 Monadnock Villages
From Walpole, take NH 12 to Keene for a stroll through downtown.

LOCAL KNOWLEDGE
BOB RAISELIS, EXHIBITS
DIRECTOR, MONTSHIRE
MUSEUM OF SCIENCE

We have about 3 miles of trails at
the Montshire, and all along these
trails are exhibits about plants, the ecology of the
area, the geology of the Upper Valley, natural history
and human history. One really lovely trail is the River
Loop. The riverside section is accessible, so it's great
for visitors in wheelchairs and those using walkers or
strollers. Just past our meadow the riverside section
begins, and visitors can walk along the Connecticut
River for quite a while, on a gentle sun-dappled trail.

length of the parking lot
and beyond, and Neptune
is way, way out there.
Located on a 110-acre site
beside the Connecticut
River, the museum
offers exhibits covering
ecology, technology and
the natural and physical
sciences. It's also the
regional visitor center for
the **Silvio Conte National
Fish & Wildlife Refuge**
(www.fws.gov/r5soc) – look

Top: Kids enjoy the Dr Seuss National Memorial Sculpture Garden
Right: Littleton

for the life-size moose and the displays that highlight local flora and fauna. In summer, water-focused and sensory exhibits in the Montshire's outdoor Science Park will fascinate younger kids. The museum is kid friendly, but adults can learn a lot too, particularly with the exhibits on the upper floors.

For details about Dartmouth and Hanover, see p220.

The Drive » Return to Hanover, taking NH 10 past the strip-mall wasteland of West Lebanon, where you pick up NH 12A south to Saint-Gaudens. For variety, the river can be tracked along US 5 in Vermont between a village or two, with regular bridges connecting New Hampshire and Vermont until you reach Walpole.

③ Saint-Gaudens National Historic Site, New Hampshire

In the summer of 1885, the sculptor Augustus Saint-Gaudens rented an old inn near the town of Cornish and came to this beautiful spot to work. He returned summer after summer and eventually bought

the place in 1892. The **estate** (www.nps.gov/saga; 139 St Gaudens Rd, Cornish; adult/child $5/free; ⏰9am-4:30pm May-Oct), where he lived until his death in 1907, is now open to the public. Saint-Gaudens is best known for his public monuments, including the Robert Gold Shaw Memorial across from the state house in Boston. Recasts of his greatest sculptures dot the beautiful grounds. Visitors can also tour his home and wander the studios where artists-in-residence sculpt. Exhibit buildings are closed in winter, but the visitor center is usually open from 9am to 4:15pm weekdays.

The Drive ≫ About 1.5 miles south is the 1866 Cornish Windsor Bridge, the longest wooden bridge in the US. And, yes, you can drive across it. Not quite a mile south, bear left onto Town House Rd at the fork for two more covered bridges, then continue south on NH 12A, which soon rejoins NH 12.

④ Fort at No 4, Charlestown, New Hampshire

Named for a 1700s land grant, the original fort was built in the 1740s to protect pioneer farmers from the French and Native Americans. The original fort, which was no longer needed by the late 1770s and no longer exists, was reconstructed in the 1960s as a **living history museum** (📞603-826-5700; www.fortat4.com; 267 Springfield Rd; adult/child 6-12yr/youth 13-17yr $10/5/7; ⏰10am-4:30pm Mon-Sat, to 4pm Sun May-Oct). Its layout is based on a detailed drawing sketched in 1746. Visitors can explore the different rooms of the fort, wander the riverside grounds and watch re-enactors, whose activities vary weekend to weekend. A Blacksmith Weekend kicked off the 2012 summer season. Check the Fort at No 4 Facebook page for current activities.

The Drive ≫ Views of rolling mountains and hills, as well as fields, railroad tracks, river views and a sugar house, decorate the 14-mile drive on NH 12 south to Walpole.

TRIP HIGHLIGHT

⑤ Walpole, New Hampshire

Locals descend from surrounding villages to dine at **Burdick Chocolate** (www.burdickchocolate.com; 47 Main St; lunch $13-23, dinner $16-24, desserts $5; ⏰7am-6pm Mon, 7am-9pm Tue-Sat, 7:30am-6pm Sun). Originally a New York City chocolatier, Burdick opened this sophisticated chocolate shop and cafe to showcase its desserts. These carefully crafted treats look like they attended finishing school – no slovenly lava cakes or naughty whoopee pies here. But you'll find more than just rich chocolate indulgences. The adjoining bistro serves creative new American dishes, plus artisanal cheeses and top-notch wines. The creamy quiche is fantastic. Purchase local art and crafts across the street at the **Walpole Artists Cooperative** (www.walpoleartisans.org; 52 Main St; ⏰10am-5pm Wed-Sat, 11am-3pm Sun), then cross Westminster St for a gander at **Ruggles & Hunt** (www.rugglesandhunt.com; 8 Westminster St; ⏰10am-6pm Mon-Sat, noon-5pm Sun), an eclectic boutique with toys, women's clothes and home furnishings.

The Drive ≫ Return to NH 12. Drive south 5 miles to the junction of NH 12 and NH 63 at the sugar house. Bear right onto NH 63 for a particularly scenic spin past the Park Hill Meetinghouse and Spofford Lake. Continue across NH 9. After Hinsdale, NH 63 swings back toward the river and soon crosses into Massachusetts. Follow MA 63 south 15 miles. Turn right at Center St and follow it to Greenfield Rd.

⑥ Montague, Massachusetts

Montague is beloved for 'books you don't need in a place you can't find.' Luckily, both claims are slightly exaggerated.

On an unassuming road in a sleepy town, the **Montague Bookmill** (www.montaguebookmill.com; 440 Greenfield Rd; ⏰10am-6pm) is a converted cedar gristmill from 1842 that now contains a big used bookstore. The maze of rooms has oodles of used books (many academic and esoteric) and couches on which to read them. The westward-facing windows overlook the roiling Sawmill River and its glorious waterfall. There are outside decks over the water where you can take your coffee.

Though the bookstore is the biggest draw, other ventures, including an art gallery, a music shop, a cafe and a restaurant, make it even easier to while away half a day at the mill.

The Drive » Leaving the mill, take a left on Greenfield Rd and an immediate left on Meadow Rd, which winds along the river, passing through scenic farmland. At the terminus, turn right on MA 47 to continue south. In Sunderland, turn left on MA 116 and continue about 10 miles into Amherst. For a quicker trip from the mill, head south on MA 47 and continue for 8 miles on MA 63 into Amherst.

TRIP HIGHLIGHT

⑦ Amherst, Massachusetts

Amherst is a sleepy little town that exudes academia. That is thanks mostly to the prestigious **Amherst College** (www. amherst.edu), a pretty 'junior Ivy' that borders the town green. Founded in 1821, Amherst College has retained its character and quality partly by maintaining its small size (1600 students).

Nearby, some pretty wooded grounds contain the two stately homes that constitute the **Emily Dickinson Museum** (www. emilydickinsonmuseum.org; 280 Main St; adult/child $8/4; ⏰10am-5pm Wed-Sun). Here, the poet lived out her years in near seclusion, penning thousands of poems.

A few miles south of the town center, **Hampshire College** (www.hampshire.edu) is an innovative center of learning, emphasizing multidisciplinary, student-led study. Stop by on your way out of town to visit the **Eric Carle Museum of Picture Book Art** (www. picturebookart.org; 125 W Bay Rd; adult/child $9/6; ⏰10am-4pm), located on campus. Cofounded by the author and illustrator of *The Very Hungry Caterpillar,* this superb museum celebrates the art of book illustration with exhibits and a hands-on art studio.

✖ 🛏 p253

The Drive » Head west on MA 9, departing Amherst and passing through the strip-mall town of Hadley. Cross the art-deco Calvin Coolidge Bridge (named for a former resident of Northampton), which yields lovely views of the Connecticut River and the Berkshire foothills. Continue east on MA 9 past the Three County Fairgrounds and into Northampton, where MA 9 becomes Main St.

⑧ Northampton, Massachusetts

In a region famous for its charming college towns, you'd be hard-pressed to find anything more appealing than the crooked streets of downtown Northampton. Old redbrick buildings, idealistic street musicians and lots of pedestrian traffic provide a lively backdrop as you wander into record shops, coffeehouses, rock clubs and bookstores.

Move a few steps west of the picturesque commercial center and you'll stumble onto the bucolic grounds of **Smith College** (www. smith.edu). The verdant 125-acre campus along Elm St holds an eclectic architectural mix of nearly 100 buildings as well as the pretty **Paradise Pond**, encircled by walking trails.

After strolling around the pond, stop by the **Lyman Conservatory** (www.smith.edu/garden; 15 College Lane; donation $1; ⏰8:30am-4pm). Visitors are welcome to explore the college's collection of Victorian greenhouses and botanical gardens,

which are packed to the brim with beautiful things in bloom.

✕ 🛏 p253

The Drive ⟫ Drive east on MA 9 and cross the Calvin Coolidge Bridge. On the east bank, veer right onto Bay Rd for about 2 miles, then turn right to head south on MA 47. The road follows the winding Connecticut River for about 6 miles, passing Skinner State Park and Bachelor Brook Resource Area before entering South Hadley.

⑨ South Hadley, Massachusetts

The southernmost and sleepiest of the Five College towns, South Hadley's tiny center contains a gazebo-dotted green with attendant brick church. Across the street, the urbanist open-air shopping mall is known as the Village Commons. Otherwise, there's not much to see in town, save the beautiful, bucolic campus of **Mt Holyoke College** (www.mtholyoke.edu), the

nation's oldest women's college. Laid out by the great American landscape architect Frederick Law Olmsted, the 800-acre campus contains lush botanic gardens, woodland trails and several waterfalls, making it a delightful strolling destination. Don't miss the gothic **Abbey Chapel**, which contains an impressive handcrafted organ.

The Drive ⟫ Head south out of town on College St (MA 116). Continue south on US 202 to I-91, which will take you south to Springfield.

TRIP HIGHLIGHT

⑩ Springfield, Massachusetts

The ongoing revitalization of downtown Springfield makes this gritty city an appropriate place to end a tour of the Connecticut River Valley. Start at the **Museum Quadrangle** (www.springfieldmuseums. org; 21 Edwards St; adult/ child/senior & student $12.50/6.50/9; ☺10am-5pm), an attractive complex that includes two art museums, a history

museum and a science museum. You'll find such diverse attractions as an extensive collection of samurai armor, a mint collection of locally produced Indian motorcycles and an impressive Dinosaur Hall. The highlight is the **Dr Seuss National Memorial Sculpture Garden** (www.catinthehat. org; admission free), at the center of the complex, dedicated to Springfield's favorite native son.

Besides the children's literary master, another American cultural icon has its birthplace here: basketball. Sports fans should swing by the **Naismith Memorial Basketball Hall of Fame** (www.hoophall.com; 1000 W Columbus Ave; adult/child/ senior $19/12/15; ☺10am-5pm), located south of the center on the riverfront. Not only will you learn about the origins of the sport, but you can also measure your hoop skills against those of the game's greatest players.

✕ p253

Eating & Sleeping

Littleton ❶

✕ Chang Thai — Thai $$

(☎603-444-8810; www.changthaicafe.com; 77 Main St; mains $10-17; ⏰lunch & dinner Mon-Sat, dinner Sun) Listen to live jazz as you savor Pad Thai, green curry and other well-seasoned dishes in this chic restaurant. Check online for jazz nights.

✕ Coffee Pot — Diner $

(30 Main St; mains up to $10; ⏰6:30am-4pm Mon-Fri, to 2pm Sat, to noon Sun) Sit at the counter and you'll be gabbing with locals before you even order your eggs. A friendly spot for getting the Littleton lowdown.

🛏 Littleton Motel — Motel $

(☎603-444-5780; www.littletonmotel.com; 166 Main St; r $68-98, ste $88-98; ⏰mid-May–Oct; ❄📶) Why, yes, I would like to stay in New Hampshire's oldest motel. But don't worry – the 19 rooms at this old-school motor inn, which opened in 1948, have refrigerators, microwaves and wi-fi.

Amherst ❼

✕ Amherst Coffee — Cafe $

(www.highercup.com; 28 Amity St; snacks $6-12; ⏰6:30am-12:30am Mon-Sat, 8am-11pm Sun) Coffee shop by day, wine and whiskey bar by night, this place is surprisingly urbane for little Amherst. The limited menu features a delectable selection of charcuterie, cheese and other Italian-style snacks. Stop in for a drink before or after catching a flick at the on-site Amherst Cinema.

✕ Antonio's Pizza by the Slice — Pizzeria $

(www.antoniospizza.com; 31 N Pleasant St; slices $2-3; ⏰10am-2am; 👪) Amherst's most popular pizza place features excellent slices made with a vast variety of toppings, flavorings and spices.

🛏 Amherst Inn — B&B $$

(☎413-253-5000; www.allenhouse.com; 257 Main St; d incl breakfast $105-195; ❄) A stately, blue, three-story Victorian with Tudor detailing, this haunted-looking B&B sits in the midst of some old shade trees with fine garden landscaping. The friendly Swedish innkeepers also operate the Allen House Inn, a half-mile out of town.

Northampton ❽

✕ Paul & Elizabeth's — Health Food $

(www.paulandelizabeths.com; 150 Main St; lunch $7-10, dinner $12-18; ⏰lunch & dinner Mon-Sat; 🌱👪) Northampton's premier natural-foods restaurant serves exquisite vegetarian cuisine and seafood, often with an Asian bent. Fish-and-chips fans, take note: the tempura-style fish with hand-cut fries may be the best you'll ever have.

🛏 Hotel Northampton — Historic Hotel $$

(☎413-584-3100; www.hotelnorthampton.com; 36 King St; d $180-250; P❄📶) This old-timer is smack in the center of Northampton and has been the town's best bet since 1927. Most of the 100 rooms are airy and well kitted out, with quilts and other frills adding to the air of historic grandeur.

Springfield ❿

✕ Chef Wayne's Big Mamou — Cajun $$

(www.chefwaynes-bigmamou.com; 68 Liberty St; lunch $8-12, dinner $10-18; ⏰lunch & dinner Mon-Sat) Patrons line up out the door for fabulous home-style Cajun fare. Ever-changing daily specials keep the regulars coming back for more, and Chef Wayne himself is almost always on hand to make sure they are satisfied. Reservations are not taken.

Meredith *This pretty town has an idyllic lakeside setting*

CHRIS CAMERON/ALAMY ©

Lake Winnipesaukee

24

This trip loops around the state's largest lake, swinging past wildlife preserves, trails, museums and a drive-in – there's something for toddlers, teens, the kids in-between and good ol' mom and dad.

TRIP HIGHLIGHTS

2 DAYS
125 MILES / 201KM

GREAT FOR...

BEST TIME TO GO
June to September: school's out and the weather is warm.

  ESSENTIAL PHOTO
The Weirs Beach Boardwalk – it's a classic!

  BEST FOR WILDLIFE
Visit Squam Lakes Natural Science Center for critter watching and live animal demos.

50 miles

Loon Center
Can you howl like a loon? Try it here

59 miles

Castle in the Clouds
Picnic like a hilltop millionaire – if only for one day

Sandwich

Moultonborough

3 **5** **6**

START/ FINISH **1**

Laconia

8

87 miles

Wolfeboro
Hike a rail trail, then catch an outdoor concert

Alton

Squam Lakes nature center
Wander past bears, mountain lions and river otters

Weirs Beach
Watch a movie the old-school way at the drive-in

19 miles

1 mile

255

24 Lake Winnipesaukee

Weirs Beach drive-in has shown movies on the big screen since 1949. Across the lake, Bailey's Bubble has scooped ice cream for generations of appreciative families. Summer camps in the area have thrived for decades, too. There's something special about this mountain-ringed lake, a place that summons people back year after year. But it's not just the beauty. It's the little moments of family fun and summer camaraderie that make it truly magical.

TRIP HIGHLIGHT

❶ Weirs Beach

Word of warning: if you're traveling with kids, they're going to want to stay here all day. With its colorful distractions – video arcades, slippery waterslides, souvenir stands and a bustling boardwalk – Weirs Beach is the lake region's center of tacky fun. Escape the hoopla on the **Winnipesaukee Scenic Railroad** (www.hoborr. com; 211 Lakeside Ave; adult/

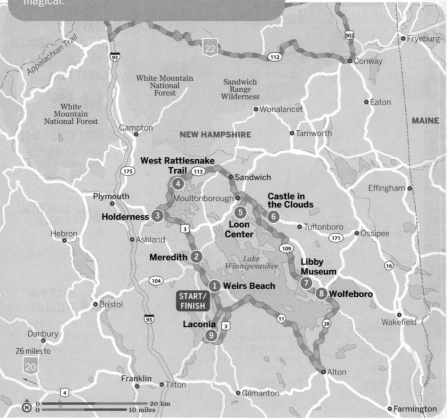

child 1hr $14/10, 2hr $15/11; ⏱11am-3pm daily late Jun-Aug, varies seasonally;), whose '20s and '30s train cars travel to the lake's southern tip at Alton Bay and back. Kids love the ice-cream-parlor car. The train depot is also the departure point for MS *Mt Washington*.

After a day on the beach, unwind with a movie at the **Weirs Drive-In** (📞603-366-4723; http://weirsdrivein.com; 76 Endicott St/Rte 3; adult/child $8.50/free; ⏱from 7pm;). Opened in 1949 and in continual operation since then, the WDI is a revered institution. Note that every car will be charged, at a minimum, for two adults.

🍴 🛏 p261

The Drive » Continue north on US 3/Endicott St, which runs parallel to the lake. Soon after passing the high-flying ropes course at Monkey Trunks

LINK YOUR TRIP

20 Ivy League Tour
Follow I-93 to the Ivies for guided tours about history and traditions.

22 White Mountains Loop
From Holderness, drive north to the Notches for trains, hiking and cascades.

CRUISING ON MS MT WASHINGTON

Boasting 183 miles of coastline, Lake Winnipesaukee is prime cruising territory. The classic **MS Mt Washington** (www.cruisenh.com; adult/child $27/14) steams out of Weirs Beach on a relaxing 2½-hour scenic lake cruise departing twice daily in July, August and late September to mid-October (reduced schedule May, June and early September). Special trips include the Sunday champagne brunch cruise and the evening sunset, fall foliage and theme cruises (tribute to Elvis, lobster fest etc) running throughout summer and fall ($43 to $49). The boat stops in Meredith on Monday and in Wolfeboro daily from Tuesday to Saturday.

(www.monkeytrunks.com), US 3's local name changes to Daniel Webster Hwy. Meredith is located 5 miles north of Weirs Beach.

② Meredith

Upscale Meredith is a lively lakeside town with attractive Colonial and Victorian homes flanking a commercial center. In Meredith village, boutiques, art and craft stores, galleries and restaurants line US 3 and Main St.

Just south of the village roundabout is **Meredith Bay Coffee House** (www.meredithbaycoffeehouse.com; 136 US 3/Daniel Webster Hwy; ⏱7am-2pm Tue-Sat) – one of those unassuming places that unexpectedly turns out to be a memorable find. The pastries are superb, the staff congenial and the cottage-y interior ready-

made for a relaxing break. Quiches, salads and sandwiches are sold for lunch. Just north of the coffeehouse, a dozen shops and restaurants can be found inside **Mill Falls Marketplace** (http://millfalls.com/marketplace; 313 US 3/Daniel Webster Hwy; ⏱from 10am), a restored linen mill tucked within a cluster of inns.

The Winnipesaukee Scenic Train and the MS *Mt Washington* (Monday only) stop in Meredith.

🍴 p261

The Drive » From Meredith, continue 5 miles north on woodsy, easy-driving US 3. Don't be surprised if you see lots of motorcyclists. Squam Lake soon nudges into view to the northeast.

TRIP HIGHLIGHT

③ Holderness

The site of the movie *On Golden Pond,* Squam Lake and Holderness remain placid and peaceful, perfect for a pair of waders and fly-fishing, or for plopping your butt in a beach chair and soaking up the sun. If you hike in the shady forests you'll frequently surprise deer, moose, or even a black bear or two.

It's all about the wildlife at **Squam Lakes Natural Science Center** (☎603-968-7194; www.nhnature.org; 23 Science Center Rd; adult/child $15/10; ◷9:30am-4:30pm May-Oct, last admission 3:30pm; 🚼), where four nature paths weave through the woods and around the marsh. The 0.75-mile **Gephardt Trail** is a highlight, leading past large trailside enclosures that hold bobcats, mountain lions, river otters and raptors. Most of the animals were orphaned or injured and unable to live on their own in the wild. The center also offers 90-minute tours of the lake ($21/17 per adult/child) and educational live animal demonstrations.

🛏 p261

The Drive » From the nature center, follow NH 113 northeast for 5 miles. About 0.25 miles after the 'Rockywold Deephaven Camps' sign, look for the 'West Rattlesnake Trail' sign. Park in one of the pull-offs on either side of the road. The trail is on the lakeside.

❹ West Rattlesnake Trail

The West Rattlesnake Trail climbs to a rocky outcrop atop Rattlesnake Mountain that yields stunning views of Squam Lake. It's less than a mile to the top, making this a good hike for families. Just watch younger kids on the rocks.

The Drive » NH 113 twists past cottages, pine trees and rock walls, offering glimpses of Squam Lake to the southeast before entering Center Sandwich. From this white clapboard village, pick up NH 109 south to NH 25/Whittier Hwy. Turn right onto NH 25 and follow it about half a mile to Blake Rd and turn left. Follow Blake Rd to Lees Mill Rd and turn right.

TRIP HIGHLIGHT

❺ Loon Center

Loons may be water birds, but their closest relatives are actually penguins, not ducks or geese. Known for their unique and varied calls (the wail sounds like a howling wolf), loons experienced a sharp decline in the 1970s.

The Loon Preservation Committee monitors the birds and works to restore a strong, healthy population. At its secluded **Loon Center** (☎603-476-5666; www.loon.org; 183 Lees Mill Rd; admission free; ◷9am-5pm Jul-early Oct, closed Sun May, Jun & early Oct-Dec, closed Sun-Wed

Jan-Apr; 🚼), wildlife enthusiasts can learn about the birds' plumage, habitat and distinctive calls and watch an award-winning video. There are also details about protecting the birds. Kid-friendly activities include interactive games, a scavenger hunt and a junior biologist's guide.

The center sits within the 200-acre **Markus**

Squam Lake

Wildlife Sanctuary
(☺dawn-dusk). The
sanctuary's **Loon Nest
Trail** is a haven for birds.
The 1.7-mile path winds
through the forest and
past a marsh to the shores
of Lake Winnipesaukee.
The best time for loon
spotting is nesting season
in June and July.

The Drive » Follow Lees Mill
Rd to Lee Rd. Turn right and
continue to NH 109. Turn right.

Continue to the junction of
NH 109 and the start of NH 171/
Old Mountain Rd. Drive about 2
miles on NH 171. The entrance
to Castle in the Clouds will be
on the left.

TRIP HIGHLIGHT

❻ Castle in
the Clouds

Perched on high like
a king surveying his
territory, the Arts and

Crafts–style **Castle in the
Clouds** (☎603-476-5900;
www.castleintheclouds.org;
455 Old Mountain Rd/NH 171,
Moultonborough; adult/child
$16/12; ☺10am-4pm, closed
mid-Oct–early May) **wows**
with its stone walls and
exposed-timber beams,
but it's the views of lakes
and valleys that draw
the crowds. In autumn
the kaleidoscope of rust,
red and yellow beats any

postcard. The 5500-acre estate features gardens, ponds and a path leading to a small waterfall. Admission includes the castle and stories about the eccentric millionaire Thomas Plant, who built it. From late June to late August, make reservations for the Monday-morning 'Walks and Talks,' about anything from birds to wild food, or for the Thursday-evening 'Jazz at Sunset' performances from late June to early September.

The Drive » Return to NH 109 south, following a woodsy route that tracks Lake Winnipesaukee, although you won't always be able to see the water. After Melvin Village, cross Mirror Lake on a pinch of land before hitting the outskirts of Wolfeboro.

7 Libby Museum

At the age of 40, Henry Forrest Libby, a local doctor, began collecting things. In 1912 he built a home for his collections, which later became the eccentric little **Libby Museum** (☎603-569-1035; http://wolfeboronh.us; 755 N Main St; adult/child $2/1; ☺10am-4pm Tue-Sat, noon-4pm Sun Jun–mid-Sep). Starting with butterflies and moths, the amateur naturalist built up a private natural-history collection that now

includes numerous stuffed mammals and birds. Other collections followed, including Abenaki relics and early-American farm and home implements. The museum sits in a lovely spot across from Winter Harbor on Lake Winnipesaukee.

The Drive » Drive 3.2 miles on NH 109 to downtown Wolfeboro.

TRIP HIGHLIGHT

8 Wolfeboro

The self-proclaimed 'Oldest Resort in America' is a nice place to wander for a few hours. The waterfront is picturesque, with a grassy lakeside park, and in summer there are lots of free concerts and art events. (It's also garnered fame as the site of Republican presidential candidate Mitt Romney's summer home.)

Stretch your legs on the **Cotton Valley Rail Trail**, which runs for 6 miles along a former railroad track. It passes two lakes, climbs through Cotton Valley and winds through forests and fields. The trail starts behind the **Wolfeboro Chamber of Commerce** (☎603-569-2200; www.wolfeborochamber.com; 32 Central Ave; ☺10am-3pm Mon-Fri, to noon Sat), inside the former train

depot, which carries a fantastic map detailing the walk. Before leaving, buy a scoop of ice cream downtown from **Bailey's Bubble** (www.baileysbubble.com; 5 Railroad Ave; 1 scoop $2.75), where they've served generations of families.

✖ 🛏 p261

The Drive » Leave NH 109 in Wolfeboro, picking up NH 28 east just south of downtown. Summer camps dot the 10-mile drive to Alton, where you pick up NH 11 north, passing the Mt Major Trail and then Ellacoya State Beach before swinging into Laconia.

9 Laconia

Plunked between I-93 and Weirs Beach, busy Laconia has the largest population in this region. There aren't any noteworthy sites, but the community does have a variety of restaurants and a number of local motels. In nearby Gilford, it's fun to sit on the upstairs porch at Patrick's Pub and sip a beer while watching airplanes swoop into Laconia Municipal Airport next door.

✖ p261

The Drive » To complete the loop, return to Weirs Beach on US 3 heading north.

Eating & Sleeping

Weirs Beach ❶

✖ NazBar & Grill   Bar $

(www.naswa.com; 1086 Weirs Blvd; mains $10-12; ⏱Jun-Sep) We're recommending this colorful lakeside bar because it's a scene. This is Weirs Beach, after all. Watch boats pull up to the dock as you sip your cocktail beside – or in – the lake. The menu includes nachos, wraps and burgers.

✖ Kellerhaus   American, Ice Cream $

(www.kellerhaus.com; 259 Endicott St/Rte 3; sundaes from $4, breakfasts from $7; ⏱8am-10pm daily late May-Oct, 10am-6pm Wed-Mon Nov-late May; 🖝) Build the creation of your dreams at the self-service sundae buffet. The tasty waffle buffet wows 'em in the morning.

🛏 Lake Winnipesaukee Motel   Motel $

(☎603-366-5502; www.lakewinnipesaukee motel.com; 350 Endicott St N; r $79-109, ste $105-140; ❄@📶🖝) Right on Lake Winn, this simple motel has cute rooms with refrigerators and microwaves.

Meredith ❷

✖ Lago   Italian $$

(☎603-279-2253; www.thecman.com/restaurants/lago; 1 US 25; mains $14-22; ⏱11:30am-3pm, 5-9pm) Inside the Inn at Bay Point, the stylishly rustic Lago serves oven-roasted salmon with artichoke salsa, lasagne with roasted eggplant and zucchini, and traditional pastas such as spaghetti *alla carbonara*. There's also a wine bar with extensive selections by the glass.

Holderness ❸

🛏 Manor on Golden Pond   B&B $$$

(☎603-968-3348; www.manorongoldenpond. com; 31 Manor Dr; r $325-490, ste $550; ❄@📶🏊) The elegant Manor has a stunning lobby that seems designed with New Hampshire's autumn in mind – greens, golds

and maroons. The rooms have stately decks, gorgeous views, Keurig coffeemakers and Frette linens; many have fireplaces. Play tennis in the morning, then enjoy high tea in the afternoon.

Wolfeboro ❽

✖ Mise En Place   French, American $$

(☎603-569-5788; http://miseenplacenh.com; 96 Lehner St; mains $16-28; ⏱5-8pm Wed-Sun, plus Tue summer) With its minimalist decoration and pleasant patio, this is a wonderful place for dinner. The 2012 summer menu included buttery steaks and a wide selection of seafood dishes, from citrus-and-lime scallops to risotto with lobster and crab. Reservations advisable.

🛏 Wolfeboro Inn   Inn $$$

(☎603-569-3016; www.wolfeboroinn.com; 90 N Main St; r $259-299, ste from $319; ❄📶) One of the region's most prestigious resorts since 1812, the Wolfeboro has 44 rooms across a main inn and a modern annex. A recent revamp added flat-screen TVs, new beds and contemporary furnishings. A restaurant and pub, Wolfe's Tavern, is on site.

Laconia ❾

✖ O Seafood & Steaks   Seafood $$

(☎603-524-9373; www.magicfoodsrestaurant group.com; 62 Doris Ray Ct; mains lunch $8-12, dinner $15-35; ⏱11:30am-2:30pm Mon-Fri, dinner daily from 5pm) Kobe beef meatballs? Yes, please. At this stylish spot with grand views of the lake, choose from steaks, fish, and lobster mac-and-cheese at dinner. Salads, burgers and fish and chips are served at lunch.

✖ Patrick's Pub   Pub $$

(☎603-293-0841; www.patrickspub.com; 18 Weirs Rd; mains $8-18; ⏱11:30am-10pm Sun-Thu, to 11pm Fri & Sat, bar to 11:30pm Sun-Thu, to 12:30am Fri & Sat) With its well-placed flat-screens, Patrick's Pub is a good place to catch a game. There's a big central bar, and the vibe is welcoming. Try the thick clam chowder.

Keene *Colorful and lively, this is a great place to stroll*

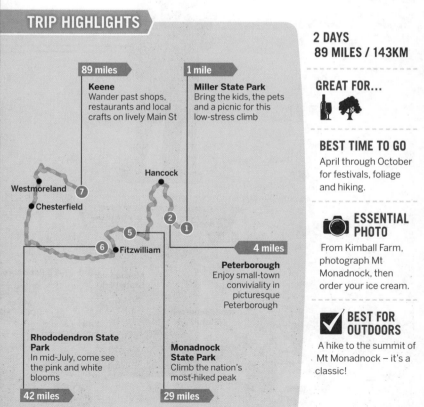

Monadnock Villages

25

Driving between the villages encircling Mt Monadnock is like gliding through a 19th-century landscape painting – one brought vividly to life with hikers, blooming rhododendrons and abundant wildlife.

TRIP HIGHLIGHTS

89 miles

Keene
Wander past shops, restaurants and local crafts on lively Main St

7

1 mile

Miller State Park
Bring the kids, the pets and a picnic for this low-stress climb

Hancock

Westmoreland

Chesterfield

2
1

5

6 ●Fitzwilliam

4 miles

Peterborough
Enjoy small-town conviviality in picturesque Peterborough

Rhododendron State Park
In mid-July, come see the pink and white blooms

42 miles

Monadnock State Park
Climb the nation's most-hiked peak

29 miles

2 DAYS
89 MILES / 143KM

GREAT FOR...

BEST TIME TO GO
April through October for festivals, foliage and hiking.

ESSENTIAL PHOTO
From Kimball Farm, photograph Mt Monadnock, then order your ice cream.

BEST FOR OUTDOORS
A hike to the summit of Mt Monadnock – it's a classic!

DANITA DELIMONT STOCK/AWL ©

263

25 Monadnock Villages

Striking peaks, birch-lined streams, white-painted villages – no wonder artists and writers such as Henry David Thoreau, Willa Cather and Thornton Wilder have found inspiration here. But the camaraderie found in the towns, with their attractive communal spaces, surely added oomph to their oohs and ahs. This convivial spirit continues today, from the shared sense of adventure on the White Dot Trail to the ice-cream fans toughing out the winds on a chilly day at Kimball Farm.

TRIP HIGHLIGHT

❶ Miller State Park

If Mt Monadnock is the main course, then Pack Monadnock is the appetizer. Just 4 miles east of Peterborough, this 2290ft mountain is the heart of **Miller State Park** (☏603-924-3672; www.nhstateparks.org; NH 101E; adult/child $4/2; ☺9am-sunset; 🚻🍴). Established in 1891, the park is New Hampshire's oldest, and a good one to visit if you're traveling with young children

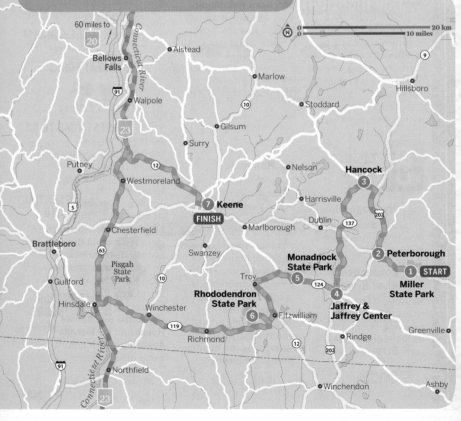

and pets. Two separate trails, the Womack Trail and the Marion Davis Trail, lead 1.4 miles from the parking lot to the summit, where you can climb a 1939 fire tower for sweeping views. Short on time? Drive the 1.3-mile paved road to the top.

- - - - - - - - - - - -

TRIP HIGHLIGHT

❷ Peterborough

This charming village of red-brick houses and tree-lined streets, with the idyllic Nubanusit River coursing through its historic center, is a particularly nice place for an extended stop, its atmosphere enhanced by the influence of the nearby **MacDowell Colony** (www.macdowellcolony.org), a century-old art colony drawing more than 250 poets, composers, writers, architects and

LINK YOUR TRIP

20 **Ivy League Tour**
For college tours, drive to I-89 from Keene via NH 9 east.

23 **Connecticut River Byway**
Swoop west from Keene on NH 12. Turn south toward Massachusetts on NH 63 or continue north on NH 12.

playwrights to the area. Playwright Thornton Wilder wrote *Our Town,* a play openly inspired by Peterborough, while at the colony.

Pop into the **Mariposa Museum** (www.mariposamuseum.org; 26 Main St; adult/child $5/3; ☺11am-5pm, closed Mon & Tue Sep–mid-Jun; 🚼) for folk art and folklore from around the world. It's a 'please touch' kind of place, and kids are encouraged to try on costumes and play the musical instruments. The indie bookstore **Toadstool Bookshop** (https://toadstool.indiebound.com; 12 Depot Sq; ☺10am-5pm) has a welcoming vibe, a good selection of books and a small cafe, Aesop's Tables (see p269).

🍴 🛏 p269

The Drive ≫ From Peterborough, follow US 202/NH 123 northwest, a woodsy route also popular with motorcyclists.

- - - - - - - - - - - -

❸ Hancock

In the first half of the 1800s, wandering artists would paint colorful landscape murals on bedroom walls in homes and inns throughout New England. Rufus Porter, an inventor who started *Scientific American* magazine, was one of the most famous of these traveling artists; unfortunately, many of his stencils and paintings were subsequently

covered, and ruined, by wallpaper. Two murals are still visible inside the **Hancock Inn** (33 Main St), a three-story B&B in the heart of town (see p269). The inn is the oldest in New Hampshire and has been in continuous operation since 1789 – when George Washington was president! Although the murals are in guest rooms, you can enjoy a Porter-style mural – with a cocktail – in the inn's sitting room before a meal at the restaurant.

🛏 p269

The Drive ≫ NH 137 winds past marshes, stone walls and lichen-covered rocks on its way to NH 101, which is 6.5 miles south. Continue south on NH 137 to Jaffrey or, if you need to break for a meal, turn left and continue to Peterborough, then head south to Jaffrey on US 202.

- - - - - - - - - - - -

❹ Jaffrey & Jaffrey Center

Jaffrey Center, 2 miles west of Jaffrey, is another tiny, picture-perfect village of serene lanes, 18th-century homes and a dramatic white-steepled meetinghouse. All of its historic sites are clustered around the wee historic district, located on both sides of Gilmore Pond Rd off NH 124. The most intriguing sights include the frozen-in-time **Little Red School House** and the **Melville Academy**, which houses a one-room museum

ANDRE JENNY/ALAMY ©

of rural artifacts. Both are open 2pm to 4pm on summer weekends. Willa Cather, a frequent visitor to Jaffrey, is buried in the **Old Burying Ground** behind the meetinghouse, with a quote from *My Antonia* gracing the headstone.

Jaffrey is perhaps best known as the home of Kimball Farm, an ice-cream shop that is favored by Mt Monadnock hikers.

The Drive » From Jaffrey, drive 2 miles west on NH 124, passing through Jaffrey Center, and turn right on Dublin Rd. Pass a church camp and follow the signs to the park.

TRIP HIGHLIGHT

⑤ Monadnock State Park

A total of 130,000 people climbed this commanding 3165ft **peak** (☎603-532-8862; www.nhstateparks.org; 116 Poole Rd; adult/child $5/2) in 2011, helping it earn the honor of the

---

🗨 LOCAL KNOWLEDGE: KIMBALL FARM

After a hike to the summit of Mt Monadnock, everyone knows that the best reward is ice cream from **Kimball Farm** (www.kimballfarm.com; 158 Turnpike Rd/NH 124, Jaffrey; scoops $3.95; ⊙10am-9pm). Consider the 40 flavors, order at the window, then find a seat at a picnic table out front. Ice-cream flavors include maple walnut, vanilla peanut butter and raspberry chocolate chip. We hear coffee Oreo is popular. Please note: scoops are huge.

Monadnock State Park Take in the views of towering Mt Monadnock

most-climbed peak in the US. Henry David Thoreau climbed it twice, in 1858 and 1860. Displays inside the visitor center explain that *monadnock* comes from the Abenaki word meaning 'special' or 'unique.' The word is now used geologically to describe a residual hill that rises alone from a plain.

Twelve miles of ungroomed ski trails lure cross-country skiers in winter, while more than 40 miles of hiking paths draw the trail-hungry hordes in summer. Numerous combinations of trails lead to the summit. The **White Dot Trail**, which joins the White Cross Trail, is the most direct route, running from the visitor center to the bare-topped peak; it's a 4-mile round trip and takes about 3½ hours. On clear days, gaze 100 miles across all six New England states.

The park's seasonal Gilson Pond Campground (p269) is well placed for a sunrise ascent. Headquarters Campground is reserved for youth groups and is not open to the general public.

🛏 p269

The Drive ›› Follow NH 124 west to NH 12. Turn left on NH 12 and drive to Fitzwilliam, marked by its town green surrounded by lovely old houses and a towering steeple. Follow NH 119 about 1 mile west, then turn right on Rhododendron Rd and drive for 2 miles.

TRIP HIGHLIGHT

⑥ Rhododendron State Park

The 16-acre rhododendron grove in this serene **park** (☎603-532-8862; www. nhstateparks.org; US 119W; adult/child $4/2; 👪) is the largest in New England. It makes for a nice stroll in mid-July, when thick

THE GREAT PUMPKIN WAS HERE

One of Keene's quirkiest annual gatherings, the **Keene Pumpkin Festival** (www.pumpkinfestival.org) brings some 80,000 visitors, who come for the magnificent tower of jack-o'-lanterns rising high above Central Sq. The event started in 1991 when local merchants, eager to keep shoppers in the area on weekend nights, displayed hundreds of pumpkins around Main St. Since then the event – which is held on the third Saturday of October – has exploded as Keene attempts to better its record of nearly 29,000 in 2003. In addition to pump gazing, visitors can enjoy a craft fair, a costume parade, a seed-spitting contest and fireworks. Live bands play and local merchants sell clam chowder, fried sausages, hot cider and pumpkin whoopee pies. If you attend, don't forget to bring your pumpkin!

stands of the giant plant *(Rhododendron maximum)* bloom white and pink along the 0.6-mile **Rhododendron Trail** circling the grove. The blooms can last for weeks and the final blossoms may occur as the leaves are turning. Listen for songbirds in the foliage while on the trail. The trail is also accessible to people with disabilities.

Hikers can hook onto the adjacent **Wildflower Trail**, where they may see mountain laurel blooms in June and berries in the fall. More ambitious ramblers can link from the Rhododendron Trail to the **Little Monadnock Mountain Trail**, which climbs to the 1883ft summit of Little Monadnock Mountain. On the way it joins the 117-mile **MetaComet-**

Monadnock Trail, which continues to the summit of Mt Monadnock.

The Drive » Drive west on NH 119, crossing NH 32 before heading into Winchester. Continue west on NH 119, passing one entrance to Pisgah State Park. Turn right on NH 63 for a bucolic spin past cows and red barns. Cross NH 9 to begin a particularly scenic drive past Spofford Lake, pine trees and the startlingly impressive Park Hill Meeting House. Turn right on NH 12 at Stuart & Johns Sugar House and drive toward Keene.

TRIP HIGHLIGHT
7 Keene

Keene is like the hub of a giant wheel, with a half-dozen spokes linking to dozens of outlying villages that encircle the city, providing an endless supply of scenic loops. You really can't go wrong with any of them.

Keene itself is a great place to explore, particularly along its pleasant and lively Main St, which is lined with indie shops and cozy eateries. For local crafts, foodstuffs and gifts, stop by **Hannah Grimes Marketplace** (www.hannah grimesmarketplace; 42 Main St; ☺10am-6pm).

Main St is crowned by a small tree-filled plaza (Central Sq) with a fountain at one end. The elegant, red-brick **Keene State College** (www.keene. edu; 229 Main St) anchors the western end of Main St and accounts for one-quarter of the town's population, as well as its youthful, artistic sensibility. The spacious, skylit halls at the **Thorne Sagendorph Art Gallery** (www.keene.edu/tsag; Wyman Way; ☺noon-5pm Wed, Thu, Sat & Sun, 3-8pm Fri Jun-Aug, daily Sep-May) showcase rotating exhibits of regional and national artists. The small permanent collection includes pieces by national artists who have been drawn to the Monadnock region since the 1800s.

In the evening, see what's doing at the 80-year-old **Colonial Theater** (www.thecolonial. org; 95 Main St), which offers a diverse line-up of entertainment.

✕ ⊨ p269

Eating & Sleeping

Peterborough ❷

✗ Aesop's Tables   Cafe $

(12 Depot Sq; mains under $9; ⊙7am-4pm
Mon-Fri, 9am-4pm Sat) Tucked inside Toadstool
Bookshop, with a few patio tables, this cafe sells
coffee, quiches, salads and sandwiches.

✗ Harlow's Pub   Pub $$

(www.harlowspub.com; 3 School St; mains lunch
$4-8, dinner $7-22; ⊙4-10pm Mon, noon-11pm
Tue, noon-midnight Wed & Thu, noon-1am Fri
& Sat) Sip draught New England brews at the
convivial bar and catch live music. Mexican and
pub grub are on the menu.

⊨ Jack Daniels Motor Inn   Motel $$

(☏603-924-7548; www.jackdanielsinn.com;
80 Concord St/US 202; r $139; ❋🛜🐾) With
its flower-bedecked entrance and scenic perch
beside the Contoocook River, the Jack Daniels
is pretty darn lovely for a motel. Rooms, on two
floors, come with microwaves and refrigerators.
A few rooms are pet friendly; add $25 per stay if
traveling with a pet.

Hancock ❸

⊨ Hancock Inn   B&B $$

(☏603-525-3318; www.hancockinn.com; 33
Main St; r $145-260; ❋🛜🐾) The inn's 14
rooms give a nod to regional personalities
and places. Features include fireplaces,
claw-foot tubs and murals in some rooms.
The 1st-floor Driver Room welcomes pets. The
restaurant (⊙5:30-8pm Tue-Sat, to 7pm Sun)
is open to the public for dinner. The seasonal
menu celebrates regional fare. The prix-fixe
Innkeeper's Supper on Sunday centers on one
comfort-minded dish ($15).

Monadnock State Park ❺

⊨ Gilson Pond
Campground   Campground $

(☏park 603-532-8862, campground 603-532-
2416; www.nhstateparks.org; 585 Dublin Rd; tent
& RV sites $25; ⊙May-Oct) Open since 2010,
this seasonal campground has 35 tent and pop-
up sites, plus five remote sites. Thirty sites are
available for reservation (www.reserveamerica.
com; there's a $9.25 reservation fee); the rest
are walk-ups. A bathhouse with bathrooms and
coin-operated showers is also on site.

Keene ❼

✗ Luca's Mediterranean Café
& the Market at Luca's   Italian $$

(☏cafe 603-358-3335; www.lucascafe.com; 10
& 11 Central Sq; cafe lunch $7-12, dinner $16-26,
market lunch $7-8, spaghetti dinner $9-12;
⊙lunch Mon-Fri, dinner daily) Enjoy excellent
thin-crust pizzas, tasty salads and gourmet
sandwiches at lunch, while dinner sees pasta,
grilled fish and pan-seared beef tenderloin. The
market is a gourmet Italian food stop that has
morphed into a casual spaghetti house.

✗ Prime Roast   Coffee Shop $

(16 Main St; ⊙7am-8pm Mon-Fri, 8am-8pm Sat,
9am-5pm Sun) A coffee shop selling a bag of
beans called 'Demon Roast' ain't messing around –
in fact they call it 'wicked' dark. Roasting is done
daily in the morning. Local artists made the
tables, and the coffee is fair trade.

⊨ EF Lane Hotel   Hotel $$

(☏603-357-7070; www.thelanehotel.com; 30 Main
St; r $189, ste $209-289; ❋🛜) This 40-room
property sits in the middle of the Main St action
and is within walking distance of the Colonial
Theater. Rooms are uniquely furnished in a classic
style. Enjoy two complimentary drinks at the
lobby bar during the Manager's Happy Hour.

STRETCH
YOUR LEGS
PORTSMOUTH

Start/Finish Colby's Breakfast & Lunch

Distance 1.5 miles

Duration Four hours

The past and present merge seamlessly on this easy stroll through a vibrant waterfront town filled with historic churches and well-preserved homes. How seamlessly? Well, there's a free wi-fi hot spot on the 300-year-old public square!

Take this walk on Trip

26

Colby's Breakfast & Lunch

If you get to **Colby's** (105 Daniel St; mains under $10; ⏰7am-1pm) after 8am on the weekend, there's going to be a wait, so give 'em your name and enjoy a cup of free coffee on the patio. Once in, egg lovers can choose from a multitude of Benedicts, and there's always the huevos rancheros and the chalkboard specials. In 2012, management posted a 'No Politicians, No Exceptions' sign on the door in the days before the presidential primary. Campaign staff and candidates were disrupting business in the 28-seat eatery.

The Walk ≫ Turn left out of Colby's and walk a block and a half to Market Sq.

Market Square

A public gathering place since the mid-1700s, this lively square, anchored by the 1854 North Church, is still the heart of Portsmouth. Nearby are open-air cafes, colorful storefronts and tiny galleries with banjo-playing buskers for entertainment on warm summer nights. There's public wi-fi here, and an information kiosk is open in summer.

The Walk ≫ Stroll down Pleasant St, passing the granite US Custom House, built in 1860. Next, on the left, is Governor John Langdon's House, where the three-term governor hosted George Washington in 1789. Turn left on Gates St, at Hancock St, then walk to Manning St and turn right. The meetinghouse and its grounds are just ahead. Turn left at the parking lot and walk beside the meetinghouse to Marcy St.

South Ward Meetinghouse

The towering **meetinghouse** (280 Marcy St), completed in 1866, replaced a parish meetinghouse that had been on the site since 1731. The 1st floor of the new building held a school, and the 2nd floor was used for meetings. Black citizens celebrated Emancipation Day here in January 1882.

The Walk ≫ From the front of the meetinghouse, cross Marcy St and walk down Hunking St.

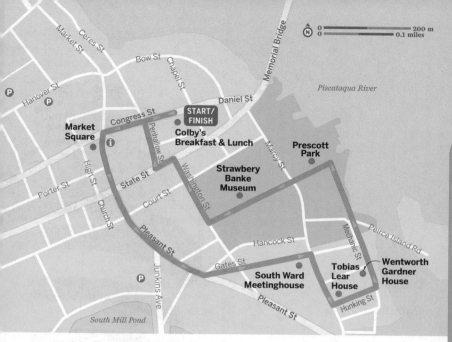

Tobias Lear & Wentworth Gardner Houses

Tobias Lear House (www.wentworthgardner andlear.org; 49 Hunking St; admission incl both houses adult/child $5/2; ☺noon–4pm Wed-Sun mid-Jun–mid-Oct), built in 1740, was in the Lear family for 120 years. The fifth Tobias Lear served as private secretary to President George Washington, who visited Lear's mother here in 1789. Around the corner is the 1760 **Wentworth Gardner House** (50 Mechanic St), one of the finest Georgian houses in the USA. Elizabeth and Mark Hunking Wentworth were among Portsmouth's wealthiest citizens, so no expense was spared in building the home, which was a wedding gift for their son.

The Walk » Turn left on Mechanic St and follow it past the windswept headstones at Point of Graves to Prescott Park.

Prescott Park

Overlooking the Piscataqua River, this leafy **park** (105 Marcy St) is the backdrop for a summer **arts festival** (www. prescottpark.org), with free music, dance and theater. The design of the shoreside Sheafe Warehouse (c 1705) made it easy for flat-bottomed boats to load and unload cargo.

The Walk » Cross Marcy St and enter the parking lot of the Strawbery Banke Museum.

Strawbery Banke Museum

Spread across 10 acres, the **museum** (www.strawberybanke.org; 14 Hancock St; adult/child $15/10; ☺10am-5pm May-Oct) is a blend of period homes dating to the 1690s. Costumed guides recount tales that took place among the 38 historic buildings. The museum includes **Pitt Tavern** (1766), a hotbed of Revolutionary sentiment, and **Goodwin Mansion**, a grand 19th-century house from Portsmouth's most prosperous time.

The Walk » Follow Washington St northwest to State St, turn left, walk a few steps then turn right onto Penhallow St and return to Daniel St.

Maine

YOU KNOW THERE'S SOMETHING SPECIAL ABOUT A STATE when its most prominent citizens donate their land for the enjoyment of all. Governor Percival Baxter provided the wilderness for Baxter State Park while John D Rockefeller and his neighbors donated land for Acadia National Park. Today, private timber companies allow recreational access to vast swaths of woodland.

For travelers, a coastal drive north from Portland swooshes past LL Bean, shipbuilding villages, Acadia National Park and first-in-the-nation sunrises. And we haven't even mentioned the lighthouses and lobster shacks. Inland, scenic byways hug rivers, lakes, forests and mountains. A lucky few may spy a moose.

West Quoddy Light Get snap happy at this lovely lighthouse (Trip 26)
DANITA DELIMONT/GETTY IMAGES ©

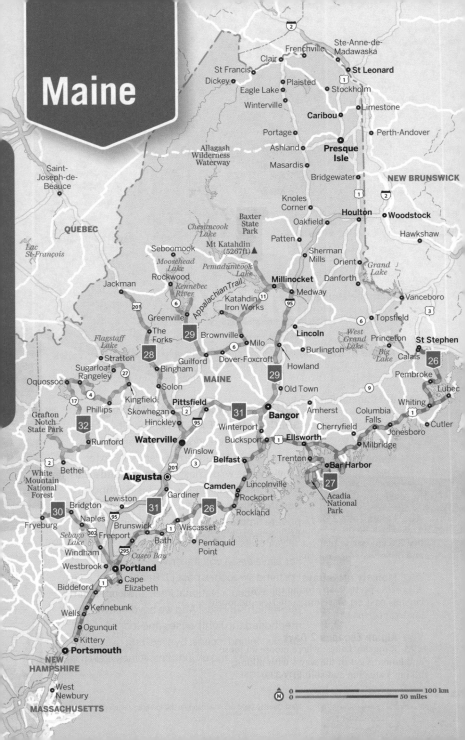

Eagle Lake (Trip 27)

☑ **DON'T MISS**

Museums & Murals
View works by American masters at the Portland Museum of Art, and snap photos of Maine-inspired murals down the street. Take them all in on Trip `31`

Lighthouse Hike
You'll earn your view of the coast after a hike across granite blocks to the Rockland Breakwater Lighthouse. Visit it on Trip `26`

Heavenly Views
Lie on the sand and ponder the universe during the Stars over Sand Beach program at Acadia National Park. Enjoy it on Trip `27`

Gifford's Ice Cream Stand
Fuel up for the North Woods with a scoop of Maine Blackberry or Caramel Caribou from Gifford's. Try it on Trip `28`

Moose Safari
Haven't spotted a moose? Increase your odds on a Northwoods Outfitters safari. Try your luck on Trip `29`

Maine *Breathe in the salt air and embrace coastal culture*

Classic Trip

Maritime Maine

26

US 1 between Kittery and Calais is a route meant for lingering: fog-wrapped lighthouses, oceanfront picnic tables, seafaring artifacts in dusty museums, and one sprawling outdoors store.

TRIP HIGHLIGHTS

63 miles

Freeport
Salute the giant boot, then find the right gear for adventuring

265 miles

Quoddy Head State Park
Crashing waves, an eerie foghorn and a lonely lighthouse

FINISH
Calais

11

9 Camden

7

6

3

78 miles

Bath
Seafaring artifacts are a link to Maine's maritime past

Ogunquit

Kittery

START

Cape Elizabeth
Snap photos of the lighthouse and wander past WWII bunkers

42 miles

Rockland Breakwater Lighthouse
A granite walkway leads to the distant beacon

127 miles

5 DAYS
285 MILES / 459KM

GREAT FOR...

BEST TIME TO GO
Summer is great, but you'll shake the crowds in September and October.

ESSENTIAL PHOTO
Stand on the rocks for a photo of Pemaquid lighthouse.

BEST FOR HISTORY
Exhibits on seafaring are captivating at the Maine Maritime Museum.

277

26 Maritime Maine

The rugged complexity of the Maine coast hits home at the visitor center in Rockland, where a giant state map – complete with lighthouses – sprawls across the floor. Islands, peninsulas, harbors – no wonder this state has such a strong maritime heritage. And it's this heritage that makes the trip memorable. The sunrises and rocky coasts are lovely, but it's the stories about lighthouse keepers, brave captains and shipyard Rosie the Riveters that make this trip different from other coastal drives.

1 Kittery

The drive to **Fort Foster Park** (www.kittery.org; car/walk-in $10/5; ⊙10am-8pm; 🚻) twists past blooming flowers, Victorian homes and tantalizing ocean glimpses. The seaside park is a nice place to picnic, and play in rocky tide pools. Look out to sea for **Whaleback Ledge** (1831), the first lighthouse on this trip.

To get here from US 1, take ME 236 to ME 103, driving just over 4 miles in total, then cross a small channel to Gernish Island. Follow Pocahontas Dr through the woods.

From Kittery, you can pop across to Portsmouth for a walking tour (p270).

🍴 p285

The Drive » Continue north on US 1. There's a nice but potentially crowded sand beach at Ogunquit. Seven miles north of Ogunquit, turn right onto Laudholm Farm Rd.

2 Wells

Wildlife lovers, bird-watchers and families enjoy wandering the 7 miles of trails at the 1600-acre **Wells National Estuarine Research Reserve** (www.wellsreserve.org; 342 Laudholm Farm Rd; adult/child $4/1; ⊙7am-sunset; 🚻), a protected coastal ecosystem. No pets permitted. Down the road, the **Rachel Carson National Wildlife**

Appalachian Trail

Bingham

Guilford

Dover
Foxcroft

Milo

Howland

Passadumkeag

West
Grand
Lake

Princeton

Calais **13**

12

FINISH St Croix Island
International
Historic Site

1

Alexander

Pembroke

Eastport

MAINE

Athens

Skowhegan

Newport

Old Town

Bangor

Amherst

Beddington

Wesley
9

Dennysville

Whiting

11

Lubec &
Quoddy
Head

Kennebec River

Norridge-
wock **28**

Pittsfield

31

Ellsworth

Bucksport

10

Hancock

1

Cherryfield

Milbridge

Columbia Falls

Whitneyville

Machias

Jonesboro

Waterville

Vassalboro

295

201

3

Belfast

Stockton
Springs

Trenton

Gouldsboro

Augusta

Gardiner

95

Lincolnville

Camden

Rockland
9 **Breakwater Lighthouse**

8 **Rockland**

Bar
Harbor

Wiscasset

Thomaston

Port Clyde

201

7 **Bath** p281

Brunswick

Pemaquid Point

N
0   50 miles
0   100 km

Dover
Foxcroft

95

6

Reserve (www.fws.gov/
northeast/rachelcarson; 321
Port Rd; ☺dawn-dusk) **holds
more than 9000 acres
of protected coastal
areas, with four trails
scattered along 50 miles
of shoreline. The 1-mile,
pet-friendly Carson Trail
meanders along tidal
creeks and salt marshes.**

LINK YOUR TRIP

28 **Old Canada
Road**

From Bath, drive to
Brunswick to wander a
museum about arctic
explorers.

31 **Mainely
Art**

In Rockland, view
paintings of local
landscapes at the
Farnsworth Art Museum.

Classic Trip

The Drive » Follow US 1 north, passing through Saco. In Scarborough, turn right onto ME 207. Follow it almost 3 miles to ME 77 and turn left. Drive just over 7 miles, passing Two Lights Rd, to Shore Dr. Turn right.

TRIP HIGHLIGHT

3 Cape Elizabeth

Good photo opportunities abound at **Fort Williams Park** (admission free; ⊙dawn-dusk), where you can explore the ruins of the fort, which was a late-19th-century artillery base, and check out WWII bunkers and gun emplacements (a German U-boat was spotted in Casco Bay in 1942). The port actively guarded the entrance to the bay until 1964.

Next door is the **Portland Head Light**, the oldest of Maine's 52 functioning lighthouses. Commissioned by George Washington in 1791, it was staffed until 1989, when machines took over. The keeper's house is now the **Museum at Portland Head Light** (www. portlandheadlight.com; 1000 Shore Dr; adult/child $2/1; ⊙10am-4pm daily Jun-Oct, Sat & Sun mid-Apr–May, Nov–mid-Dec), which traces the maritime and military history of the region.

✗ p285

The Drive » Drive north 1 mile on Shore Dr, then turn right onto Preble St. Drive another mile, then turn right on Broadway then left onto Breakwater Dr. Just ahead, turn right onto Madison St.

4 Portland

Maine's largest city and port is graced by a handful of handsome lights, including the 1875 **Portland Breakwater Light**, with Corinthian columns. Dubbed the 'Bug Light' because of its tiny size, it sits in a small park in South Portland with a panoramic view of downtown across the harbor. You can't enter the Bug Light, but you can traipse over the stone breakwater and walk around the light's exterior.

The **Liberty Ship memorial**, across the park, describes the site's history as a shipyard during WWII, when more than 30,000 people, including about 3750 women, were employed here to build cargo vessels, called Liberty Ships. For views of approaching boats, grab a seat on the deck at Joe's Boathouse next door. If you'd like to explore Portland further, see p318 and p322; see p336 for a walking tour.

🛏 p285

The Drive » Follow I-295 north and take exit 17. DeLorme Map Store will be on your right

off the ramp. You can also follow US 1 north from Portland.

5 Yarmouth

Eartha, a giant 52,300-sq-ft globe, rotates in a lofty atrium beside the inviting **DeLorme Map Store** (www.delorme.com; 2 DeLorme Dr; ⊙9am-6pm Mon-Sat, to 5pm Sun). Maker of the essential *Maine Atlas* and *Gazetteer*, DeLorme creates maps and software for every destination in the US. This welcoming shop will transport you to a thousand different places via maps, travel guides and books about Maine and the great outdoors.

The Drive » Follow US 1 north 4.5 miles past outlet stores and motels to LL Bean. There's a large parking lot on the left between Howard Pl and Nathan Nye St.

TRIP HIGHLIGHT

6 Freeport

A century ago Leon Leonwood Bean opened a shop here to sell equipment and provisions to hunters and fisherpeople. His success lured other retailers and today nearly 200 stores line US 1, leading to traffic jams in summer.

Fronted by a 16ft hunting boot, the flagship **LL Bean store** (www.llbean. com; 95 Main St; ⊙24hr) is a Maine must-see. In 1951 Bean himself removed the locks from the doors, deciding to stay open 24 hours a day, 365 days a year. With almost three million visitors annually, the store is one of the state's most popular tourist attractions. There's an archery range, a 3500-gallon aquarium, a stuffed moose and a coffee shop – not to mention outdoor clothing and gear.

The store celebrated its 2012 centennial by donating $2.5 million to causes that encourage kids to enjoy the outdoors. A new Bootmobile supports this mission on the road. The **LL Bean Outdoor Discovery School** (☎888-552-3261; www.llbean.com/ods) offers fly-fishing, paddleboarding, kayaking and archery courses and runs biking and canoe tours.

✕ ⊨ p285

The Drive » Follow US 1 north 18 miles through Brunswick to Bath. Pass Middle St, then turn right on Washington St and drive 1.2 miles to the museum.

TRIP HIGHLIGHT

7 Bath

This quaint Kennebec River town was once home to more than 20 shipyards producing more than a quarter of early America's wooden ships. Bath Iron Works, founded in 1884, is still one of the largest and most productive shipyards in the nation.

On the western bank of the Kennebec, the **Maine Maritime Museum** (☎207-443-1316; www.mainemaritimemuseum.org; 243 Washington St; adult/child $15/10; ⊙9:30am-5pm) preserves the town's traditions with paintings, models and exhibits that tell the tale of the last 400 years of seafaring. Landlubbers and old salts alike will find something of interest, whether it's an 1849 ship's log describing the power of a hurricane or a hands-on tugboat pilot's house. On the grounds, look for the partial remains of the *Snow Squall*, a three-mast 1851 clipper ship that foundered near the Falkland Islands, and a life-size sculpture of the *Wyoming*, the largest wooden sailing vessel ever built.

In summer, the museum offers a variety of short **boat cruises** (per person $25-40), including a lighthouse cruise and a wildlife tour.

The Drive » Return to US 1 and continue north 40 miles, taking a moment to ogle the long line at Red's, a popular lobster shack in Wiscasset known for its lobster rolls, which are stuffed with the meat from one whole lobster. Continue north to Rockland.

8 Rockland

This thriving commercial port boasts a large fishing fleet and a proud year-round population. Settled in 1769, it was once an important shipbuilding center and a transportation hub for river cargo. Today, tall-masted ships still fill the harbor because Rockland, along with Camden, is a center for Maine's busy **Windjammer cruises**

↱ **DETOUR:**
PEMAQUID POINT

Start: just beyond 7 **Bath**

Maine's most famous lighthouse these days is **Pemaquid Point Light**, which was featured on the special-edition Maine quarter. Perched dramatically above rock-crashing surf in **Lighthouse Park** (☎207-677-3499; www.bristolparks.org; adult/child under 12yr $2/free), the 1835 lighthouse is one of 61 surviving lighthouses along the Maine coast; 52 of them are still in use. The keeper's house now serves as the **Fisherman's Museum** (⊙10am-5pm). Staffed by volunteers, it displays fishing paraphernalia and photos. From Damariscotta, between Wiscasset and Waldoboro, follow ME 130 south.

JEFF GREENBERG/ALAMY ©

RANDY DUCHAINE/ALAMY ©

WHY THIS IS A CLASSIC TRIP
AMY C BALFOUR, AUTHOR

There's a certain thrill in joining the crowds at the iconic spots along the coast. But it's also fun to follow up on unexpected recommendations. In Brunswick I was directed to a tiny convenience store, **Libby's Market** (42 Jordan Ave; lobster rolls $9-18), a few turns from the main drag. I sat at a picnic table by the parking lot and ate what was surely the perfect lobster roll, a toasted bun with chunks of lobster and the right hint of mayo. Welcoming service, too. It was a great find.

Top: Maine Maritime Museum
Left: Red's lobster shack, Wiscasset
Right: Portland Head Light

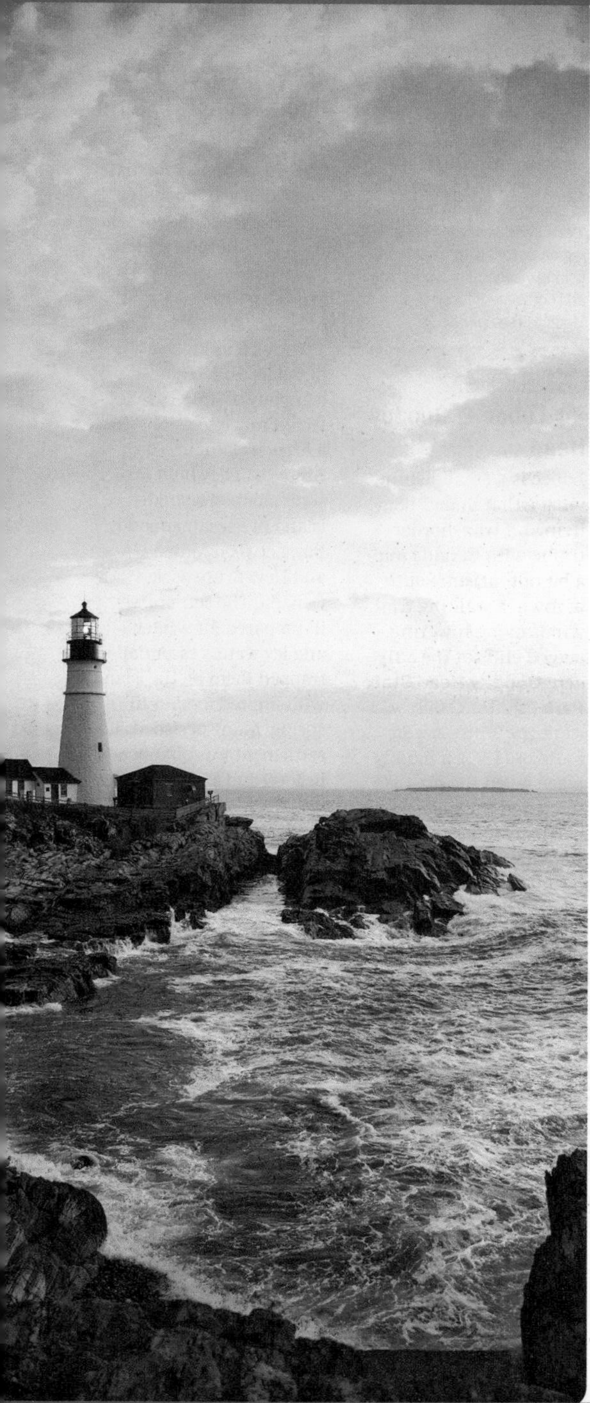

THOMAS NORTHCUT/GETTY IMAGES ©

(www.sailmainecoast.com), which are multiday treks on wind-powered schooners.

A map of Maine's coast, with all of its lighthouses, spreads across the floor of the **Penobscot Bay Regional Chamber of Commerce** (207-596-0376; www.mainedreamvacation.com; 1 Park Dr; 9am-5pm Mon-Fri) beside Rockland Harbor. Ask for the list that identifies the lighthouses on the map. The chamber of commerce shares a roof with the **Maine Lighthouse Museum** (www.mainelighthousemuseum.org; 1 Park Dr; adult/child under 12yr $5/free; 9am-5pm Mon-Fri, 10am-4pm Sat Jun-Oct, closed Sun-Tue Nov-May), which exhibits vintage Fresnel lenses, foghorns, marine instruments and ship models.

For information about the Farnsworth Art Museum, see p326.

The Drive » Follow Main St/US 1 north just over 1 mile from downtown to Waldo Ave. Turn right and drive half a mile. Turn right onto Samoset Rd, following it to a small parking lot.

TRIP HIGHLIGHT

9 Rockland Breakwater Lighthouse

Feeling adventurous? Tackle the rugged stone breakwater that stretches almost 1 mile into Rockland Harbor from Jameson Point at the

harbor's northern shore. Made of granite blocks, this 'walkway' – which took 18 years to build – ends at the **Rockland Breakwater Lighthouse** (www.rocklandharborlights. org). Older kids should be fine; just watch for slippery rocks and ankle-twisting gaps between stones. Bring a sweater, and don't hike if a storm is on the horizon.

The Drive » US 1 hugs the coast as it swoops north past the artsy enclaves of Rockport, Camden and Belfast, curving east through Bucksport before landing in Ellsworth, about 60 miles from Rockland.

⑩ Ellsworth

Cooks and coffee lovers, this stop's for you. In old-school Ellsworth, pull over for **Rooster Brother** (www. roosterbrother.com; 29 Main St; ⏱ store 9:30am-5:30pm Mon-Sat, coffee from 7:30am), a kitchenware boutique that also sells amazing roasted coffee. Step downstairs from the retail store for a free coffee sample – but be careful, you'll likely end up buying a full cup or a pound to go. Check out the excellent fresh cookies, especially the super-tasty molasses. Wine, chocolate, cheese and fresh bread are also for sale.

The Drive » From Ellsworth, drive north on US 1. Just east of the ME 3 junction, take ME 182, the most direct route north, or follow US 1 south onto the Schoodic Peninsula (see p287). ME 182 hooks back onto US 1 at Cherryfield. From here, enter 'down east' Maine, an unspoiled region dotted with traditional fishing villages. For a good meal and convenient lodging, stop in Machias (see p285).

TRIP HIGHLIGHT

⑪ Lubec & Quoddy Head

Lubec is a small fishing village that makes its living off transborder traffic with Canada and a bit of tourism. South of town, a walking trail winds along towering, jagged cliffs at the 531-acre **Quoddy Head State Park** (☎207-733-0911; www. maine.gov; 973 S Lubec Rd; adult/child $3/1), a moody place when the mist is thick and the foghorn blasts its lonely wail. The tides here are also dramatic, fluctuating 16ft in six hours. Look for whales migrating along the coast in summer. The park is also the site of the 1858 **West Quoddy Light**, which looks like a barber's pole.

The Drive » Return to US 1 north, passing Pembroke and Perry. About 3 miles north of Perry look for a pull-off on the left marking the 45th parallel, the halfway point between the North Pole and the equator. Continue 8.5 miles north.

⑫ Saint Croix Island International Historic Site

The site of one of the first European settlements in the New World is visible from this **historic park** (www.nps.gov/sacr; admission free; ⏱9am-5pm late May-Jun & Sep-early Oct, 8:30am-6pm Jul & Aug), 8 miles south of Calais. In 1604, a company of settlers sailed from France to establish a French claim in North America. They built a settlement on a small island in Passamaquoddy Bay, between Maine and New Brunswick, Canada. The settlers were ill-prepared for winter, and icy waters essentially trapped them on the island with limited food until spring. Many perished. The settlement was abandoned in 1605 and a new home was established in Port Royal, Nova Scotia. A trail winds past bronze statues and historic displays.

The Drive » Return to US 1 and drive 5 miles north to a rest area on your right. If you end up in Canada – or pass the local high school – you've gone too far.

⑬ Calais

Maine's northernmost lighthouse is **Whitlocks Mill Light** (http://stcroix historical.com), visible from a rest area 3.5 miles south of Calais. To spot the lighthouse, look for the sign, walk down to the fence and look north.

Eating & Sleeping

Kittery ❶

🍴 Bob's Clam Hut
Seafood $$

(www.bobsclamhut.com; 315 US 1; mains $5-23; ⏱11am-7:30pm, to 8:30pm Fri & Sat) The view of suburban sprawl is uninspiring, but everything else is first rate. Come here for down-home service and big baskets of fried seafood and clam chowder.

Cape Elizabeth ❸

🍴 Lobster Shack at Two Lights
Seafood $$

(☎207-799-1677; www.lobstershacktwolights. com; 225 Two Lights Rd; mains $4-20; ⏱11am-8pm, to 8:30pm Jul & Aug) Crack into lobster at this well-loved seafood shack, with killer views of the crashing Atlantic from indoor and outdoor seating areas.

Portland ❹

🛏 Portland Regency Hotel
Hotel $$$

(☎207-774-4200; www.theregency.com; 20 Milk St; r from $339; ✳🛜) Portland's former armory, this redbrick building is in the heart of Old Town. Ask for one of the newly renovated rooms on the 3rd or 4th floor for the most up-to-date furnishings. Parking is $12 per night.

Freeport ❻

🍴 Harraseeket Lunch & Lobster
Seafood $$

(☎207-865-3535; www.harraseeketlunch andlobster.com; 36 Main St, South Freeport; ⏱lunch & dinner May-Oct) Head down to the

marina to feast on lobster at this iconic red-painted seafood shack. Grab a picnic table or do as the locals do and sit on the hood of your car. Finish with blueberry pie. BYOB. No credit cards, but there's an ATM on the premises.

🍴 Gritty McDuff's Brew Pub
Pub $$

(www.grittys.com; 187 Lower Main St; mains $9-15; ⏱lunch & dinner) Kids getting cranky, and momma needs a beer? Let the young ones run wild on the back lawn while you sip an IPA and savor a cheeseburger on the deck. This offshoot of the popular Gritty's in Portland is 2 miles south of LL Bean.

🛏 Harraseeket Inn
Inn $$$

(☎207-865-9377; www.harraseeketinn. com; 162 Main St; r incl breakfast $205-305; ✳@🛜♨🐾) This big, white clapboard inn with a lodge-style lobby is a Freeport tradition. Most of the rooms have florals and wall-to-wall carpet. Within walking distance of LL Bean.

Machias

🍴 Helen's Restaurant
American $$

(www.helensrestaurantmachias.com; 111 Main St/US 1; mains $4-20; ⏱breakfast, lunch & dinner) Think seafood with a hint of verve: the fresh haddock is moist, flaky and seasoned with a touch of lemon, while crabmeat pastas have thick dollops of organic local ricotta. Long known for its pies.

🛏 Machias Motor Inn
Motel $$

(☎207-255-4861; www.machiasmotorinn. com; 103 Main St/US 1; r $119; ✳🛜🐾) Next to Helen's, this roadside lodge has 38 spacious rooms with refrigerators and microwaves. Most have views of the Machias River out back. It's $10 per pet per night.

Cadillac Mountain *Greet the morning with sublime views*

Classic Trip

27

Acadia Byway

For adventurers, Mt Desert Island is hard to beat. Mountain hiking. Coastal kayaking. Woodland biking. Bird-watching. When you're done exploring, unwind by stargazing on the beach.

TRIP HIGHLIGHTS

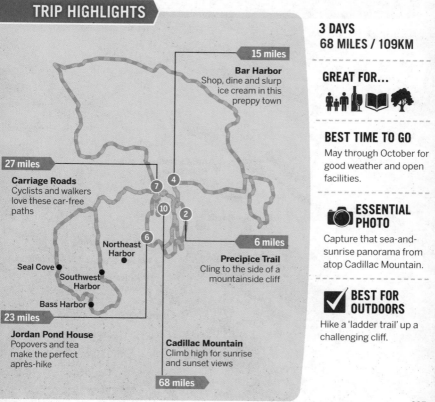

15 miles

Bar Harbor
Shop, dine and slurp ice cream in this preppy town

27 miles

Carriage Roads
Cyclists and walkers love these car-free paths

7
4
10
2
6

Northeast Harbor

Seal Cove
Southwest Harbor
Bass Harbor

6 miles

Precipice Trail
Cling to the side of a mountainside cliff

23 miles

Jordan Pond House
Popovers and tea make the perfect après-hike

Cadillac Mountain
Climb high for sunrise and sunset views

68 miles

3 DAYS
68 MILES / 109KM

GREAT FOR...

BEST TIME TO GO
May through October for good weather and open facilities.

ESSENTIAL PHOTO
Capture that sea-and-sunrise panorama from atop Cadillac Mountain.

BEST FOR OUTDOORS
Hike a 'ladder trail' up a challenging cliff.

27 Acadia Byway

Drivers and hikers alike can thank John D Rockefeller Jr and other wealthy landowners for the aesthetically pleasing bridges, overlooks and stone steps that give Acadia National Park its artistic oomph. Rockefeller in particular, before donating the lands, worked diligently with architects and masons to ensure that the infrastructure – for both carriage roads and motor roads – complemented the surrounding landscape.

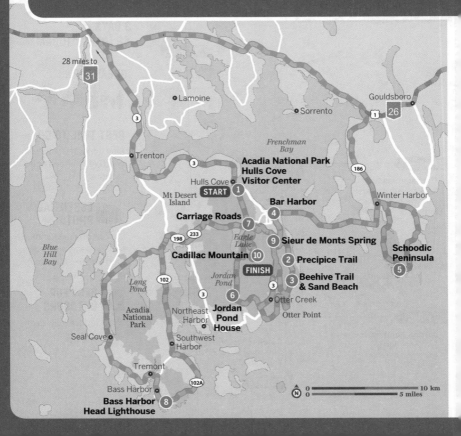

1 Acadia National Park Hulls Cove Visitor Center

Whoa, whoa, whoa. Before zooming into Bar Harbor on ME 3, stop at the **park visitor center** (📞207-288-3338; www.nps. gov/acad; ⏰8am-4:30pm Apr 15-Oct, extended hours Jul-Sep) to get the lay of the land and pay the admission fee (see the box, p291). Inside, head directly to the large diorama, which provides a helpful overview of Mt Desert Island (MDI). As you'll see, Acadia National Park shares the island with several non-park communities, which are tucked here and there beside Acadia's borders.

From the visitor center, the 27-mile Park Loop Rd circumnavigates the northeastern section of the island. The loop is part of the **Acadia All American Road** (http://

byways.org), a national scenic byway.

The Drive ≫ From the visitor center, turn right onto the Park Loop Rd, not ME 3, which leads into Bar Harbor. Take in a nice view of Frenchman Bay on your left before passing the spur to ME 233. A short distance ahead, turn left to begin the one-way loop on Park Loop Rd.

TRIP HIGHLIGHT

2 Precipice Trail

What's the most exciting way to get a bird's-eye view of the park? By climbing up to where the birds are. Two 'ladder trails' cling to the sides of exposed cliffs on the northeastern section of Park Loop Rd, dubbed Ocean Dr. If the season's right, tackle the first of the ladder trails, the 2.2-mile round-trip Precipice Trail, which climbs the side of Champlain Mountain on iron rungs and ladders. (Note that the trail is typically closed March through to the middle of August because it's a nesting area for peregrine falcons. If it is closed, you might catch volunteers and staff monitoring the birds through scopes from the trailhead parking lot.) Skip the trail on rainy days.

The Drive ≫ Drive south on Park Loop Rd. The Beehive Trail starts 100ft north of the Sand Beach parking area.

3 Beehive Trail & Sand Beach

Another good ladder trail is the Beehive Trail. The 1.6-mile (round-trip) hike includes ladders, rungs, narrow wooden bridges and scrambling – with steep drop-offs. If it's crowded, you can loop back down on a neighboring trail.

Don't let the crowds keep you away from Sand Beach. It's home to one of the few sandy shorelines in the park, and it's a don't-miss spot. But you don't have to visit in the middle of the day to appreciate its charms. Beat the crowds early in the morning, or visit at night, especially for the **Stars over Sand Beach** program. During these one-hour talks, lie on the beach, look up at the sky and listen to rangers share stories and science about the stars. Even if you miss the talk, the eastern coastline along Ocean Dr is worth checking out at night, when you can watch the Milky Way slip right into the ocean.

The Drive ≫ Swoop south past the crashing waves of Thunder Hole and then turn right onto Otter Cliff Rd, which hooks up to ME 3 north into town.

LINK YOUR TRIP

26 **Maritime Maine**
Enjoy Bass lighthouse? Hop on US 1 for more photogenic beacons.

31 **Mainely Art**
Take US 1 south to Rockland for galleries, museums and local artists.

④ Bar Harbor

Tucked on the rugged coast in the shadows of Acadia's mountains, Bar Harbor is a busy gateway town with a J Crew joie de vivre. Restaurants, taverns and boutiques are scattered along Main St, Mt Desert St and Cottage St. Shops sell everything from books to camping gear to handicrafts and art. For a fascinating collection of natural artifacts related to Maine's Native American heritage, visit the **Abbe Museum** (📞207-288-3519; www.abbemuseum.org; 26 Mt Desert St; adult/child $6/2; 🕙10am-4pm, closed Jan). The collection holds more than 50,000 objects, such as pottery, tools, combs and fishing instruments spanning the last 2000 years, including contemporary pieces. There's a smaller summer-only **branch** (🕙10am-5pm late May-early Oct) in Sieur de Monts Spring (see p294).

Done browsing? Spend the rest of the afternoon, or early evening, exploring the park by water. Sign up in Bar Harbor for a half-day or sunset kayaking trip. Both **National Park Sea Kayak** (📞800-347-0940; www.acadiakayak.com; 39 Cottage St) and **Coastal Kayaking Tour** (📞207-288-9605; www.acadiafun.com; 48 Cottage St) offer trips along the jagged coast.

🍴 🛏 p295

The Drive » Drive north 16 miles to US 1 north, following it about 17 miles to ME 186 east. ME 186 passes through Winter Harbor and then links to Schoodic Point Loop Rd. It's about an hour's drive one way. Alternatively, hop a Downeast Windjammer ferry (see p341) from the pier beside the Bar Harbor Inn.

✓ TOP TIP: PARK SHUTTLES

With millions of visitors coming to the park each summer, parking can be a hassle. On arrival, drive the Park Loop Rd straight through for the views and the driving experience. Then leave the driving to others by using the **Island Explorer** (www.exploreacadia.com; 🕙late Jun-early Oct), free with park admission. Shuttles run along eight routes that connect visitors to trails, carriage roads, beaches, campgrounds and in-town destinations. They can even carry mountain bikes.

⑤ Schoodic Peninsula

The Schoodic Peninsula is the only section of Acadia National Park that's part of the mainland. It's also home to the Schoodic Point Loop Rd, a rugged, woodsy drive with splendid views of Mt Desert Island and Cadillac Mountain. You're more likely to see a moose here than on MDI – what moose wants to cross a bridge?

Much of the drive is one way. There's a picnic area at **Frasier Point** near the park entrance. Further along the loop, turn right for a short ride to **Schoodic Point**, a 440ft-high promontory with ocean views. For historic details about sites along the drive, ask for the Schoodic National Scenic Byway brochure at the Hulls Cove Visitor Center.

The full loop from Winter Harbor is 11.5 miles and covers park, town and state roads. If you're planning to come by ferry, you could rent a bike beforehand at **Bar Harbor Bicycle Shop** (📞207-288-3886; www.barharborbike.com; 141 Cottage St, Bar Harbor; rental per day $24-35; 🚲) – the Schoodic Point Loop Rd's smooth surface and easy hills make it ideal for cycling.

In summer, the Island Explorer Schoodic

ISLAND VISIT PLANNER

Acadia National Park

Orientation & Fees

Park admission is $20 per vehicle from mid-June to early October, $10 per vehicle late in spring and mid-fall, and $5 for walk-ins and cyclists. Admission is valid for seven days. No admission fee is charged from November to April.

Camping

There are two great rustic **campgrounds** (📞877-444-6777; www.nps.gov/acad, reservations www.recreation.gov; 🏕) on Mt Desert Island, with more than 500 tent sites between them. Both are densely wooded and near the coast. Four miles west of Southwest Harbor, **Seawall** (tent & RV sites $14-20; ⊙late May-Sep) has by-reservation and walk-up sites. Five miles south of Bar Harbor on ME 3, **Blackwoods** (tent & RV sites May-Oct $20, Apr & Nov $10; ⊙year-round) requires reservations in summer. Both sites have restrooms and pay showers.

Bar Harbor & Mt Desert Island

Before your trip, check lodging availability and connect to hotel, motel and B&B websites via the **Acadia Welcome Center** (📞207-288-5103; www.acadiainfo.com; 1201 Bar Harbor Rd/ME 3, Trenton; ⊙8am-6pm Jun-Aug, to 5pm Mon-Fri low season) website, run by the Bar Harbor Chamber of Commerce. Staff can also mail you a copy of the visitor guide. Otherwise, stop by the welcome center itself for lodging brochures, maps and local information. It's located north of the bridge. From here you can call various hotels, motels and B&Bs directly for reservations.

Shuttle runs from Winter Harbor to the peninsula ferry terminal and south along the Schoodic Peninsula. It does not link to Bar Harbor.

The Drive » Return to the Park Loop Rd on MDI. Pass Otter Point then follow the road inland past Wildwood Stable. The Jordan Pond House is 1 mile ahead on the left.

- - - - - - - - - - - - -

TRIP HIGHLIGHT

⑥ Jordan Pond House

Share hiking stories with other nature lovers at the lodge-like **Jordan Pond House** (📞207-276-3316; www.jordanpond.com; Park Loop Rd; afternoon tea $9.50, lunch $10-17, dinner $19-27;

⊙lunch 11:30am-5:30pm, dinner 6-9pm), where afternoon tea has been a tradition since the late 1800s. Steaming pots of Earl Grey come with hot popovers (hollow rolls made with egg batter and strawberry jam). Eat on the broad lawn overlooking the lake. On clear days the glassy waters of 176-acre Jordan Pond reflect the image of Mt Penobscot like a mirror. Take the 3-mile self-guided nature tour around the pond after finishing your tea.

The Drive » Look up for the rock precariously perched atop South Bubble from the pull-off almost 2 miles north. Continue north to ME 233, following it on

a westerly course to parking at Eagle Lake.

- - - - - - - - - - - - -

TRIP HIGHLIGHT

⑦ Carriage Roads

John D Rockefeller Jr, a lover of old-fashioned horse carriages, gifted Acadia with some 45 miles of crisscrossing carriage roads. Made from crushed stone, the roads are free from cars and are popular with cyclists, hikers and equestrians. Several of them fan out from Jordan Pond House, but if the lot is too crowded continue north to the parking area at Eagle Lake on US 233 to link to the carriage road network. If you're

LOCAL KNOWLEDGE
SONJA BERGER,
PARK RANGER

If you're feeling adventurous, and you're not scared of heights, then some of the ladder trails are really fun and really challenging. My favorite is Jordan Cliffs, which is over by the Jordan Pond area. It has an interesting mix of ladders and other kinds of trail-building options that get you up the sheer cliff face and across. Then you've got the popovers and lobster stew at the Jordan Pond House to eat. You can burn off all the calories on the ladder trails.

Top: Bass Harbor Head Lighthouse
Right: Mt Desert Island

planning to explore by bike, the Bicycle Express Shuttle runs to Eagle Lake from the Bar Harbor Village Green from late June through September (see p290 for bike-hire info). Pick up a Carriage Road User's Map at the visitor center.

The Drive » Take ME 233 toward the western part of MDI, connecting to ME 198 west, then drop south on ME 102 toward

Southwest Harbor. Pass Echo Lake Beach and Southwest Harbor, then bear left onto ME 102A for a dramatic rise up and into the park near the seawall.

---

8 Bass Harbor Head Lighthouse

There is only one lighthouse on Mt Desert Island, and it sits in the somnolent village of Bass Harbor in the far southwest corner of the park. Built in 1858, the 36ft lighthouse still has a Fresnel lens from 1902. It's in a beautiful location that's a favorite of photographers. The lighthouse is a coast guard residence, so you can't go inside, but you can take photos. You can also stroll to the coast on two easy trails near the property: the **Ship Harbor Trail**, a 1.2-mile loop, and the **Wonderland Trail**, a 1.4-mile round-trip. These trails are spectacular ways to get through the forest and to the coast, which looks different to the coast on Ocean Dr.

The Drive » For a lollipop loop, return on ME 102A to ME 102 through the village of Bass Harbor. Follow ME 233

back to the Park Loop Rd and the Wild Gardens of Acadia.

- - - - - - - - - - - -

⑨ Sieur de Monts Spring

Nature lovers and history buffs will enjoy a stop at the Sieur de Monts Spring area at the intersection of ME 3 and the Park Loop Rd. Here you'll find a nature center and the summer-only branch of the **Abbe Museum** (adult/child $6/2), which sits in a lush, nature-like setting. Twelve of Acadia's biospheres are displayed in miniature at the **Wild Gardens of Acadia** (admission free), from bog to coniferous woods to meadow. Botany enthusiasts will appreciate the plant labels. There are also some amazing stone-step trails here, appearing out of the talus as if by magic.

The Drive » To avoid driving the full park loop, you can follow ME 3 into Bar Harbor and then hook back onto ME 233 northwest to the exit leading to Cadillac Mountain.

- - - - - - - - - - - -

TRIP HIGHLIGHT

⑩ Cadillac Mountain

Don't leave the park without driving – or hiking – to the 1530ft summit of Cadillac Mountain. For panoramic views of Frenchman Bay, walk the paved 0.5-mile **Cadillac Mountain Summit loop**. The summit is a popular place in the early morning because it's long been touted as the first spot in the US to see the sunrise. The truth? It is, but only between October 7 and March 6. The crown is passed to northern coastal towns the rest of the year because of the tilt of the earth. But, hey, the sunset is always a good bet.

Eating & Sleeping

Bar Harbor 4

✖ 2 Cats
Cafe $

(130 Cottage St; mains $6-12; ⏲7am-1pm Jan–mid-fall) Cat paws are painted on the tabletops inside this sunny cottage where weekend crowds line up for smoked-trout omelets and homemade muffins. Lunch offers slightly heartier fare. The five-pepper hot sauce is HOT – and sold by the bottle. You might see a cat or two strutting around inside.

✖ Mache Bistro
French $$

(☎207-288-0447; www.machebistro.com; 135 Cottage St; mains $17-24; ⏲5:30-9pm Wed-Sat May-Oct) Savor contemporary, French-inflected dishes in a stylish cottage with an interior that looks a bit like a French nightclub. The changing menu highlights local riches – seafood stew with haddock and scallops, and wild blueberry trifles. Open some Mondays and Tuesdays in summer; check the website.

✖ Mt Desert Island Ice Cream
Ice Cream $

(www.mdiic.com; 7 Firefly Lane; scoops $3.75, milkshakes $5; ⏲11am-10pm Apr-early fall) A cult hit for edgy flavors such as salted caramel, boozy White Russian and blueberry basil sorbet, this postage stamp–sized ice-cream counter is a post-dinner must.

✖ Side Street Cafe
American $$

(www.sidestreetbarharbor.com; 49 Rodick St; ⏲lunch & dinner) At this happenin' bar and eatery, pub grub comes with the occasional twist – think build-your-own mac and cheese and heartbreaker hot dogs with bacon, jalapenos and onions. Plenty of burgers and sandwiches, too.

🛏 Acadia Inn
Hotel $$

(☎207-288-3500; www.acadiainn.com; 98 Eden St; r incl breakfast $189; ❄🛜🛗) This traditional three-story hotel with helpful staff is beside a trail leading into the park. The good-sized rooms are comfortable, there's a laundry on site and the park shuttle stops here in summer. Can get crowded with convention attendees.

🛏 Aurora Inn
Motel $$

(☎207-288-3771; www.aurorainn.com; 51 Holland Ave; r $169; ❄🛜) This retro motor lodge has 10 clean rooms and a good location within walking distance of downtown. Guests can use the pool and laundry at nearby Quality Inn. Rates drop significantly outside high season (July to early September).

🛏 Bass Cottage
B&B $$$

(☎207-288-1234; www.basscottage.com; 14 The Field; r incl breakfast $230-380; ⏲May-Oct; ❄🛜) The 10 light-drenched guest rooms here have an elegant summer-cottage chic. Tickle the ivories on the parlor's grand piano or read a novel beneath the Tiffany stained-glass ceiling of the wood-paneled sitting room. Its fine-dining restaurant, 10 Tables (www.10tablesbarharbor.com), serves innovative New England fare in an intimate setting.

🛏 Holland Inn
B&B $$

(☎207-288-4804; www.hollandinn.com; 35 Holland Ave; r incl breakfast $140-185; ❄🛜) In a quiet neighborhood near downtown, this restored 1895 house and adjacent cottage have nine homey, unfrilly rooms. The ambience is so low-key you'll feel like you're staying in a friend's private home.

Kennebec River *A churning backdrop to history-filled towns*

Old Canada Road

28

The Kennebec River offers a stunning backdrop for photographers, a link to the past for history students, a white-water mecca for rafters and a source of inspiration for, well, everyone.

TRIP HIGHLIGHTS

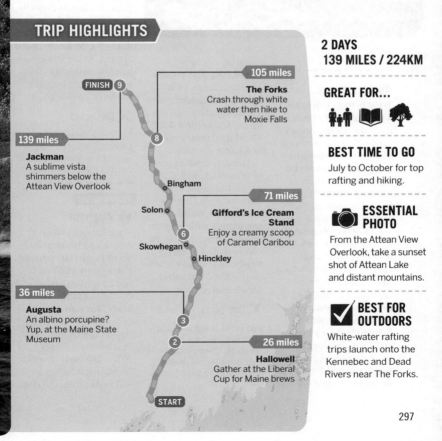

105 miles

The Forks
Crash through white water then hike to Moxie Falls

FINISH 9

139 miles

Jackman
A sublime vista shimmers below the Attean View Overlook

8

Bingham

71 miles

Solon

Gifford's Ice Cream Stand
Enjoy a creamy scoop of Caramel Caribou

6

Skowhegan

Hinckley

36 miles

Augusta
An albino porcupine? Yup, at the Maine State Museum

3

2

26 miles

Hallowell
Gather at the Liberal Cup for Maine brews

START

---

2 DAYS
139 MILES / 224KM

GREAT FOR...

BEST TIME TO GO
July to October for top rafting and hiking.

ESSENTIAL PHOTO
From the Attean View Overlook, take a sunset shot of Attean Lake and distant mountains.

BEST FOR OUTDOORS
White-water rafting trips launch onto the Kennebec and Dead Rivers near The Forks.

28 Old Canada Road

The Old Canada Rd is a 'hands-on' museum for history buffs. Stretching north from Hallowell to the Canadian border along US 201, it tracks the Kennebec River for most of the drive, passing farms, old ports, private timberlands and rafting companies – all of the industries that have sustained the region over the last few centuries. You're also following the trail of Benedict Arnold, who marched this way for George Washington during the Revolutionary War.

① Brunswick

What better place to start a road trip than a museum dedicated to an intrepid explorer? On the campus of Bowdoin College, the **Peary-MacMillan Arctic Museum** (www.bowdoin.edu/arctic-museum; 9500 College Station, Hubbard Hall; 10am-5pm Tue-Sat, 2-5pm Sun) displays memorabilia from the expeditions of Robert Peary and Donald MacMillan, who were among the first explorers to reach the North Pole – or a spot pretty darn close to it. Exhibits include an oak-and-rawhide sledge used to carry the expedition to the pole and Peary's journal entry reading 'The pole at last!' Also notable are MacMillan's B&W arctic photos and displays examining the Inuit people and arctic wildlife. The stuffed polar bear looks...not so cuddly.

The surrounding town of Brunswick, which sits on the banks of the Androscoggin River, is a handsome, well-kept community with a pretty village green and historic homes tucked along its tree-lined streets. For info on the Bowdoin College Museum of Art, see p323.

✕ 🛏 p303

The Drive » Follow US 201 north past meadows, fruit stands, old Chevy pickup trucks and Dunkin' Donuts (they're everywhere!) on this 30-mile stretch.

TRIP HIGHLIGHT

② Hallowell

Hallowell, a major river port for many years, thrived on the transportation of granite, ice and timber. There's a nice view of the town and the Kennebec River from the **Kennebec-Chaudière Corridor Information Panel**, located at a small pull-off south of town and describing the 230-mile international heritage trail between Quebec City and Fort Popham, ME. Hallowell dates from 1726, and the compact downtown, dubbed a 'Museum in the Streets,' holds numerous historic buildings and an easy-going pub, the Liberal Cup (see p303).

✕ 🛏 p303

The Drive » From Hallowell, follow US 201 just 1.5 miles north to downtown Augusta and the State Capitol complex.

TRIP HIGHLIGHT

③ Augusta

What happens when a moose and his rival lock horns in mortal combat? Their interlocked racks end up in the Cabinet of Curiosities at the **Maine State Museum** (207-287-2301; www.mainestatemuseum.org; 230 State St, State House Complex; adult/child $2/1; 9am-5pm Tue-Fri, 10am-4pm Sat, plus 1-4pm Sun late Jun-late Nov) in Augusta, the state

capital. The museum, a four-story ode to all things Maine, is situated around a multistory mill that churns by waterpower. The newest permanent exhibit, At Home in Maine, looks at homes throughout the years; in the mod 1970s house you can watch a family filmstrip and dial a rotary phone. Groovy!

Across the parking lot, take a guided tour of the **State House** (www. maine.gov; ⏰8am-5pm Mon-Fri, tours on the hour 9am-noon), built in 1832 and enlarged in 1901. It was designed by Boston architect Charles Bullfinch, the same architect behind the nation's Capitol building in Washington, DC.

The Drive » On the 19-mile drive to Winslow you'll cross the river and pass a barn or two, a taxidermy shop, pine trees, creeks and small churches.

LINK YOUR TRIP

29 Maine Highlands
From Jackman, take ME 6 east to Rockwood to tour Maine's largest lake.

31 Mainely Art
Visit the Bowdoin College Museum of Art in Brunswick, then stroll through galleries along the coast.

❹ Waterville & Winslow

The oldest blockhouse fort in the US is located at the **Fort Halifax State Historic Site**, a small park on the banks of the Kennebec River in Winslow. Built by British Americans in 1754 and 1755, the log fort was part of a larger garrison built to guard against attacks by the French and their allied Native American tribes. In 1987 the fort's logs came apart during a flood and floated downstream. They were recovered, and the fort was rebuilt. The fort sits on US 201 a mile south of the Winslow-Waterville Bridge.

✕ ⊨ p303

The Drive » Cross the Winslow-Waterville Bridge and continue on US 201 north through downtown Waterville. From here it's a 9-mile drive. Look out for logging trucks as the road approaches Hinckley.

❺ LC Bates Museum

Any road-trip guidebook worth its stripes includes at least one quirky museum. This guide earns its stripes – and its spots and feathers – with the nicely nonconformist **LC Bates Museum** (☎207-238-4250; www.gwh. org; US 201, Hinckley; adult/ child $3/1; ⊗10am-4:30pm Wed-Sat, 1-4:30pm Sun, closed Sun mid-Nov–Mar). Housed in a 1903 brick school building on the Good Will-Hinckley educational complex south of Hinckley, the museum embraces the concept of the 20th-century Cabinet of Curiosities with an assortment of natural, geologic and artistic artifacts. On the 1st floor, look for an amazing array of taxidermied birds. The basement holds stuffed mammals (including one of the last caribou shot in Maine), rocks, minerals and fossils. There are treasures here, and staff members are glad to point out the more interesting finds and answer questions. **Hiking trails** meander through the forest out back.

The Drive » The Kennebec stays in the picture on the 10-mile drive to Skowhegan, former home of Margaret Chase Smith, the first female US senator.

TRIP HIGHLIGHT

❻ Gifford's Ice Cream Stand

At the hard-to-resist **Gifford's** (http:// giffordsicecream.com; 307 Madison Ave/US 201, Skowhegan; scoops $3; ⊗noon-9pm mid-Mar–mid-Oct), every ice-cream flavor sounds delicious, from Maine Blackberry to Caramel Caribou to Moose Tracks with peanut-butter cups and fudge. To celebrate LL Bean's centennial in 2012, the Gifford folks

NORTH WOODS RIVER RAFTING TRIPS

Some of the best white water in America rushes through Maine's North Woods. From May to mid-October, dozens of companies run organized rafting trips on the Kennebec, Dead and Penobscot Rivers. Bingham and The Forks serve as bases for rafting companies, and trips range in difficulty from Class II to Class V. For a one-day trip on the Kennebec, expect to pay between $89 and $119, with prices at their highest in July and August.

Recommended rafting companies:

Crab Apple Whitewater (☎207-663-4491; www.crabapplewhitewater.com; 3 Lake Moxie Rd, The Forks)

Northern Outdoors (☎207-663-4466; www.northernoutdoors.com; 1771 US 201, The Forks)

Three Rivers Whitewater Inc (☎207-663-2104; www.threeriverswhitewater.com; 2265 US 201, The Forks)

Moscow Set against the Kennebec River

created Muddy Bean Boots – vanilla ice cream with caramel ripples and brownie bites. If you don't pull over for a scoop, you'll never hear the end of it from your kids or your co-pilot. But don't worry, these creamy concoctions are delicious.

The Drive » From Skowhegan, drive 10 miles north to the junction of US 201 and ME 43, which marks the start of the Old Canada Road National Scenic Byway – a particularly lovely stretch of the longer Old Canada Rd.

- - - - - - - - - - - -

⑦ Robbins Hill Scenic Area

Take a picnic and your camera to the overlook at Robbins Hill near the start of the national byway. Look west for views of Saddleback Mountain, Mt Abraham and other mountains in Maine's Rangeley Lakes region. Signboards detail the history of the communities along the Old Canada Rd, from the region's agricultural beginnings in the late 1700s to the effects of the railroad to the arrival of the timber industry.

The Drive » Pass white clapboard houses in Solon

301

BENEDICT ARNOLD SLEPT HERE

About 12 miles north of Bingham, on the left side of the road, a small stone memorial marks the spot where Benedict Arnold and his soldiers left the Kennebec River in October 1775 during the Revolutionary War. Arnold, at the time still loyal to America, had been placed in command of 1100 men by George Washington. His mission? To follow the Kennebec and Dead Rivers north to defeat the British forces at Quebec. The soldiers used bateaux to travel up the Kennebec and encountered numerous difficulties along the way. Many men were lost through desertion and illness. A weakened force of about 500 reached Quebec, where they were ultimately defeated.

and another roadside pull-off, this one overlooking the Kennebec River. Here you'll find informational plaques about the railroad and the logging industries, including a picture of the last American log drive here in 1973. Continue past rafting businesses and brewpubs.

TRIP HIGHLIGHT

8 The Forks

After passing through Bingham and Moscow, US 201 follows a gorgeous stretch of river into The Forks. At this dot on the map, the Dead River joins the Kennebec River, setting the stage for excellent white-water rafting (see p300). At the junction of US 201 and Lake Moxie Rd, there's a small rest area with picnic tables, an information kiosk and a footbridge over the Kennebec River. From here, drive 2 miles east on Lake Moxie Rd to the trailhead for the easy walk (0.6 miles one way) to the dramatic **Moxie Falls**. At 90ft, this is one of the highest waterfalls in the state.

🍴 p303

The Drive » On this 20-mile push, you'll ascend Johnson Mountain before reaching the Lake Parlin overlook, where there are details about the American moose – which can reach speeds of 35mph.

TRIP HIGHLIGHT

9 Jackman

Jackman knows how to throw out the welcome mat. Just south of town, the **Attean View Overlook** greets road trippers with a dramatic view of Attean Lake and distant mountains – a landscape that sweeps into Canada.

The lake and overlook are named for Joseph Attean, a Penobscot Indian leader who guided Henry David Thoreau on trips through the Maine woods in 1853 and 1857. Attean died during a log drive on July 4, 1870. Legend says that his boots were hung from a pine knot near where his body was found, a tradition for river drivers killed while working the waterway. Today, Jackman is a good base for outdoor fun, including rafting, canoeing, hiking, biking, snowmobiling and cross-country skiing.

🛏 p303

Eating & Sleeping

Brunswick ①

✕ Frontier Cafe   Cafe $$

(www.explorefrontier.com; 14 Maine St; mains $11-16; ⊙ lunch & dinner, closed Mon) Massive windows overlook the Androscoggin River at this raw, loft-like space that's part cafe, part cinema, part bar and part art gallery. It serves cranberry chicken salad, fish tacos, pancetta-wrapped pork tenderloins and a few vegetarian dishes. Located at the back of Fort Andross.

🛏 Inn at Brunswick Station   Inn $$

(☎207-837-6565; www.innatbrunswick station.com; 4 Noble St; r/ste $189/249; ⬤) Monochromatic earth tones and crisp white linens give rooms modern style. Enjoy flat-screen TVs, full-length mirrors and proximity to Bowdoin College.

Hallowell ②

✕ Liberal Cup   Pub $

(www.theliberalcup.com; 115 Water St/US 201; mains $7-14; ⊙ 11:30am-9pm Sun-Thu, to 10pm Fri & Sat) Wash down your haddock sandwich with a pint of Old Hallow Ale at this friendly local brewpub in a renovated downtown storefront. The pub stays open until 1am.

✕ Slates Restaurant
& Bakery   Modern American $$

(☎207-622-9575; www.slatesrestaurant.com; 167 Water St/US 201; pastries, cookies & bread $2-9, mains lunch $9-17, dinner $12-28) Bakery to the right, cafe to the left inside this yellow house. The sprawling menu includes crabmeat crepes, grilled pesto pizzas and beef tenderloin au poivre. You can also order to-go sandwiches. The bakery serves breakfast goodies, breads, desserts and coffee.

🛏 Maple Hill Farm B&B   B&B $$

(☎207-622-2708; www.maplebb.com; 11 Inn Rd; r incl breakfast $115-205; ❄🛜) Host Scott Cowger, a former Maine state senator and

staffer with the Department of Environmental Protection, is committed to using energy wisely. With solar panels and a wind turbine, the B&B generates half of its power from renewable sources. The eight rooms are bright and comfortable; amenities include a pub, a sauna and an outdoor hot tub. The property is on a farm, so enjoy fresh eggs for breakfast.

Waterville & Winslow ④

✕ Big G's   American $

(www.big-g-s-deli.com; 581 Benton Ave, Winslow; mains under $9; ⊙ 6am-7pm) The sandwiches are big and inexpensive, making Big G's a good stop for travelers on a budget. Breakfast is available, too.

🛏 Fireside Inn & Suites   Hotel $$

(☎207-873-3335; www.firesideinnwaterville. com; 356 Main St, Waterville; r incl breakfast $149; @🛜❄🐾) Common areas are a bit worn, but rooms are very clean and come with a fridge and a microwave.

The Forks ⑧

✕ Kennebec River Pub
& Brewery   Pub $$

(☎207-663-4466; www.northernoutdoors. com; 1771 US 201; mains breakfast $6-9, lunch & dinner $8-22; ⊙ closed Dec & Apr) After a day of rafting, enjoy a chili burger and a Kennebec 'logger.' The on-site Kennebec Brewery is a stop on the Maine Beer Trail. The pub is part of the Forks Resort Center.

Jackman ⑨

🛏 Bishops Country Inn Motel   Motel $

(☎207-668-3231; www.bishopsmotel.com; 461 Main St; r incl breakfast $90-100; ❄🛜) The spacious rooms work well for gear-laden adventurers and come with microwave, refrigerator and flat-screen TV.

Moosehead Lake Silver-blue and dotted with islands, the lake is one of the state's most glorious places

Maine Highlands

29

Welcome to the highlands, a land of superlatives where you can hike Maine's highest mountain, canoe its largest lake and ogle the stomping grounds of America's spookiest author – if you dare.

TRIP HIGHLIGHTS

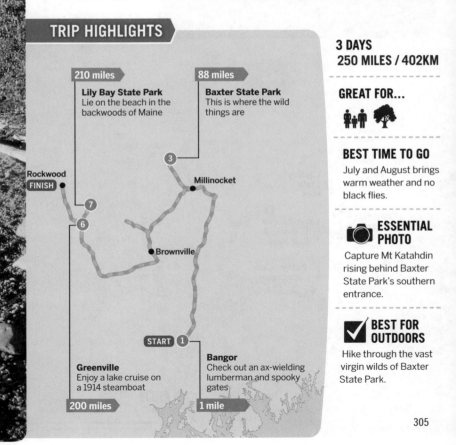

210 miles

Lily Bay State Park
Lie on the beach in the backwoods of Maine

88 miles

Baxter State Park
This is where the wild things are

Rockwood
FINISH

Millinocket

Brownville

START 1

Greenville
Enjoy a lake cruise on a 1914 steamboat

200 miles

Bangor
Check out an ax-wielding lumberman and spooky gates

1 mile

3 DAYS
250 MILES / 402KM

GREAT FOR...

BEST TIME TO GO
July and August brings warm weather and no black flies.

ESSENTIAL PHOTO
Capture Mt Katahdin rising behind Baxter State Park's southern entrance.

BEST FOR OUTDOORS
Hike through the vast virgin wilds of Baxter State Park.

305

29 Maine Highlands

Texts. Tweets. Twenty-four hours of breaking news. If you need a respite from the modern world, grab your map — a paper one! — and drive directly to the Maine highlands, part of the sprawling North Woods. What will you find? Silence and solitude. Water and pines. The unfettered wildness of Baxter State Park. And access to 175,000 acres of private forest thrown open for public recreation.

TRIP HIGHLIGHT

① Bangor

Bangor is the last city on the map before the North Woods. So it seems appropriate that a towering **statue of Paul Bunyan** (Main St btwn Buck & Dutton Sts) stands near the center of downtown, in the middle of the 500 block of Main St. The 37ft statue has watched over Bangor since the 1950s, but the ax-wielding lumberman isn't getting much love these days. His view of the Penobscot

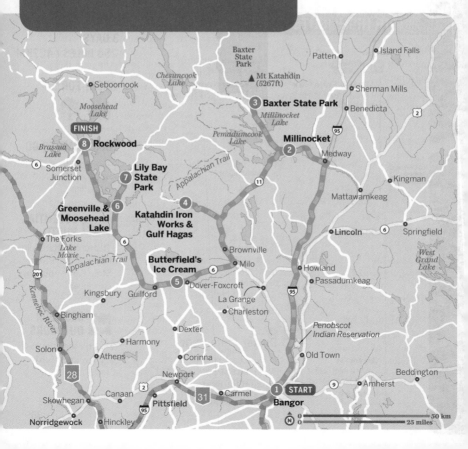

River is now blocked by a casino, and a new Bangor Arena and Conference Center is rising quickly behind him. There have been calls to move him to a more scenic spot.

But Paul's not the only star in town. Stephen King, the mega-selling author of horror novels such as *Carrie* and *The Shining* resides in an appropriately Gothic red Victorian **house** (West Broadway), off Hammond St. You can't go inside, but you can snap a photo of his splendidly creepy wrought-iron front gate that's adorned with spider webs. The house is in a residential neighborhood, so please keep your shrieking and personal creepiness to a minimum.

 p311

The Drive » The 60-mile drive on I-95 north to exit 244 for Millinocket isn't that interesting.

LINK YOUR TRIP

28 Old Canada Road

Head west to US 201 from Rockwood for rafting and riverside history.

31 Mainely Art

In Bangor, visit the University of Maine Museum of Art for contemporary art.

But it's efficient, and the rest of the drive will blow this ho-hum stretch from your memory. From exit 244, drive northwest on ME 11/157.

- - - - - - - - - - - - - -

② Millinocket

Baxter State Park is far, far off the beaten path, and many of its rules and policies differ from those at other Maine state parks. For these reasons, do a bit of planning before driving out here. The town of Millinocket, with its motels, inns and eateries, works well as a base camp. Eighteen miles from the park, it's also the closest town to the southern entrance. For park information and a copy of *Windnotes,* the helpful park visitor guide, stop by the **Baxter State Park Authority Headquarters** (☎207-723-5140; www.baxterstateparkauthority.com; 64 Balsam Dr; ⊗8am-4pm daily Jun-early Oct, Mon-Fri early Oct-May); it's just east of the McDonald's.

 p311

The Drive » The drive from Millinocket to Baxter State Park takes in bogs, birches and pine trees and then some very narrow roads. Gape at Katahdin from the Keep Maine Beautiful sign, then continue to Togue Pond Gate and visitor center.

- - - - - - - - - - - - - -

TRIP HIGHLIGHT

③ Baxter State Park

In the 1930s, Governor Percival Baxter began buying land for **Baxter State Park** (www.baxterstateparkauthority.com; per vehicle per day $14), using his own money. By the time of his death in 1969, he had given, in trust, more than 200,000 acres to the park as a gift to the people of Maine. **Mt Katahdin** is the park's crowning glory. At 5267ft it is Maine's tallest mountain and the northern endpoint of the 2179-mile Appalachian Trail.

Baxter also left an endowment fund for the support and maintenance of the park. His greatest desire was for the land to remain wild and to serve as a 'sanctuary for beast and birds.' To ensure that his vision is followed, the park is kept in a primitive state and there is very little infrastructure inside its boundaries. And what a difference that makes. Baxter is Maine at its most primeval: the wind whips around 47 peaks, black bears root through the underbrush and hikers go for miles without seeing another soul.

See p308 and p310 for more information.

 p311

The Drive » From Millinocket, follow ME 11 south for about 25 miles. Turn right onto Katahdin Iron Works Rd, and drive 6 miles on a mostly dirt road. If you get to Brownsville Junction on ME 11, you missed Katahdin Iron Works Rd.

④ Katahdin Iron Works & Gulf Hagas

A reminder of a time when blast furnaces and charcoal kilns smelted iron all day, the **ironworks** (www.maine.gov; ⏰Jun-Aug) was built in 1843 and used for about 30 years. Eventually the costs of operating in such isolation made the facility unable to compete with foundries in Pennsylvania and other states, and it closed in 1890.

Katahdin Iron Works Rd also leads to **Gulf Hagas** (📞207-965-8135; www.northmainewoods.org; day-use adult/child $10/free; ⏰6am-9pm early May-early Oct), dubbed the Grand Canyon of Maine. The gorge features a stunning 500ft drop studded with waterfalls over the course of its 5 miles. Carved over five million years by water eroding the slate bedrock, the gulf is a national natural landmark and is surrounded by some of Maine's oldest white pines. An 8-mile hiking loop at the site is remote and challenging, so come very prepared. Gulf Hagas is within the Ki-Jo Mary Multiple-Use Forest, which is owned and managed by private timber interests but allows public use. Pay the entrance fee at the checkpoint across the road from Katahdin Iron Works. Visit the North Maine Woods website for maps as well as details about fees and access to Gulf Hagas.

The Drive » From Brownville, south of Brownsville Junction, continue south on ME 11. Take ME 6 west to Dover-Foxcroft.

⑤ Butterfield's Ice Cream

It's a bit of a haul between the ironworks and Greenville. This route swings below the private logging roads of the North Woods. Take a break for **Butterfield's** (946 W Main St; scoops $2.50; ⏰11:30am-8pm) in Dover-Foxcroft. Walk up to the window, choose your scoop, grab a seat and enjoy your licks beside the smiling cow.

The Drive » Follow ME 6 west through Guilford and Abbot Village. North of Monson, look for a pull-off on your right beside the Appalachian Trail. From this trailhead it's 112 miles north to

BAXTER STATE PARK

Admission

Only so many visitors are allowed in each day, so arrive at the entrance very early. Baxter's two main gates are **Togue Pond Gate** (⏰6am-10pm early May-late Jun, 5am-10pm late Jun-Aug, low season varies) in the south, where there is a **visitor center** (⏰7am-3pm Mon-Thu, to 6pm Fri-Sun late May-early Oct, low season varies), and **Matagamon** (⏰6am-10pm early May-early Oct, to 7pm rest of year) in the north. Maine residents enjoy a $1 to $2 admission discount at most state parks. At Baxter, Mainers have an even better deal: they're exempt from the $14 vehicle-admission fee.

Hiking

Read the park's website thoroughly. To hike, you need a parking reservation. A few spots may be available on a first come, first served basis, but don't count on that on a summer weekend. Parking reservations can be made online at the park's website for a $5 fee or by calling 📞207-723-3877/5140. For an easy day in the southern part of the park, try the mile-long walk to Katahdin Stream falls or the pleasant 2-mile nature path around Daicey Pond. Visit the park's website for maps and details about hiking Mt Katahdin.

The road from Millinocket to Baxter State Park

Katahdin. This trailhead marks the southern start of a very remote section of the trail. The pull-off is about 11 miles south of Greenville.

TRIP HIGHLIGHT

6 Greenville & Moosehead Lake

Silver-blue and dotted with islands, Moosehead Lake sprawls over 120 sq miles of North Woods wilderness. Named, some say, after its shape from the air, it's one of the state's most glorious places. Greenville is the region's main settlement.

Owned and maintained by the Moosehead Marine Museum, the 115ft steamboat **SS Katahdin** (www.katahdincruises.com; adult/child 3hr cruise $33/18, Mt Kineo cruise $38/21; ⊙3hr cruise Tue-Sat late Jun–early Oct, Mt Kineo cruise limited dates) was built in 1914. It still makes the rounds on Moosehead Lake from Greenville's center, just like it did in Greenville's heyday. The lake's colorful history is preserved in the **Moosehead Marine Museum** (⊙10am-4pm Mon-Sat late Jun–early Oct), next to the dock. For moose safaris, white-water rafting, guided

309

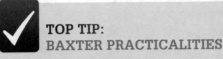

TOP TIP:
BAXTER PRACTICALITIES

» No pets are permitted inside the park boundaries.

» Bring insect repellent. Black flies and no-see-ums bite in the spring and mosquitoes appear in June. Green deer flies and black moose flies can also bite in the middle of summer.

» Pack warm clothes, even in summer, as well as water, a flashlight and rain protection.

» There are no treated water sources inside the park, so bring your own or carry purifying tablets.

» Cell phones and iPads don't work in the park. Handheld GPS devices work with reasonable accuracy, but always hike with a map and compass. Vehicle GPS units can be less reliable. Staff regularly get reports that visitors have been directed onto Golden Rd, a nearby logging road, and missed the park entrance. Use written directions after Millinocket Lake, near the south entrance. (See http://www.baxterstateparkauthority.com/maps/directions.php.)

fishing trips and guided/self-guided canoe trips, stop by **Northwoods Outfitters** (📞207-695-3288; www.maineoutfitter.com; 5 Lily Bay Rd; ⏰8am-7pm) in the center of town. It also sells outdoor gear and hot coffee.

The **Moosehead Lake Region Chamber of Commerce** (📞207-695-2702; www.mooseheadlake.org; 480 Moosehead Lake Rd; ⏰10am-4pm) runs a good visitor center south of downtown.

✗ ➡ p311

The Drive » Tantalizing glimpses of Moosehead Lake peek through the trees on the 8-mile drive from Greenville on Lily Bay Rd.

TRIP HIGHLIGHT

7 Lily Bay State Park

To camp on the shores of Moosehead Lake, pitch your tent at one of the 90 campsites at this 925-acre **park** (📞207-695-2700, camping 207-624-9950; www.maine.gov, www.campwithme.com; 13 Myrle's Way; tent sites $24; ⏰year-round, staffed mid-May–early Oct). Relax on the sandy beach, bird-watch and stroll the lakeside trail. The park is also a good base for other area hikes.

The Drive » Return to Greenville, then drive 20 miles north on ME 6, passing the

Lavigne Memorial Bridge and marker, memorializing a local son who died in WWII.

----

8 Rockwood

The distinctive **Mt Kineo** is a 1769ft rhyolite mountain rising from the bottom of Moosehead Lake. For a good silhouette of its steep, towering face, which juts more than 700ft above the lake, pull over in the village of Rockwood north of Greenville. From Rockwood, return to Greenville or continue 26 miles through the woods on a lovely ribbon of road with lake views to US 201 near Jackman.

Eating & Sleeping

Bangor ❶

✖ Bagel Central   Deli $

(www.bagelcentralbangor.com; 33 Central St; mains under $7; ⏱6am-6pm Mon-Thu, to 5:30pm Fri, to 2pm Sun) Bagel Central bakes 16 varieties of bagels, which are then transformed into sandwiches spilling over with smoked salmon and other tasty fillings. Omelets and other breakfast fare served all day.

✖ Fiddlehead   Modern American $$

(☎207-942-3336; www.thefiddleheadrestaurant. com; 84 Hammond St; mains $15-22; ⏱dinner Tue-Sun) The menu puts an international spin on local seasonal ingredients, from red and yellow lentil curry with naan to grilled shrimp with hoisin and ginger glaze. Craft cocktails served too.

Millinocket ❷

✖ River Drivers Pub   Pub $

(☎207-723-8475; www.neoc.com/riverdrivers; 30 Twin Pines Rd; mains lunch $7-12, dinner $17-26; ⏱lunch & dinner Jan, Feb & Jun-Aug) At this restaurant at Twin Pines Camp, off Black Cat Rd, enjoy sandwiches, seafood, steak and pasta with a view of Mt Katahdin.

⛏ Five Lakes Lodge   B&B $$$

(☎207-723-5045; www.5lakeslodge.com; Fire Rd No 4; r incl breakfast $225-275; ❄🌐) Rustic goes modern at this inviting lakeside lodge off ME 11, where the view of Mt Katahdin is a stunner. The five rooms have lake views, custom-made log beds, fireplaces, refrigerators and Jacuzzi tubs. A stone fireplace anchors the lofty den.

⛏ Twin Pines Camp   Cabins $$

(☎207-723-5438, reservations 800-634-7238; www.neoc.com; 30 Twin Pines Rd; cabins $245-607; ♿🌐) Part of the New England Outdoor Center, these spiffy lakeside cabins are close to Baxter State Park and have views of Mt Katahdin. Play volleyball and paddle canoes on the lake. It's $20 per pet per night; there's wi-fi in the restaurant.

Baxter State Park ❸

⛏ Baxter State Park   Campground $

(☎207-723-5140; www.baxterstatepark authority.com; dorm bunks $11, tent sites $30, cabins $55-130) Reserve your spot well in advance. There are 11 campgrounds and numerous backcountry sites. Each backcountry site has an untreated water source, an outhouse and a fire ring (except David Pond). Backcountry tent sites are $20.

Greenville & Moosehead Lake ❻

✖ Auntie M's   American $

(13 Lily Pond Rd; mains under $10; ⏱5am-3pm) Eat breakfast all day at this cozy eatery near the center of town. Burgers, wraps and Mexican pizza served at lunch. Also sells $6 bag lunches with a sandwich and snacks. Cash only.

⛏ Blair Hill Inn   B&B $$$

(☎207-695-0224; www.blairhill.com; 351 Lily Bay Rd; r incl breakfast $350-495; ⏱dinner Thu-Sat mid-Jun–mid-Oct; 🌐) The view of Moosehead Lake from this hilltop B&B and restaurant is astounding. The B&B has eight plush rooms with in-room fireplaces. The restaurant serves exquisite five-course creations ($59) of local seafood and house-grown veggies and herbs.

⛏ Moose Mountain Inn   Motel $

(☎800-792-1858; www.moosemountaininn. com; 314 Rockwood Rd/ME 15; r $90-110; ❄🌐♿🐾) Owned by Northwoods Outfitters, this two-story motel offers 15 simple rooms with refrigerators, microwaves and flat-screen TVs. Pets $10 per night.

Lake Sebago As the sun sets, take to a canoe, or simply enjoy the serenity

Lakes Tour

30

Bright blue lakes dapple the landscape like drops from Mother Nature's paintbrush, luring travelers with sandy beaches, excellent kayaking, small-town strolling and New England's favorite state fair.

TRIP HIGHLIGHTS

3 miles

Saco River Canoe & Kayak
Load up the canoe and hit the lazy river

18 miles

Bridgton
The Magic Lantern movie house charms with great service and a pub

27 miles

Naples
Mark Twain would envy the views from the *Songo River Queen II*

③
②
START

④

⑥
⑦

● Windham

● Portland
FINISH

Fryeburg Fair
Ride the Ferris wheel, watch the lumberjacks or visit the ox barn

1 mile

Sebago Lake State Park
Who needs a resort when you've got lakeside camping?

30 miles

**2 DAYS
60 MILES / 97KM**

GREAT FOR...

BEST TIME TO GO
To enjoy swimming and boating, visit from May to October.

ESSENTIAL PHOTO

Stake your position on the Naples causeway for sweet pics of Long Lake.

BEST FOR FAMILIES

Spend a lazy afternoon canoeing the Saco River near Fryeburg.

313

30 Lakes Tour

US 302 in southeast Maine is the quickest link between North Conway's outlet stores and the LL Bean store just north of Portland, but the road is also the lifeline for the stunning Lakes Region. Filled with glacier-made lakes and ponds, this summer hot spot is home to the state's most popular campground as well as a beloved paddle wheeler and the family-friendly Saco River. Lovely B&Bs encourage lingering with water views and scrumptious breakfasts.

❶ Fryeburg Visitor Information Center

Just east of the Maine state line, this state-run **visitor center** (📞207-935-7670; www.exploremaine.org; US 302, Fryeburg; ⏰9am-5:30pm Nov-Apr, 8am-6pm May-Oct) can prepare you for an adventure anywhere in the Pine Tree State. It's well stocked with brochures, and the staff is very helpful. Want to stretch your legs? A 1.5-mile section of the new **Mountain Division**

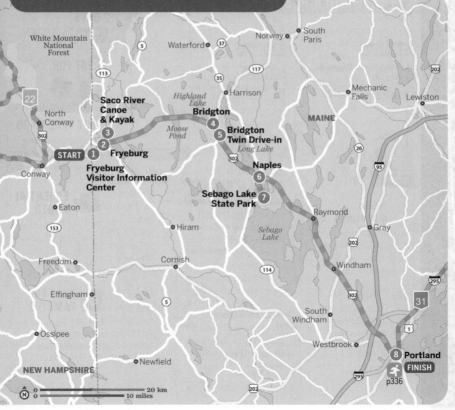

Trail begins just behind the visitor center. If all goes to plan, the hiking and biking trail will eventually extend 52 miles from Fryeburg to Portland.

The Drive » From the visitor center, follow US 302 east into downtown.

TRIP HIGHLIGHT

2 Fryeburg

Sitting prettily on the banks of the Saco River, Fryeburg is best known for hosting the annual **Fryeburg Fair** (☏207-935-3268; www.fryeburgfair.com; 1154 Main St; admission $10, parking $5; ☺late Sep-early Oct), an eight-day state agricultural fair that started in 1851. Today it attracts more than 300,000 people. Events and attractions include everything from livestock and flower shows to a whoopee pie

contest, a pig scramble (local pigs only, please), a horse-pulling contest and a Woodsman's Day, when male and female lumberjacks chisel poles of timber with their chainsaws and hurl their mighty axes.

The rest of the year, the big draw is the Saco River. If you want to feel the sand under your feet after hiking through the White Mountains in next-door New Hampshire, relax on **Weston's Beach**. To get there, take a left onto ME 113/River Rd just before entering Fryeburg from the visitor center. Parking is ahead on the right after crossing the river.

🛏 p319

The Drive » Follow ME 5 north for 0.5 miles from the junction of US 302 and ME 5, where signs advertising chowder suppers and community dinners tempt weary travelers.

TRIP HIGHLIGHT

3 Saco River Canoe & Kayak

Ready to get out on the water? The friendly folks at **Saco River Canoe & Kayak** (☏207-935-2369; www.sacorivercanoe.com; 1009 Main St), who've run self-guided trips for more than 40 years, will set you up on the family-friendly Saco River. The river flows about 120 miles from Saco Lake in New Hampshire's

upper White Mountains through Crawford Notch and into Maine. In Maine, the Saco runs parallel to US 302 as it makes its way to the Gulf of Maine southwest of Portland. The river is particularly pleasant around Fryeburg, with leafy banks and sandy shores, mountain views and gentle conditions. Trips can range from one hour to several days. Canoe and kayak rentals run from $30 to $45 per day, depending on watercraft and season. Delivery and pick-up services are charged separately, and cost $6 to $16 per trip (minimum charge from $10). Service to the nearby Swans Fall access point is free.

The Drive » US 302 passes Christmas-tree farms and diamond-blue lakes on its 15-mile run east to Bridgton.

TRIP HIGHLIGHT

4 Bridgton

Bridgton is prime digs for a weekend getaway. Main St runs for 1.5 miles past a museum, a movie house, an inviting park and an eclectic array of indie shops (see p316). The well-regarded **Rufus Porter Museum** (☏207-647-2828; www.rufusportermuseum.org; 67 N High St; adult/child $8/free; ☺noon-4pm Wed-Sat mid-Jun–mid-Oct) looks at the work of 19th-century Renaissance man Rufus Porter. Porter

LINK YOUR TRIP

22 **White Mountains Loop**
Take US 302 west to North Conway, NH, to hop a train ride to the Presidential Range.

31 **Mainely Art**
For inspiration, check out the American landscapes at the Portland Museum of Art.

is recognized throughout New England for the landscape murals he painted in hundreds of houses in the region between 1825 and 1845. Also an inventor, he sold the concept of the revolving rifle to Samuel Colt in 1844 and created *Scientific American* magazine.

Take a moment to walk through the photogenic Bob Dunning Memorial Bridge – built by district craftsmen in 2007 to honor a local conservationist. It marks the entrance to **Pondicherry Park** (www.pondicherrypark.org), a 660-acre woodland park filled with trails and wildlife. The park sits behind the **Magic Lantern** (207-647-5065; www.magiclanternmovies.com; 9 Depot St; adult/child $6.50/5), a beloved community movie house – and the site of a tannery in the

1800s – that anchors downtown. Congenial staff, a pub with a 23ft screen and three new, themed theaters, make this a pleasant spot to catch a blockbuster, an indie flick or the big game.

✗ ⊨ p319

The Drive » From downtown Bridgton drive 1 mile east on US 302.

- - - - - - - - - - - -

⑤ Bridgton Twin Drive-in

One of just five drive-ins remaining in the state, **Bridgton Twin Drive-in** (207-647-8666; 383 Portland Rd; adult/child $7.50/5; ☉Apr-Sep; ♿) shows movies on two screens, and is a popular choice with families. Visit its Facebook page to see what's playing.

The Drive » US 302 rolls east of out Bridgton, turning in a more southerly direction as it

approaches Naples, 8 miles to the south.

- - - - - - - - - - - -

TRIP HIGHLIGHT

⑥ Naples

Restaurants and shops cluster around the Causeway in downtown Naples, which sits on a spit of land between Long Lake and Brandy Pond. A walk along the Causeway affords grand views of bright blue Long Lake. The big draw here, beyond the eateries and bars with lake views, is the red-and-white **Songo River Queen II** (207-693-6861; www.songoriverqueen.net; US 302; tours adult/child 1hr $12/6, 1½hr $16/8, 2hr $20/10; ☉daily mid-Jun–Aug, Sat & Sun mid-May–mid-Jun & early Sep–mid-Oct), a 93ft paddle wheeler with a covered upper deck. The boat churns up the east coast of the lake, then comes back down the west side (or vice versa). You'll get a look

SHOPS OF BRIDGTON

Welcoming proprietors and an eclectic mix of shops in close proximity make downtown Bridgton a great spot for an hour or two of shopping. A few stores are included below; check websites for hours not listed, which vary seasonally.

Bridgton Books (140 Main St; ☉9:30am-5:30pm Mon-Sat, 11am-6pm Sun) Large inventory of new and used books. Helpful staff.

Gallery 302 (www.gallery302.com; 112 Main St) Sixty-member artists co-op displays and sells art in all its forms.

Harry Barkers Emporium (www.harvesthills.org; 142 Main St; ☉10am-5pm) In partnership with Harvest Hills Animal Shelter, Harry Barker (get it?) sells an eclectic mix of antiques from a dozen vendors. Inventory changes daily.

Reny's (www.renys.com; 151 Main St) Reny's is a discount mini department store in Maine with 14 locations. Look for clothing, housewares and a bit of this and that.

Fryeburg Fair Enjoying some maple-sugar cotton candy

317

at Mt Washington and the Presidential Range during the cruise. The *Songo* holds 350 people, so reservations are not typically needed.

In the spring of 2012, a new fixed-span bridge replaced the 60-year-old swing bridge that connected the eastern and western shores beside the Causeway. Traffic, which used to stop when a boat passed between the pond and lake, should flow more smoothly.

✖ p319

The Drive » From the Causeway, turn left onto ME 114 and drive 2 miles south. Turn left onto State Park Dr and take a woodsy cruise to the park entrance.

TRIP HIGHLIGHT

❼ Sebago Lake State Park

With 250 campsites scattered throughout the woods beside the sandy shores of Lake Sebago, this 1400-acre **state park** (☎207-693-6231; www. maine.gov; 11 Park Access Rd; adult/child 5-11yr $6.50/1; ⊙year-round, camping late

May-early Sep; 🚹) is a popular and scenic place to swim, picnic and camp on the way into Portland. Lake Sebago is Maine's second-largest lake at 45 sq miles. If the beach gets too hot, just step into the woods, where you can wander several miles of easy to moderate trails or bike the roadways. There's also a nature center. In summer, rangers lead talks, hikes and canoe trips; look for details on the bulletin board at the park entrance. The trails and nature center are open to campers only, not day-use visitors, but the latter can enjoy the beaches, grills and picnic tables. The park is known for keeping restrooms super clean. Pets are not allowed on the beaches or in the campground.

🛏 p319

The Drive » Continue east on US 302, passing through Windham. Suburbia and development creep in as Portland approaches.

❽ Portland

Well, hello there. Is that a brew house at the eastern end of US 302, on the fringes of downtown Portland? Yes? Cheers, we say! And welcome to the **Great Lost Bear** (GLB; www. greatlostbear.com; 540 Forest Ave, ⊙noon-11pm; 🛜), a fun and quirky place in a fun and quirky city. Decked out in Christmas lights and flea-market kitsch, this rambling bar and restaurant is a Portland institution. Sixty-nine taps serve 50 different northeastern brews, including 15 from Maine, making the GLB one of America's best regional beer bars. Atmosphere is high energy, though you might see someone tapping away at their laptop at the bar. On the menu look for nachos, burgers, burritos, cheese steaks and a decent selection of vegetarian options. For more coverage of Portland, see p280 and p322; for a walking tour, see p336.

✖ 🛏 p319

Eating & Sleeping

Fryeburg ❷

🛏 Oxford House Inn   B&B $$

(📞207-935-3442; www.oxfordhouseinn.com;
548 Main St; r incl breakfast $179-199) Enjoy
Saco River views from this 100-year-old house
with four traditional but stylish rooms. The on-
site restaurant serves contemporary American
dishes (mains $22 to $32) from a seasonal
menu; much of the produce is sourced from
Weston Farms behind the property. A cozy,
inviting pub, Jonathan's, recently opened on the
lower level.

Bridgton ❹

✘ Campfire Grille   American $$

(www.thecampfiregrille.com; 646 N High St/US
302, Watford; mains breakfast $5-10, lunch &
dinner $9-19; ⏱11am-10pm Mon-Wed, to 11pm
Thu-Sat, 8am-10pm Sun) Tucked between US
302 and Beaver Pond – with views of the latter –
this easy-going eatery serves pub-grub dishes
with gourmet flair.

🛏 Noble House Inn   B&B $$

(📞207-647-3733; www.noblehousebb.com; 81
Highland Rd; r incl breakfast $165-265; ❄🛜🐾)
Did you say bottomless cookie jar? Yup, and
that's just one of the details that make the nine-
room Noble House Inn so inviting. Breakfasts
are baked from scratch and typically sourced
from locally grown, organic ingredients. Wildlife
carouses on the lawn or in the adjacent pine
grove, while Highland Lake beckons across the
street.

🛏 Bear Mountain Inn   B&B $$

(📞207-583-4404; www.bearmtninn.com; 364
Waterford Rd; r incl breakfast $120-175; ste
$325; ❄🛜🐾) Eight miles north of Bridgton,
this attractive inn sits on a 25-acre site on a
hill overlooking Bear Pond. The hillside deck,
with a tree-framed lake view and BBQ grill, is a
guest favorite. The 11 rooms have rustic-chic
flair; there's a cabin that sleeps eight and a pet-
friendly cottage.

Naples ❻

✘ Rick's Cafe   American $$

(www.rickscafenaples.com; Roosevelt Trail/
US 302; mains $9-21; ⏱from 11:30am late May-
early Sep) In the thick of the Causeway action,
Rick's is good for camaraderie, drinks and lake
views. Serves burgers, seafood and Mexican
dishes.

Sebago Lake State Park ❼

✘ Sebago Lake State
Park Campground   Campground $

(📞park 207-693-6231, reservations 207-624-
9950; www.campwithme.com; resident/non-
resident $15/25, with hook-ups $27/38; ⏱late
May-early Sep) This uber-popular campground
starts accepting reservations on February 1 at
9am. All sites become first come, first served
after mid-September. Prices do not include the
$2 reservation fee or the 7% state lodging tax.

Portland ❽

✘ Susan's Fish & Chips   Seafood $$

(www.susansfishnchips.com; 1135 Forest Ave/
US 302; mains $7-19; ⏱11am-8pm) Pop in for
fish and chips at this no-fuss eatery on US 302,
where the tartar sauce comes in mason jars.
Located in a former garage.

✘ Hot Suppa   American $$

(www.hotsuppa.com; 703 Congress St; mains
breakfast $5-12, lunch $9-12, dinner $9-16;
⏱7am-2pm Mon, 7am-2pm & 5-9pm Tue-Sat,
7:30am-2pm Sun) A little hip, a little home-
style, Hot Suppa wows at breakfast with egg
scrambles and corned beef hash. The menu
speaks Cajun at dinner, cher, offering po'boys,
cornmeal-crusted catfish, and boudin balls,
which are made of deep-fried pork. You'll also
find odds and ends like chicken and waffles and
pulled pork.

Portland Museum of Art What's an art tour without a coffee break?

Mainely Art

31

Up the river, into the woods and down the coast. On this drive you'll view the work of Maine's finest painters inside art museums and lovely galleries, then cruise past the landscapes that inspired them.

TRIP HIGHLIGHTS

160 miles

Belfast
A seaside town with galleries, indie shops and a 19th-century Main St

● Bangor

● Augusta

Freeport ●

⑤

⑦

⑨

178 miles

Camden
The river meets the sea in this inviting gourmet town

②
FINISH

① **START**

187 miles

Rockland
The Wyeths are in the spotlight at the Farnsworth Art Museum

Portland
It's an easy walk between museums and galleries

Brunswick
Take a pretty stroll from downtown to the art museum

1 mile

27 miles

**3 DAYS
200 MILES / 322KM**

GREAT FOR...

BEST TIME TO GO

May through October is high season for art walks.

ESSENTIAL PHOTO

Andre the Seal in Rockport is a local celeb. Aaark! Aaark!

BEST FOR CULTURE

Galleries, museums and a mural keep Portland cutting-edge.

321

31 Mainely Art

Art museums in Maine spotlight native sons and daughters and other American masters who found inspiration here. It's a talented bunch that includes Winslow Homer, George Bellows, Edward Hopper, Louise Nevelson and the Wyeths. But really injecting energy into the contemporary art scene are the fantastic special exhibits that explore the issues of our day, from conservation to urban planning to social networking, in unexpected but thought-provoking work.

TRIP HIGHLIGHT

1 Portland

Is it art? Is it graffiti? Does it matter as long as it catches your eye? Whatever its classification, the **mural** (Free St) splashed across the back wall of the Asylum nightclub, east of Center St, captures the artistic spirit of Portland. At press time, the vibrant mural, painted by eight Maine-based graffiti artists, was a postcard for the city, with an image of the Portland

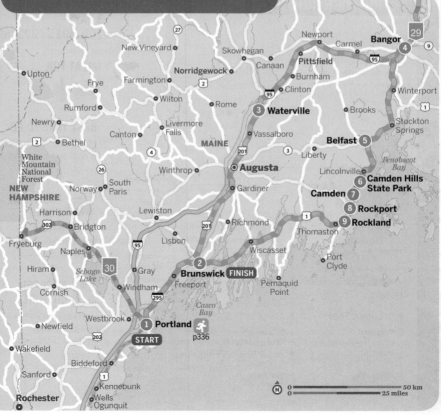

Head Light and a rocky coast. In 2011, the mural, which is changed annually, paid homage to the stories of Stephen King.

Things are a bit more formal at the nearby **Portland Museum of Art** (☎207-775-6148; www.portlandmuseum.org; 7 Congress Sq; adult/child $12/6, 5-9pm Fri free; ⊙10am-5pm Tue-Thu, Sat & Sun, to 9pm Fri), founded in 1882. This well-respected museum houses an outstanding collection of American works. Maine artists, including Winslow Homer, Edward Hopper, Louise Nevelson and Andrew Wyeth, are particularly well represented. You'll also find a few paintings by European masters.

For more on Portland, see p280 and p318; for a walking tour, see p336.

 p327

LINK YOUR TRIP

29 Maine Highlands

From Bangor, a short drive on I-95 leads to the North Woods and Mt Katahdin.

30 Lakes Tour

Hop on US 302 in Portland and head west for Rufus Porter murals.

LOCAL KNOWLEDGE: GRACE

For craftsmanship of a different kind, step into **Grace** (☎207-828-4422; www.restaurantgrace.com; 15 Chestnut St, Portland; ⊙5-10:30pm Tue-Sat), an 1850s Gothic revival–style Methodist church that was closed and sold due a declining congregation. In 2010, after a $2-million renovation that adhered to strict historic guidelines, it reopened as an upscale restaurant and cocktail bar, where the pulpit serves as the hostess desk and diners sit on refurbished pews beneath 27 stained-glass windows. Sacrilegious? Or a stunning 'adaptive reuse' of a historic structure? The Redemption sangria may help you decide.

The Drive » If you want to make good time, hop on I-295 and drive 25 miles north to Brunswick. For LL Bean and the outlet stores, make a detour onto US 1 at Freeport.

- - - - - - - - - - - -

TRIP HIGHLIGHT

❷ Brunswick

Tidy Brunswick, with its well-kept central green and dramatic perch over the Androscoggin River, is a landscape painting come to life. The view stays inspiring on the Bowdoin College campus, where stately buildings surround a tree-dotted quad. The dramatic glass entrance pavilion at the **Bowdoin College Museum of Art** (☎207-725-3275; www.bowdoin.edu/art-museum/; 9400 College Station, Bowdoin quadrangle; admission free; ⊙10am-5pm Tue, Wed, Fri & Sat, to 8:30pm Thu, 1-5pm Sun) injects this pastoral scene with a bit of modernity, and sets a compelling tone

for further exploration. The 15,000-piece collection is particularly strong in the works of 19th- and 20th-century European and American painters. See p298 for details about Bowdoin's Peary-MacMillan Arctic Museum.

🛏 p327

The Drive » For inspiring views of the Kennebec River and time on the historic Old Canada Rd, follow US 201 north. The quickest route for the 50-mile drive is I-295 north to I-95 north.

- - - - - - - - - - - -

❸ Waterville

At press time, the **Colby College Museum of Art** (☎207-859-5600; www.colby.edu/museum; 5600 Mayflower Hill; admission free; ⊙10am-5pm Tue-Sat, noon-5pm Sun) was undergoing a 26,000ft expansion that includes the construction of a new pavilion fronted by towering glass-paneled walls. The space will display works from a nearly 500-piece collection gifted to Colby by Peter and Paula Lunder. Valued at about $100 million, it is one of the largest gifts of art to a liberal-arts college. Highlights from the current collection include works by American masters and modern pieces by Agnes Martin, Chuck Close and Alex Katz. A few galleries are open during construction, which should be completed by 2013.

The Drive » From Waterville, I-95 swoops along the edges of the Maine highlands as it angles north and then east on its 55-mile swing to Bangor.

- - - - - - - - - - -

❹ Bangor

The small **University of Maine Museum of Art** (☎207-561-3350; www.umma.umaine.edu; 40 Harlow St; admission free; ☺10am-5pm Mon-Sat) in Bangor is the northernmost art museum on the Maine Art Museum Trail (www.maineartmuseums.org). It's not the largest

or most impressive collection in the state, but Bangor is a pleasant gateway for exploring the moody Maine highlands to the north and the mid-coast art towns just south. The university's collection spotlights mid-century modern American artists as well as contemporary pieces by David Hockney, Roy Lichtenstein, Andy Warhol and others. The special exhibits can really shine, so check the online calendar to see what's on display.

✗ p327

The Drive » This 45-mile jaunt south on US 1A west to US 1 south passes the Paul Bunyan statue (p306) in downtown Bangor then tracks the Penobscot River, passing the informative Penobscot Marine Museum (www.penobscotmarinemuseum.org) in Searsport.

- - - - - - - - - - -

TRIP HIGHLIGHT

❺ Belfast

There aren't any art museums in Belfast, but this working-class

community with Scots-Irish roots does have an inviting downtown with 12 or so galleries and studios. The oceanfront town is also the site of the nation's oldest shoe store, **Colburn Shoe** (www.colburnshoe.com; 79 Main St), which opened in 1832! Stop by **High Street Studio & Gallery** (www.highstreetgallery.com; 149 High St; ☺11am-5pm Mon-Thu, to 8pm Fri, 10am-4pm Sat) for bright paintings by a trio of local women. The art-deco **Colonial Theater** (☎207-338-1930; www.colonialtheater.com; 163 High St; adult/child $8/5) has shown movies since 1912, luring moviegoers with a neon sign and a rooftop elephant. On the way out of town, see what's happening at **Waterfall Arts** (www.waterfallarts.org; 256 High St; ☺10am-5pm Tue-Fri), a three-gallery arts center that celebrates Maine as a natural backdrop.

The Drive » Follow US 1 south for 16 miles, mostly along the coast, passing Ducktrap and Lincolnville.

- - - - - - - - - - -

❻ Camden Hills State Park

A favorite hike in **Camden Hills State Park** (☎207-236-3109; www.maine.gov; 280 Belfast Rd; adult/child $4.50/1), is the half-mile climb up **Mt Battie**, offering exquisite views of Penobscot Bay.

✓ TOP TIP:
GALLERY GUIDE & ART NEWS

For a list of galleries and studios throughout the state, pick up the free **Maine Gallery & Studio Guide** at art museums and galleries. It's available online at www.mainegalleryguide.com. An up-to-date listing of openings is provided at the **Cafe des Artistes blog**, maintained by the *Bangor Daily News* at http://cafedesartistes.bangordailynews.com.

MAURICIO HANDLER/GETTY IMAGES ©

Camden harbor View from Camden Hills State Park

The Drive » Drive 2 miles south on US 1 to downtown Camden.

- - - - - - - - - - -

7 Camden

Camden and its picture-perfect harbor, framed against the mountains of Camden Hills State Park, is one of the prettiest sites in the state. The Megunticook River crashes dramatically into the sea beside the public landing, behind US 1 in the center of town. At the landing you'll also find the helpful **Penobscot Bay Regional Chamber of Commerce** (📞207-236-4404; http://mainedreamvacation.com; 2 Public Landing; ⊙9am-5pm Mon-Fri). Camden offers windjammer cruises (www.sailmainecoast.com) – anything from two-hour rides to multi-day journeys up the coast. There are also galleries, fine seafood restaurants and back alleys for exploring. Enjoy good meals at **Waterfront Restaurant** (www.waterfrontcamden.com; 40 Bayview St) or **Francine Bistro** (www.francinebistro.com; 55 Chestnut St).

🛏 p327

The Drive » By the time you get your seatbelt buckled you're already in Rockport, just a 2-mile drive south on US 1.

- - - - - - - - - - - - - - -

⑧ Rockport

Photographers flock to Rockport, a sleepy harborside town, for more than just the picturesque coast. Rockport is the home of the world-renowned **Maine Media Workshops** (www.mainemedia.edu; 70 Camden St), one of the world's leading instructional centers in photography, film and digital media. The institute offers more than 250 beginner- through professional-level workshops throughout the year. Student and faculty works are displayed in **Union Hall**

(18 Central St). But let's not forget the most important attraction in town: the granite statue of **Andre the Seal** (Rockport Marine Park, Pascal Ave), about 0.5 miles off US 1 via Main St. Andre was a crowd-pleasing showboat who swam to the harbor every summer from Boston from the 1970s until his death in the mid-'80s. He was the subject of a children's book, *Andre the Seal*, and a 1994 movie.

The Drive » Leave Andre behind as you turn left onto Pascal Ave, following it to US 1. Rockland is 6 miles to the south.

- - - - - - - - - - - - - -

TRIP HIGHLIGHT
⑨ Rockland

Rockland is a cool little town. Its commercial port adds vibrancy, and its bustling Main St is a window into the city's socio-cultural diversity, with working-class diners, bohemian cafes and high-end bistros beside galleries and old-fashioned storefronts.

Just off Main St, the **Farnsworth Art Museum** (📞207-596-6457; www.farnsworthmuseum.org; 16 Museum St; adult/child $12/free; ⏰10am-5pm daily, to 8pm Wed Jun-Oct, closed Mon Apr, Nov & Dec, closed Mon & Tue Jan-Mar) is one of the country's best small regional museums. The collection spans 200 years of American art. The 'MAINE in America' permanent exhibit spotlights artists who have lived or worked in the state. Exhibits about the Wyeths – Andrew, NC and Jamie – are housed in galleries throughout the museum and in the Wyeth Center, a former Methodist church across the garden.

The wonderful **Archipelago Fine Arts** (www.thearchipelago.net; 386 Main St; ⏰9:30am-5:30pm Mon-Fri, to 5pm Sat, 11am-4pm Sun), in partnership with the conservation-minded **Island Institute** (www.islandinstitute.org), sells jewelry, paintings and arts and crafts by artists living on Maine's islands and coast.

From Rockland, continue south along the coast on US 1 to loop back to Brunswick.

✕ p327

MID-COAST ART WALKS

If it's a Friday night in July or August, and you're driving along Maine's mid-coast, you're going to drive past an art walk:

Bath 5pm to 8pm, third Friday of the month, June to September; www.artwalkmaine.org/bath.

Belfast 5:30pm to 8pm, first Friday of the month, June, September, October and December, every Friday July and August; http://belfastartwalk.com.

Brunswick 5pm to 8pm, second Friday of the month, May to October; www.artwalkmaine.org/brunswick.

Portland 5pm to 8pm, first Friday of the month year-round; www.firstfridayartwalk.com.

Rockland 5pm to 8pm, first Friday of the month year-round; www.artsinrockland.org.

For a list of art walks throughout the state, visit www.artwalkmaine.org.

Eating & Sleeping

Portland ❶

✕ DuckFat
Sandwiches $$

(www.duckfat.com; 43 Middle St; sandwiches $6-12; ⏱ lunch & dinner) **The french fries are fried in duck fat – and so, so good: shatteringly crisp with melt-in-your-mouth fluffy centers, plus dipping sauces. The fancy panini are also excellent.**

✕ Fore St
Modern American $$$

(☎207-775-2717; www.forestreet.biz; 288 Fore St; mains $25-50; ⏱ dinner) **Chef-owner Sam Hayward has turned roasting into high art at this much-lauded restaurant. Chickens turn on spits in the open kitchen as chefs slide an iron kettle into the wood-burning oven. Eco-friendly.**

✕ Two Fat Cats Bakery
Bakery $

(www.twofatcatsbakery.com; 47 India St; whoopee pies $2.25; ⏱ 8am-6pm Mon-Fri, to 5pm Sat, to 4pm Sun) **Whoopee pies. Cupcakes. Cookies. Meow.**

🛏 Danforth
B&B $$$

(☎207-879-8755; www.danforthmaine.com; 163 Danforth St; r incl breakfast $275-345; ❄ 🛜) **Shoot pool in the wood-paneled game room (a former speakeasy) or climb to the rooftop cupola for harbor views. The eight rooms are decorated with a breezy, stylish mix of antiques and modern prints. The new restaurant, Carmen at the Danforth, is spicing up the Portland dining scene with Latin-infused seafood dishes.**

🛏 Inn at St John
Hotel $$

(☎207-773-6481; www.innatstjohn.com; 939 Congress St; r incl breakfast $82-250; ❄ @ 🛜) **This quirky but cool three-story inn is one of Portland's best deals. It has a Victorian-era feel, with old-fashioned pigeonhole mailboxes and narrow, sweetly floral rooms. The cheapest rooms have shared bathrooms. There's no elevator, and the stairs are steep, so reserve a 1st-floor room if you have bad knees.**

Brunswick ❷

🛏 Brunswick Inn
B&B $$

(☎207-729-4914; www.brunswickbnb.com; 165 Park Row; r incl breakfast $145-195, cottages $260; 🛜) **Overlooking the town green, this elegant guesthouse has 12 rooms, each uniquely designed in an airy, farmhouse-chic style. The 1st-floor bar is a great place to enjoy a glass of wine. There's also a carriage house that works well for families.**

Bangor ❹

✕ Friars Bakehouse
Bakery $

(21 Central St; mains under $7; ⏱ 8:30am-1:45pm Tue-Fri) **Two Franciscan monks preside over this tiny bakery, serving fresh pastries at breakfast and soups and sandwiches at lunch. Tables are shared. No credit cards or cell phones.**

Camden ❼

🛏 Lord Camden Inn
Hotel $$

(☎207-236-4325; www.lordcamdeninn.com; 24 Main St; r incl breakfast $199-279; ❄ 🛜 🍽) **Exposed-brick walls and in-room Keurig coffeemakers add verve to this boutique property in the heart of the turn-of-the-20th-century downtown. The house-made granola at breakfast is so darn good that we'll forgive that the parking lot is not adjacent to the property. New carpets were being installed at press time.**

Rockland ❾

✕ Atlantic Baking Co
Bakery, Sandwiches $

(www.atlanticbakingco.com; 351 Main St; mains under $7; ⏱ 7am-6pm Mon-Sat, 8am-4pm Sun, closed Sun & Mon winter) **This cheery bakery near the Farnsworth sells tasty sandwiches on fresh-made bread. Pastries, soups and salads are also available.**

Screw Auger Falls This 23ft waterfall crashes dramatically through a narrow gorge

Alpine Escapes

32

This trek feels akin to flying. Leafy byways soar up the sides of mountains. Pristine forests float beneath lofty overlooks. And bumpy frost-heaves add swoop-de-doo turbulence on the back roads.

TRIP HIGHLIGHTS

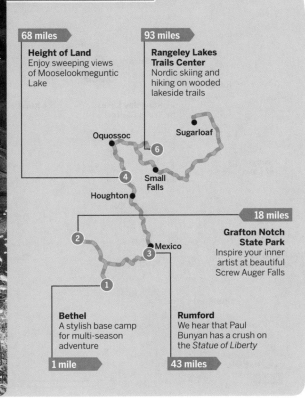

68 miles

Height of Land
Enjoy sweeping views of Mooselookmeguntic Lake

93 miles

Rangeley Lakes Trails Center
Nordic skiing and hiking on wooded lakeside trails

Oquossoc

Sugarloaf

6

4

Small Falls

Houghton

18 miles

Grafton Notch State Park
Inspire your inner artist at beautiful Screw Auger Falls

2

3 Mexico

1

Bethel
A stylish base camp for multi-season adventure

1 mile

Rumford
We hear that Paul Bunyan has a crush on the *Statue of Liberty*

43 miles

2 DAYS
160 MILES / 257KM

GREAT FOR...

BEST TIME TO GO

June through March is good for hiking, leaf-peeping and skiing.

 ESSENTIAL PHOTO

Frame a shot of Mooselookmeguntic Lake from the Height of Land overlook.

 BEST FOR WILDLIFE

ME 16 between Rangeley and Phillips is a local moose alley.

32 | Alpine Escapes

The first time you see a moose standing on the side of the road, it doesn't seem unusual. You've been prepped by all of the moose-crossing signs. But then it registers. 'Hey, that's a moose!' And you simultaneously swerve, slam on the brakes and speed up. Control these impulses. Simply slow your speed and enjoy the gift of wildlife. Then share your good fortune on Facebook, of course.

TRIP HIGHLIGHT

① Bethel

If you glance at the map, tiny Bethel doesn't look much different from the other towns scattered across this alpine region. But look more closely. The town is cocooned between two powerful rivers, and several ski resorts and ski centers call the community home. Four state and national scenic byways begin within an 85-mile drive (see p331).

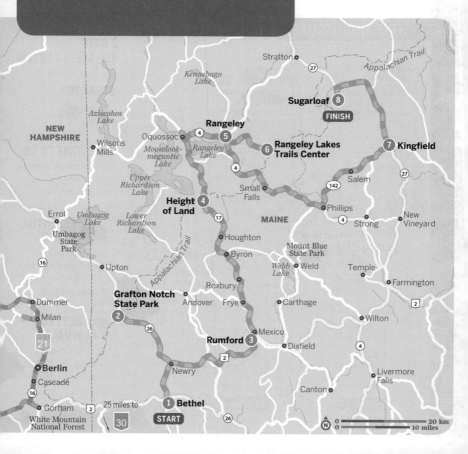

Of the ski resorts, **Sunday River** (📞207-824-3000; www.sundayriver.com; 15 South Ridge Rd, Newry; ski lift adult/child $80/68; 🚠) is the biggest draw, luring skiers with eight peaks, 132 trails and a host of winter activities. From July until early October, the resort opens 30 mountain-bike trails and runs trips up to North Peak on its fast-moving **Chondola** (adult/child $12/8; ⏰10am-4pm Fri-Sun). There's also a six-line **zip-line tour** (tickets $49; ⏰9am, noon & 3pm Thu-Sun). Several outdoor centers, including the **Bethel Nordic Ski Center** (www.caribourecreation.com; ⏰mid-Dec–Mar), are base camps for cross-country skiing and snowshoeing.

 p335

The Drive » Follow ME 5/ME 26/US 2 north from Bethel, tracking the Sunday River about 6 miles north. Keep left

LINK YOUR TRIP

21 **Woodland Heritage Trail**

Take US 2 west to learn the history of logging on the Androscoggin River.

30 **Lakes Tour**

Follow the Pequawket Trail Scenic Byway along ME 113 to a riverside beach in Fryeburg.

SCENIC BYWAYS IN THE LAKES & MOUNTAINS REGION

Grafton Notch Scenic Byway From Bethel, follow ME 5/26 north, then take ME 26 toward Grafton Notch State Park at Newry.

Pequawket Trail Scenic Byway Follow the Androscoggin River west from Bethel on US 2. Turn south onto ME 113 at Gilead and follow it to Fryeburg.

State Route 27 Scenic Byway From stop 7, in Kingfield, follow ME 16/27 to Sugarloaf, then continue north on ME 27 to Canada.

Rangeley Lakes National Scenic Byway Drive east on US 2 from Rumford to Mexico, then turn north on US 17. The byway begins about 15 miles north, just beyond the town of Byron.

on NH 26 as it leaves ME 5/US 2 and becomes Bear River Rd, which leads to the park 11 miles west.

- - - - - - - - - - -

TRIP HIGHLIGHT

② Grafton Notch State Park

Tucked beside the Grafton Notch Scenic Byway within the Mahoosuc Range, this rugged **park** (📞May 15-Oct 15 207-824-2912, low season 207-624-6080; www.maine.gov; Bear River Rd) is a stunner. Carved by a glacier that retreated 12,000 years ago, the notch is a four-season playground, chock-full of waterfalls, gorges, lofty viewpoints and hiking trails, including 12 strenuous miles of the **Appalachian Trail**. Peregrine falcons build nests in the cliffs, helping the park earn

its spot on the **Maine Birding Trail** (www.mainebirdingtrail.com); the best viewing is May to October. Cross-country skiers and snowshoers enjoy the park in winter. If you're short on time, simply wander the trail beside **Screw Auger Falls**, off the main parking lot. This 23ft waterfall crashes dramatically through a narrow gorge. If you have more time, try the 2.2-mile round-trip hike up to **Table Rock overlook** or the walk to **Eyebrow Loop** and **Cascade Falls**, with excellent picnicking opportunities beside the falls.

The Drive » Return to US 2 north. On the 16-mile drive, you'll pass stone walls and antique stores, and enjoy the Androscoggin River tagging along on your right.

KEVIN SHIELDS/ALAMY ©

TRIP HIGHLIGHT

③ Rumford

How do you know you've arrived? When the giant, ax-wielding **Paul Bunyan** says 'Hey there.' According to legend, the red-shirted lumberman was born in Maine but was later sent west by his parents. Today, he stands tall beside the **River Valley Chamber of Commerce Visitor Center** (⊙207-364-3241; www.rivervalleychamber.com; 10 Bridge St; ⊙9am-5pm daily May-Oct, 10am-2pm Mon-Sat Nov-Apr). Walk a few steps beyond the visitor center building for a fantastic view of the wild and woolly **Pennacook Falls**. The highest falls east of Niagara, they drop 176ft over a granite ledge. The small park here holds a black marble memorial honoring local son and former US senator Edmund Muskie, who authored the Clean Water Act.

The Drive » Leave Rumford and US 2, picking up ME 17 north in Mexico. From here ME 17 runs parallel to pines, farms, meadows and the rocky Swift River. Snap a photo of the river barreling through metamorphic rock at the Coos Canyon Rest Area in Byron, then swoop-de-doo north (you'll see), picking up the Rangeley Lakes National Scenic Byway north of Houghton.

TRIP HIGHLIGHT

④ Height of Land

The entrance to this photogenic **overlook** sneaks up on you – it's on the left as you round a bend on Brimstone Mountain, just after a hiker warning sign. But don't slam on your brakes and swerve across the grass divider if you miss the turn (we saw this happen), because there's another entrance just north. But you should pull over. The expansive view of island-dotted **Mooselookmeguntic Lake**, the largest of the Rangeley Lakes, as it sweeps north towards distant mountains is astounding. Views of undeveloped forest stretch for up to 100 miles; you can even see the White Mountains in New Hampshire. The dogged **Appalachian Trail** runs alongside the viewpoint, and an interpretive sign shares a few details abut the 2179-mile footpath.

The Drive » Drive north to the village of Oquosocc, then turn right onto ME 4/16. Take a photo at the Rangeley Lake overlook, where there is a panoramic view of Rangeley Lake. This overlook is about 6.5 miles from Height of Land. From here, continue east.

⑤ Rangeley

An adventure hub, with tidy inns and down-home restaurants, Rangeley makes a useful base for skiing, hiking, white-water rafting and mountain biking in the nearby mountains. Snowmobilers can zoom across 150 miles of trails. For information, stop by the **Rangeley Lakes Chamber of Commerce** (⊘207-864-5364; www.rangeleymaine.com; 6 Park Rd; ⊙10am-4pm Mon-Sat, plus noon-3pm Sun Jul & Aug), **which**

Rangeley Lakes Park

has handouts about restaurants, lodging options, local trails and moose watching. Just behind the visitor center, **Rangeley Lakes Park** (☺5am-10pm) is a nice spot to enjoy a picnic by the lake. On rainy days, ask at the chamber about the local museums.

✕ ⊨ p335

The Drive » ME 4 breaks from ME 16 in downtown Rangeley. From the chamber of commerce, follow ME 4 east. Turn left onto Dallas Hill Rd, then in 2.5 miles bear right on Saddleback Mountain Rd and continue another 2.5 miles.

TRIP HIGHLIGHT

6 Rangeley Lakes Trails Center

A green yurt marks your arrival at the **Rangeley Lakes Trails Center** (☎207-864-4309; www. rangeleylakestrailscenter.com; 523 Saddleback Mountain Rd; day pass during snow season adult/child $18/10, by donation rest of year), a four-season trail system covering gorgeous woodland terrain beside Saddleback Lake. Here there are more than 34 miles of trails for cross-country skiing

and snowshoeing during snow season. You can rent equipment inside the yurt. In summer, the cross-country trails double as hiking trails, and the snowshoe trails allow single-track biking. The yurt is closed in summer, but trail maps are available at the adjacent information kiosk and the chamber of commerce. Visit the website for details about the hiking trails.

The Drive » Follow ME 4 southeast, passing another Rangeley Lake overlook. Continue southeast. You'll pass another Appalachian Trail crossing before entering prime

HERE A MOOSE, THERE A MOOSE

Moose-crossing signs are as ubiquitous as logging trucks in these parts. But spotting one of these chunky beasts, which can reach a height of 7ft at the shoulder and weigh anywhere from 1000lb to 1400lb, is trickier. You'll most likely see them eating on the side of the road in the morning, in the evening and between noon and 2pm. According to a handout from the Rangeley Lakes Chamber of Commerce, these are some of the top moose-spotting sites in the area:

Route 4 Phillips to Rangeley (we saw one here in late April, early in the evening).

Route 16 Rangeley to Stratton; Wilsons Mills to the New Hampshire border.

Route 17 Between the Height of Land overlook and the Rangeley Lake overlook.

Route 16/27 Stratton to Carrabassett Valley.

When driving these routes stay extra vigilant and slow down, particularly at night. Moose don't always leap out of the way like deer, and in the dark your vehicle's headlights won't always reflect off the animals' eyes, due to their height. If you come upon a moose standing in the road, do not get out of the car (they can charge the vehicle) or drive around it. Wait for the moose to mosey off the road.

moose country. Follow ME 12 east to NE 16/27 north.

7 Maine Huts & Trails Office

If you enjoy hiking and cross-country skiing, but not backpacking, consider a hut-to-hut trip through **Maine Huts & Trails** (📞877-634-8824; www.mainehuts.org; 496 Main St, Kingfield; r $79-199), a non-profit organization operating three overnight eco-lodges along a remote 45-mile trail near Sugarloaf. Choose a dorm bed or a private room and enjoy dinner, breakfast and a variety of room configurations. Pillows and blankets are provided, but not

bedding. A second office and information center sits beside NE 16/27 in the Carrabassett Valley north of Kingfield. This trail-and-hut network is a work-in-progress, and the plan is to extend the trail to 180 miles, with more huts along the way. The trail system is open to the public free of charge. There is no vehicle access to the huts.

The Drive » From Kingfield, NH 16 joins ME 27, unfurling beneath the pines, with the Carrabassett River tumbling merrily alongside.

8 Sugarloaf

Rangeley's most popular **ski resort** (📞207-237-2000; www.sugarloaf.com;

5092 Sugarloaf Access Rd, Carrabassett Valley; adult/child $79/55; 🚡), Sugarloaf has a vertical drop of 2820ft, with 153 trails and glades and 14 lifts. This is Maine's second-highest peak (4237ft). Summer activities include lift rides, zip lines and golf. The resort village complex has an enormous mountain lodge, an inn and rental condos.

Near Sugarloaf's slopes, the **Sugarloaf Outdoor Center** (📞207-237-6830; www.sugarloaf.com/outdoorcenter; adult/child $20/12) has nearly 56 miles of groomed cross-country trails and an NHL-size skating rink.

Eating & Sleeping

Bethel ❶

✖ Cho Sun   Asian $$

(📞207-824-7370; www.chosunrestaurant.com; 141 Main St; mains $17-25, sushi from $5; 🕐5-9pm Wed-Sun) Korea smashes into Maine at this unassuming Victorian house. Try dishes from the owner's native South Korea, like *bibimbap* (rice pot with meat and veggies) or kimchi stew. There's also a sushi bar.

✖ Café DiCocoa   Cafe $

(www.cafedicocoa.com; 125 Main St; mains under $8; 🕐7am-6pm daily Jul-early Oct, Thu-Sun low season, closed early Oct-late Nov, Apr & May; 🔊) This funky orange bungalow is a morning must for espresso-based drinks. It also serves wholegrain baked goods and vegetarian lunches.

✖ Good Food Store   Sandwiches, Self-Catering $

(www.goodfoodbethel.com; 212 Mayville Rd/ME 26; salads & sandwiches under $7, heat-and-eat meals $10-14; 🕐store 9am-8pm, takeout 11am-6pm) Buy sandwiches, salads and heat-and-eat meals at this gourmet organic market and wine shop. The homemade cookies and dried fruit are fantastic. BBQ by Smokin' Good BBQ is sold here Thursday through Sunday.

🛏 Chapman Inn   B&B $

(📞207-824-2657; www.chapmaninn.com; 2 Church St; dm $35, r $99-139; 🔊) Nine private rooms are done up in florals and antiques, with slightly sloping floors attesting to the home's age. In winter, skiers bunk in the snug dorm, complete with a wood-paneled game room. Breakfast, a lavish spread of homemade pastries and made-to-order omelets, will keep you full for a day on the slopes.

Rangeley ❺

✖ Red Onion   American $

(http://rangeleyredonion.com; 2511 Main St; mains $7-13; 🕐lunch & dinner; 👶) This boisterous Italian-American joint in the heart of downtown is known for its pizzas and its 1970s wood-paneled bar. A big plate of chicken parmesan after a day on the slopes has been a Rangeley tradition for years.

🛏 Rangeley Inn   Inn $

(📞207-864-3341; www.rangeleyinn.com; 2443 Main St; r $84-125; 🔊) Relax by the fire and admire the mounted bear in the lobby of this big, creaky turn-of-the-20th-century lodge. Rooms are simple and old-fashioned, with Victorian wallpaper and brass beds.

🛏 Loon Lodge Inn   Inn $$

(📞207-864-5666; www.loonlodgeme.com; 16 Pickford Rd; r $85-150; 🔊) Hidden in the woods by the lake, this log-cabin lodge has nine rooms, with wood-plank walls and handmade quilts. No TVs or telephones, but there is wi-fi.

STRETCH YOUR LEGS
PORTLAND

Start/Finish International Museum of Cryptozoology

Distance 2 miles

Duration Four hours

This walk winds past museums both quirky and inspiring before dropping to the bars and shops of the hard-charging Old Port District. Re-energize along the working wharves, then make a final push up into the West End for a sun-dappled finale among the mansions.

Take this walk on Trips

26 30 31

International Museum of Cryptozoology

Bigfoot, yetis, specter moose and other cryptids share the spotlight at this **museum** (www.cryptozoologymuseum.com; 11 Avon St; adult/child $7/5; ⊙ noon-4pm Mon, 11am-4pm Wed-Sat, noon-3:30pm Sun; 🚻). Cryptids are animals thought by mainstream science not to exist; this two-room museum, the brainchild of Loren Coleman, delves into the stories surrounding them. Evidence includes yeti fur and casts of bigfoot footprints. There's also a color-coded pinboard of Maine that shows the locations of alleged sightings. Get a photo of yourself beside the furry, 9ft-tall bigfoot. Cash and checks only.

The Walk » Turn left onto Avon St and walk to Congress St. Cross Congress St and follow it left into downtown. Pass Coffee by Design, a local coffeehouse, then cross High St to the museum entrance on Free St.

Portland Museum of Art

Paintings by Winslow Homer and other Maine artists are highlights at the **museum** (www.portlandmuseum.org; 7 Congress Sq; adult/child $12/6, 5-9pm Fri free; ⊙10am-5pm Tue-Thu, Sat & Sun, to 9pm Fri, plus 10am-5pm Mon Jun-Aug), which anchors the city's Arts District. The collection sprawls across three separate buildings. Most pieces are in the postmodern Charles Shipman Payson Building, designed by the firm of IM Pei. Don't miss the flying staircase in the 1801 Federal-style McClellan House in the back.

The Walk » Leave the museum and turn right onto Free St. You'll pass the Children's Museum. Turn left on Oak St and return to Congress St. Turn right and follow Congress two blocks. The Wadsworth-Longfellow House is on the left.

Wadsworth-Longfellow House

The revered American poet Henry Wadsworth-Longfellow grew up in this Federal-style **house** (www.mainehistory.com;

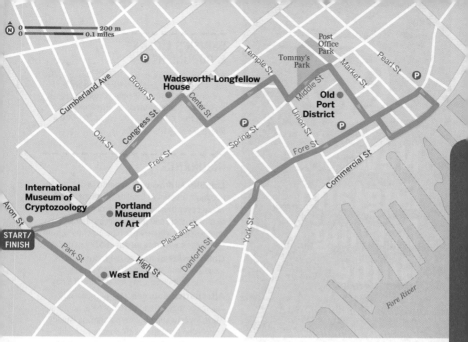

489 Congress St; adult/child $12/3; ⏲10am-5pm May-Oct), built in 1788 by his Revolutionary War–hero grandfather. The house has been impeccably restored to look as it did in the 1800s, complete with original furniture and artifacts. The ticket price includes admission to the Maine Historical Society Museum next door, which has rotating exhibits about life in Maine over the past few centuries.

The Walk » Return to Free St, passing the eye-catching mural on the back wall of the Asylum nightclub. Turn right on Temple St and walk one block. Turn left onto Middle St, following it to Exchange St.

Old Port District

Handsome 19th-century brick buildings line the streets of Old Port, with the city's most enticing shops, pubs and restaurants. By night, flickering gas lanterns add to the atmosphere. Wander down Exchange St and its offshoots for fresh seafood, local microbrews and tiny galleries. To sign up for a sightseeing boat tour or order lobster to ship home, walk down to the wharves.

The Walk » Follow Fore St west to its junction with Danforth St, where there's a statue of movie director and native son John Ford. Continue west on Danforth St.

West End

Portland's loveliest neighborhood is a hillside enclave of brick town houses, elegant gardens and stately mansions; some date from the neighborhood's founding in 1836. This is a fairly mixed community along the gay–straight, young–elderly divide, with pockets of smaller, working-class families among higher-mortgage-paying neighbors. Be sure to walk past the **Victoria Mansion** (www.victoriamansion.org; 109 Danforth St). This Italianate palace, whose exterior would work well in a Tim Burton movie, dates to 1860.

The Walk » Return to the cryptid collection by taking Park St northwest to Congress St.

New England Driving Guide

Let us answer all your questions about driving in New England, including where to pahk your cah.

Driving Fast Facts

→ **Right or left?** Drive on the right
→ **Legal driving age** 16
→ **Top speed limit** 75mph (on interstate in rural Maine)
→ **Best bumper sticker** 'Wicked Cool Bumpah Stickah'

DRIVER'S LICENSE & DOCUMENTS

All drivers must carry a driver's license, the car registration and proof of insurance. If your license is not in English, you will need an official translation or an International Driving Permit (IDP). You will also need a credit card to rent a car.

INSURANCE

Liability All drivers are required to obtain a minimum amount of liability insurance, which would cover the damage that you might cause to other people and property in case of an accident. Liability insurance can be purchased from rental-car companies for about $12 per day.

Collision For damage to the rental vehicle, a collision damage waiver (CDW) is available from the rental company for about $18 a day.

Alternative sources Your personal auto insurance may extend to rental cars, so it's worth investigating before purchasing liability or collision from the rental company. Additionally, some credit cards offer reimbursement coverage for collision damages if you rent the car with that credit card; again, check before departing. Most credit-card coverage isn't valid for rentals of more than 15 days or for exotic models, SUVs, vans and 4WD vehicles.

RENTING A CAR

Rental cars are readily available at regional airports and in major towns. Rates usually include unlimited mileage. Dropping off the car at a different location from where you picked it up usually incurs an additional fee. It always pays to shop around between rental companies, utilizing price-comparison websites.

Renting a car without a major credit card is difficult, if not impossible. Without one, some agencies simply will not rent vehicles, while others require prepayment, a deposit slightly higher than the cost of your rental, pay stubs, proof of round-trip airfare and more.

The following companies operate in New England:

Alamo (www.goalamo.com)
Avis (www.avis.com)
Budget (www.budget.com)
Dollar (www.dollarcar.com)

Enterprise (www.enterprise.com)
Hertz (www.hertz.com)
National (www.nationalcar.com)
Rent-A-Wreck (www.rentawreck.com)
Rents cars that may have more wear and tear than your typical rental vehicle but are actually far from wrecks.
Thrifty (www.thrifty.com)

BORDER CROSSING

Generally, crossing the US–Canada border is straightforward. The biggest hassle is usually the length of the lines. All travelers entering the USA are required to carry passports, including citizens of Canada and the USA.

MAPS

Detailed state-highway maps are distributed free by state governments. You can call or write to state tourism offices in advance to request maps, or you can pick up the maps at highway tourism information offices ('welcome centers') when you enter a state on a major highway.

Road-Trip Websites

American Automobile Association (AAA; www.aaa.com) Provides maps and other information, as well as travel discounts and emergency assistance for members.

Gas Buddy (www.gasbuddy.com) Find the cheapest gas in town.

New England Travel Planner (www.newenglandtravelplanner.com) Routes, reviews and other travel resources.

Traffic.com (www.traffic.com) Real-time traffic reports, with details about accidents and traffic jams.

Another excellent map resource is **DeLorme Mapping Company** (www.delorme.com), which publishes individual state maps – atlas-style books with detailed coverage of backcountry roads. The scales range from 1:65,000 to 1:135,000. The New England box set includes all six states for $75.

Road Distances (miles)

	Boston, MA	Provincetown, MA	Portsmouth, NH	Portland, ME	Bar Harbor, ME	Burlington, VT	Brattleboro, VT	Norwich, VT/Hanover, NH	Hartford, CT
Provincetown, MA	114								
Portsmouth, NH	58	171							
Portland, ME	108	221	51						
Bar Harbor, ME	267	380	210	159					
Burlington, VT	217	330	207	209	334				
Brattleboro, VT	120	220	124	175	354	151			
Norwich, VT/Hanover, NH	127	240	116	167	346	96	69		
Hartford, CT	101	206	150	201	380	236	85	152	
Providence, RI	50	120	106	157	336	265	137	175	86

ROADS & CONDITIONS

New England roads are very good – even the warren of hard-packed dirt roads that crisscross Vermont. A few hazards to be aware of:

➡ Some of the region's big, old cities can be difficult to navigate. Boston in particular is notorious for its scofflaw drivers and maddening maze of one-way streets. Park your car and use alternative means to get around (see p26).

➡ Traffic is heavy around urban areas during rush hour (7am to 9am and 4pm to 7pm Monday through Friday).

➡ Some roads across northern mountain passes in Vermont, New Hampshire and Maine are closed during the winter, but good signage gives you plenty of warning.

Toll Roads

You are likely to encounter tolls for some roads, bridges and tunnels while driving around New England:

➡ Blue Star Turnpike (New Hampshire Turnpike; I-95)

➡ Claiborne Pell Newport Bridge, Rhode Island

➡ Frederick E Everett Turnpike (Central New Hampshire Turnpike)

➡ Maine Turnpike (I-95)

➡ Massachusetts Turnpike (I-90)

➡ Mt Equinox Skyline Dr, Vermont

➡ Mt Mansfield Auto Toll Rd, Vermont

➡ Mt Washington Auto Rd, New Hampshire

➡ Spaulding Turnpike, New Hampshire

➡ Sumner Tunnel, Massachusetts

➡ Ted Williams Tunnel, Massachusetts

➡ Tobin Bridge (Mystic River Bridge), Massachusetts

New England Playlist

Sweet Baby James James Taylor

The Impression that I Get The Mighty Mighty Bosstones

Farmhouse Phish

New Hampshire Matt Pond PA

Let the Good Times Roll The Cars

ROAD RULES

The maximum speed limit on most New England interstates is 65mph, but some have a limit of 55mph. (One stretch of I-95 in rural Maine has a speed limit of 75mph.) On undivided highways, the speed limit will vary from 30mph to 55mph. Police enforce speed limits by patrolling in police cruisers and in unmarked cars. Fines can cost upwards of $350 in Connecticut, and it's similarly expensive in other states.

Other road rules:

➡ Driving laws are different in each of the New England states, but most require the use of safety belts.

➡ In every state, children under four years of age must be placed in a child safety seat secured by a seat belt.

➡ Most states require motorcycle riders to wear helmets whenever they ride. In any case, use of a helmet is highly recommended.

➡ All six New England states prohibit texting while driving, while Connecticut has banned all handheld cell-phone use by drivers.

PARKING

Public parking is readily available in most New England destinations, whether on the street or in parking lots. In rural areas and small towns, it is often free of charge. Many towns have metered parking, which will limit the amount of time you can leave your car (usually two hours or more).

Parking can be a challenge in urban areas, especially Boston. Street parking is limited, so you will probably have to pay for parking in private lots. Where necessary, parking recommendations are provided in this book in the trips' Drive text. See p26 for more information about parking in Boston.

FUEL

Gas stations are ubiquitous and many are open 24 hours a day. Small-town stations may be open only from 7am to 8pm or 9pm.

Most stations require that you pay before you pump. More modern pumps have credit-/debit-card terminals built into them, so you can pay with plastic right at the pump. At 'full-service' stations, an attendant will pump your gas for you; no tip is expected.

Driving Problem-Buster

What should I do if my car breaks down? Call the service number provided by the rental-car company, and it will make arrangements with a local garage. If you're driving your own car, it's advisable to join the AAA (see the box, p339), which provides emergency assistance.

What if I have an accident? If any damage is incurred, you'll have to call the local police (☑911) to come to the scene of the accident and file an accident report, for insurance purposes.

What should I do if I get stopped by the police? Always pull over to the right at the first available opportunity. Stay in your car and roll down the window. Show the police officer your driver's license and automobile registration. For any violations, you cannot pay the officer issuing the ticket; rather, payment must be made by mail or by internet.

How do the tolls work? Most tolls are payable in cash only. Tolling stations are usually staffed, so exact change is not required. Alternatively, consider purchasing an E-Z Pass for the state you will be traveling in (this is not transferable to other states).

What if I can't find anywhere to stay? In summer and autumn, it's advisable to make reservations in advance. Most towns have tourist information centers or chambers of commerce that will help travelers find accommodation in a pinch.

SAFETY

New England does not present any particular safety concerns for drivers. That said, travelers are advised to always remove valuables and lock all car doors, especially in urban areas. Be extra cautious driving at night on rural roads, which may not be well lit and may be populated by deer, moose and other creatures that can total your car if you hit them the wrong way.

RADIO

Maine WCYY (94.3FM) plays oldies and newbies out of Portland, with Alternative Mornings from 6am till noon.

Massachusetts Boston is blessed with two public radio stations – WGBH (89.7FM) and WBUR (90.9FM) – broadcasting news, classical music and radio shows.

New Hampshire The Freewaves (91.3FM) is run by the students of the University of New Hampshire, offering indie, classical, jazz and folk.

Vermont WRUV (90.1 FM) – also known as Burlington's Better Alternative – is a nonprofit student- and volunteer-run radio station, playing a mix of music at DJs' discretion, but no songs that were EVER in Billboard's Hot 100 can be played.

FERRY CROSSINGS

Unfortunately, you can't drive to New England's offshore islands. Park your car in port ($10 to $20 per day) and hop on a boat. In addition to the high-speed catamarans listed below, Hy-Line and Steamship also offer traditional ferry crossings (half the price but twice the time). They can also bring your car ($400 to $450), but you'll need to book well in advance.

See p55 for information on ferries to Martha's Vineyard.

Block Island Ferry (www.blockislandferry. com) Ferry between Point Judith, RI, and Block Island, RI. Car-and-passenger ferries take an hour; high-speed passenger ferries ($35.85 round-trip) take 30 minutes.

Downeast Windjammer (www. downeastwindjammer.com; adult/child $30/20, bikes $6) Passenger-only ferry between Bar Harbor, ME, and Winter Harbor, ME, allowing exploration of the island and mainland sections of Acadia National Park.

Hy-Line Cruises (www.hylinecruises.com; 220 Ocean St; round-trip adult/child $77/51) Catamaran between Hyannis, MA, and Nantucket, MA.

Steamship Authority (www.steamship authority.com; South St; round-trip adult/child $67/34) Catamaran between Hyannis, MA, and Nantucket, MA.

BEHIND THE SCENES

SEND US YOUR FEEDBACK

We love to hear from travelers – your comments help make our books better. We read every word, and we guarantee that your feedback goes straight to the authors. Visit **lonelyplanet. com/contact** to submit your updates and suggestions.

Note: We may edit, reproduce and incorporate your comments in Lonely Planet products such as guidebooks, websites and digital products, so let us know if you don't want your comments reproduced or your name acknowledged. For a copy of our privacy policy visit lonelyplanet.com/privacy.

OUR READERS

Many thanks to the travelers who used the last edition and wrote to us with helpful hints, useful advice and interesting anecdotes: Richard Hemingway, Nancy Voigts

AUTHOR THANKS

MARA VORHEES

I am grateful to my fabulous coauthors for their cooperation and efficacy and to Dianne Langeland and Eddie Horgan for divulging their best secret spots. Special thanks to my three favorite men for keeping me company on some of these trips and for holding the fort at the pink house while I was away on others.

AMY C BALFOUR

Thank you, Mara, Paula and Caroline! Many thanks to those who shared their local knowledge: Laurel Nelson, Ron Mattson, Pat Sirois, Steve Sirois, Mike Mattson, Lindsey Martinez, Laura Orcutt, Bill Orcutt, John Stone and Whit Andrews, and experts Sonja Berger and Bob Raiselis. Special cheers to Amy Stone Scannell and Ames and John Shea for their hospitality.

PAULA HARDY

I'd like to thank the following for sharing the best of Connecticut and Rhode Island: Anne McAndrews, Dave Fairty, Pat and Wayne Brubaker, Rick Walker, Sanjeev Seereeram, Ira Goldspiel, Allie and her doughnuts, Harry Schwartz, Elizabeth MacAlister and the Preservation Society of Newport; also thanks to Rob Smith for the laughs along the way.

CAROLINE SIEG

Thanks to the countless Vermonters who gave me guidance and made me laugh – you rock. *Danke* to my parents for instilling in me a lifelong zest for travel. And, last but not least, thanks mucho to Jennye Garibaldi for giving me this gig.

PUBLISHER THANKS

Climate map data adapted from Peel MC, Finlayson BL & McMahon TA (2007) 'Updated World Map of the Köppen-Geiger Climate Classification,' *Hydrology and Earth System Sciences*, 11, 1633–44.

Cover photographs: Front (clockwise from top): Farm, Vermont, Mark Newman/ Getty Images; Restored 1938 pickup truck, Rhode Island, Stephen Simpson/Alamy; Brant Point Lighthouse, Nantucket, Megapress/Alamy. Back: Portsmouth harbor, Jerry and Marcy Monkman/Alamy.

Photograph of Bob Raiselis (p248) © Montshire Museum of Science.

THIS BOOK

This 2nd edition of *New England's Best Trips* was researched and written by Mara Vorhees, Amy C Balfour, Paula Hardy and Caroline Sieg. The previous edition was written by Ray Bartlett, Gregor Clark, Dan Eldridge and Brandon Presser.

Commissioning Editor Jennye Garibaldi Coordinating Editors Sarah Bailey, Carolyn Boicos Coordinating Cartographer Gabriel Lindquist Coordinating Layout Designer Wendy Wright Managing Editors Bruce Evans, Andi Jones Managing Cartographers Shahara Ahmed, Anita Banh Managing Layout Designers Chris Girdler, Jane Hart Assisting Editors Janet Austin, Elin Berglund, Kate Daly Assisting Cartographers Karusha Ganga, Cameron Romeril Assisting Layout Designers Yvonne Bischofberger, Mazzy Prinsep Cover Research Timothy O'Hanlon Internal Image Research Rebecca Skinner Thanks to Jennifer Bilos, Laura Crawford, Piotr Czajkowski, Janine Eberle, Ryan Evans, Joshua Geoghegan, Liz Heynes, Laura Jane, Jennifer Johnston, David Kemp, Wayne Murphy, Trent Paton, Jessica Rose, Mik Ruff, Julie Sheridan, Laura Stansfeld, Matt Swaine, John Taufa, Gerard Walker, Juan Winata

INDEX

Paula Hardy As I'm the British half of an American-British couple, I spend a lot of time hopping across the pond, torn between the bright lights of London town and Boston, where weekending in the New England countryside is a near-weekly activity. Research for this book, though, took me way off the beaten path into Connecticut's sugar shacks, dairy barns and wine-tasting rooms, and Rhode Island's tiny East Bay villages, where lasting memories of Allie's doughnuts aren't easily forgotten.

My Favorite Trip `10` **Connecticut Wine Trail** for the Philip Johnson Glass House, where I'd very much like to live.

Caroline Sieg My relationship with New England began when I briefly lived in Boston. Subsequent trips to the region yielded countless hikes in the Green Mountains, excessive beer and cheese tasting in Vermont, and a profound obsession with blueberry pie and apple-cider doughnuts. I also believe that one of the best ways to embrace the area is to explore its ubiquitous lakes and waterways by boat. These days, I visit New England as often as I can.

My Favorite Trip `16` **Vermont Back-Roads Ramble** for the quirky puppet museum, and my favorite beer, brewed up on a hill well off the beaten track.

OUR WRITERS

OUR STORY
A beat-up old car, a few dollars in the pocket and a sense of adventure. In 1972 that's all Tony and Maureen Wheeler needed for the trip of a lifetime – across Europe and Asia overland to Australia. It took several months, and at the end – broke but inspired – they sat at their kitchen table writing and stapling together their first travel guide, *Across Asia on the Cheap*. Within a week they'd sold 1500 copies. Lonely Planet was born.

Today, Lonely Planet has offices in Melbourne, London and Oakland, with more than 600 staff and writers. We share Tony's belief that 'a great guidebook should do three things: inform, educate and amuse'.

Mara Vorhees I'm not a native New Englander, but I can bang a U-ey with the best of them. I'm the coordinating author of Lonely Planet's *New England* and sole author of Lonely Planet's *Boston City Guide*. When not exploring the region's highways and byways, I live in a pink house in Somerville, MA, with my husband, two kiddies and two kitties. You can follow my adventures online at www.maravorhees.com.

My Favorite Trip `3` **Cape Cod & the Islands** for seaside bike trails, secluded swaths of sand and oysters on the half shell.

Amy C Balfour I fell for the White Mountains during a hut-to-hike 12 years ago when I tromped between Greenleaf and Galehead. Since then I've returned to New Hampshire for more hiking, and expanded my horizons to Maine for shopping and lobster-roll testing. On this trip, south of Rangeley, ME, I flipped when I saw my first moose in the wild. I'm sure the moose had a good laugh.

My Favorite Trip `27` **Acadia Byway** for its multisport appeal and well-designed roads that complement the surrounding beauty.

← MORE WRITERS

Published by Lonely Planet Publications Pty Ltd
ABN 36 005 607 983
2nd edition – Feb 2013
ISBN 978 1 74179 811 1
© Lonely Planet 2013   Photographs © as indicated 2013
10 9 8 7 6 5 4 3
Printed in China

Although the authors and Lonely Planet have taken all reasonable care in preparing this book, we make no warranty about the accuracy or completeness of its content and, to the maximum extent permitted, disclaim all liability arising from its use.

MIX
Paper from responsible sources
FSC™ C021741

Paper in this book is certified against the Forest Stewardship Council™ standards. FSC™ promotes environmentally responsible, socially beneficial and economically viable management of the world's forests.